Information Management

Information Management
Organization, management and control of computer processing

Donna S. Hussain

K.M. Hussain
Professor Emeritus
New Mexico State University

Prentice Hall

NEW YORK · LONDON · TORONTO · SYDNEY · TOKYO · SINGAPORE

First published 1992 by
Prentice Hall International (UK) Ltd
Campus 400, Maylands Avenue
Hemel Hempstead
Hertfordshire HP2 7EZ
A division of
Simon & Schuster International Group

Typeset in 10 on 12 pt Palacio
by MHL Typesetting Ltd, Coventry, UK.

Printed and bound in Great Britain by
Dotesios Printers Limited, Trowbridge, Wiltshire

Library of Congress Cataloging-in-Publication Data

Hussain, Donna.
    Information management / by Donna S. Hussain, K.M. Hussain.
        p.cm.
    Includes bibliographical references and index.
    ISBN 0-13-553777-0 (pbk.)
    1. Information resources management. I. Hussain, Khateeb M.,
1924–   . II. Title.
T58.6.H89 1992   92—11989
004'.068--dc20   CIP

British Library Cataloguing in Publication Data

A catalogue record for this book is available
from the British Library

ISBN 0-13-553777-0 (pbk)

1 2 3 4 5 96 95 94 93 92

To Salima and Masood Ali Baig

Contents

Preface

Computers today are used for operations, control, and planning. They help managers collect, store, and analyze data, and contribute to the decision-making process. Clearly, computers are beneficial to management, but they do add to a manager's work because computing resources require supervision. This book describes how to acquire, organize, monitor, and control information resources, and describes management problems unique to computer environments. While many of the references in the text are business oriented, most of the issues discussed refer to computer use in government and non-profit organizations as well. The chapters are addressed primarily to managers (or students of management) but should also be of interest to information processing professionals.

This book began as a new edition to the textbook *Information Resource Management* which we first published in 1984. However, so many changes have occurred in the field of computing since that time that a new book evolved during the rewrite. Today, managers are concerned not only with mainframe computing by information professionals but with end-user computing (use of computers by persons who lack an information processing background). They want to know how to control use of desktop micros, how to initiate micro to mainframe links, how to utilize computer networks, and how to employ information as a strategic weapon. We have addressed these topics by adding new sections to almost every chapter of the original text, and by updating those remaining. We have also added two new chapters of interest to managers: 'Global issues related to information management' (Chapter 15) and 'The future of computing' (Chapter 16). In addition, we have written case studies with an international focus for each chapter, asking readers to apply the principles introduced in the text to real-life situations.

We have made some deletions from the contents of *Information Resource Management* as well. To make the reworked text manageable in size, we have eliminated four chapters that reviewed basic computer concepts and terminology. As a result, the book is no longer a stand-alone text; it requires at least a basic course on computing as a prerequisite.

The expected audience of this textbook is the upper division undergraduate or the master's student. The book serves as a companion volume to *Information Systems for Business*, also published by Prentice Hall International, which deals with ways computers assist managers in their jobs.

Each chapter includes a list of key words, discussion questions and case studies. To assist students who desire supplementary reading, current references are listed in the bibliographies of each chapter.

1 Introduction

The old world was characterized by a need to manage things. The new world is characterized by a need to manage complexity.
Stafford Beer

Worldwide, computers are a billion-dollar industry. Every year, the number of installed computers is on the increase, as is the number of employees who need a working knowledge of computers to carry out their jobs. We are an information-based society with more than half of our workforce engaged in the production of information or employed by organizations that manufacture or sell information products. No wonder the development of computers with the ability to process and manipulate information on a large scale has had a revolutionary effect on the way business is conducted around the globe.

Modern information machines emerged during the Second World War. The emphasis at that time was on data processing, the use of machines to reduce both clerical costs and the volume of paperwork. Early computers processed business transactions primarily for financial applications. The use was economically justified since the computers performed some of the functions of clerks and helped to increase their productivity.

As performance improved with advances in technology and as equipment became cheaper, more robust, and portable, computer applications expanded. Companies began to use computers to process information related to production, marketing, inventory control, and other business functions. With this expansion, focus shifted away from systems that would simply save money toward computers that would improve methods of operation. By the mid-1960s, when computers with miniaturized solid logic technology and integrated circuits reached the market, the computer revolution was launched.

Today, the intense competition facing modern business is a force driving information technology (IT). Most corporations recognize that information is an asset and can be a weapon to enhance the corporations's posture in local and world markets. As illustrated in Figure 1.1, information can improve a firm's product and its relationship with clients. Consider the following ways in which information technology has helped suppliers of goods and services to become low-cost producers, to stake out a market niche, or to differentiate their product from the products of competitors.

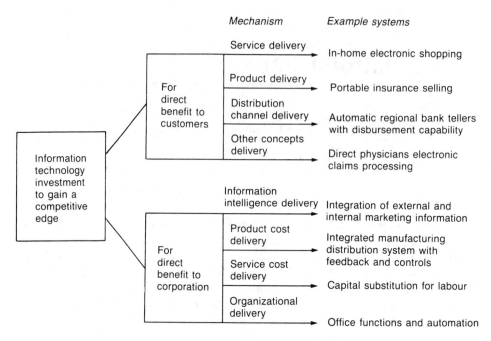

Figure 1.1 *The information system as a weapon (Source: Ives and Learmouth, 1984)*

- Mitsubishi uses microcomputers to control body roll during cornering, making swerving for an emergency at high speed easier and safer. Electronic suspension also eliminates the tendency of a car's nose to dive when brakes are applied hard or its tail to squat with sudden acceleration. The smooth ride of the car gives the company a sales advantage.
- In launching its new chocolate bar, Wispa, Cadbury orchestrated its strategy from one personal computer (PC) using Delta database products. To catch competition off guard, orders were generated and processed in almost total secrecy in each new market. The speed of order processing and the quality of information analysis that the computer produced helped Cadbury win a market niche for Wispa.
- On days with few races or in the evenings, the Tote (Horserace Totalization Board) earns extra revenues by using its computers and telecommunications equipment for a telemarketing bureau.
- The German television station ZDF, which developed its Sphinx system to store news agency flashes and to respond to complex queries by journalists, is marketing this system to other news organizations with similar information needs: the asking price, DM 124,000.
- British Airways plans to put PCs with touch sensitive screens on the back

of passengers' seats to attract travellers to its flights. The PCs will allow people to order goods, rent a car, and obtain information about their destination while in the air.

■ The Washington Hotel in Tokyo uses a robot to check in guests. Many tourists are drawn to the hotel because of its novel registration procedures.

■ Exxon is developing a debit-card network to give customers the convenience of a credit card but the same discount given cash receipts. The cost of a purchase is immediately debited from the customer's bank account through this network.

Throughout this book we will cite other examples of ways information technology serves modern business. Organizations that do not implement IT are likely to loose customers and their markets. The challenges that business managers face is to utilize information technology to improve the strategic position of their companies.

Management of information systems

So much information is being produced these days that the term information glut has been coined. In order to utilize information effectively and efficiently, managers at all organizational levels are being forced to learn better ways of managing information resources. No longer can responsibility for these resources be delegated to computer professionals as in the past. Managerial skills in the areas of personnel management, planning, resource acquisition and allocation, computer applications and networks are required in order to ensure that the information generated by computers meets organizational goals. This explains why responsibility for information resources, particularly in the area of systems development, operations and control, is shifting to corporate management, especially managers of functional departments that use information generated by computers.

In many organizations, responsibility for information resource management is also shifting to end-users at operational levels. A number of technological advances have led to this development. For example, advances in telecommunications facilitate distributed data processing and the independence of processing nodes. The establishment of computer networks, improved user interface, the marketing of database management systems, and the widespread use of microcomputers have contributed to the ability of users to manage information resources. Today, end-users frequently choose equipment, design and develop new systems, and handle their own computer operations. End-users, as well as managers, are faced with the problems of how to:

■ Select and acquire hardware and software.
■ Provide enough computer power to satisfy demand.

- Make technology as accessible and easy to use as possible.
- Reduce applications backlogs.
- Plan, budget, and monitor information systems.
- Improve investment payoffs.
- Minimize systems maintenance effort.
- Ensure the privacy and security of data.
- Mitigate 'people problems' associated with computerization, such as resistance to change.
- Speed development of new systems.

Purpose of book

The purpose of this book is to help train you in information resource management for your future role as manager or as user of information technology. You will discover that concepts applicable to the management of things (such as property, depletion, monopoly, and depreciation) do not apply to information. For example, information when used, is not depleted as are raw materials such as coal and iron. Information, when exchanged, does not become the exclusive property of one individual but is shared. Information has a tendency to leak. To hoard or monopolize information is only possible in specialized fields and then only for short periods of time. Traditional hierarchies of power have been based on ownership, access, or control of physical resources. These hierarchies crumble when the resource is information. Clearly, many of the basic assumptions in the management of materials and manufactured goods do not apply to information.

No wonder a course in information resource management — one that teaches how to manage an enterprise's information requirements, using contemporary technology in a profitable way — has been added to the curriculum of most business schools. This explains why so many corporate managers and information users in the field are studying textbooks such as this one.

Book outline

This textbook is divided into four parts, as shown in Figure 1.2.

The organization of information resources is the focus of Part One. The design of a computer room and the structure of computer departments are described, as is the organization of centralized and distributed processing. Also presented is the concept of an information centre to assist end-users in learning how best to utilize the information function. Computing services, oversight mechanisms, and IT staffing are examined as well.

Once a computer system is operational, the information resources of that system

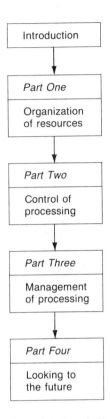

Figure 1.2 *Organization of book*

must be controlled. Part Two describes how to evaluate systems to ensure that resources are being fully utilized, how to monitor processing to minimize machine and human error, how to protect the privacy of data, and how to secure resources from misuse or abuse. The role of auditing in a computer environment is also discussed. All of the mechanisms of control described in this part must be incorporated in the system's design.

Part Three on the management of processing discusses day-to-day concerns of managers responsible for information resources. Scheduling, budgeting, standards and management of resistance to change are subjects of the chapters in this part.

Finally, Part Four discusses the impact of computing on corporate management, technology transfer to the Third World, transborder flow and the future of computing.

Case studies, a list of key words, and a set of discussion questions follow each chapter in addition to a bibliography recommending supplementary reading.

Case study: 'Factory of the future' proves to be a headache

Automobile manufacturers have designed their new plants to be showcases for industrial high technology. Unfortunately, many of these plants are building fewer cars per hour than originally expected. So many problems have resulted from the use of robots on the assmebly line, from use of automated guided vehicles to deliver parts, and from use of laser beams and computers to inspect and control the manufacturing process, that management of these plants has become a monumental headache.

To give an example, cars starting down the assembly line at GM's Hamtramck plant are equipped with a programmable 'box' that specifies the car's make, model, colour, and equipment. Along the line, electronic scanners read the box. This information, fed to a computer, is used to program robots and other machines to build that particular car. In addition, codes are displayed on a monitor telling workers who add parts by hand what fixtures to install. The problem is that the computer sometimes flashes the wrong codes. This leads to errors like the bolting of Cadillac bumpers onto Oldsmobiles.

In other factories, robots, assigned the task of applying sealants to a car's joints sometimes miss the right places and drip the glue-like sealant on the floor. Lack of proper depth perception in vision-equipped robots that set windshields in place has resulted in breakage because the robots push too hard. The hoses on robots that twist and turn to spray-paint car bodies have burst because of constant bending. Robots have spray-painted each other and painted cars so unevenly that they have had to be repainted with old-fashioned handheld spray guns. In one factory, a robotic system designed to make 100 welds in 27 seconds smashed into a car body and stopped the assembly line altogether.

Because of problems such as these, some car manufacturers are scaling back their automation plans. For example, GM has cancelled several robot orders for plants that will build its new generation of mid-sized cars. According to a spokesman, the company is going to phase in automation more slowly than originally planned. *Source:* Amal Nag, 'Auto makers discover factory of the future is headache just now', *The Wall Street Journal*, vol. 124, no. 93 (13 May 1986), p. 1.

Questions

1 Why is the automobile industry interested in the implementation of information technology in car manufacture?
2 Why are car manufacturers having problems with their automated systems? How can they resolve these problems? What is the role of corporate management and computer centre management in this regard?
3 Do you believe that the problem has been one of absorbing new technology? According to one automobile executive, it may be necessary to slow the process of automation and the use of computer technology until the workforce has been carefully trained and the goodwill of unions has been gained. Comment.
4 'High technology, like strong medicine, must be taken in carefully measured doses.' How does this statement apply to automobile construction? To all growth industries that use computer technology?
5 The Japanese are emphasizing new technology more in cars themselves than in car plants, according to one reporter. Who in a car manufacturing plant makes such a decision? How will such a strategy affect the organization and management of computer resources?

Bibliography

Dickson, Gary, and Geraldine de Sanctis. 'The management of information systems: research status and themes', in *Research Issues in Information Systems*, A.M. Jenkins, H.S. Siegle, W. Wojtkowski and W.G. Wojtkowski (eds). Dubuque, Ia: William C. Brown, 1990, pp. 45–82.

Earl, Michael J. *Management Strategies for Information Technology*. New York: Prentice Hall, 1989, pp. 1–38.

Goodman, S.E. 'The globalization of computing: prospectives on a changing world', *Communications of the ACM*, vol. 34, no. 1 (January 1991), pp. 19–21.

Gunton, Tony. *Infrastructure*. Hemel Hempstead: Prentice Hall, 1989.

Ives, Blake and Gerald P. Learmouth. *Communications of the ACM*, vol. 27, no. 12 (December 1984), p. 1197.

Kaye, David. *Game Change: The impact of information technology on corporate strategies and structures*. Oxford: Heinemann, 1989.

King, John Leslie and Kenneth L. Kraemer. 'Information resource management: is it sensible and can it work?', *Information and Management*, vol. 15, no. 8 (August 1988), pp. 7–14.

Mensching, James R. and Dennis A. Adams. *Managing an Information System*. Englewood Cliffs, NJ: Prentice Hall, 1991.

O'Brien, James A. and James N. Morgan. 'A multidimensional model of information resource management', *Information Resources Management*, vol. 2, no. 2 (Spring 1991), pp. 2–12.

Scarrott, G.G. 'The nature of information', *The Computer Journal*, vol. 32, no. 3 (June 1989), pp. 262–6.

Scott, James and Wiliam Perkins. 'Infostructures: how to survive and prosper through the information revolution' in A.M. Jenkins, H.S. Siegle, W. Wojtkowski and W.G. Wojtkowski (eds), *Research Issues in Information Systems: An Agenda for the 1990s*. Dubuque, Ia: William C. Brown, 1990, pp. 1–26.

Sharratt, John and Alastair McMurdo, 'Introduction to information management' in *Managing the Information Explosion*. Bradford: MCB University Press, 1991, pp. 6–12.

PART ONE
Organization of resources

Part One describes how a firm organizes its computing resources. Chapter 2 opens with a discussion of the location of computer departments within a firm's organizational structure. Some companies favour the centralization of computing resources; others, the distribution of resources to dispersed processing sites with hardware connected in a network. Still another mode of processing is end-user processing in which people who use computer output, many of whom have little or no data processing background, manage their own computers, such as stand-alone microcomputers (micros). Because these users often need advice and guidance from information technology professionals, many firms establish information centres to provide such services. The chapter closes with a look at human relationships in a computer environment.

Large computer systems, the management of which require the expertise of information specialists, are usually located in a computer centre. The design of such a centre is discussed in Chapter 3, including capacity planning, site selection and preparation, and facility layout.

Chapter 4 focuses on in-house computer staffing. The jobs of systems analysts, programmers, operators, data administrators, and other information specialists are described. The chapter also covers job design, hiring, turnover, career development, training and technostress.

Chapter 5 deals with the role of management and steering committees in the oversight of computing.

Finally, Chapter 6 covers service organizations that can supplement in-house computer resources. Considered are consultants, vendors, facilities management, service bureaux, remote processing, and computer utilities.

2 Organization of computing

You can't sit on the lid of progress. If you do, you will be blown to pieces.
Henry Kaiser

All organizations, be they business firms, manufacturing plants, governmental departments or agencies, service organizations such as hosptials and schools, research labs, or charitable groups like the Red Cross, generate information. In today's world, most depend on computer hardware and software to process this information. The location of hardware/software resources within the organization is one facet of the organization of computing. Another is the placement of people who operate or manage these resources in the group's organizational hierarchy.

This chapter traces the organization of computer resources from the 1950s, when computer facilities were commonly under the auspices of subdepartmental units, to the mix of organizational modes of the 1990s. You will learn that most large organizations today retain a department for computing services, commonly called an **information systems (IS) department**, the term we use in this text. Other names for this department are management information system centre, information processing centre, or some similar title. The IS department is usually assigned responsibility for planning and control of processing, the maintenance of hardware and software, the development of new computerized information systems, and the processing of applications that require the expertise of computer processing professionals. Decentralized processing options are also described, including distributed data processing and end-user computing.

In the 1950s, only those with computer expertise, including programming skills and knowledge of operations, could interact with computers. Today, many employees with little knowledge of computer science spend their work hours at computer terminals or depend on computer-generated information in their jobs. Conflicts often arise between these employees and computer personnel because of differences in outlook, training, and level of computer expertise. In organizing the computer function, managers must look for ways to keep such conflicts to a minimum and provide mechanisms for problem resolution as described in this chapter.

Misunderstandings may arise between corporate managers and computer processing personnel as well. Again the cause may stem from differences in background and experience with computer systems. The way in which processing

n facilitate communication between these two groups as you will

apter looks at ways in which the workload of information workers
ᵤ_d by the dynamic nature of the computer industry. The continual
introduction of advanced hardware/software products requires frequent
reorganization of computing resources within a single organization.

Location of computing resources

Many locations for a computer department are possible within the organizational
structure of a firm. Six alternatives are shown in Figure 2.1.

When computing was in its infancy, most businesses and industries used
computers to process accounting and financial applications. At that time, a
subdepartmental unit for **electronic data processing (EDP)** was common (see Case
1, Figure 2.1). Although companies might have several computers located in
dispersed departments, no centralized authority coordinated their activities.

When more resources were devoted to computing and computers began to play
a larger role in information processing, EDP rose in the organizational hierarchy
of most firms. This placed computer processing personnel directly under a
department head (Case 2) or a division chief (Case 3).

Later, as the need for expensive data processing resources grew and applications
extended to all functional areas (for example, marketing and production), sharing
of data and equipment across division lines was initiated to cut costs. This gave
impetus to **centralized data processing**, the establishment of a single computer
department reporting directly to top management (Case 4). Planning, computer
operations, the development of new computer systems, and control over
hardware, software, and corporate data were consolidated. **Common databases**
(pooled data integrated for shared use by computer professionals and employees
dependent on information processing for their jobs) were established. The
expectation was that costs would drop. Indeed, studies showed that a single large
installation was less expensive to run than small dispersed centres. It was also
expected that information processing would be more responsive to management
needs than formerly; that the delivery speed of information would increase; that
redundancy in data collection, storage, and processing would be eliminated; and
that security and control of information would be tightened.

Unfortunately, these expectations were not all realized. Lack of communication
between information users and processing personnel continued under
centralization. Information users resented the hours required to justify and
document requests for computer processing service and felt isolated from
computing facilities. They complained that centralized data processing was
unresponsive to their needs, that the bureaucracy of centralization was inept at
mediating conflicts. Computer professionals chafed at the criticism. They believed

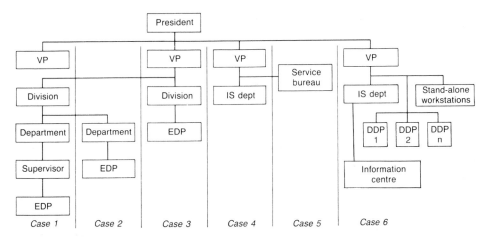

Key:
EDP *Electronic data processing*
IS dept *Information systems department*
DDP *Distributed data processing*

Figure 2.1 *Alternative locations of EDP within a firm's organizational structure*

that the length of time required for the development of computer systems in response to information requests was simply not understood by users.

In spite of these problems, centralized computing is the organizational structure of many firms today. However, the name EDP centre has become outmoded since computer processing nowadays includes text and image processing as well as data processing. We now speak of information systems (IS) departments rather than EDP centres because the term is more inclusive. Many organizations supplement their internal computing capacity by contracting jobs with outside service bureaux (Case 5). (**Service bureaux** provide computer equipment, software, or personnel to clients according to their needs.)

However, in recent years, a large number of firms, disenchanted with centralized computer centres, have once again decentralized much of their information processing (Case 6). A number of technological advances have made this an attractive option. Micro- and minicomputers with capabilities exceeding many former large computers are now on the market at low cost. In addition, experience with computer processing has given information users confidence that they can manage and operate their own processing systems. This has led to **end-user computing** (processing by non-computer professionals) and facilities to support end-users (for example, information centres), subjects we will explore later in this chapter in greater depth.

Furthermore, recent strides in telecommunications mean that computer processing networks can today link dispersed processing sites (called **nodes**) at

Table 2.1 *Some alternative centralization—decentralization combinations*

Alternative	Development personnel	Equipment and operation	Development activities	Database	Planning
1	C	C	C	C	C
2	D	C	C	C	C
3	D	D	C	C	C
4	D	D	D	C	C

C = Centralized
D = Decentralized

low cost, making **distribution data processing (DDP)** an expeditious mode of processing. With DDP a worker sitting at a computer terminal can access the computing power of a distant computer facility. The argument is now advanced that information users are better served and computer applications more easily implemented and maintained under DDP.

To centralize or distribute processing is not an either/or proposition. As shown in Table 2.1, a variety of combinations is possible. Alternative 4 has become increasingly popular in recent years with operations and development activities placed under local control, but planning and database control centralized.

Centralized computing

A sample organizational chart for a centralized computing facility is illustrated in Figure 2.2. Note that computer processing is subdivided into three functional areas: systems development, operations and support. To understand fully the ramifications of the centralization—decentralization issue, you need to understand the jobs of computer professionals in each of these functional areas, which we explain in Chapter 5. For the purposes of this chapter you should recognize the complexity of modern computing operations, which this figure illustrates. As you learn about problems with distributed processing and end-user processing in sections that follow, you will understand why some organizations decide that centralized control of their computing facilities is the best way to effectively utilize their computer resources, given the number of people and variety of skills required to meet information requirements of modern workers.

Distributed computer systems

Let us now take a closer look at distributed data processing (DDP). Among computer scientists, the definition of DDP is still evolving. For the purposes of

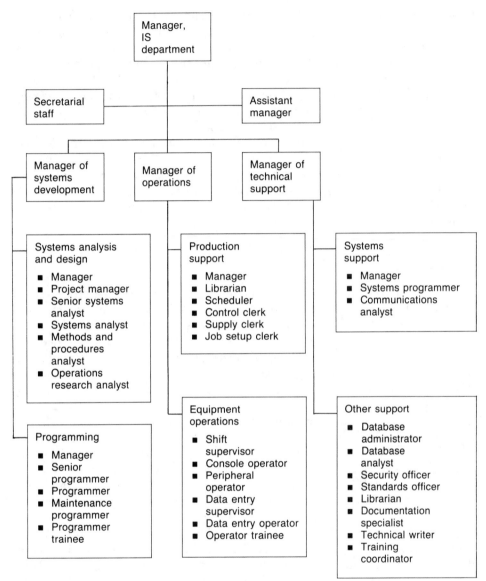

Figure 2.2 *Sample organization chart for a computer department*

this text, we shall define DDP as many separate computing processing centres all belonging to a single organization. Each node has computer facilities for program execution and data storage. Yet linkage between the nodes enables them to cooperate in processing tasks. A DDP network can be spread over a large or small area. Some DDP systems are global (for example, air traffic control systems).

Others may be local, within a single room, building, or group of buildings.

The distributed computer concept applies age-old management principles to new technology. For example, DDP permits division of labour, the increase of productivity through parallelism. It incorporates the concept of specialization of labour, since computers (like people) vary in the tasks that they do best. Furthermore, DDP promotes the delegation of responsibility because management at remote nodes commonly controls hardware/software acquisitions, operations and the development of systems for local use.

Distributed computing is a simple concept but it is not simple to put into practice. DDP is more than relocating hardware from a centralized computer centre to dispersed locations. The design of operating systems, databases, and applications are affected. Job descriptions, departmental structures, the flow of corporate information, and relationships between management and workers are altered. So is the process of decision making.

Equipment configurations

The difference between distributed data processing and dispersed processing in the 1950s is linkage: DDP involves a communications network to link decentralized processors. Figure 2.3 shows sample DDP network configurations. In a **star network**, failure of a central computer impairs the entire system. The **ring network** structure overcomes this problem, because rerouting is possible should one processing centre or its link fail. A ring network allows interaction and **offloading** (the transference of processing from one site to another) without dependence on a central host.

Both star and ring configurations are essentially horizontal systems. That is, each node processor is equal although the hardware may be unique to each node, which means that not all computer resources in the organization are purchased from the same vendor. The advantage is that users can acquire hardware/software that incorporate the latest technology on the market. However, this flexibility has a negative aspect: it increases problems of linkage and compatibility between nodes.

Hierarchical distribution is the configuration that many firms prefer. This configuration, illustrated in Figure 2.4, has a central host computer and common database with minis and micros at dispersed sites. Generally, all equipoment and software in hierarchical systems are supplied by the same vendor, minimizing problems of compatibility between nodes. Because many computers have either a **fail-safe capability** (ability to continue operations, in spite of breakdown, due to the existence of backup) or a **fail-soft capability** (the ability to continue with a degraded level of operations), a breakdown in the hierarchy should not incapacitate the entire system.

Of course, Figure 2.4 is merely a model. Firms design hierarchical configurations with a mix of devices at different nodes according to their needs.

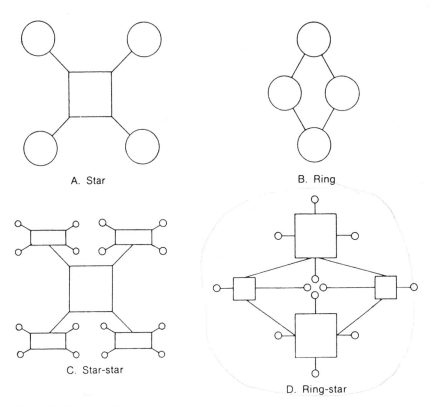

Figure 2.3 *Sample DDP network configurations*

Distributed database configurations

With distributed processing networks, a decision also needs to be made regarding the organization of the company's databases. In such networks, should all data be centralized, or should processing nodes store database segments that they need for daily operations? Perhaps data stored centrally should be replicated for use at local sites. Options for data organization are discussed next.

Centralized database
Centralization of data is possible under DDP, but costs are high when all data must be transmitted to distributed nodes for processing. A centralized database is appropriate when infrequent access to that data is needed or when updating needs to be strictly controlled.

Segmented distributed database
The storage of parts of the database at local nodes is called **segmented distributed database** organization. The segments might be data from a function or data

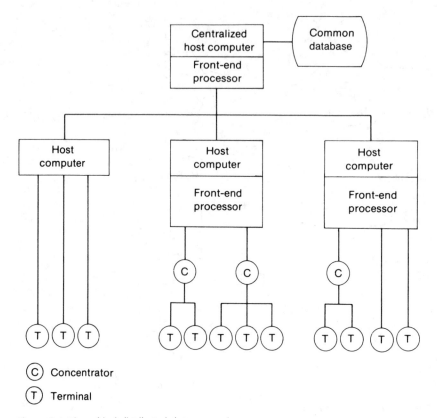

C Concentrator

T Terminal

Figure 2.4 *Hierarchical distributed data processing*

pertaining to the geographic area — data that allows the node to be virtually independent, although other nodes may also use the data as a shared resource.

Replicated distributed database

When more than one dispersed processor needs the same data, a common approach to database organization is to store the database at a central repository with duplicate segments needed for local processing stored at each node. A database organized in this fashion is called a **replicated distributed database**. The local bases used for processing, including online real-time operations, are then periodically used to update the centralized database. From the updated centralized base, the replicated databases at distributed sites are updated in turn.

Large regional banks frequently adopt this form of database organization. Central processing takes place after banking hours, and replicated distributed databases are then created for branch offices. These replicated databases consist essentially of working files used for local transactions, such as deposits and withdrawals. At the end of each working day, the central database is again updated by incorporating data on transactions conducted at the branches during the day. Then the cycle begins once again with the creation of updated databases for distribution to the branch offices.

In general, the centralized database includes all control and summary data, whereas transactional data and local data are in the replicated distributed databases. Branch offices still have to access the centralized data during the course of the day. This occurs if a customer of the bank wishes to cash a cheque at a branch that does not have a record of his or her account. In this case, the transaction has to be routed through the central database.

One advantage of replicated databases is that they provide backup. As a result, the system is less vulnerable should failure occur at the central location. An additional advantage is that systems are more responsive to local needs when data are managed locally (an advantage that applies to segmented databases as well). In particular, maintenance and updating of large and complex databases are more effective when portions of the base are under local control. Certain types of processing are also more efficient. For example, retrieval by indexes requires careful cross-indexing. Personnel on location with a need for the retrieved data will be more highly motivated to update and maintain indexes and retrieval software and are more knowledgeable about user needs than programmers at a centralized database.

A major problem with replicated distributed databases is redundancy. For efficient processing, no more data than absolutely necessary should be stored at remote sites. Unfortunately, the distributed centres' exact need for data is not easily determined.

Hybrid approach

Some firms both segment and replicate their databases. This is the **hybrid approach** to database organization. For example, a large national business may segment its database geographically, giving regional headquarters segments relevant to their operations. Replicated data from these headquarters are then distributed to branch offices within each region. Warehouse inventories are often controlled in this manner.

Micro—mainframe link technology

Although microcomputer use for stand-alone processing has been common in the business world since the early 1980s, recent advances in technology today make it feasible to integrate microcomputers (and minis) into distributed processing networks. Sales of **micro—mainframe link** products, including software, modems, and emulation boards, are on the rise. The number of vendors for such products is also increasing.

The original impetus for linkage was the desire of users to download data from mainframes to micros. But today, uploading is viewed as a major application of the technology as well. In the future, mainframes may be used as database machines, while much local processing will take place on network microcomputers.

Many technological problems still must be resolved. Software to facilitate micro—mainframe communications is needed, as are ways to handle different people working on the database at the same time. Security is a major issue. Corporate proprietary data that are downloaded to portable floppy disks are in jeopardy. How can access to data (and disks) be controlled? The possibility that users may upload incorrect information processed on their microcomputers is also a concern. Ways to check and verify data before they are uploaded need to be devised.

Other problems that affect microcomputer—mainframe linkage are:

- The cost of micro—mainframe products and the speed with which such products are developed for the marketplace.
- Problems of incompatible data formats. Data downloaded from the mainframe may require processing before they can be used for microcomputer applications.
- Lack of open-architecture links. At present, most micro—mainframe systems are based on proprietary architectures. The micro—host software will only access data residing on the same vendor's mainframe software.

Rewards and risks of DDP

Improved systems reliability is one of the primary functional advantages of DDP. The fact that work is modularized means that tasks are less complex and therefore less vulnerable to failure. Furthermore, natural compartmentalization can reduce the scope of errors, failures, and damage. Should one module fail, another can provide backup service.

A DDP system facilitates growth without disruption of service. System upgrades can take place in small increments. For example, modules can be replaced or modernized one at a time so that conversion can be easily managed. There is built-in flexibility that allows systems to meet new requirements, to bypass failed components, to integrate new services or new technologies, and to extend systems' life expectancy. What's more, throughput and response time are improved because communication delays and queueing are avoided when local nodes process local databases. Less complex software is required, a fact that reduces the cost of systems development, maintenance, and training.

With on-site processing, the need for communications with a centralized processor is lessened. This helps to reduce costs, as does improved systems response. Shared resources minimize the need for duplication of resources. Modularity can improve procurement competition and can likewise improve cost—performance ratios because of economies of specialization. (A system can cater to the needs of a particular group rather than service the complex needs of diverse groups.)

Certainly, this list of benefits should include increased motivation among distributed staff, resulting from greater independence and local control of processing. With a smaller user base, fewer political and priority conflicts need to be resolved. Staff can concentrate on systems optimization instead. There is also a psychological advantage when users find services tailored to their needs and have more voice in computing decisions, such as hardware and software upgrades. In addition, the geographical location of facilities is no longer an important factor.

In spite of these advantages, the initiation of DDP involves multiple risks. Among the more common are poor systems design resulting from inexperience, redundancy among nodes, problems with interface, costs that are hidden or that escalate, and employee resistance to change. For example, distributed computing requires more planning than centralized systems. More attention must be paid to the efficiency of information flow and distribution. Standards for data elements and interfaces need to be designed, monitored, and enforced. Four thorny data distribution issues need to be resolved:

- Where to store data.
- How to find needed data efficiently.
- How to keep data synchronized and maintain integrity.
- How to protect data from security and privacy abuse and fraud.

Distributed architectures are still in the early stages of development. To date, most of the work has centred on how to connect hardware components. A number of issues, such as how to build a distributed network operating system, still need more research. Clearly, new technology means new potential yet also heightens risk. And designing a multiple-processor system is much more difficult than designing a single-processor system.

When to implement DDP

Distributed data processing is not applicable to all organizations. How does a firm decide whether it is appropriate? What **organizational considerations** are important in the decision? Unfortunately, no formula or precise decision rule exists to guide management in reaching a DDP implementation decision. However, firms with geographically dispersed outlets, firms with a matrix structure rather than functional organization, multinationals, project-based companies (such as construction firms), and conglomerates have organizational structures that lead naturally to decentralization and the distributed mode.

In less obvious cases, a grid analysis may help determine the appropriateness of DDP. A sample is shown in Table 2.2. Here, a hypothetical firm with Sites A, B, C, and D has informational needs satisfied by Processes 1–3 and Files 1–3. The informational requirements of each site are marked on the grid. Since Process 1 and File 2 are required by all sites, centralization of their processing is indicated.

Table 2.2 *Illustration of grid analysis*

Informational sites / Needs	A	B	C	D
Process 1	X	X	X	X
2	X			
3		X	X	
Files 1	X			
2	X	X	X	X
3			X	X

Since Process 2 and File 1 are needed by only a single site, they are clear candidates for the distributed mode. Process 3 and File 3 are possible candidates.

However, before implementation, management should assess DDP's impact on the firm. How will DDP affect corporate decision making? Is DDP economically feasible? If a firm has centralized processing, a switch to DDP is usually not considered unless there is dissatisfaction with centralization. It is up to management to decide whether this dissatisfaction with operations can be remedied by DDP and whether the benefits of DDP will be worth the cost and disruption that reorganization entails.

End-user computing

It is predicted that in the 1990s, 50 per cent of computer users will generate information without calling upon the services of computer professionals (see Alavi and Weiss, 1985–6: 5–20). They will access distant computer facilities through telecommunications or utilize stand-alone minis or micros. They will purchase packages or write their own software instead of requesting systems development by their company's IS department. Already, large numbers of employees belong to this category. They apply information technology to their jobs without the intermediary of trained computer processing personnel, although most have no formal training in computer science.

In the effort to distinguish such users of computer resources from computer professionals, the term *end-user* has been coined. Not only is the name poorly chosen but agreement on its definition is lacking. Usually the term is applied to non-computer professionals who design, program, purchase and/or operate their own applications.

End-user computing is a relatively new phenomenon, attributed to recent advances in information technology that make modern computers easy to use, program and administer. Corporate management has a responsibility to plan carefully for the expanded, productive use of end-user computing tools.

A number of risks associated with end-user computing can readily be identified:

- Risks related to problem analysis. In developing applications, end-users may proceed without adequate problem specification and end up solving the wrong problem.
- Development risks. Persons who do not have systems development training and experience are more susceptible to modelling errors. They may fail to apply documentation standards when developing new sytems and fail to test their solutions.
- Redundancy. End-users may spend time and effort developing applications that have already been developed.
- Unprofitable expenditure of time and effort. It is questionable whether people with professional skills should spend time developing applications rather than concentrating on their area of expertise.
- Waste of computing resources. End-users may be unaware of underlying operational costs as well as hardware/software costs. Without budgetary restraints, their use of computing resources may be uneconomical.
- Threat to data privacy and security. Physical access, custodianship controls, backup and recovery issues are seldom addressed by end-users.
- Lack of computing efficiency and effectiveness. Few end-users establish procedures for performance evaluation of their systems or subject them to audits.
- Incompatibility of end-user tools and devices. Standards for acquisitions may be lacking.

The controls that need to be installed by management for end-user computing fall into three categories: preventive, detective and corrective. The preventive category includes policies, procedures, and authorization structures to minimize the possibility that the risks will occur. For example, a cost—benefits analysis might be required before computer equipment is purchased by end-users; computer training might be mandatory; and rules on diskette access, storage and backup might be promulgated. Detective controls might include procedures such as supervisory review of logs and performance. The changing of a password could be categorized as a corrective control.

This brief discussion points out that there are valid reasons to control end-user computing. What make controls difficult to install are the dispersed nature of end-user computing and the fact that control policies are often viewed as a frontal attack on employee/professional productivity. The organization and control of end-user computing are subjects widely discussed today in management circles and among information processing professionals. There is not yet consensus on how to resolve problems of organization and control, just recognition that problems exist.

Information centres

The concept of a computer support group to provide information workers with guidance and training in computer use, as well as with hardware/software tools, evolved during the 1970s and 1980s as organizations looked for ways to maximize the efficiency and effectivness of their computer processing. A number of terms have been used to describe this support, such as client service centre, solution centre, resource centre, and business systems support centre. However, the term **information centre**, coined by IBM Canada in 1976, is the name most widely used today.

Information centre services

Typically, information centres are designed to support end-users, not computer professionals. Here is a sampling of the type of services that may be offered.

Aid in problem resolution
User assistance usually begins by staffing a telephone hot line and a help desk. Requests for service may range from a simple query regarding the meaning of a message on a computer screen to an appeal for help when a system malfunctions or breaks down. When a problem cannot be resolved quickly, the user will be referred to a staff member with expertise in that area.

Consultation
Typically, the role of a consultant in an information centre is to help end-users plan for effective use of their computing resources, to advise them in ways to computerize their work, to evaluate proposed computer applications, to assist in product selection, and to answer specific questions regarding hardware and software.

Training
Computer literacy is the main objective of educational programmes. Training may consist of self-study methods, such as computer-based training and audio-visual presentations, or be instructor led. Self-study is favoured when:

- Immediate training is required and the centre does not have time to plan and deliver a course on the subject.
- The schedule of the employee in need of training precludes class attendance.
- Training is needed at a remote site that instructors cannot reach.

Individualized instruction may be given when an employee needs to develop a specialized skill not needed by others. More commonly, workshops and classroom instruction are the teaching mode. Popular courses include word processing, file creation, electronic mail, and how to use software such as Lotus 1—2—3, Multimate, Omnilink, and dBase III. Classes may last half a day (for example, an introduction to the personal computer) or for as long as a week to 10 days (for example, application engineering to teach techniques in prototyping, data modelling and structured analysis).

Technical support
Technical assistance is provided by the centre when user problems are too large or complex to be solved without the aid of technical specialists, but only if the solution is not extensive modification of a large applications system or new systems development. (Those problems will be referred to persons in the IS department responsible for development projects.) 'Fast-response report group', a name some information centres give to their technical support team, helps explain the team's assignments. In addition to problem solving, staff may be asked to help audit systems performance, establish backup and recovery procedures, plan data access, assist with the design of security, plan projects or document user requirements. In effect, technical support is an extension of the centre's consulting service.

Product support
Software packages may reside at the information centre to provide end-users with services such as graphics, spreadsheets, decision support, modelling capability, financial analysis, fourth-generation query languages, database management, applications generators and so on. Staff may demonstrate how the software is used, perhaps by providing a sample problem solution walkthrough. In addition, they may help end-users interpret reference manuals, suggest tips and techniques for using the product and give debugging assistance if needed. Aid of this nature will also be given to end-users when they purchase new software.

Hardware access
Terminals, microcomputers, printers, plotters, microfilm and microfiche readers and other equipment may be available for use, or hardware may be on display to help end-users decide what equipment to acquire. Sometimes the information centre serves as an in-house computer store. End-users can try out equipment, receive advice about the relative merits of models produced by different manufacturers and then lease or purchase the equipment directly from the centre. This eliminates the lengthy acquisition procedures that are required when dealing with outside vendors. The centre offers 'one-stop shopping', and the prices may be lower than those of retail stores. Furthermore, the centre can provide training, configuration assistance and maintenance after the lease or purchase.

Staffing
Some information centres provide backup assistance for end-users who have a temporary need for information processing personnel.

Computer resource planning and justification

The centre can help end-users analyze their workloads, make projections of future needs and prepare (and justify) requests for additional funding for computer resources. One of the more important roles of the centre is to nurture end-user awareness of the importance of standardization and integration of resources.

New-service evaluation

In order to provide better services to end-users, centre staff will keep abreast of users' needs. When new products (both hardware and software) come on the market, these products will be evaluated to see whether they will increase end-user self-sufficiency and productivity. If appropriate, the centre may then initiate a proposal to management for acquisition of the product.

Administrative services

This category of service commonly includes:

- Promotion and advertising of information centre activities (for example, a newsletter or bulletin board notices).
- Orientation workshops or open houses to introduce end-users to the information centre.
- New-product announcements.
- A library of computer-related materials.
- Equipment maintenance and service.
- Accounting and billing for centre use.

Delivery of services

Most information centres are the responsibility of the firm's IS director, who monitors and controls the centre's usage and growth. The ways in which services are delivered varies from organization to organization.

In some centres, a person on the staff will work with an end-user from start to finish. That is, the staff member will analyze the user's problem and requirements, select appropriate packages, train the end-user if needed, and support the end-user in developing the problem solution. In this way, the staff member will have time to become thoroughly familiar with the end-user's environment (perhaps even be able to identify hidden problems) and will be able to develop a close working relationship with the end-user. The drawback is that a single individual may lack some of the skills needed to solve the problem.

At other centres, someone at the help desk may first analyze the end-user's problem, then pass the end-user to staff members who have expertise in that specific problem area. A number of specialists from the centre may work with the end-user over a period of time.

Most information centres being opened today are microcomputer oriented. But training is not limited to stand-alone computing: remote computing is supported as well, since microcomputers are often used as intelligent terminals when connected with minis or mainframes. Within the centre, computers may belong to a local area network or be networked with computers in other departments. An important role of many information centres is to promote the acquisition of computers with a set of data communication standards, so that linkage of all corporate computers will be facilitated in the future.

Future of information centres

Since the inception of information centres, a debate has raged in professional circles over the following question: Are the centres here to stay, or are they a temporary phenomenon? It is generally agreed that end-users will always need troubleshooting, training, and consultation in order to take full advantage of their computing resources. The focus of the controversy is whether such services will be the responsibility of departmental experts working in functional areas or whether they will remain in the information centre in the future.

Judging by the content (and number) of current articles on the subject, information centres are not likely to disappear soon. Centres may remain the central focus for guiding and supporting end-user computing, as long as centres keep up to date on new applications and technology, maintain quality staff and address issues of user concern.

Integration of information services

When information services are the responsibility of a number of departments, coordinating and integrating their activities becomes necessary. Many firms appoint a vice president of information services to oversee this integration. (The exact title of this position may vary from firm to firm. Vice president of information resource management is also frequently used.) Figure 2.5 is an example of a sample organizational structure for **integration of information services**. Of course, not all firms are organized in this manner. Some will place record-keeping in the IS department, others will join word processing with reference services.

Whatever structure is chosen will be temporary at best, because advances in computer technology will undoubtedly lead to the development of new computer applications in the future. Over time, it becomes necessary to restructure departments to incorporate new technology.

Human relationships in a computer environment

The organization of computer resources within a business or industry establishes lines of communication between information workers and computer professionals, and shapes the interaction of these two groups with corporate management.

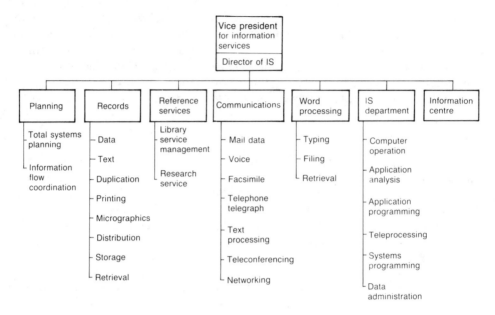

Figure 2.5 *Horizontal integration under vice president for information services*

Problems arise in every computing facility. Their resolution may well depend on harmony in the working relationships within the organization.

Relations between information users and computer personnel

Unfortunately, most information users (be they clerks, professionals like engineers, or business managers) have a negative view of computer technicians, especially systems analysts and programmers. Users see such individuals as overzealous in changing existing procedures, disdainful of others (even of employees with years of experience in the firm), long on theory but short on common sense and lacking in both humility and company loyalty. Computer personnel are also criticized for the impersonality of their reports, inability to relate to clientele, non-responsiveness to enquiries, insensitivity to user desires, lack of functional involvement, and occasional dishonesty, such as the unauthorized sale of address lists or other information.

This long list of complaints makes all too evident the antagonism that is commonly directed towards computer specialists. Perhaps one factor contributing to this antagonism is that programmers and analysts have high job mobility. The rate with which they change jobs prevents them from forming deep interpersonal relationships with other corporate employees and gives them little time to improve their image.

On the other side of the coin, computer personnel complain that users often do not know what they want, fail to articulate their needs even when they do know and keep changing their minds throughout the development of information systems and their implementation. Wouldn't it be unreasonable for a client to ask an architect to build a two-storey building, then demand an additional storey halfway through construction? Yet, the equivalent is commonly demanded of analysts and programmers during a systems development project, and the analysts and programmers get blamed for time/cost overruns that result.

One way of reducing friction between information users and computer technicians is through educational programmes. Such programmes can teach users about computer technology and educate analysts about business management, so that each group understands the other's viewpoint and function. Another approach is to establish an ombudsman position to resolve or arbitrate complaints. Sometimes committees (such as a feasibility study group or project management group) mediate conflicts and provide interface between technicians and users.

To lessen friction during projects to develop new information systems, procedures for formal user approval of progress are helpful. The life cycle of most development projects includes a feasibility study, user specification, design, testing and conversion to the new system. Users for whom the system is being developed are expected to monitor the work during each stage, then sign their approval of the project's status at the completion of each stage. A sign-off procedure of this nature protects computer professionals from charges that the project, once completed, is not what was originally requested.

Since problems in the operation and maintenance of newly developed systems can also cause friction between users and computer personnel, it is sometimes helpful to appoint a member of the development team to help implement new systems and to act as a liaison between the IS department and users when things go wrong. Because of their familiarity with the new systems, such individuals can often trace the cause of problems quickly and recommend corrective action that will prevent a recurrence of problems.

Computing advances — non-procedural languages, prototyping, software packages, applications generators and other techniques — can help computer centres respond more quickly to users' requests for service. This helps to improve relationship between users and IS departments. Furthermore, new technology encourages end-user computing, which reduces the need for interaction between computer personnel and users and, hence, lessens potential areas of discord.

The history of computing has been one of constant shifts in the relationship between computer departments and users, as reflected in Figure 2.6. For example, note how responsibility for the database has switched back and forth. Originally, local data was kept by users (1950–60). With the centralization of EDP and the advent of common databases, data processing departments assumed jurisdiction over data (1960–75). Today's minis enable local sites to manage local data, while distributed data processing technology permits users to control replicated or segmented parts of the common database as well. So again, responsibility for data is reverting back to the user (since 1975).

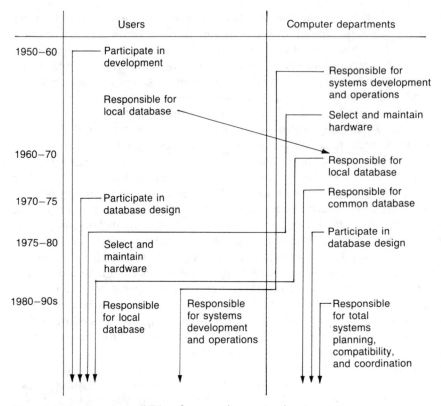

Figure 2.6 *Changing responsibilities of users and computer departments*

Whenever changes in the responsibilities of computer professionals occur, reorganization of computer departments is triggered. Such reorganizations keep relationships between users and computer personnel in a continual state of flux. Technological advances will certainly bring still other organizational changes to computer departments in the future, so one can expect that interaction between users and computer personnel will always be volatile.

Strains between corporate management and IT professionals

Corporate managers and computer professionals (called **information technology (IT) personnel**) have different backgrounds, a major cause in misunderstandings between the two groups. The former have a business background: the latter, technical training. No wonder problems are not viewed in the same light.

Another factor that affects the relationship between upper-echelon managers and IT personnel is attitude toward change. Corporate managers seek stability, whereas computer personnel are committed to change. Indeed, change and motion are viewed as constants in the field of computing. From a computer specialist's point of view, stability within change is a viable concept and not a contradiction of terms.

A divergence also exists in attitude toward the dissemination of information. Generally, corporate executives favour restrictions on the distribution of information, lest the information be misused. (The charge is often made that the real reason management wants information controlled is to keep unfavourable reports quiet.) IT personnel favour the free and wide distribution of information.

Friction between the two groups can often be attributed to the belief of computer personnel that corporate executives do not give them the recognition or status that is their due. Rarely are IS managers included (as are other department heads) in key decisions on new products or budgets, although information processing can contribute analysis and decision support for such determinations. Too often, the road to other executive positions is blocked for IS managers, creating a dead-end career path: computer managers are seldom promoted to top managerial echelons of the firm, because corporate executives see them as computer technicians, disregarding their managerial skills.

Resentment against corporate management is further fuelled by the manner by which the performance of IS managers is commonly judged. The evaluation is based on quantitative measures (budget variances, for example) and general efficiency measures that poorly reflect important performance characteristics of IS administration, according to the viewpoint of computer personnel. Moreover, corporate executives blame IS management when embarrassing mistakes are made but rarely give those managers credit when the computer centres function well — at least, that is the perception of many persons in data processing. The belief of IS managers that their services are unappreciated and undervalued is a source of much of the tension that exists in their relations with corporate management.

The first step in improving the working relationship between corporate executives and IS managers is to determine the sources of friction. Only then can steps be taken to resolve misunderstandings. Although the action taken will depend on the nature of the problem, many companies look toward educational programmes for answers. Presumably, an understanding of information processing on the part of corporate executives and an understanding of business management problems by IT personnel will promote accord between the two groups.

Because it is easier and faster to train senior management about computers than for technicians to acquire the prerequisites for managing a firm, most companies provide in-house training programmes on computer technology for high-level management, sponsoring group seminars or videotape programmes acquired from consulting firms or software houses. Some firms release time for managers to attend educational programmes in their home communities. Others organize pilot studies, demonstrations and briefings. Another method of keeping management technically up to date is to circulate journals and pertinent literature.

All of these educational approaches attempt to smooth communication between corporate management and computer personnel. When the two groups use the same vocabulary and when corporate managers have enough background to understand computing problems, relations between the groups generally improve. Improved relations, in turn, can speed resolution of computer-related problems and raise employee morale, leading to higher productivity.

Summing up

Describing where computer departments fit into a firm's organizational schema is no simple task, because technological advances have changed the nature of information processing over time and, as a consequence, altered the location of computer centres within the hierarchy of firms. In the 1950s, computers were generally found in subdepartmental units wherever processing was needed. As more resources were allocated to computing, centralization was favoured in order to take advantage of economies of scale and to ensure better integration and management of computer facilities. Today, distributed data processing is becoming popular, with local autonomy over development activities and operations and centralization for planning, standards, and management of common systems. In fact, available today for the delivery of information services are a number of options, or combinations of options, including:

- Centralization of computing facilities.
- Large, online interactive, database systems that operate under the direction of computer professionals.
- User-operated stand-alone minicomputers and microcomputers.
- Distributed processing networks.
- Information centres, where computer staff train and support users in accessing, analyzing, and generating the information they need.

The problem for corporate managers is to choose and implement the computer systems that best match user requirements. In doing so, they alter the traditional relationship of computer personnel with corporate management and users, and create organizational problems and tensions that require resolution.

The position of computer departments within the organization is still evolving. Unfortunately, employee frustration and anger over the expanding role of computers is commonly vented on IT personnel, who have demonstrated little sympathy for the non-technician in the past, thereby exacerbating tensions. This chapter identifies many sources of misunderstandings and suggests ways to improve relations between IT personnel and management/users, such as educational programmes, sign-off procedures, ombudsmen, or interface committees that provide a forum for airing problems and reaching collective decisions.

Crises in computing need not embitter relationships among employees of a firm. It has been noted that the Chinese expression for 'crisis' has two characters. The first represents danger, the other opportunity.

Case study: Organization of computing at United Distillers

United Distillers produces whisky, gin and bourbon in thirty-two distilleries in Scotland. In each distillery, PCs collect data directly from cask filling heads (information on date, distillery, and characteristic of each barrel of whisky), information loaded automatically in an in-house database. Nightly, data are downloaded to the distilling centre in Elgin and eventually sent to the Edinburgh head office for mainframe processing. This sytem allows tracking of 7 million separate barrels, information used by masters responsible for the blends of the Scotches. (Each bottle of whisky that is blended at one of United Distillers bottling plants may draw from forty different malts stored in one of six warehouses throughout Scotland.) The information also keeps the customs and excise department at bay. (A fine of up to £5,000 per barrel can be levied if the company cannot account for each and every one of its 7 million barrels.)

Departmental computers, usually a Bull, DEC Vax or Hewlett Packard mini, act as a fileserver to access data in corporate mainframes for operating groups within the company. From there the data can be retrieved by individual PCs. This is to avoid the problem of a large number of people searching for information in the mainframes all at once.

Distributors worldwide are given 'agreed autonomy' over computer systems in their local offices as long as rules in the areas of interconnectability and communications are followed. Within the United Kingdom, however, applications software and PC make are standardized because this results in discounts from suppliers. 'In fact, the purchasing power we can exert has actually been more important in the UK than the need for communications compatibility', says a company spokesperson.
Source: David Dobson, 'Whisky Business', *Which Computer*, vol. 14, no. 4 (April 1991), pp. 126–8.

Questions

1 Why is a distributed computer environment necessary at United Distillers?

2 Describe how the data on barrel characteristics are distributed in the organization.

3 Corporate mainframes are principally transaction processors, but also act as corporate dataservers, 'barrels of information into which an operator in London, or wherever, can dip when necessary'. How does this organizational structure benefit United Distillers? What are some of the disadvantages with this structure?

4 Do you think that it is likely that United Distillers has a security system in place to control access to corporate data so that employees can only get the information they require for their jobs? Why?

5 In recent years United Distillers has purchased more of its distributors, up from 20 per cent to 80 per cent. What problems in the organization of computing resources do such acquisitions create?

Case study: Information centre at Texas Instruments

Texas Instruments Incorporated (TI) has fifty manufacturing plants in seventeen countries and employs approximately 79,000 people. In 1983 when the company decided to implement its first information centre, more than a quarter of company employees were using the organization's worldwide network for messaging and computing. Many of the corporate data were already computerized, but not all employees knew how to access them. With computer literacy high and the expectation that over half of TI total computing resources would be in the hands of end-users by 1990, the need of a centre to guide end-user computing before it grew out of control was recognized.

The first centre opened with a staff of fourteen people and supported one mainframe product — the fourth generation language Focus. By 1987 the company had thirty-two information centres serving 10,000 employees in twenty-nine locations. The difficult economic conditions of the mid-1980s contributed to the large number of employees using the centres — they discovered that they could save money by doing their own computing. By 1987 the centres supported seven mainframe software products and six TI professional computer packages in the areas of financial planning, graphics, electronic mail, electronic filing, decision support and database reporting and inquiry.

Source: 'Creating an information centre strategy', *EDP Analyzer*, vol. 25, no. 2 (1987), pp. 1–16.

Questions

1 How does TI's information centre strategy contribute to the following:
   (a) End-user self-sufficiency.
   (b) Better use of information system resources.
   (c) The corporate financial picture.
2 What mission do the centres have?
3 Glenn Fischer, the information centre manager, believes that TI has already trained all of the 'early adopters' — those employees who are eager to use computers. Now he wants to focus on the 'reluctant users' and make such users comfortable with computing. What strategies should the centre adopt to attract this clientele?
4 Do you think analysts will like working in information centres? Give reasons for your view.
5 Is the TI model of an information centre transferable to other organizations? Give reasons for your view.

Case study: PC support at British Airways

PC HQ, a section of the Information Management Department at British Airways, is responsible for consultancy, support and general promotion of the use of personal computers. In addition, the section helps organize the purchase and maintenance of PCs and is concerned with systems integration so that PC users can access mainframe data. 'The mainframes are the key systems for the airline', says Hilary Henning, a PC HQ spokeswoman. 'BA depends so much on them for operational use. When it comes to PCs it's a supplementary activity — decision support based on corporate data.'

PC HQ, with a staff of thirty experts in PC topics, also provides direct support for end-user departments. For example, it produces guides and leaflets, gives demonstrations and runs seminars. To help end-users make the best use of information resources, PC HQ will also go out into a department and monitor its hardware/software for a four to six week period using a package called PC Checker, then issue a

report on resource usage. The department is then advised on ways to improve its operations. 'The PC world is so complex now that it's easy to buy the wrong combination', says Ms Henning.
Source: Kate Lloyd Jones, 'Case study two: British Airways', *Which Computer*, vol. 13, no. 8 (August 1990), p. 92.

Questions

1 Does BA's Information Management Department provide the services of an information centre? Explain.

2 According to Ms Henning, the company has 6,000 PCs and is adding a couple of hundred a month. What problems does this growth present to PC HQ? To top management of British Airways?

3 Many PCs at British Airways act as mainframe terminals with data manipulation facilities. What type of problems can arise in this environment?

4 BA maintains a list of recommended PC software products. Give reasons why such a list is helpful.

5 British Airways employs 50,320 people scattered in 2,000 locations. What problems does this pose for integrating computer systems? For the purchase and maintenance of PCs? For the training of personnel?

Key words

Centralized data processing
Common database
Distributed database
Distributed data processing (DDP)
Electronic data processing (EDP)
End-user computing
Fail-safe capability
Fail-soft capability
Hierarchical

distribution
Human relations in a computer environment
Hybrid approach
Information centre
Information systems (IS) department
Information technology (IT) personnel
Integration of information services

Micro—mainframe link
Nodes
Offloading
Organizational considerations
Replicated distributed database
Ring network
Segmented distributed database
Service bureau
Star network

Discussion questions

1 What are the central issues in the controversy between centralization and decentralization of computer resources?

2 Does the decision to centralize or decentralize depend on:
(*a*) Firm size?
(*b*) Whether the firm is multinational?
(*c*) Whether the firm has branch offices? Explain.

3 Should the location of the computer department in an organization be a function of:
(*a*) Size of the computer department and its maturity?

(b) Organization's size?

(c) Power politics of the organization?

(d) Industry of the organization?

(e) Computer executive's personality?

4 Describe the essential elements of a distributed processing system. What are the characteristics of DDP? Which activities should be distributed? Which centralized? Would this distribution change with:

(a) Size of organization?

(b) Organizational structure of firm?

(c) Geographical distribution of branches?

5 What configuration of computer equipment in a DDP environment would you select for the following situations:

(a) A bank with many branches?

(b) A wholesaler with many warehouses?

(c) A factory with distributed plants, each of which manufactures a different component?

6 What problems arising out of personnel conflicts and power struggles should be expected in the transition from centralized computing to DDP? What can be done to minimize the harmful effects of such conflicts?

7 Why is a micro—mainframe linkage more difficult technologically than linkage between two mainframes?

8 What management problems are unique to micro—mainframe linkage?

9 What are the problems of control, security, and privacy to be expected in a DDP environment? How can one overcome such problems?

10 What type of business or industrial environment lends itself to DDP? What factors should be taken into consideration in deciding whether to implement DDP?

11 Discuss the benefits of DDP.

12 What are the risks associated with end-user computing? How can these risks be resolved?

13 Comment on the following statement. End-user computing frees employees from channelling all processing requests through IT personnel; this independence, the main benefit of end-user computing, would be lost if end-user processing controls were installed. What organizational structure would you recommend for end-user computing?

14 What measures should be taken to foster a smooth working relationship between computer personnel and users?

15 How can understanding between corporate management and computer personnel be promoted?

16 Do you agree with the concept of an ombudsman as an arbitrator and facilitator between the frustrated user and the computing centre? If so, what qualifications should the ombudsman have?

17 Do you believe that computer technology will soon make users totally independent of computer departments? Explain.

18 Are conflicts between corporate management and computer personnel based on differences in educational background? Or do differing attitudes and biases contribute to dissension? Explain.

19 Although the concept of a support centre for end-users is not new, it was not until the 1980s that the concept gained widespread support. Why?

20 What is the difference between an information user and an end-user? Should an information centre distinguish between the two? Why? What distinction should be made?

21 Can an information centre reduce end-user frustration in the use of computer resources? How?

22 How does the IT department benefit from the establishment of an information centre?

23 Discuss the services that information centres commonly provide. Who should decide whether a request for information centre service is legitimate and reasonable? What criteria should be used?

24 Suppose that the advice given to the end-user by the information centre conflicts with the view of the end-user's supervisor. How should the conflict be resolved? Should the information centre be passive or 'battle' for what it believes?

25 Do you think that information centres are here to stay or just a passing fad? Give your reasoning.

Bibliography

Abdul-Gader, Abdulla H. 'End-user computing success factors: further evidence from a developing nation', *Information Resources Management Journal*, vol. 3, no. 1 (Winter 1990), pp. 1–14.

Alavi, Maryam and Ira R. Weiss. 'Managing the risks associated with end-user computing', *Journal of Management Information Systems*, vol. 1 (Winter 1985–6), pp. 5–20.

Altman, R. 'Are you ready for cooperative processing?', *Information Center*, vol. 6 (April 1990), pp. 20–31.

Amoroso, Donald L. 'Understanding the end user: the key to managing end-user computing', *Managing Information Resources in the 1990s*, Proceedings of 1990 Information Resources Management Association International Conference, Hersey, Pennsylvania, 14–16 May 1990, pp. 10–18.

Earl, Michael J. *Management Strategies for Information Technology*. Hemel Hempstead: Prentice Hall, 1989, pp. 127–57.

Gunton, Tony. *Enduser Focus*. Hemel Hempstead: Prentice Hall, 1988.

Henderson, John C. 'Plugging into strategic partnerships: the critical IS connection', *Sloan Management Review*, vol. 31, no. 3 (Spring 1990), pp. 7–17.

Hunt, Gary E. 'Challenge of the 90s: harmonizing business and technology for commercial advantage', *Journal of Information Technology*, vol. 5 (1990), pp. 105–9.

Jones, R. 'Time to change the culture for information systems departments',

Information and Software Technology, vol. 31, no. 2 (March 1989), pp. 99–104.

Kerr, Jim. 'The management information center', *Computerworld,* vol. 25, no. 44 (5 December 1990), pp. 125–7.

Lemming, Anne. 'Creating a business-oriented IT department', *Journal of Information Technology,* vol. 5 (1990), pp. 175–7.

Meiklejohn, Ian. 'New forms for a new age', *Management Today,* (May 1989), pp. 163, 166.

Rathswohl, Eugene J. 'Information resource management and the end user: some implications for education', *Managing Information Resources in the 1990s,* Proceedings of 1990 Information Resources Management Association International Conference, Hersey, Pennsylvania, 14–16 May 1990, pp. 81–5.

Saunders, Carol S. and Richard W. Scamell. 'Organizational power and the information services department: a reexamination', *Communications of the ACM,* vol. 29, no. 2 (February 1986), pp. 142–7.

Simmons, Laurette Poulos. 'The impact of information centers on end-user computing', *Information Resources Management Journal,* vol. 2, no. 2 (Spring 1989), pp. 13–23.

3 Design of a computer centre

When possible make the decisions now, even if action is in the future. A reviewed decision usually is better than one reached at the last moment.
William B. Given, Jr

Organizations with centralized computing resources usually house these resources in a facility called a **computer centre**. This computer centre, under the jurisdiction of the IS department, contains mainframes, minis, communications equipment, printers, plotters and other peripherals that are shared by information workers in the firm's employ. This chapter describes how a computer centre is planned, how the layout of the centre is designed and what problems must be resolved regarding site preparation before hardware is actually installed.

Not all of the computers in modern corporations are centralized. As described in Chapter 1, computer equipment may be located in functional departments but linked by telecommunications to the centre. In addition, employees may have stand-alone microcomputers on their desks and manage their own computing resources. Nevertheless, in most large corporations, the bulk of information generated by computer is processed by computer centres.

Planning overview for a computer centre

A new computer centre — or one that is being relocated, renovated or expanded — requires meticulous planning. The amount of floor space required will depend on the equipment to be installed, which in turn depends on the projected workload of the centre. That is why the design of a computer centre begins with **capacity planning** (Box 1 in Figure 3.1). Resource needs and area requirements are determined for both current and future information requirements. Next, the site is selected (2) and planning takes place for the physical layout of the centre (3) and the room layout (4). Site preparation (5) will include consideration of special environmental support facilities such as air-conditioning, electrical power and security measures. Each of these design stages is discussed in the sections that follow.

A full-time **project manager** is often needed to oversee a computer centre overhaul or a new construction. This person should have six to ten years of

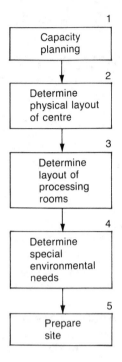

Figure 3.1 *Planning process for a computer centre*

experience operating a computer centre and also have a technical background. The project manager needs a thorough understanding of the operational aspects of a computer centre, good project management skills and some knowledge of structural problems that may be encountered in site preparation.

One of the first duties of a project manager, and one of the most critical to project success, is to identify personnel needed to support the project. Cooperation and assistance from computer processing personnel who will work in the new centre and from representatives of functional departments to be served by the centre is required when plans for the centre are formulated. The project manager also needs the expertise of electrical and mechanical engineers, vendors of computer equipment, representatives from the local telephone company, an interior designer/architect, a lighting consultant, an acoustical consultant, a security specialist, a fire control consultant, insurance staff members, a telecommunications expert and someone knowledgeable about local building codes. (The role of each of these experts will become apparent as this chapter progresses and planning stages are discussed.)

The project manager makes design decisions based on the recommendations of these experts and oversees the actual construction and occupancy of the computer centre in accordance with blueprints based on these decisions. What's more, the project manager makes sure that the construction does not interfere with the ongoing delivery of information services and is completed within funding and time constraints.

Capacity planning

Once a decision has been made by corporate management to build (or expand) a computer centre and a project manager has been chosen, planning can begin. The objective of capacity planning, the first planning stage, is to determine an efficient mix of resources in order to achieve and then sustain the level of information services expected by corporate management for workloads in the future. Generally, planners can only project usage two or three years ahead with any degree of accuracy, although estimates may be made for a longer time horizon.

Capacity planners first study the work processes and information needs of employees and how computer technology is presently used on the job. Then they look ahead, anticipating problems and how they might be solved using the information technology of tomorrow. This requires an in-depth knowledge of technological trends, coupled with the ability to make forecasts based on current data, estimates, hunches, intuition and experience. Capacity planners must also consider possible future organizational changes that may increase computing load: for example, a merger or acquisition of another firm.

Clearly, capacity planning is a risky proposition. If planners fail to project the future environment with accuracy, the corporation may either lack adequate resources and processing power to meet information requests in coming years or have excess unused capacity, a costly waste.

Collecting data on goals and objectives

Projections for future computer centre requirements are based on the answers to a number of basic questions. One of these questions is: What goods or services does the company plan to produce in the future?

The answer can be found by studying the organization's long-range plan, which outlines business goals and objectives. Departmental strategic plans (including those of the IS department) will likewise provide insights into the expected direction of the company. From this information, the capacity planner estimates what information resources will be needed to accomplish stated goals.

A review of other organizations that have already placed similar goods and services on the marketplace is another way to estimate future requirements. By analyzing what business transactions are involved when producing and marketing such goods and services, the role of information processing to support the transactions can be ascertained. Once this role is known, the planner can then extrapolate hardware, software and personnel needs.

Questionnaires and interviews with information users are also useful ways of gathering data on information resource requirements for the future. Suppose a user states that an online system to handle inventory queries is high on his or her department's applications' wish list. On learning this application priority, the planner can map out which support resources should be available: input/output devices, memory, communication facilities and so on.

Gathering data from a large number of information users can be time consuming and costly. Fortunately, this is not necessary. Only a small proportion of workers account for a major portion of a computer centre's workload. According to one rule of thumb, the ratio is 80 to 20: that is, 80 per cent of the resources are used by 20 per cent of information users. Capacity planners can identify employees who place heavy demands on information services and direct questions to these workers. On the basis of the information collected, a projection of service demands for the entire information user population can be made.

Another data source on which to base projections is historical records. However, caution is in order here: straight-line projections from historical data have proven notoriously inaccurate. There are simply too many variables that can cause a dramatic alteration in computer centre use. For example:

- A change in the attitude of the workforce towards information technology or the learning of new skills.
- The hiring of people who use information services heavily.
- The demand for or introduction of new hardware and software products as a result of technological advances.
- The demand for new types of information to meet the challenge of competitors.

Software tools are available to help in the data collection and analysis phase of the planning process. Programs can be purchased for the task of matching, merging and validating data from several different sources. Other packages help in determining the amount of information resources that will be required by new applications. Also available are performance/capacity planning software packages and capacity planning graphics/reporting software packages.

Service-level expectations

Another question that the capacity planner must consider is what level of service the computer centre should provide. Client departments perceive service in terms of reliability, ease of use and response time. They generally will give planners range estimates of service requirements. For example, an information user may state that a 3-second response time is desirable, a 5-second response time is adequate and a 10-second response time is intolerable.

The ability of the centre to meet service requirements will depend, in part, on the volume of service the centre will have to deliver. That is why workloads must be forecast. Many capacity planners subdivide current workload into major processing subsystems, then ask 'what if' questions, using analytical modelling software tools to help them make their forecasts. They take into account activity periods (during both day and year) in which the workload may peak, as well as periods of nominal activity. An important decision of the capacity planner is whether to provide computer resources to fulfil all requests for service during **peak time zones** or whether to allow some of the demand to spill into **shoulder zones** (contiguous non-peak zones). One way to cut down the amount of funding that must be spent for information resources is to allow spillover.

A difficulty in making workload projections is that workloads tend to rise with increased capacity, a phenomenon sometimes called the **latent workload**. This occurs because departments may not depend on the computer centre for their information needs when service is poor, but become clients when service improves.

Preliminary configuration of resources

The design of the resource mix for a new computer centre can begin once the information demands that will be placed on the new computer centre have been identified. The first step is to evaluate existing processing capacity. How reliable is the delivery of information services at the present? How much demand is currently being processed? Are resources on hand being used to full capacity? Could a reconfiguration of resources lead to a more effective utilization of facilities or personnel?

Next to be assessed are hardware and software in the marketplace, as well as products being readied for market introduction. Their features, limitations and cost are examined, as are constraints imposed by management. How much money can be spent on the new computer facility? What is the time frame of the project? What will be the staff size and the qualifications of people working in the new centre? What types of backup will be required? Planning issues faced by the project manager are similar to those facing a systems development team. That is, the configuration of information resources for a computer centre will depend on technological, economic, financial and organizational constraints similar to those that affect the design of new application systems.

Figure 3.2 summarizes the factors to be taken into consideration by the project manager determining the preliminary resource configuration for the new computer centre.

Use of analytical and simulation models

Fortunately, software is on the market to assist planners in the evaluation of proposed **resource configurations**. For example, some programs will generate analytical standard reports on performance and service levels for given resource configurations. Others will make a technological assessment or financial analysis of a preliminary configuration. Some suggest configuration alternatives.

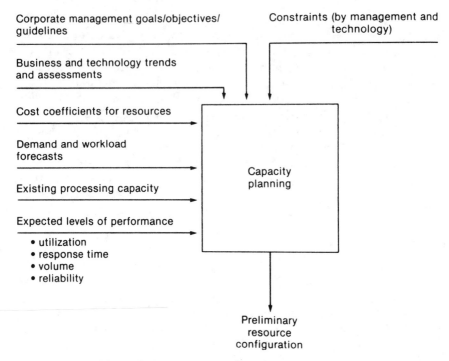

Figure 3.2 *Determining preliminary resource configuration*

Simulation models can answer 'what if' questions, such as: 'What if the demand for service of User B is increased by 100 per cent?' The answer might be calculated in terms of the impact on other information users with regard to average and maximum waiting times, length of queue, average and maximum response times, and so on. (ISERT and SCERT are models of this nature.) 'What if' questions might also be asked about a possible change in hardware or software resources: for example, what if a different model of a central processing unit (CPU) with different operating systems (or different peripherals) were used?

Contingency planning
Simulation models are particularly helpful in **contingency planning** — planning for disaster or some abnormal shutdown of operations for an extended period of time. By asking 'what if' questions (for example, what if there were a power failure for six hours during a peak load period?), the planner can determine the effect on operations of an earthquake, flood, fire, bomb or some other calamity, information that is needed in designing backup facilities for the centre. (See Table 3.1 for a list of events that can cause confusion or havoc in a computer centre.)

Consideration of **backup** is crucial at this planning stage because special

Table 3.1 *Potential calamities*

Acts of God	Other calamities
Dust storm	Collapse of structure
Earthquake	Hardware operational faults
Flood	Human errors, omissions and negligence
Hail	Industrial accidents and fires
Hurricane	Mechanical failure
Intense cold weather	Power failure
Intense heat and/or humidity	Software failure
Lightning	Telecommunications failure
Rain	Utility (gas, water) failure
Snow	Arson
Tidal waves	Bomb
Tornadoes	Holding hostage:
Volcanic eruptions	Data
Windstorms	Humans
	Programs
	Theft:
	Computer time
	Data
	Programs

equipment to warn against disaster (such as alarms, scanners or sensors) may require physical space within the centre and funding from the centre's budget. What's more, duplicate or supplementary resources placed in the centre or in a separate facility may be essential in order to restore vital operations following a calamity. No corporation can protect itself from every possible disaster. In narrowing the field, in deciding what disasters are likely and what measures are most cost effective in protecting resources, simulation models are useful tools. They can also be used to calculate both the resources needed to restore vital operations and the cost of such recovery.

Usually, corporate management makes decisions regarding backup levels and policies. These decisions will be based on management's aversion to risk and a judgement on whether the cost of backup is worth the benefits. The responsibility of a project manager is to present contingency options to top management. It is important that backup strategies be decided before the resource configuration for the new computer centre has been finalized so that space for backup resources can be allocated and funds for their acquisition can be budgeted.

Analysis and consultation

Before finalizing the resource configuration of the new computer centre, the project manager should consult with computer processing professionals, future information users and corporate management.

Finalization of resource configuration

Sometimes, no detailed disclosure is made of the finalized plan to avoid disappointment or frustration should the plan require modification at a later date. More commonly, however, the **capacity plan** is publicly announced. This commits corporate management to the plan and makes the project manager accountable for its implementation.

Some organizations go a step further and formalize their commitment to the capacity plan with a **service-level agreement** (SLA), a document that guarantees information users a given level of service in terms of transaction volumes and response times. The SLA may also specify the price structure for services. The advantage of this agreement is that users know what information services the centre will deliver and planners know that they will not be accountable should users suddenly increase their service demands.

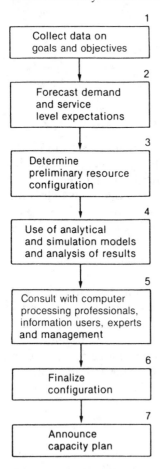

Figure 3.3 *Stages in capacity planning*

The most time-consuming and difficult stage of planning a computer centre is capacity planning, the steps of which are reviewed in Figure 3.3. A capacity planner should keep a record of what scenarios are assumed, what information is collected, what planning tools are used and what predictions are made. This record can guide future planners when the centre needs further expansion. And should forecasts be off the mark, the record can be analyzed to determine what went wrong so that the mistakes won't be repeated.

Site selection

Ideally, a decision regarding the location for a new computer centre should follow capacity planning, so that adequate space will be allowed for current operations of the centre and for projected growth. In companies building a new office facility that will include a computer centre, the **site selection** team should include the project manager for the centre to ensure that the special needs of the centre are taken into consideration in the site decision. (For example, the desire of Shearson/ American Express for a security facility with controlled access led to the selection of a Lower Manhattan site large enough for a 10-storey structure surrounded by considerable open space.)

Space allocation for the computer centre within a new facility should be based on convenience of access for the users of the centre and special construction requirements, such as floor load ratings, access to service lifts, ceiling heights and fire barriers. (More on computer centre site preparation appears later in this chapter.) Here again, the expertise of the computer centre project manager is invaluable. In practice, however, critical site decisions are often made without a computer specialist on the planning team. This can later lead to innumerable and costly problems in computer centre construction.

Facility layout

The **layout** of a computer facility follows finalization of the resource configuration for the centre. Figure 3.4 shows the layout of a typical small computer centre, with rooms for job receipt, data conversion, library, job assembly, teleprocessing, CPUs and peripherals, output preparation and distribution, storage and offices. In larger computer centres, more rooms for offices and support (such as rooms for vendors, customer engineers or backup power) will be needed.

What decides the location of one room in relation to other? **Workflow**. Room placement is designed to facilitate the smooth and efficient movement of work from the time a processing job is received by the centre to output distribution. For example, job assembly should take place near the room that houses processing hardware. Storage rooms for paper supplies should be in close proximity to the printers and plotters that use the paper. Although the offices for supervisory

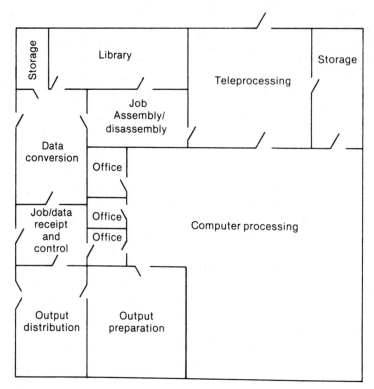

Figure 3.4 *Layout of a small computer centre*

personnel should be near operations, access to these offices should not be through operational areas to prevent the possibility of someone causing a malfunction by bumping into sensitive equipment.

Figure 3.5 illustrates the order in which computer centre tasks are performed. In general, this sequence of tasks dictates room assignments when computer centres are being designed. (Note that the computer centre layout in Figure 3.4 is based on the workflow model in Figure 3.5.)

Sometimes, factors other than task sequence influence layout decisions. For example, the need for controlled access to CPUs may result in the placement of security checkpoints that interfere with a smooth, efficient workflow. Or the necessity of large outside doors for equipment delivery may dictate the location of the room in which processing takes place. The project manager may have to make compromises in workflow efficiency for a variety of reasons, but will do so only with reluctance.

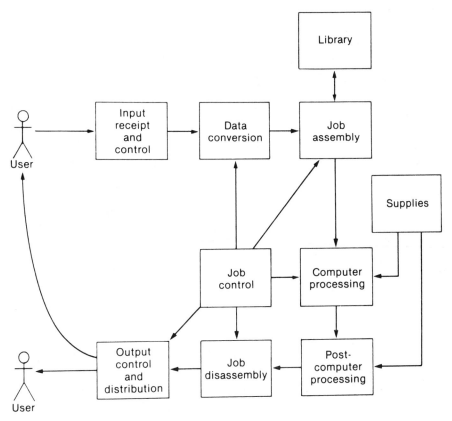

Figure 3.5 *Work flow in processing of a computer job*

Room layout

After a decision is made regarding the arrangement of facilities in the computer centre, the layout of individual rooms is planned. Here again, workflow is important. In equipment rooms, machines should be placed so that operators can move efficiently from one task to another. Vendors generally supply templates (like those in Figure 3.6) for their equipment, to be used when planning the location of machines. The shaded portion of each template in Figure 3.6 shows the machine in operation; the dotted and arced lines indicate the amount of space needed around each machine for opening equipment panels for maintenance and for ventilation and cooling.

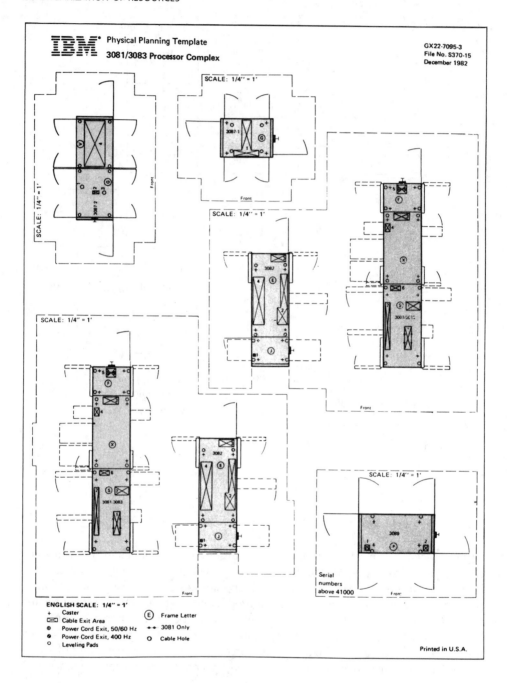

Figure 3.6 *Configuration of a computer room*

Site preparation

A computer centre has highly specific needs with regard to room construction, power supply, wiring, air-conditioning, fire protection and security. Let us now turn to problems of this nature that confront a project manager in **site preparation**.

Room construction

The size and weight of computer hardware to be installed in the new centre will dictate ceiling height, floor loading capacity, room dimensions, door size and the location of loading docks. (Vendors will supply information on equipment requirements to the project manager.) Floors raised in height from 12 to 24 inches are standard in computer centres. This allows space for power cables, telecommunication lines, heavy-equipment supports and air circulation under the floor and around pipes, wires, fire protection equipment or whatever else needs to be installed there. In earthquake areas, sway bracing and flexible joints should be part of the room construction to ensure that equipment stays upright. Where flooding is a possibility, adequate drainage and sump pumps should be added at the time of construction.

In areas where radio frequency interference is a problem, the computer room will have to be shielded to suppress this interference. Even low to moderate levels of interference can cause read/write errors. High levels can be a hazard to operating personnel and equipment components. Shielding techniques include grounding computer equipment, using copper screens on windows and installing equipment away from outside walls and windows.

Another special need is the inclusion of sound-absorbent materials in walls, ceilings and room furnishings. Soundproofing will help reduce the noise level in operational areas and help isolate equipment noise from office areas and meeting rooms.

Chapter 9 describes security precautions that should be taken at a computer centre site, including restricted access through a single entrance, guard stations, locks, window grills, alarms and so on. Many centres include three perimeter barriers: an outside wall or fence, interior walls, and locked cabinet and storage vaults within the centre. Security is also taken into consideration in the design of manholes, door frames, ventilation ducts and the roof.

A variety of detectors are available to protect facilities from intrusion. Some are triggered when an electric circuit is broken: for example, when a door is opened or when the lights are switched on. Others are activated when a light beam or laser beam is interrupted. Vibration monitors will detect a presence; ultrasonic and radar waves can be used to detect movement. Closed-circuit TV and time-lapse cameras, which snap frames at preset intervals, can assist security guards in surveillance of the centre. Protective measures of this nature should be planned at the time the centre is designed, not added later as an afterthought.

Power

The **power** requirements of a computer room will depend on the type and amount of equipment to be installed. Power needs for lighting, air-conditioning, heating, administrative office equipment and future growth must also be taken into consideration.

A backup power supply is commonly planned. There is always the danger that lightning or a storm will cause a blackout. A power outage for a period as short as four milliseconds can interrupt millions of computer operations and may result in equipment damage and data loss. Voltage problems, such as spikes, surges, dips, noise or brownouts, can be equally destructive. If a computer centre is to perform critical functions and must remain continuously online, then the purchase of a constant voltage transformer, motor generator or uninterruptible power supply (UPS) is an answer. Some companies maintain large sets of batteries for power backup. Table 3.2 lists the causes and characteristics of common outage and voltage problems, describes their impact and recommends solutions.

Following a calculation of power requirements, the placement of power outlets and electrical conduits is decided. Floor sockets or roof sockets instead of wall sockets are useful. They allow the placement of equipment away from walls for ventilation without danger of employees tripping over and possibly damaging exposed cables. Electrical wiring can run under the floor when the room is designed with raised floors.

Air-conditioning

Temperature regulation of a computer centre is a top priority because machine heat that is generated during computer operations can damage equipment and lead to the deterioration of tapes and disks. Excessive humidity can likewise cause damage. In designing a computer room, a project manager will consult vendors regarding the limits of heat and humidity for their products. It is the manager's responsibility to ensure that the site has adequate provision for air circulation, heating and cooling, and humidity control.

Fire protection

In a computer centre, **fire protection** is more than planning for fire extinguishers and sprinkler systems. It begins with room construction using fire-resistant materials, the erection of fire barriers such as fire doors, the placing of alarms and the installation of fireproof vaults for the storage of critical records and documentation. The facility should have an independent air-conditioning system to minimize the possibility of a fire spreading from an external location. A decision on hardware location and density also has fire safety implications. To minimize potential fire damage, computer centres generally separate CPUs rather than place them side by side.

Table 3.2 *Power disturbances in a computing centre*

Type of problem	Characteristics	Cause	Impact	Solution
Spikes	Sudden rise in power	Lightning Heavy equipment switching	Burns electronic hardhare Wipes out data	Voltage regulator
Surge	Increase in power	Opening or closing of switch Lightning	Burns electronic components	Suppressors Voltage regulator
Dip	Sudden drop in power	Voltage drops over distances	Erases data Causes CPU malfunction	Voltage regulator
Noise	High voltage High-frequency interference on power line	Lightning Ground faults Poor motor–brush contact Switching power supplies Heavy electrical equipment	System malfunction Data loss	Ultraisolation transformer
Brownout	Temporary reduction of voltage, ranging from 10 to 35 per cent	Smoothing demand, causing 5–15 per cent variation temporarily	Motors run hotter and slower on equipment designed for 10–15 per cent variation	Backup system
Blackout	Complete loss of service	Storm Inadvertent shutoff	Data loss Computer damage	Standby power supply (SPS) or uninterrupted power supply (UPS) Backup system

Heat-sensing devices that activate an alarm when room temperature rises suddenly or reaches a predetetermined level may be installed. A drawback of this system in a computer environment is that electrical fires are generally localized. As a result, the alarm may not be triggered until extensive damage is done.

Smoke detectors are another fire prevention device. In general, such detectors are placed in ceilings, in ducts and under the raised floors of computer centres. Unfortunately, smoke detectors are prone to false alarms. That is why some systems are designed to alert an operator of the presence of smoke rather than to set off automatic extinguishers and alarms. The operator is responsible for activating firefighting systems. Other smoke detection systems are controlled by a microprocessor and programmed to shut down computer equipment and air-conditioning, then release extinguishers following a short delay. The delay allows operators to override automatic firefighting systems in the case of a false alarm.

Sprinkler systems are recommended when the computer room is built of or stores combustible materials. Water cools a fire quickly, prevents flashbacks and is inexpensive to use. As long as equipment is de-energized, water will not cause permanent damage. But water sprinkled on machines with the power still on will create shorting and arcing and will ultimate damage equipment. The steam created can ruin magnetic media as well. What's more, the computer centre will have to be cleaned up and dried out before it can go back online.

For this reason, some computer centres rely on carbon dioxide extinguishers to suffocate the fire. The danger is that humans will be suffocated as well, which is why carbon dioxide is used primarily to extinguish fires in unattended facilities. If used in areas where people work, safeguards should be added for their protection. For example, the room should have numerous exits, oxygen should be available, the gas should have a delayed release and staff members should be highly trained in emergency procedures.

Another extinguisher is **halon gas**, a form of Freon that is safe for humans for short periods of time when in low concentrations. However, the gas does decompose into a toxic substance in an intense fire. A major disadvantage of halon is its expense. Whereas a water sprinkler system will generally protect a 20 × 20 foot area for $2,000, halon for the same area would cost around $20,000. Another problem is that halon pipes are custom-cut. They must be carefully cleaned of metal filings before installation since the filings can cause electrical glitches in computer equipment.

Of course, hand-operated fire extinguishers should be placed in the computer centre. In addition, space for storing waterproof and fireproof machine covers should be provided in all equipment rooms. Another fire safety feature is the placement of clearly marked and unobstructed master switches at all main doors to power down equipment.

Fire protection equipment should be carefully tested and properly maintained. When a fire occurred in one computer room, employees discovered that fire-fighting equipment installed just outside the computer centre would not fit through the door.

Other features of special concern

Because of the importance of telecommunications to modern computer centres, consultants from the telephone company generally participate in the design of such centres. They help plan networks and the supporting communication facilities, including loop wiring, carrier lines, patch panels and control centres. Sometimes, a special room for telecommunications equipment is strategically located in the computer centre.

Lighting consultants help ensure that computer rooms are well lit for daily operations and they can offer advice on the ways to use lighting as an after-hours security measure.

Expert advice may also be sought regarding the installation of alarms to alert the police and fire departments of computer centre emergencies. Sometimes, a centre has special plumbing requirements. Water from leaks in pipes, air-conditioning units or sprinkler systems can damage equipment; this water may collect under the raised floors, eventually seeping into cables and plugs. To prevent such damage, water detection systems may be installed.

Summing up

This chapter has dealt with planning issues that are unique to computer centres, such as how to determine capacity needs, decide on appropriate information resources and design layouts. Special problems in site preparation have also been discussed. (See Figure 3.7 for a computer centre that incorporates many of the

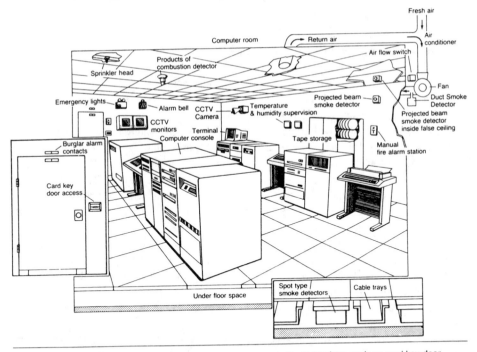

Note: Many means are shown for obtaining computer room security and safety, such as card-key door access and CCTV camera surveillance, and for detecting fire, such as smoke detectors, or in ceiling and air-conditioning ducts. A particularly interesting feature is automatic notification to a monitoring station of an emergency.

Figure 3.7 *Computer room layout (Source: ADT Security Systems, New York)*

features discussed in this chapter.) Because of the speed with which computer technology is advancing and because of escalating demand for information services, the design of a computer centre is a continuous process. Quite often, planning for a new round of construction or remodelling begins as soon as the last round has been completed. In one centre with which the authors are familiar, there were four changes in the CPU over a period of six years. And each required a new resource configuration and remodelling, including changes in the location of walls and false floors, a different power supply, altered ducts for air-conditioning and so on.

The number of factors that a project manager has to take into account in site preparation makes the job a demanding one. Experience, technical knowledge, leadership, patience, the ability to listen to others, flexibility, organization, an instinct for cost control and common sense are all needed to do the job well.

Fortunately, many technical manuals have been written to assist a project manager in designing a computer centre. And many experts can be called in to consult on technical problems, such as the design of raised floors, the wiring for teleprocessing or the installation of security devices.

Case study: Security against terrorist attack

During a raid, police found a terrorist hit list containing the names of 78 companies, including two German firms, MBP and SCS. Informed that an attack might be imminent, both companies increased their security. For example, MBP hired special guards to patrol its offices and grounds, and SCS, whose computer operations were visible from the street, installed reinforced glass in its windows. But the terrorists were not deterred. At MBP, an explosion knocked a hole in the building and wrecked two minicomputers; at SCS, an explosion caused more than £40,000 in damages.

Even companies that do not believe they are targets are taking added security precautions in view of the increase in world terror. Once terrorists realize how sensitive computer centres are, they fear that bombing attacks may escalate. SCS director, Jocchim Schweim, reportedly has a philosophical attitude towards protection in general. He is quoted as saying, 'There is a limit to how much of a "fence" you can throw up around a building and still allow people to carry out their normal work.'

Questions

1 Do you agree with Mr Schweim regarding the limits of security? Explain. What anti-terrorist measures might interfere with 'normal work'?

2 What protective measures do you think MBP and SCS should have taken in view of the police tip-off that their names appeared on a target list?

3 If you were responsible for the design of a new computer centre, what security features would you include to protect the facility against terrorism? What factors might limit the number of protective measures that you install?

4 Should security measures against terrorism be relaxed or eliminated when the threat of terrorism is reduced or eliminated? How is this determined and by whom? Is this a decision by IT management or corporate management?

Case study: Fire protection design

In 1989, a fire swept through a computer centre designed with a portable gas generator and fire extinguisher system on wheels so that the equipment could be moved to all parts of the computer room. The storage closet for this equipment was in the hallway leading to the computer centre. When the fire was discovered, employees ran to the closet to find it locked. When the key was located, they discovered that the firefighting equipment was too bulky to pass through the computer centre door.

By the time fire engines arrived, the fire had spread to tapes in the data library. Although located in a special fireproof vault, the librarian was moving tape reels in and out of the vault that morning by trolley, so had wedged the door ajar. Flames swept through the open door destroying billions of bytes of data.

Questions

1 What design features contributed to this disaster?
2 It would appear that the firefighting equipment had not been tested in the computer centre. Who was at fault for this lack of testing? The supplier of the equipment? The director of the computer centre? Explain.
3 What design features might help a computer centre recover from a fire like this one?
4 Who should be responsible for disaster planning for a computer centre? Who should design equipment, layout and procedures to prevent (or contain) fires like this one? Discuss both the formulation and implementation of disaster plans.

Key words

Analytical and
    simulation models
Backup
Capacity plan
Capacity planning
Computer centre
Contingency planning
Fire protection

Halon gas
Latent workload
Layout
Peak time zones
Power
Project manager
Resource configurations

Service-level agreement
    (SLA)
Shoulder zones
Site preparation
Site selection
Temperature regulation
Workflow

Discussion questions

1 Why are the planning and design of a computer centre important? Who are the interested parties?
2 Because of the widespread use of stand-alone computers, are large computer centres becoming obsolete? Explain your answer.
3 Who should be responsible for the design of a computer centre: a person from corporate management, a computer processing professional, a user of computer services or a consultant? Why?
4 Give some of the reasons why a new computer centre may be needed.

5 What are the inputs and outputs of planning a new computer centre?
6 What is capacity planning for a computer centre? How can one predict future capacity needs?
7 How can computer programs like SCERT help in planning a computer centre configuration? Does use of the model help with hardware only or also with software planning? What types of reports from SCERT are relevant to capacity planning?
8 What are the advantages, dangers and limitations of gathering information from computer users regarding their expected future computing needs?
9 What, if any, should be the role of consultants in designing and implementing a new computer centre?
10 What are the dangers of making straight-line projections of computer demand?
11 What is disaster planning? Why is it needed? How do you check to ensure that planning for disaster is adequate?
12 Discuss security issues in planning a computer centre.
13 What is the relevance of a service-level agreement? Whom does it protect and how?
14 What are some of the factors to be considered in the layout of a:
    (*a*) Computer centre building?
    (*b*) Computer centre room?
15 What is the importance of workflow in the design of a computer centre? Give examples of how workflow can be impeded or facilitated by room design.
16 What is a template? How can it be used in layout? Where can one get templates?
17 How can a computer centre be designed to detect or prevent:
    (*a*) Fire?
    (*b*) Water leaks?
    (*c*) Power failures?
    (*d*) Security violations?
    (*e*) Air-conditioning failure?
    Should these events occur despite protective measures, how would you deal with them?
18 Why is an uninterrupted power supply necessary to a computer centre? How can it be obtained?

Bibliography

'Consolidating multiple data centers', *I/S Analyzer*, vol. 28, no. 11 (November 1990), pp. 1–16.

Davis, D.B. 'IS automates for data center survival', *Datamation*, vol. 36, no. 22 (15 November 1990), pp. 95–8.

Devlin, Edward S., Harris Devlin and James A. MacMicking. 'Contingency planning: preparing for the worst', *Insurance Software Review*, vol. 14 (December/January 1989), pp. 60–2.

Gerald, T. 'Evaluating a disaster recovery plan', *Insurance Software Review* (January 1989), pp. 6–7.

Joseph, Gilbert W. 'Computer virus recovery planning: an auditor's concern', *Journal of Accounting and EDP*, vol. 6 (Spring 1990), pp. 26–30.

'Making the case for data center automation', *I/S Analyzer*, vol. 29, no. 4 (April 1991), pp. 1–16.

Niedzielski, Vince. 'Determining automation needs: seven critical concerns', *Datacenter Manager*, vol. 2, no. 2 (March/April 1990), pp. 35–7.

Nonnenberg, L. 'The changing role of support providers in the data center', *Datacenter Manager*, vol. 2 (September/October 1990), pp. 14–15.

Parker, Claire M. 'Developing an information systems architecture: changing how data resource managers think about systems planning', *Data Resources Management*, vol. 1 (Fall 1990), pp. 5–11.

Radding, Alan. 'Improve it or lose it', *Computerworld*, vol. 25, no. 19 (13 May 1991), pp. 71–4.

Ring, Tim. 'The balance of power', *Which Computer?*, vol. 14, no. 2 (1991), pp. 42–52.

Waller, Mark. 'Planning data center design', *Datamation*, vol. 35, no. 21 (1 November 1990), pp. 73–82.

Yourdon, Edward. 'A manager's guide to interface issues', *Dataquest* (India) (June 1991), pp. 82–8.

4 Computer personnel

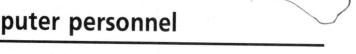

*The extension of man's intellect by machine, and
the partnership of man and machine in handling
information may well be the technological advance
dominating this century.*
Simon Ramo

Although computerized societies are often pictured as machine dominated, with humans subservient to technology, computers exist to serve people and to aid managers in reaching decisions. And they cannot execute given tasks without the assistance of a large number of **information technology (IT)** professionals and support personnel.

For example, input — be it data, operating instructions, or applications programs — is initiated by humans. It takes analysts to assess the needs of information users, and skilled programmers to convert these needs into bits, the only medium understood by machine. Collection and updating of data are an iterative human activity. Programmers are needed for the preparation of computer instructions, and many technicians are required for operating and servicing the computer itself. Without analysts, programmers, operators, managers, clerks, librarians, schedulers, and other support personnel, computers are unable to produce the information users request.

This chapter focuses on staffing an IS department. First, the duties and responsibilities of computer personnel are described. Job design, hiring, and turnover are discussed next. Since studies have shown that computer people place a high value on professional growth, both career development and training are also addressed in the chapter. The chapter closes with a section on job stress in the computing field.

Jobs in computing

Who are the professionals and support personnel needed to run a computing facility? Information processing is usually subdivided into three functional areas: systems development, operations, and support, as shown in Figure 4.1. Programmers and analysts fall in the first category, operators in the second, with

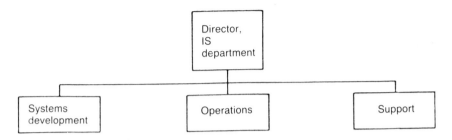

Figure 4.1 *Organizational structure of a typical IS department*

librarians, standards officers, schedulers, supply clerks, training coordinators, and others providing technical support in the third.

A breakdown of job classification in each of these three categories appeared in Figure 2.2 in Chapter 2.

The actual percentage of employees in each category varies from one company to another depending on the size of the firm, the amount of resources devoted to computing and the manner in which they are organized and the industry that the company represents. For example, a distributed processing configuration generally requires more operational and fewer support personnel at each node. A centralized computer installation has the opposite mix: more support and fewer operational personnel.

Even within a given facility, positions are not static, since needs are constantly changing. A salary survey by *Datamation* in the early 1950s listed 27 computer positions. A similar survey in the 1980s listed 55. This increase can be attributed to the growth of computing facilities and the complexity of computer operations today. Not all computer centres have 55 positions, however. Small companies may have far fewer positions, with a single individual filling several jobs.

Every year, the number of people choosing IT careers grows.

In the sections that follow, the work of analysts, programmers, operators, and technical writers is described. The duties of a database administrator, data administrator and chief information officer are also presented. Check the index to find where in the text the duties of other information processing personnel are discussed. For example, the responsibilities of schedule officers and librarians are covered in Chapter 10, the work of the IS director in Chapter 5.

Systems analysts

A **systems analyst** is a technican who participates in the development, implementation and maintenance of systems. The analyst studies a problem and decides what procedures, methods, or techniques are required for a computer solution to the problem. Analysts also gather and analyse data, document systems, design forms and test systems.

In addition, analysts serve as the link between users and the IS department staff, interpreting client needs and formulating user specifications for systems development teams. Analysts are also responsible for explaining the capabilities and limitations of computing to users with no technical background. And analysts are the persons who resolve complaints and serve as mediators in user—IS staff disputes. Indeed, the position of systems analyst was originally designed to bridge the gap between information users and programmers in order to resolve the classic computing problem: how to develop computer systems when users (who want results) and programmers (who know how to make things happen) have difficulty communicating with one another. The idea was to train a computer professional with the knowledge of what computers can do, someone familiar with the jargon of programming, able to talk to and translate for end-users.

Figure 4.2 outlines the responsibilities of systems analysts in each phase of a computer system's development. During the feasibility study, analysts make

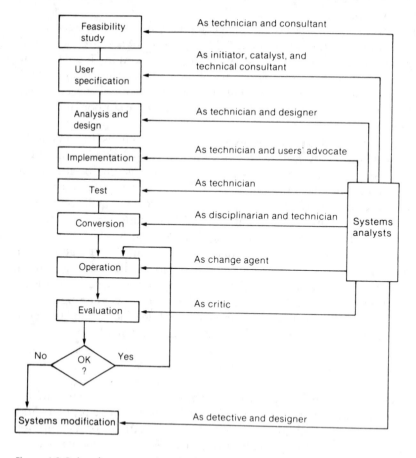

Figure 4.2 *Roles of systems analysts in development of a computer system*

cost−benefits estimates and advise the development team on the technological feasibility of proposals. During the user specifications phase, analysts take an active role in structuring the problem, quantifying objectives, and helping to synthesize and crystallize user desires so that systems specifications can be prepared. When conflicting user interests arise, analysts must find a compromise.

When the design phase is reached, analysts have technical concerns: design specifications for output, input, files, forms, and procedures. In implementation, analysts become users' advocates, working with programmers for solutions that consider human factors. During conversion, analysts may seem to switch sides. Their job is to prod reluctant users procrastinating over conversion and to refuse user requests for late specification changes, working on behalf of the IS department to resolve technical problems and speed conversion.

Although most analysts are assigned other projects when a system is finally operational, some may assist management in planning and implementing strategies to reduce employee resistance to the new system. Analysts can advise management as to how new technology will affect daily operations, and they may be astute in gauging the amount of change an organization can comfortably absorb. Analysts may also assist in orientation and training programmes, effectively acting as change agents to promote favourable attitudes towards computing. Once systems are operational, analysts often participate in systems evaluation. They identify errors and recommend system modifications.

Most firms have a number of systems analysts so that no individual analyst would be assigned all of these functions. As a matter of fact, it is unwise for a single analyst to have prime responsibility for all stages of systems development. That would violate the principle of separation of duties, a management principle that stipulates that those who plan and design a system should not take part in testing and approval decisions. Since complex projects require the expertise of many analysts, this division of responsibility can usually be enforced. It is over the life of a number of projects that an individual analyst may be required to perform the spectrum of roles shown in Figure 4.2. However, small firms with limited personnel may require a single analyst to work on all phases of development.

The ideal systems analyst should have the characteristics listed in Table 4.1. One look at the list should explain why good analysts are in scarce supply. Because the ability to handle people is as important as technical competence and because knowledge of an organization, its power structure, policies and procedures is essential to analysts, many firms like to hire analysts from their organization's labour pool. Individuals who have demonstrated aptitude for systems analysis and have the right temperament are hired even if they lack some of the skills needed in the job. They are then given appropriate technical training. It is thought by some that analysts hired and trained in this fashion are more quickly of value to the firm than analysts hired from outside who have technical qualifications but are unfamiliar with key personalities and how the company is run. Not everyone agrees with this viewpoint, however.

Table 4.1 *Desirable characteristics of a systems analyst*

Technical expertise in systems analysis and systems design.
Working knowledge of hardware, software, databases, operating systems and telecommunications.
Detailed knowledge of a programming language, such as COBOL for business applications.
Creative mind.
Ability to think in the abstract, to work with symbols and problem logic.
Receptivity to different approaches to problem solving, analysis and design.
Ability and patience to teach and train both professionals and non-technical users.
Good listening skills.
Project management skills.
Enjoys working with people.
Sensitivity to people and knowledge about human factors.
Knowledge about clients, their business, and industry.
Sensitivity to the company's power structure.
Ability to work in non-structured, ill-defined, and conflict-prone environments.
Ability to function well under pressure, resolve conflicts and balance trade-offs.
Ability to work in a team.
Halo — if possible.

Programmers

The job of a **programmer** is to write and test the instructions that tell the computer what to do. Unlike analysts, who have to deal with the marriage between people and machines and often with unpredictable human emotions, programmers solve problems of logic in a more predictable environment — a machine environment. They first decide how to solve a problem, then prepare a logic chart, code instructions in a language the computer can understand, establish input/output formats, follow testing procedures, allocate storage, and prepare documentation.

Although some of a programmer's duties overlap with those of analysts, programmers do not require the social skills of analysts. Indeed, the typical programmer is reclusive, an individual who wants to work alone, without much social interaction or managerial direction. Many programmers are highly strung and overspecialized and reject externally imposed structure and routine. Most have no desire to enter into managerial or executive ranks. A large number of young, mobile, unmarried people with technical bents enter the field, which helps explain why programming is a high-turnover profession.

Sometimes, small firms that cannot afford a large staff merge the responsibilities of analysts and programmers in one position. Even large firms like the analyst–programmer combination, since it helps reduce the misunderstandings that often arise between the two professional groups and eliminates finger pointing and blame shifting when things go wrong. The problem is finding qualified personnel. The development of special-purpose, high-level languages that makes programming easier has contributed to a number of analysts doing their own programming, so the analyst–programmer may become more common in the future.

With regard to programming skills, there is great diversity among programmers. Some specialize in COBOL, FORTRAN, or other high-level languages. Others specialize in packages for decision support systems or languages for such support, like GPSS and SIMSCRIPT. Still others, schooled in operations research, focus on simulation. Systems programmers with expertise in hardware deal with low-level languages (assembler or machine languages). These programmers work more closely with operations than with applications development.

Operators

Since the early days of computing, the job of **operator** has changed greatly for both peripheral and computer operators. Formerly, operators loaded machines with tapes, disks, or cards and monitored relatively simple machine consoles. Vocational or junior college training was adequate for the job. Today's operators, because they operate sophisticated systems, must be knowledgeable about hardware, software, and databases. An estimated 80—90 per cent of an operator's time is in software-related activities, where knowledge of the system's job control language is required in order to optimize the system's resources.

Operators have responsibility for the security and privacy of data and hardware as well. Operating errors can lead to damage to expensive equipment, necessitate reconstruction of the database, require costly reruns, or result in lost business due to delay or inconvenience to users.

Database administrator

The training of specialists to assist in systems development and implementation has arisen as information technology has grown more complex. For example, the position of **database administrator (DBA)** has emerged in recent years. This administrator is responsible for the coordination and use of data stored under the control of a database management system. For example, it is the job of the DBA to minimize the cost of the machinery or hardware involved in data management and to minimize disk space and the time it takes to access data.

The position entails the upkeep of data (updates, additions, deletions, and database reorganizations), data maintenance (this may entail moving data from one storage media to another for quick and efficient access), maintenance of historical data (including modification of files when definitions of data elements and classifications change), and the purging of useless data. Any changes to the database, data directories or data element dictionaries must also be approved and supervised by the DBA. In addition, the DBA resolves conflicts when users dispute data classifications or who should create data, establishes policies for segmented or replicated databases and determines the distribution of data.

The role of the DBA is both technical and non-technical: mainly, the DBA interacts with technical staff (analysts and programmers) and with end-users. Persons in this job need training in database management systems, physical and

Table 4.2 *Functions of a database administrator*

Database design	Retrieval
Content	Search strategies
Create	Statistics
Reconcile differences	Access
Dictionary/directory	Frequency of processing
Create	Spare use
Maintain	User utlization
Data compression	Response time
Data classification/coding	Operational procedures design
Data integrity	Access to database
Backup	Access for testing
Restart/recovery	Interfaces
	Testing system
Database operation	
Data element dictionary custodian/authority	*Monitoring*
Maintain	Data quality/validity
Add	Performance
Purge	Efficiency
Database maintenance	Cost
Integrity	Use/utilization
Detect losses	Security/privacy
Repair losses	Audit
Recovery	Compliance
Access for testing	Standards
Dumping	Procedures
Software for data element	
dictionary/data dictionary	*Other functions*
Utility programs	Liaison/communications with:
Tables, indexes, etc., for end-user	End-users
Storage	Analysts/programmers
Physical record structure	Training on database
Logical-physical mapping	Consulting on file design
Physical storage device assignments	
Security/access	
Assign passwords	
Assign lock/key	
Modify passwords/keys	
Log	
Encrypt	
Modify	

logical database design, data planning, relationship modelling, data standardization, data dictionaries, data security and operating systems.

Table 4.2 lists the numerous responsibilities of the DBA. Because of the scope of these activities, most large organizations provide DBAs with a staff including data specialists and analysts experienced in public relations and liaison with users. Usually, the DBA reports to the IS department director, but some firms give the position independent status, with the DBA reporting directly to a user committee.

Data administrator

A specialist who shares responsibility with the DBA for managing and controlling data is the **data administrator**. This individual generally handles the coordination and use of all data collected by an enterprise. In some organizations, the data administrator is allocated responsibility for the logical organization of data while the DBA focuses on physical database design. That is, the data administrator may be responsible for the global management, control, and documentation of information that the organization uses, while the DBA designs, implements and maintains databases and database management systems. In other organizations, however, the division of responsibility may be made along different lines.

The positions of DBA and data administrator are relatively new and still evolving. A great deal of variation still exists among firms in both job descriptions and titles of computer specialists assigned the task of data control and management. One of the challenges of a computer processing director is to organize and manage personnel in such a way that specialists (including data specialists) work in harmony as cohorts and co-workers, not as antagonists and competitors.

Technical writer

Today, computers are in the hands of many people who have no training in information technology. As a result, an increased responsibility has been placed on the developers of both hardware and software to provide clear and complete descriptions of their projects and instructions for their use. **Technical writers** perform this role. In addition, they document computer and clerical procedures within an organization. This documentation helps to provide continuity when personnel turnover occurs and facilitates operations, programming maintenance and audits.

A new trend is to add technical writers to systems development teams. This helps the writer gain a clear knowledge of the product. In addition, the writer's skill as a technical communicator can be used to improve the quality of the writing in systems specifications, planning documents, and analysis statements prepared by analysts and programmers.

Chief information officer

The position of **chief information officer (CIO)** is being introduced in organizations where information plays a key role. Usually, the CIO is a senior vice president who acts as an information resource representative and technology adviser to the chief executive officer and other members of the executive committee.

The job of CIO is generally a staff position, with no direct responsibility for line activity. Perhaps the term *technology facilitator* best describes the CIO's work.

Date processing job description — Page 1	Classification No. 222

Job title: Maintenance programmer	Grade

Reports to: Manager of programming

Job titles supervised directly: None	Approximate no. of positions:

Natative description
Performs maintenance and modification of programs currently in production to keep them responsive to user needs and to assure efficient operation in the production environment. Modifies or expands coding to accomplish specified processing changes. Tests modified programs to ensure that changes operate correctly and that changes have no adverse impact on program or system operation. Updates program historical and procedural documentation to reflect modifications. Creates special reports and file extracts from existing databases, using generalized routines.

Responsibilities
1 Analyzing existing program logic to determine best method of accomplishing required changes or causes of program malfunction.
2 Designing change modules and adjustments to existing coding to accomplish correction or modifications.
3 Testing modified programs.
4 Maintaining installation test database.

Duties
1 Analyze production programs to isolate problems or to determine more efficient methods.
2 Design program logic to eliminate problems, accomplish needed changes, or increase operational efficiency.
3 Expand test data to perform more thorough validation and to reflect requirements of program modifications.
4 Update program documentation to include changes
5 Fulfil user requests for data extracts and special reports.
6 Fulfil administrative reporting requirements.

External job contacts
1 Systems designers and analysts.
2 Operations personnel.
3 Applications programmers.

Qualifying experience
1 High school diploma and two to four years of college.
2 Programming fundamentals.
3 Six to 12 months as a programmer trainee.
4 Proficient in at least one of the programming and job control languages used in the department.

Achievement criteria

Figure 4.3 *Sample job description: maintenance programmer (Source: IBM, Organizing the Data Processing Installations, C20-1622-2, White Plains, NY: IBM)*

CIOs act as advisers and coordinators, relying on their ability to express and sell ideas to peers and subordinates to get things done. Most have a good technical background in data processing, knowledge of the industry, and management experience. Their exact role will differ from one organization to the next, but the key functions that usually fall under their jurisdiction are information processing, office automation, communications and sometimes planning.

Job design

As mentioned earlier, the responsibilities assigned to a given position will vary somewhat from firm to firm. When organizing an IS department, **job descriptions** will be prepared by management for each computing position and these descriptions will be used when hiring and evaluating personnel. A sample job description, that of a maintenance programmer, appears in Figure 4.3.

How does the manager of an IS department decide what duties to assign a given job? One design technique is to first draw up a list of all responsibilities of staff, then to distribute the workload among the positions funded. A sample from such a **task list** appears in Table 4.3.

Many managers like to customize assignments to individuals in their employ, matching aptitude, skill and preference while rotating unpopular duties. They prefer general job descriptions so that a change in a given employee's duties will not require a corresponding change in title and job. Figure 4.4 shows how such

Table 4.3 *Task list sample*

---

1 Act as coordinating point for all data processing plans in the organization.
2 Be responsible for achieving the agreed annual data processing revenue.
3 Agree and maintain data processing priorities.
4 Maintain staff records.
5 Direct and control systems feasibility studies.
6 Prepare user procedure manuals for new systems.
7 Document written programs in accordance with departmental standards.
8 Prepare, agree on and maintain the department's five-year hardware plan.
9 Control the process of hardware selection.
10 Direct induction training for recruits engaged in the systems function.
11 Ensure that computer run job streams are scheduled to obtain maximum utilization of equipment.
12 Conduct routine purges of files in order to release redundant files.
13 Record data preparation work done and maintain appropriate logs.

Note: A task list of an IS department typically includes hundreds of activities like these.

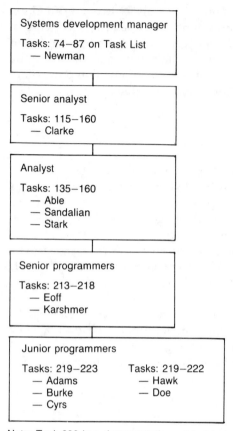

Note: Task 223 is a documentation-related task

Figure 4.4 *Sample task assignments for systems development personnel*

flexible assignments might be made. Note that although both Adams and Hawk are junior programmers, Hawk is not responsible for Task 223. This could be for any number of reasons. Perhaps Hawk is poor at documentation, or as a recent trainee, is still learning the firm's documentation standards. Maybe Hawk has just served as a maintenance programmer and is now being rotated to other duties. Perhaps Hawk strongly dislikes documentation.

Making job assignments from a task list has many advantages. It serves as a checklist to ensure that all tasks are allocated and that backup for crucial tasks is assigned. In computing, where continual adjustment must be made to new hardware, software and changed environmental conditions, new tasks are constantly being identified. The list helps a manager restructure jobs to incorporate the new tasks or plan changes to allow for job enlargement and job enrichment. In addition, the list can serve as a basis for evaluation when using the management-by-objective approach to evaluation.

Another useful managerial tool when designing jobs is a job diagnostic survey. Such surveys give employees an opportunity to express views on their own jobs and to recommend changes. Suggestions should be adopted for humanizing jobs, for making them more enjoyable as well as more challenging and efficient. A follow-up attitude survey will help managers evaluate the effectiveness of implemented changes. In computing, job redesign should be an ongoing process. Jobs cannot remain static when information technology is moving at such a fast pace.

Hiring

Computer personnel, especially those in professional classifications, are in demand. The shortage of qualified professionals is creating delays in the development of new computer systems and means large financial rewards for professionals who are willing to job-hop. To find experienced personnel, organizations engage in a variety of **recruiting** practices. Vacancies are advertised in 'help wanted' sections of national newspapers, in professional journals and on the radio. Many companies send personnel representatives to recruit at universities and may also have members of their computing staff visit to explain what kinds of work they are doing. This sparks student interest and helps sow the seeds for future hiring. Other firms turn to recruitment agencies and search firms, even though the agency fees are high for a referred prospect who is subsequently hired.

Corporations with a large number of openings in many departments may hold an open house for prospective employees. Sometimes, an IS director is looking for persons with a more diverse educational background than computer science (someone with a qualification in accounting, finance, or engineering and with some computing experience is often preferred over the pure computer science graduate). The open-house setting allows the director to interview candidates who might not realize that their backgrounds qualify them for information processing positions.

Setting up booths at professional job fairs is another recruiting technique. Most people find that a fair is a non-threatening environment for job hunting and like being able to shop around and compare available jobs. Recruiters like the opportunity of meeting a large number of prospects face to face.

Some organizations have formalized internal employee referral services that have proven highly effective. They ask employees to inform recruiters when they learn of professional colleagues who have entered the job market. Succession planning, a form of internal recruitment, is another way to fill openings. It may be as simple as designating successors to key positions, or it can encompass detailed career planning and career ladders.

Because there are seldom enough qualified job applicants in computing, firms may have to hire inexperienced programmers and analysts or train people to fill openings. Unfortunately, predicting aptitude or potential is difficult for many computing positions. A few multiple-choice tests for programmers have been developed, but those in existence are used so often that applicants in the job market will probably be given the same test over and over. Before applying to firms of their choice, many try to gain experience with the test by first interviewing with companies low in their preference list. To make testing effective, a battery of tests is needed, or a large database of questions should be prepared from which a test can be generated at random.

As a result of the demand for qualified IT personnel and the shortage of suitable candidates, the already high salaries in IS departments are constantly rising. Personnel officers must guard against hiring new, inexperienced employees at a higher rate than the salary received by employees on the same job that were hired earlier. Compression, the reduction of salary differentials because of inflation, can also be the source of employee dissatisfaction if new employees are hired at high pay. Salaries should synchronize so that employees who change to other occupational ladders (switching from operator to programmer, for example) do not experience loss of pay.

Sometimes, a fringe benefit package that will attract applicants is negotiated, or an appealing career path or promotion schedule is offered. Competition for applicants may be so keen that companies may even give bounties to employees who succeed in enticing (raiding) experienced IT personnel from competitors or other firms, although most managers consider this practice unethical.

Turnover

Because of the lack of qualified personnel in job markets, **turnover** is a major concern of IS directors. They try to create a work environment in their departments that will encourage employees to remain on the payroll. Research which tries to identify positive and negative motivational factors in the workplace is of great interest to them.

Although many studies have been done on employee motivation in the past, the question that needs to be addressed is whether IT personnel are different from other groups in the workforce. When Jac Fitz-enz asked 1,500 computer personnel to rank a list of job 'satisfiers and dissatisfiers' (criteria drawn from an earlier study by Fred Herzberg whose work is still widely referenced in industrial training), he found that achievement, possibility for growth, work itself, recognition and advancement rated highest. Salary and status were much lower in the rankings than expected.

In another study, J. Daniel Couger and R.A. Zawacki compared the attitudes of 2,500 computer employees with the findings in a survey done by J.R. Hackman and Greg Oldman, using the same diagnostic survey instrument. The two main findings of Couger and Zawacki are that analysts and programmers express a greater need for personal growth and development than the 500 other occupational groups surveyed and they express a lower social need strength (desire to interact with others) than any other job category analyzed. More-recent studies agree that computer people seek personal fulfilment and growth from their work and are less motivated by money and job titles than other employee groups.

In acknowledgement of such differences, corporate managers have developed strategies to motivate and reward computer professionals other than the traditional rewards of pay, title and promotion. To reduce turnover, they:

- Keep on the leading edge of technology. Most computing people prefer to create new systems than to spend their time maintaining outdated ones.
- Provide challenges. Reduce routine.
- Pay attention to the needs and desires of individual workers. (When work tools are lacking, job-hopping may follow.)
- Make sure that each employee sees that the work he or she does is used and that it plays an important role in making a product (or project) successful.
- Provide training and educational opportunities.
- Create attractive career paths that allow for individual growth.
- Work together with IT staff to develop equitable ways to measure and evaluate performance. (The problem of performance evaluation in the field of computing is discussed in Chapter 7.)
- Establish informal lines of communication with co-workers and management.
- Decentralize the company's structure to allow for more individual autonomy and decision making on the job.
- Recognize and reward contributions. (When a cash bonus or promotion is not appropriate, how about two tickets to a London show, a posh dinner, or a four-day weekend?)
- Involve employees in planning. This instils a commitment on the part of the employee to make the plans work.
- Provide work that increases the number of skills used on the job.
- Rotate unpopular assignments, such as systems maintenance.
- Move people from project to project to keep them from getting bored.
- Institute flexible working hours. Explore telecommuting.
- Offer stock-purchase plans or profit sharing as long-term incentives.

Of course, good personnel administration is also needed, the features of which are found in general business texts and will not be repeated here.

Career development

Since computer personnel place a high value on professional development, a computing facility should offer employees career paths that progress in

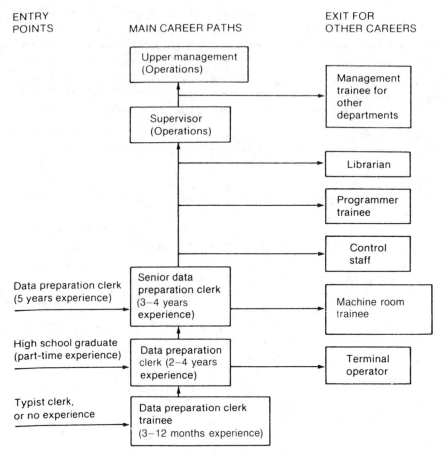

Figure 4.5 *Career paths for data preparation clerk*

responsibility, authority and compensation. These paths should allow employees to move from any position laterally or upward in the hierarchy of the IS department. (The possibility of a career track for technical employees that does not necessarily lead to promotion into management should be considered. Many IT specialists lack the interest in and aptitude for management.) The pipeline concept has been adopted by many firms: they encourage employees to prepare themselves for higher-level jobs and give employees first consideration for positions as they open up.

Figures 4.5 and 4.6 illustrate how such **career paths** work. An applicant's education and previous experience determine level and salary when hiring a data preparation clerk. Different entry levels mean that employees who transfer to the position from other jobs can be placed at a level with equal responsibility and authority, receiving a salary commensurate with or better than their former pay.

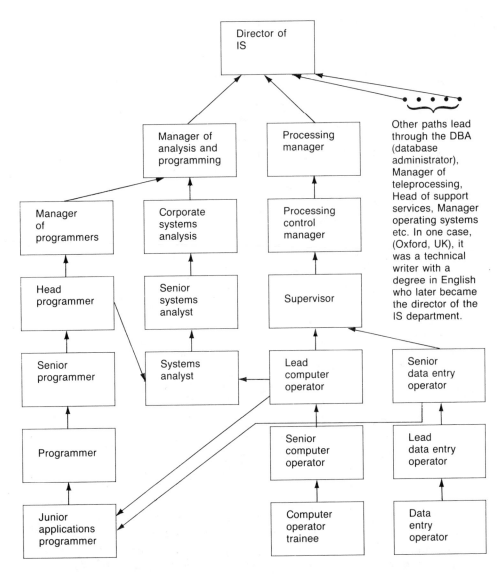

Figure 4.6 *Some career paths in information technology*

Data preparation clerks can exit laterally to other computer jobs as they gain experience and learn new skills, or they can work up to a supervisory position and then switch to other departments as a management trainee.

Career ladders should be developed for all computing positions, with entries and exits, and lists showing the body of knowledge and skills that belong to each professional position should be available to employees. These lists help employees

Table 4.4 *Knowledge required for job as sytems analyst or programmer, by priority rankings*

Prerequisite	Systems analyst	Programmer
Introductory computer and information systems concepts	1	1
Computer security controls and auditing	13	13
Planning and controlling of systems development projects	9	14
Improving computer centre productivity	18	18
Human relations in systems development	4	9
Software package analysis	15	17
Computer scheduling	16	16
Legal aspects of computing	19	19
Human factors in equipment design and layout	7	13
Telecommunications concepts	8	7
Hardware characteristics	10	8
Database management systems	6	5
Operating systems characterization	11	4
Information-gathering techniques	2	11
Minicomputer characteristics and uses	14	2
Systems design topics	12	6
Applications programming languages	5	3
Computer simulation	17	19
File design	3	2
Job control languages	12	3
Introductory statistics	20	20
Statistical decision theory	23	21
Regression analysis and sampling theory	24	22
List processing	21	15
Sorting	22	10

Source: Adapted from Paul H. Cherney and Norman R. Lyons, 'Information systems skill requirements: a survey', *MIS Quarterly*, vol. 4, no. 1 (March 1980), p. 42.

select career paths and guide them in planning the training they need. Table 4.4 is an example of one such list. It ranks occupational prerequisites for systems analysts and programmers in order of importance according to a survey of 32 information systems managers. Once introductory computer and information systems concepts are mastered, each job has different priorities of required knowledge.

Each job in a career ladder should also be associated with a set of required skills, so that an employee knows what training or experience is necessary to move up the ladder. Since computer technology is not static, these requirements are subject to frequent change. For example, analysts today have to know about personal computers, word processing, spreadsheets, graphics and voice synthesizers — subjects not part of their jobs ten years ago. In addition, since there are optimal times for switching from one job ladder to another, employees should be cognizant of how jobs mesh. For example, Figure 4.6 shows that an operator wishing to become a programmer should make the switch no later than senior operator or control clerk. If the operator has risen to the position of production manager, a switch to the programming ladder will result in a loss of pay, since the only level at which an inexperienced programmer can enter this ladder is as a junior applications programmer.

Sometimes, certain courses or a university degree are prerequisites for advancement along a career path. Firms differ in their policies regarding released time or financial support for studies, but all should offer advice and encouragement to employees willing to make an educational commitment in order to advance their careers. Indeed, management should encourage job mobility, since it is in the interest of a firm to have an experienced core of employees who know the organization and can provide backup for a number of jobs. And since career development is a key to job satisfaction, advancement within the firm should help foster company loyalty and reduce job-hopping to other companies.

Although an employee should theoretically be able to cross over and move up career ladders to reach any desired position in computing by gaining qualifications and experience, openings must be available and management willing to promote or transfer the employee. Sometimes, however, managers turn down requests for promotion or transfer. For example, programmers who wish to switch to the more prestigious career ladder of systems analyst may lack the requisite temperament, although they may have the required technical competence. (Programmers tend to be loners who shun interpersonal relationships, whereas analysts need to be perceptive of group dynamics and at ease when dealing with people.) Such an individual may find a career path or choice blocked in some organizations, even though jobs have been designed to allow for vertical or lateral movement.

Training

Many computer departments sponsor **training** programmes to provide employees with the background knowledge, skills, and up-to-date information needed to support the firm's hardware and software. The programmes may also be designed to promote career development of personnel. The justification for the expense of the career programmes is that they help reduce turnover, improve productivity, instil cooperation and loyalty to the firm, attract applicants, and also help retrain at less cost than firing/hiring when new computer applications upset the job structure of the firm.

The approaches used by corporations in training IT personnel are much the same as those used to train employees in other departments of a firm. Programmes range from on-the-job training, briefings and seminars to course work that rivals degree programmes at many universities.

Many software houses and manufacturers of hardware provide training materials, such as programmed instructions that come in manuals or a package for a terminal. The primary advantages of computer-based training over formal classwork is that the course is self-paced and can be scheduled at the employee's convenience. (Unfortunately, many people lack the self-discipline required to take a course of this nature.) Vendors may also sponsor training programmes of their own at reasonable cost for their corporate clients.

Some firms organize training by setting up an educational matrix that identifies groups of employees and courses needed by those groups, scheduling courses on the basis of the matrix. Other firms build courses around jobs, scheduling courses needed for becoming a programmer or manager, for example. Still others provide counselling to employees, customizing the training for individual career development. Table 4.5 shows a sample training status report of one employee under such a programme. The company draws up a list of training needs prepared from the status reports and then plans and schedules courses accordingly.

Although training based on individual needs is expensive, it may prove the solution to firms otherwise unable to fill openings due to the low supply of and high demand for qualified IT personnel. Also, such training may be the only way to get needed specialists, such as employees trained in computer-aided design or in languages such as APL that are used in numerical control.

Technostress

Before closing this chapter, a few words are in order on the impact of **stress** (mental, emotional or physical tension) on workers in computer-related professions. Although moderate levels of stress can motivate and challenge, the negative effects of stress are becoming increasingly apparent in the computing

Table 4.5 *Sample training status report*

Name	Karen Dallenbach
Current title	Programmer
Manager's name	Marion Latch
Interests	Working with people
Personal dislikes	Documentation
Future job	Systems analyst
Training needs	
Internal	Courses on systems analysis
	Basic course in accounting
	Assignment to development projects, especially accounting-oriented projects
External	Computer auditing
Other recommendations	Courses on DBMS
Target date of achievement	1994
Last date of update	5/2/91
Date of run	12/6/91

field. Too often, stress is associated with low morale, decreased efficiency, hair-trigger tempers, ulcers, heart disease, nervous conditions, neuroses and job-hopping.

Some stress can be attributed to physical discomforts in a computer environment. For example, eyestrain may result from screen flicker or from terminal glare. Backache may be triggered by poorly designed or positioned equipment. Many people are sensitive to the cold temperature of computer installations and to the loud noise of many peripherals, such as high-speed printers.

Other stress factors are attributed to the fast pace of the computer industry. Innovative products and technologies are continually emerging; IT professionals must keep abreast of advances in the field and adapt to them. Frequently, new procedures must be learned and new hardware mastered. The scope of computer jobs has to be altered and information processing departments reorganized. The tension that accompanies such changes is often compounded by unrealistic management and user demands, heavy workloads, and backlog pressures. Furthermore, many computer installations are run in a day-to-day crisis mode. Technostress, a 'disease that results when the delicate balance between people and computers is violated', may also result from inadvertent disk erasure, system breakdown, slow response time, or similar frustrations associated with computer use.

An important role of management in a computerized organization is to identify the causes of stress and to initiate programmes that will reduce it. For example, planning can help minimize strain during periods of heavy workload. Contingency planning and well-tested recovery procedures can lessen turmoil during and following system breakdown, while careful planning for project development should prevent unrealistic time schedules. It is no longer uncommon for firms to use the services of industrial psychologists and psychotherapists when planning social structures to relieve strain in the workplace.

Many companies also help employees learn how to alleviate stress. (For stress symptoms, see Table 4.6.) They offer seminars in stress control that teach time management techniques and physical remedies, such as special exercises. At career workshops, employees may play-act stressful situations and be counselled on ways to cope with job tensions. Since exercise is a good way to relax, firms may provide recreational facilities for their employees and sponsor sports teams.

The first step in alleviating computer-related stress is to acknowledge that the problem exists. Rather than debate whether information processing is more stressful than other professions, the focus should be on planning programmes to control and alleviate pressures associated with computer use.

Summing up

In the 1950s, when firms first introduced computing, a single employee may have acted as a programmer, analyst and operator. As computing grew, more positions

Table 4.6 *Stress signs**

Rapid breathing
Heart rate increase
Nervousness and tiredness
Energy level lower or higher than usual
Headaches
Pain or irritation in neck, jaw, lower back, or outer body regions
General tension of body muscles
Changes in sleeping and eating patterns
Feeling of fear, anger, and sadness
Circular thought processes
Excessive preoccupation with a single problem or situation

Source: National Employee Services and Recreation Association.

*Although the listed symptoms may occur when people are in stressful situations, no single sign is a good stress indicator. Consider the context in which these signs occur and remember that the presence of injury or disease may cause many of these same signs.

were added to computing departments. This is graphically portrayed in Figure 4.7. Note that the temporal evolution of computing corresponds with growth of firm size and that some new jobs were introduced in the 1970s and 1980s. These include database administrator, security officer, word processing specialists, problem analysts (who might be compared to earlier time-and-motion experts, tracing back to Taylor), and policy analysts (who evaluate information processing input and output for policy implications). Yet companies with limited electronic data processing today may still retain the computing structure of the 1950s, consolidating operations, programming, and analysis.

Computer personnel can be grouped in three categories: systems development, operations, and support. The systems development group, consisting of analysts and programmers, is concerned with long-term projects. Operations concerns daily activities. Maintenance programmers, production personnel, and operators of peripherals fall into this category. The support function includes system programmers, the database administrator, security and standards officers, the librarian and training personnel. This chapter has outlined the duties and responsibilities of some of these employees and described how their jobs are designed.

Hiring, motivation, evaluation and training of IT personnel should be consistent with traditional theories of personnel management, such as Fred Herzberg's theories on work (mentioned earlier), Abraham Maslow's on motivation, and Edgar Schein's on organizational psychology. Special attention, however, should be paid to the emphasis IT personnel place on challenging work and career

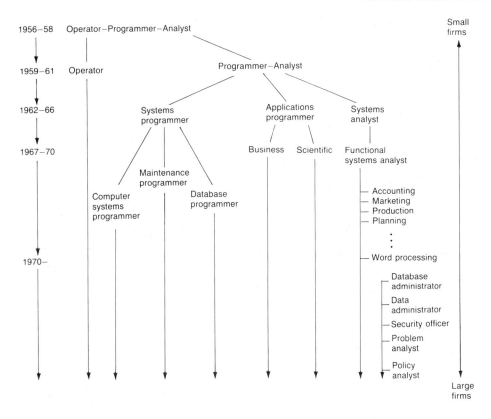

Figure 4.7 *Correlation of temporal and size evolution in computing personnel configurations*

development. Because many computer-related jobs are stressful, an important management concern in computer centres is to implement strategies to control and alleviate job tensions.

IT personnel in the 1990s will need skills and knowledge in database management, networks, telecommunications, artificial intelligence, fourth-generation languages, multiprocessor systems and ergonomics (human factors) — to name but a few areas where new technology is being introduced. This need will exacerbate shortages of qualified personnel, although the increased level of computer literacy in schools and universities should lead to more persons entering the computer field. Unions for computer personnel may be in the offing, demanding higher salaries, shorter workweeks and more employee participation in job-related decisions. Managing an IS department in the future should be quite a challenge.

Case study: **Ways to reduce stress**

Here are some suggestions for IT personnel of ways to reduce stress.

- Learn to play politics. Just doing a good technical job is not enough. You must develop good working relationships with management and users.
- Be open to change. Accept the fact that nothing in an IS department stays the same for long.
- Remember you are not a solo act. Use support resources that the IS department offers.
- Accentuate the positive. Some pressure can add colour and excitement to your work.
- Know your limits. Keep a balanced, realistic attitude about what you can do.
- Realize that you've got plenty of company. Long work hours are found in many other professions.
- Take time off. Don't put off that scheduled vacation.
- Get more training if you find yourself falling behind technologically.
- Plan your career. Explore other career options if you fear burnout.
- Look for the 'right' company. Make sure the corporate culture matches your own personality.
- Keep in touch with users. Nip problems in the bud.

Source: Alan J. Ryan, 'Before you burn out, chill out', *Computerworld*, vol. 24, no. 47 (19 November 1990), pp. 111–12.

Questions

1 Describe the personality profile of an IT professional who should listen to, and follow, the above advice. Is your profile 'typical' of IT personnel? Can one, should one, stereotype IT professionals? Explain.
2 If you were the manager of the individual you describe in your answer to Question 1, what steps would you take to pass on this stress-reducing advice? To ensure that the advice is followed?
3 As an IS manager, what measures could you take independently to reduce stress in the workplace?
4 How can an IS manager assess whether the level of stress among employees is high.

Case study: **Training at Abbey National**

Abbey National believes that company success depends on a well-rounded, well-trained staff. Indeed training is at the very heart of company strategy, says Julian Wakely, manager of the firm's distance learning group. Included in the contract of every staff member is a clause stating that the employee will receive training.

Recently, the company began the process of installing new Olivetti financial systems in its 687 branches. Managers and staff members at each branch are being sent on a three-day training course which begins with a video to introduce the new systems, followed by hands-on tutorials. A supplementary computer-based training package, written by Mr Wakely's department, is available for use once back at local branches. (Each branch has one terminal available at all times for staff training. Mr Wakely's department sends out 2,000 copies of training packages when new applications are introduced.) In addition, training programmes are embedded in the new systems to serve as help tutorials on the job.

Source: 'Case study: Abbey National', *Which Computer*, vol. 14, no. 5 (May 1991), p. 72.

Questions

1 Course-based training can run to several hundreds of pounds per day. Cheaper options, like audio-tape, video, and software packages to provide introductory training, are available for between £50 and £200. The time employees spend on training also is a cost factor. How can a firm, like Abbey National, justify such expenditures on training?

2 Abbey National has a performance appraisal system for all of its 15,500 staff. How can this system be used by management to appraise training needs?

3 This case describes Abbey National's three-tier training strategy. Which purpose does each tier serve? Do you think all tiers are necessary? Which is most cost-effective in your point of view?

4 Do you think it is a good strategy for Abbey National to send branch managers as well as staff to the three-day training courses? Why?

Case study: Japan Air Lines robot competition

Japan Air Lines (JAL) recently sponsored a robot competition, giving several workshops and maintenance teams Y5 million (£16,000) each to design a robot to reduce airline costs or enhance operations. Prizes were awarded to a team that designed a robotic aircraft-wash (resembling a car-wash but 80 feet high, 200 feet wide) and one that designed a robot that makes it easier to inspect parts for cracks. (The parts are sprayed with light-sensitive dye, cleaned, then placed under ultraviolet lamps. Dye that shows up is in cracks. The robot's contribution is to automate some of the spraying.)

Another robot idea which did not win but has since been implemented, saving the airline Y162 million (£0.52 million) a year, is a robot to polish the windows of jumbo jets. Since the soft acrylic windows of aeroplane windows scratch easily, they were periodically removed in the past and taken to a laboratory for polishing — a tedious operation taking three hours per window. The new robot hangs from the fuselage, allowing the windows to remain in place. It scrapes off precisely 130 microns using three different pads, an abrasive, polishing liquid and a coolant, and takes only a half hour per window. Six of these robots are currently in use at Haneda airport and will soon appear at Tokyo's Narita international airport as well. In addition, the robots are being sold by JAL to other airlines for around £14,000 apiece.

The company owns the robot patents. The winners received some prize money for further research and for a 'booze-up'.

Source: 'Glittering prizes', *The Economist*, vol. 312, no. 7613 (29 July 1989), p. 94.

Questions

1 Why do you think JAL planned this competition?

2 Do you think that this robot competition affected the morale of IT workers at JAL? How?

3 Wouldn't a competition like this just add stress to the workplace? Wouldn't this added stress be counterproductive? Comment.

4 What does this case tell you about JAL's style of personnel management?

Key words

Career paths	Information technology	Stress
Chief information	(IT) personnel	Systems analyst
officer (CIO)	Job descriptions	Task list
Data administrator	Operator	Technical writers
Database administrator	Programmer	Training
(DBA)	Recruiting	Turnover

Discussion questions

1 Are personnel concerns in an IS department different from personnel concerns in other departments of a firm? Explain.

2 Should authority over personnel reside within the IS department, or should the personnel office of a firm handle personnel matters for all departments of the firm?

3 Are computer staffs given privileges or special treatment? Explain. Does this create tension and dissatisfaction among other employees? How can a firm minimize or eliminate dissatisfaction arising from unequal treatment?

4 Once development, input preparation and output generation are shifted to the information user, the nature of personnel problems in IS departments will change. Comment.

5 Is it true that IT personnel do not mix well with other employees in a firm? Explain.

6 Is the danger of becoming professionally obsolete any different for a computer technician than for an engineer? How can IT professionals keep abreast of new technology?

7 Is the current shortage of IT personnel a temporary problem? How can this problem be solved?

8 Are employee-motivation personnel policies that are studied in personnel administration applicable to IT personnel? Explain.

9 Many employees believe evaluation procedures for computer jobs are irrelevant and unfair. Comment. What evaluation procedures and criteria would you use to evaluate the work of programmers, analysts, computer managers and other IS department personnel?

10 Why is there high turnover among IT personnel? How can turnover be reduced?

11 Is a user-friendly computer environment just a matter of improving personal relations between information users and computer technicians, or does it also require the special design of hardware, software, and data systems in order to bridge the gulf between the user and IT personnel? Explain.

12 What is the role of a:

(*a*) Systems analyst?
(*b*) Programmer?
(*c*) Operator?
(*d*) Database administrator?
(*e*) Technical writer?
(*f*) Chief information officer?
Name other positions commonly found in large computer centres.

Bibliography

Brown, Eric H., Kirk R. Karwan, and John R. Weitzel. 'The chief information officer in smaller organizations', *Information Management Review*, vol. 4, no. 2 (Fall 1989), pp. 25–40.

Brumm, Eugenia K. 'Chief information officers in service and industrial organizations', *Information Management Review*, vol. 5, no. 3 (Winter 1990), pp. 31–46.

Burnes, Bernard. 'Managerial competence and new technology: don't shoot the piano player: he's doing his best', *Behaviour and Information Technology*, vol. 10, no. 2 (1991), pp. 91–109.

Cougar, D. 'Motivating analysts and programmers', *Computerworld*, vol. 24, no. 1 (1 January 1990), pp. 73–6.

Duret, D., T. Ferrare, U. Debrun, E. Werner and P. Degoul. 'Custom-made information and the information engineer', *Technovation*, vol. 112, no. 2 (1991), pp. 113–19.

Gilmore, Ron V. 'CIO perils, and day or two later', *Canadian Information Processing* (April/May 1991), pp. 8–11.

Lyon, Lockwood. 'Appraising MIS personnel: techniques to make IT work in your organization', *Information Executive*, vol. 4 (Winter 1991), p. 6–7.

Mayo, Andrew. 'Management development: the ICL experience', *Management Decision*, vol. 29, no. 2 (1991), pp. 9–14.

McCuster, Tom. 'Why business analysts are indispensible to IS', *Datamation*, vol. 36, no. 2 (15 January 1990), pp. 76–8.

Meiklejohn, Ian. 'Whole role for hybrid', *Management Today* (March 1990), pp. 113–16.

Mullins, Carolyn, 'Training gifts for the 1990s', *Information Center*, vol. 3 (March 1989), pp. 16–18.

Ruhl, J. 'An MIS manager's guide to hiring programmers', *Journal of Information Systems*, vol. 7 (Spring 1990), pp. 47–54.

Stokes, Stewart L. 'The new IS manager for the 1990s', *Journal of Information Systems Management*, vol. 8, no. 1 (Winter 1991), pp. 44–50.

Watson, Hugh, Dale Young, Sheila Miranda, Barry Robichaux and Ron Seerley. 'Requisite skills for new MIS hires', *Data Base*, vol. 21, no. 1 (Spring 1990), pp. 20–9.

Watson, Richard T. and James C. Brancheau. 'Key issues in information systems management', *Information and Management*, vol. 20 (1991), pp. 213–23.

Westeman, John and Pauline Donoghue. *Managing the Human Resource*. Hemel Hempstead: Prentice Hall, 1989.

Wolman, Rebekah. 'Managing technical professionals', *Information Center*, vol. 6, no. 3 (March 1990), pp. 11–19.

5 Oversight of computing

All the time the Guard was looking for her, first
through a telescope, then through a microscope, and then
through an opera-glass. At last he said, 'You are
travelling the wrong way'
Lewis Carrol, *Through the Looking-Glass*

Information System (IS) departments have often been called **'a business within a business'**. But for reasons described in this chapter, they are under the direction of corporate management. Information user departments also exercise a measure of control over IS departments through their representatives on steering committees and project development teams. The sections that follow will describe the many ways in which activities of IS departments are subject to supervision and how steering committees, top management, information users and IS department directors interact in their oversight roles.

Each firm has a unique environment. Although this chapter describes how the **oversight function** is typically carried out, companies vary considerably regarding supervisory practices.

A business within a business

Within the organizational framework of a firm, an IS department is merely one of many departments. In structure, however, it may resemble an independent business. Indeed, the department can be compared to a manufacturing concern, since it operates as a job shop (in batch mode) or a continuous-production shop (real-time processing) to provide a product (information). There is a correlation in specific activities as well, as shown in Table 5.1. For example, facilities planning in manufacturing could be compared to computer configuration and network planning, tooling might be compared to programming, and a product line resembles the department's applications portfolio. The primary difference is product disposal: IS departments do not have to rely on market mechanisms for pricing or selling. Their product is often for a captured market, when sold to other departments in the company, or considered as a service when provided to information user departments without charge.

Table 5.1 *Parallel computer centre and manufacturing business activities*

Manufacturing business	Information processing centre
Product planning	Information systems planning
Facilities planning	Computer configuration and network planning
Market research	Computing demand forecasting
Product research	Keeping abreast with computer technology
Market development	User education
Product design	Systems design
Problem analysis	Systems analysis
Tooling	Programming
Production scheduling	Job scheduling
Production	Computing and operations
Production control	Production/operations control
Inventory control	Supplies inventory
Quality control	Input/output and information quality control
Consumer survey	User satisfaction survey
Consumer services liaison	User liaison
Personnel management	Personnel management
Administration	Administration
Product for sale	Information (sold or as a service)
Product line strategy	Applications development strategy
Product cost analysis	Applications project estimation
Pricing policy	Charge policy

Nevertheless, IS departments do seek to provide a product that is competitive with outside information processing centres. To do so, they must be managed with efficiency and effectiveness. Usually, a steering committee plays an oversight role.

Steering committee and subcommittees

A **steering committee** might be considered a board of directors for computing: it ensures that computing strategy is in line with corporate strategic planning objectives. That is, the steering committee usually establishes corporate policy towards information systems, makes long- and short-range plans for the IS department, sets information processing priorities, and allocates computing resources. It may also set standards and performance levels; schedule, monitor, and control operations; approve acquisitions; evaluate interfunctional applications; and resolve conflicts concerning user needs.

See Table 5.2 for a summary of the responsibilities of a typical steering committee. These functions can be classified in five general areas:

Table 5.2 *Functions of a typical steering committee*

Establishes corporate policy for information systems.

Formulates strategy to reach corporate objectives.

Assures coordination of information systems policy with corporate goals, objectives and policies.

Approves strategic, tactical, long- and short-range plans.

Recommends to top management the allocation of resources (budgetary decisions).

Designs organizational structure to ensure effective use of computers within the company.

Evaluates and approves proposals for resource acquisition and development of projects.

Reviews and monitors milestones of major development projects.

Establishes criteria and levels of performance for computing operations.

Establishes evaluation procedures.

Monitors and controls operations and schedules.

Resolves and arbitrates conflicts on priorities and schedules.

Formulates standards, guidelines, and constraints for both development and operations.

Allocates scarce resources.

Exercises funding discipline over major expenditures.

Oversees staffing.

Provides communication link between computer centre and corporate management.

Provides forum for feedback from information users.

- Direction setting — links corporate strategy with computer strategy.
- Rationing — reconciles the commitment of corporate resources to information systems with commitments to other business activities.
- Structuring — settles the centralization versus decentalization issue and charters various organizational units.
- Staffing — selects top computer managers.
- Advising and auditing — assists in problem solving and checks to ensure that the department's activities are on track.

Top management should be represented on steering committees, as should management representatives from user groups. Sometimes, consultants will be added to a committee to ensure a balance between technically oriented members and those knowledgeable about the goals, objectives, and policies of the organization. A balance between line and staff representatives is also advisable, as is a balance between planners, production personnel, and individuals from accounting and finance. With such representation, committees become a forum for IS management and information user departments to express their views, air their problems and reconcile their differences with regard to information systems.

Some steering committees are more successful than others. (Many computer managers consider them bureaucratic nonsense, rubber-stamp committees of little value.) Those that function effectively do so because they involve senior management as well as IT personnel and information users. Indeed, most steering committees today are chaired by a corporate manager, and it is probable that as information technology becomes more intertwined with corporate strategy, the trend toward top management chairmanship will continue. Another characteristic of successful steering committees is that they make long-range plans instead of approving projects singly. Furthermore, they involve information users in project planning and require them to justify their requests for information services.

According to some observers and practitioners, steering committees that meet too frequently get bogged down in details and find that they do not have enough knowledge to deal with the issues. Quarterly meetings that focus on strategic issues work best. The ideal committee size seems to range between five and ten members. Larger committees often result in one-way communication, not an open discussion of problems.

Organizations with a small computing facility may find that a single steering committee suffices. But organizations with large IS departments that offer complex services will undoubtedly require a hierarchy of lower-level steering committees. For example, a project review committee may be given responsibility for project development, while a tactical steering committee has responsibility for operations. Other common subcommittees and their reporting units are listed in Table 5.3.

Table 5.3 *List of committees and their reporting units*

Committee	Responsible to

Standing committees
  Steering committee
  Tactical steering committee
	Top management

Operating committee Users' committee for operations Project priority committee (for development, maintenance, and redevelopment) Resource planning committee	Steering committee
Database committee	Steering committee or director of systems

Ad hoc committees
  Resource selection committee
    Hardware committee
    Software committee
  Resource acquisition and implementation committee
  Security advisory committee
  Privacy advisory committee
  Control advisory committee
	Steering committee

Project team	Project manager and project review committee

The function of standing committees differs from that of ad hoc committees, which are created to solve an immediate problem, then dissolved after a solution is reached. The former have ongoing responsibilities.

At times, the steering committee may act as a crisis centre. Ideally, however, problems should be brought to the attention of the committee before reaching crisis proportions. Computing activities should be constantly monitored by steering subcommittees. Feedback and control systems (such as exception reporting) should alert committee members to problems. In addition, the IS director has the responsibility of bringing problems to the committee before they get out of hand.

Oversight role of top management

Let us now focus on **senior management oversight** of IS departments. As explained in the preceding section, representatives from senior management serve on steering committees. Although user representatives and IT personnel are also on the committees, two factors add weight to management's importance: (1) usually, the chair is drawn from senior management and (2) corporate management oversees the steering committees themselves. That is, the function of steering committees is decided by corporate managers, and they are the persons who appoint committee members in the first place.

Since corporate managers are also users of information systems, representatives from the top echelons of the firm participate in the development activities of many projects. For example, managers, as future information systems users, will participate in feasibility studies and help draw up systems specifications when new applications are initiated. They will help evaluate testing to see that systems that are developed do, in fact, meet managerial needs. As illustrated in Figure 5.1, senior managers have an oversight role in computing through development team membership as well as through steering committee stewardship. Furthermore, corporate management has budgetary control over development activities. It makes Go/No Go decisions following feasibility studies, selects

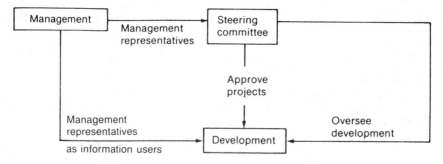

Figure 5.1 *Management's oversight role in development*

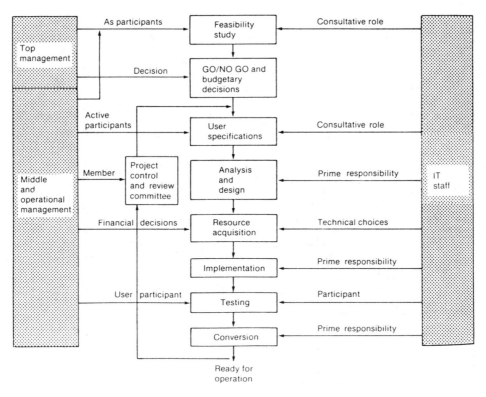

Figure 5.2 *Role of management and IT staff at various developmental stages*

methods of financing projects, and approves major resource acquisitions. This can be seen in Figure 5.2, which also clarifies the relationship of top management and IT staff to each stage of development.

With regard to daily operations, management again has multiple supervisory roles. As a user of information services, management can exercise a measure of control by refusing to accept output that fails to adhere to systems specifications. Through membership in the steering committee, management will appoint auditors to evaluate efficiency and effectiveness of daily operations. Approval of maintenance or redevelopment and the setting of priorities are also responsibilities of the steering committee, which gives management control over operations. Finally, management supervises the activities of an IS department through the budgetary process. Expenditures for ongoing operations require the approval of the financial officers of the firm. By holding the purse strings, top management controls operations. Figure 5.3 illustrates the many ways in which management participates in daily operations as an information user while engaging in a supervisory role at the same time.

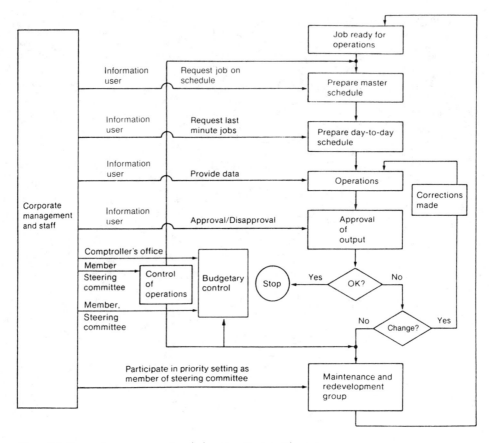

Figure 5.3 *Corporate management's role in computer operations*

Oversight role of information users

This chapter has already discussed the role of senior managers as users of computer services. Users are also found in non-managerial levels of an organization. They may be clerks, accountants, programmers, secretaries, warehouse personnel, engineers, sales representatives, planners — the list could go on and on. At all levels in the organizational hierarchy of a firm, there is **user oversight** of computing. For example, information user representatives serve as members of the steering committee and participate in the development of new systems, just as management representatives do. They also provide feedback to the steering committee and to the IS director regarding weaknesses in processing systems that they use in their jobs.

To collect and act on user feedback requires (1) mechanisms for identifying and classifying users, (2) instruments for determining user satisfaction, and (3) procedures for evaluating user criticisms and improving service.

Identification and classification of information users

Opinion regarding effectiveness of operations is sought from all information users, regardless of their level in the organizational hierarchy of a firm. But organizations do attempt to classify users according to:

- Skill level in computing use (novice, intermediate, expert).
- Intensity of computing use (frequent, occasional, infrequent).
- Position of the user in the organization's hierarchy.
- Type of systems used. Static systems (for example, database searches, programming, text editing) versus dynamic systems (for example, process control).

Users' opinions are then weighed according to classification and problem at hand. For example, data entry clerks would have more voice in workstation layout than infrequent management users. However, experienced users would have more say than novices in the development of a database management system. (The classifications also aid IT staff in identifying major user groups so that services can be tailored to their needs.)

User satisfaction determination

In small companies, word of mouth may be adequate to determine user satisfaction. In organizations where information users are free to choose between in-house computing and an external facility, market mechanisms are at play. Satisfied users remain customers. Dissatisfied users demand improved service or take their business elsewhere. Large organizations that do all their own computing usually rely on formal **survey instruments** to gauge user satisfaction. Such surveys may be designed for specific user classifications or for specific computing environments, such as inventory control or word processing. Some may survey user attitudes toward service, while others may concentrate on evaluation of performance criteria.

Whatever the instrument's approach, the purpose should be to help the steering committee and computing staff identify areas where efforts to improve quality of service should be concentrated. Figure 5.4 is a sample survey instrument, showing the types of questions that users might be asked.

Corrective action

Usually, an individual (or committee) from the IS department will be assigned responsibility for analyzing the responses to user surveys. Problems that can be

A. *User inventory*
    Name:
    Department:
    Position:
    Relationship to computer centre:
    Participation in computer centre organization (committees):
    Computer centre resources used:

Resource	Frequency and degree of usage

Knowledge of computing:
Interest in computing:

B. *Satisfaction survey* (You may wish to answer some of the questions below for each output you use.)
    Development:
    ■ Was your project developed on time?
    ■ Was your project adequately tested?
    ■ Did your project meet your initial needs? Changing needs?
    ■ Is your application using the most recent technology available?
    ■ Is your application satisfactorily integrated with other applications?

    Operations:
    ■ Is your report:
      (a) Timely?
      (b) Accurate?
      (c) Well packaged?
      (d) Corrected promptly when errors occur?
      (e) Available in mode desired?
      (f) Easy to use/understand/verify for accuracy?
    ■ Are computer centre personnel helpful and cooperative?
    ■ How can your existing reports be improved?
    ■ How can the service to you be improved?
    ■ How can the computer centre be more responsive to your needs?
    ■ How can the structure of the computer centre be changed to improve:
      (a) Performance?
      (b) Responsiveness?
    ■ Is user orientation and training:
      (a) Adequate?
      (b) Timely?

Figure 5.4 *Sample user satisfaction questionnaire*

quickly solved are differentiated from those requiring long-term solutions. The former are sent to the appropriate IT staff member for action, the latter to the steering committee or relevant project team for study.

Surveys may indicate a demand for an added peripheral, such as a faster printer or plotter. They may identify problems that require program maintenance or point to the need for development of a new application. A common user complaint is lengthy turnaround time. In response, many IS departments (especially those with a database management system environment) institute a quick-response service for users needing fast service for short, simple reports — the equivalent of the express lane in a grocery store. Many complaints can be resolved at small incremental cost, yet yield a high payoff in user goodwill. IT staff can then count on the support and cooperation of users when tackling problems that have long-term solutions.

In summary, user opinion helps the steering committee and the IS director determine how computer service might be improved. User representatives on the steering committee are in a position to see that user concerns, once identified, are followed by corrective action. So users perform an oversight role in two ways: by reporting problems and by participating as members of steering committees.

Role of the IS director

The **information system (IS) director** is responsible for daily operations of the IS department. In some companies with a steering committee, the IS director is hired/fired by the committee and may approach top management only through the committee. In others, the director is directly responsible to senior management, reporting to a vice president of information services or some similar officer.

Oversight function

Like other departmental managers in a firm, the IS director must plan departmental activities, prepare and control budgets, schedule work assignments, monitor work in progress, and select, hire, train, and evaluate personnel. The personnel roster of an IS department includes individuals with a wide range of skills: from clerks engaged in repetitive tasks and having hourly deadlines and a short-term outlook to highly trained IT professionals with long-term vision engaged in experimental systems design. Such diversity complicates management. So does the fact that many of the people working in high-tech fields are task-oriented, creative individuals who like working alone, dislike interruptions and small talk, and work with a sense of urgency that makes them insensitive to the status quo.

It is up to the IS director to establish a work environment that provides freedom of creative expression, yet promotes orderly organizational processes at the same time. The director has to command the technical respect of employees and be responsive to innovative ideas. Yet, the manager's knowledge must extend beyond technology to people, equipment resources, user relations, and budgeting and capital expenditures. At the same time, the director needs to understand the corporate environment outside of the department, be comfortable in relationships with senior management and be knowledgeable about the industry to which the company belongs. The director should be prepared to make and stand behind a decision, willing to get involved in risky projects or play the role of a change agent.

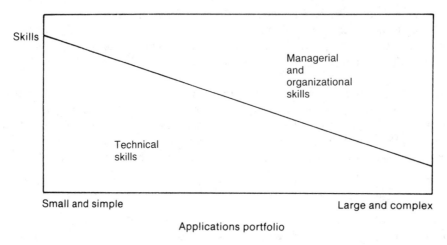

Figure 5.5 *Required IS director skills as a function of application portfolio size*

Clearly from this list, the director needs both behavioural and technical skills. Unfortunately, many IS directors have been promoted from systems engineering ranks and have no managerial training other than on the job. Only recently have universities begun to add information management to their master of business administration programmes.

The relative importance of behavioural and technical skills on the job is determined to some degree by the size of the applications portfolio that an IS director must oversee. When the portfolio is limited (a small budget and few computer employees), the director's job is more technical and less managerial. As the size and complexity of applications increase, however, technical tasks will be delegated to analysts and specialists, freeing the executive for managerial concerns associated with an enlarged staff and budget. Figure 5.5 shows that the skill requirements of a director's job are a function of portfolio size and complexity.

The position of IS director is very stressful and has a high turnover. This can be attributed largely to the element of risk in the job. Technical risks are run when trying to incorporate the latest computer advances in new systems. Financial risks are high due to the probability of time and cost overruns in systems development. Security of computer resources and privacy of data are vulnerable to assault, while reputation and credibility depend on user satisfaction.

Tension in the job can also be attributed to the fact that computer technology tends to upset traditional organizational and operational patterns, sending disruptive reverberations throughout the firm. It is the IS director who is responsible for orchestrating the introduction of new computer applications, for setting up interface committees to interpret technology to information users, and for smoothing conversion to new systems. Hostility may be exhibited toward the IS department, and toward the IS director in particular, by persons who resent the intrusion of computers in their work spheres.

The IS director cannot seek solace from other department heads, who may themselves harbour resentment against the IS department. They are piqued that computing is given favoured status, yet produces no tangible product or benefit of ascertainable market value. They are embittered that the failure rate accepted in computer projects would cost them their jobs.

A strain may also exist in the relationship between the IS director and corporate management. This strain is based, in part, on differences in their backgrounds, technical orientations, and objectives but can also be traced to problems in communication. Technical jargon and computer acronyms are not always understood outside the computing field. 'Talking down' to senior management is also inappropriate, for management is becoming increasingly knowledgeable about computer capabilities. A genuine dialogue should be sought: corporate management sharing its vision of the firm's future, the IS director explaining in non-technical terms how computer advances (such as microtechnology, telecommunications, networking, office automation, computer-aided design and manufacturing, and robots) can further corporate goals. Corporate management can help moderate the pressure on the IS director by being accessible for counsel and by establishing a fair approach to evaluation of the director's performance.

The new breed of IS managers

Because of the large funds involved in information processing and the long lead time required for equipment delivery and systems development, planning has always been a major concern of IS directors. 'What can the IS department do for you?' was the question traditionally asked of users. Today, however, the style of computer management is becoming more aggressive. Directors, as change agents, offer innovative ideas instead of waiting for service requests, saying, 'Here is what we can do and should do for you.'

The new breed of IS directors is more political, able to recognize power bases and win converts. Such directors are also integrators, able to merge computers, communications, and databases into effective delivery systems. But not all have the same outlook regarding the primary function of their IS departments. Some endorse the concept that IS departments should be profit centres and that information users should determine what services are offered by their willingness to pay. Others view their departments as service agencies. They are less concerned with departmental profits than with developing systems to improve corporate performance. Perhaps, the ideal IS director would be a combination of the two: a profit-conscious, service-oriented manager.

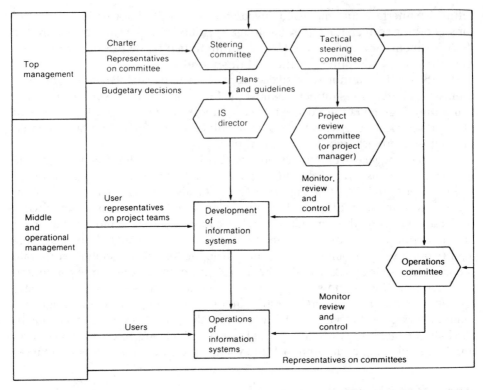

Figure 5.6 *Sample configuration of a steering committee and subcommittees in relation to corporate management and the IS director*

Summing up

Computing involves a web of relationships between corporate management, computing personnel, and information users. This chapter has focused on committees that provide the formal structure for interaction between these groups in the oversight of computing. In Figure 5.6, which illustrates a sample configuration of oversight relationships, the IS director reports directly to a steering committee. The steering committee also receives reports on performance from subcommittees that oversee developmental activities and operations. Some steering committees require that all computing be done in-house. Others allow information users within the firm to request bids for jobs, placing in-house computing facilities in competition with outside service centres.

Top management controls computing by chartering the steering committee, making budgetary decisions, and serving with other users as members of the steering committee and subcommittees. Management is also a receiver of computing services and so participates in development projects as a team member and criticizes output, just as other users do.

Information users are found at all levels of an organization, from data clerks to company presidents. The steering committee and IS director need a method of determining whether the services offered meet users' needs. Many firms conduct user surveys for this purpose.

New responsibilities are continually being added to the job of IS director. The expansion of applications, the addition of word processing to traditional data processing, and the movement towards distributed processing centres require technical expertise and business skills that former EDP heads did not need when computing was a mere back-shop operation. The IS director of the future will be an information manager who takes the initiative in business information planning, one who discovers opportunities for improving the effectiveness of information utilization and 'sells' these options when appropriate and beneficial to the company.

IS directors with demonstrated proficiency in managing modern IS departments have administrative talent that should not be wasted. An IS director should not have a dead-end job but should have a career path leading to corporate management.

Case study: **Oversight at a bank**

In a regional bank, management was dissatisfied with the bank's information processing, as were departmental information users within the bank. The bank officers were concerned about the information processing budget. User departments felt that information processing should be of greater service but weren't sure how. The IS director worried about staff turnover and how best to allocate computing resources. There was general agreement that the bank needed an organizational body to provide direction and control to computing.

The first step in setting up a guiding body was to establish objectives for such a group. It was agreed that the group would be responsible for setting information processing directions and services and for the establishment of priorities for information processing activities and development.

An Executive Steering Committee (ESC) was then chartered. It asked a consulting firm to assist bank personnel in evaluating the bank's information processing. Systems maintenance and enhancement were found to be inadequate, and efficiency pressures had gone too far, resulting in damage to many systems and technical resources. The ESC then formulated an information processing funding evaluation strategy and established new funding directors for the bank's information processing. In time, the committee broadened its scope to include more technical oversight of information processing.

The ESC has proved effective in its oversight role. Keys to the committee's success are that the ESC members have developed (1) a working relationship with employees and (2) analysis procedures that lead to consensus regarding the current status of information processing, issues, and resolution of problems. They are also able to communicate this consensus in business language and business structure to bank officers.

Source: Richard L. Nolan, (ed.) *Managing the Data Resource Function*, 2nd edn. St. Paul, Minn.: West Publishing, 1982, pp. 381–3.

Questions

1 Why do you suppose that the ESC turned to a consulting firm for oversight assistance?

2 Should the establishment of procedures for oversight wait until problems become apparent? Explain.
3 Why do some companies fail to provide oversight of computing?
4 What lessons can be drawn from this case?

Case study: **Horse-race betting in Hong Kong**

The Royal Hong Kong Jockey Club has a technological infrastructure able to process 1,600 betting transactions per second at peak periods, an infrastructure that generates annual betting revenues in excess of HK$24.4 billion. The club's complex distributed network allows nine types of bets to be placed at racecourses, 128 offtrack centres, or through handheld Customer Input Terminals distributed to 11,000 of its 450,000 telephone account holders. The equipment to process these bets consists of a host of PDP 11/44s, PDP 11/84s, MicroVAX IIs, as well as six VAX 8600s.

Two types of transactions are required to aggregate the betting pool. First is computing the standard bets — win, place, Quinella and double. 'The system just keeps on collating the amount of wager on each horse for the standard bets, and the win collation is used to calculate the odds', said Daniel Lai, the club's information systems operations manager.

The second type of transaction involves exotic bets with handsome dividends — Treble, Six Up, Double Quinella and Double Trio. For example, Double Trio is picking first, second and third in correct order for two races. Prior to the installation of its real-time online network, the large number of permutations involved in calculating such exotic bets was time-consuming and cumbersome. Exotic tickets had to be validated at betting centres, brought to data centres to be microfilmed, then read by optical scanners.

The Jockey Club is a non-profit organization. Betting revenues are shared with Hong Kong's charitable groups, including hospitals, community centres and art societies.
Source: Marsha Johnson, 'Betting on a transaction network', *Datamation*, vol. 36, no. 9 (1 May 1990), pp. 99–101.

Questions

1 What type of oversight structure do you think would be appropriate for information processing at the Jockey Club?
2 Would you classify the Royal Hong Kong Jockey Club as a business? In what way does the Club differ from a conventional business, such as a store, a manufacturing plant, or a bank? How should Club oversight of information processing differ from these types of businesses?
3 Who should be members of oversight committees? IT personnel? Board members of the Jockey Club? Representatives of the betting public? Representatives from the charitable organizations receiving revenues? Government officials? Explain.
4 Who should have responsibility for introducing new information technology to the racetrack? For developing new applications of IT? For making decisions regarding hardware/software acquisitions? What is the relationship of oversight to planning?
5 How can satisfaction of the betting public with track betting operations be ascertained? Is it

important to know this information? Why? What is the relationship of public opinion regarding the type of bets the track offers and information technology acquired by the Jockey Club?

6 What qualifications and experience do you think would be desirable for the IS director for the Royal Hong Kong Jockey Club?

Key words

Business within a business

Information system (IS) director

Oversight function

Senior management oversight

Steering committee

Survey instruments

User oversight

Discussion questions

1 How does corporate management oversee IS department operations?
2 How can the following functions be controlled in an IS department?
  (*a*) Spending.
  (*b*) Standards.
  (*c*) Scheduling.
  (*d*) Integration of systems.
  (*e*) Honesty and integrity of staff.
  (*f*) Priorities for maintenance jobs.
3 In what ways do computing departments differ from:
  (*a*) Wholesale business?
  (*b*) University?
  (*c*) Government office?
  (*d*) Public library?
4 What mechanisms should be implemented to achieve a satisfactory interface with users in:
  (*a*) Conversion?
  (*b*) Debugging user programs?
  (*c*) Meeting user hardware needs?
5 Can the same user interface mechanisms be used in centralized and decentralized processing?
6 When managing a computer department, is the element of risk the same for both:
  (*a*) Small and large computing systems?
  (*b*) Centralized and distributed systems?
  (*c*) Functional and integrated systems?
  (*d*) Batch and online systems?

(e) A large computer and a network of minis?

7 At what point and under what circumstances should a steering committee delegate its authority and responsibility to other committees?

8 What is the purpose of classifying information users? How best can this be done?

9 What qualities and qualifications are desirable in an IS director?

10 Should IS directors have technical or business management backgrounds? Explain.

11 What qualifications would you recommend for appointees to a steering committee?

12 What are the main risks faced by IS directors and steering committees? How can they be minimized or eliminated?

13 What role (if any) should the IS director play in corporate policy decision making?

14 How should information user satisfaction be determined?

Bibliography

Gupta, Yash P. and T.S. Raghunathan. 'Impact of information systems (IS) steering committees on IS planning', vol. 20, no. 4 (Fall 1989), pp. 777–93.

Karten, Naomi. 'Surviving the PC challenge demands management skills', *Data Management*, vol. 23, no. 9 (September 1985), pp. 14–18.

McConnell, Vicki and Karl Kock. 'Misuse of power', *Computerworld*, vol. 25, no. 4 (28 January 1991), pp. 67–9.

McKeen, J.D. and Tor Guimaraes. 'Selecting MIS projects by steering committee', *Communications of the ACM*, vol. 28, no. 12 (November 1985), pp. 1344–51.

McLean, Ephraim R., Stanley J. Smits and John R. Tanner. 'Managing new MIS professionals', *Information and Management*, vol. 20 (1991), pp. 257–63.

Meiklejohn, Ian. 'CIOs search for a role', *Management Today* (September 1989), pp. 137–8.

Meiklejohn, Ian. 'Whole role for hybrid', *Management Today* (March 1990), pp. 113–14.

Ryan, Hugh W. 'The third wave: user as producer', *Journal of Information Systems Management*, vol. 8, no. 1 (Winter 1991), pp. 71–4.

Umbaugh, Robert E. 'Corporate responsibility and the MIS manager', *Journal of Information Systems Managment*, vol. 4, no. 1 (Winter 1987), pp. 58–62.

Watson, Richard T. 'Influences on the IS manager's perceptions of key issues: information scanning and the relationship with the CEO', *MIS Quarterly*, vol. 14, no. 2 (June 1990), pp. 217–31.

Wolman, R. 'Managing technical professionals', *Information Center*, vol. 6 (March 1990), pp. 9–11.

6 Computing services

If you want to make a long trip through
a far wilderness, find a guide who has made
the journey before.
Old proverb

A large computing service industry has developed over the years to provide organizations with computer expertise to supplement and enhance in-house processing capability. For example, a company may contract with an outside firm for remote processing. Data will be transmitted by telecommunications to this outside source for processing. Another segment of the computing service industry provides consulting services. When the problem is lack of personnel to manage and run a corporate computing facility, a facilities management company can be contracted on a short- or long-term basis to operate the centre.

Firms with no computers of their own may turn to a service bureau or a utility for information processing. Such service firms are also used by companies that want access to computing power to supplement in-house capability and by those needing access to hardware or software that they lack in-house.

This chapter will discuss the advantages and disadvantages of each of the above types of computing services, stressing that these alternatives are not mutually exclusive. A variety of mixes is possible. For example, a firm with an in-house computer centre may assign certain jobs to a service bureau. Or a firm that contracts for facilities management may also use remote processing to access a utility's specialized database.

Remote processing

Remote processing is defined as the processing of computer programs through an input/output device that is remotely connected to a computer system. That is, jobs are submitted online to a computer from a terminal that is physically distant from the central processing unit (CPU).

One type of remote processing is distributed data processing (DDP), introduced in Chapter 2, whereby an employee sitting at a terminal is able to access a company computer located in another room, on another floor, or in another company

he terminal is connected to the CPU by in-house cable or by
ications.) The term remote processing is also used to describe access
g power from an external source, such as another firm with excess
power or a utility that specializes in meeting the computing needs
(Utilities will be described later in this chapter.) This latter type of remote
processing is categorized as a computing service, the subject of this chapter.

Remote processing may be either **continuous processing** or **batch processing**.
That is, data can be transmitted online as they are generated for instantaneous
processing (**active online processing**) or can be stored upon receipt by the
computer for later batch processing (**passive online processing**). An example of
active online processing would be an airline system that allows a travel agent
to ascertain seat availability for a given flight and to confirm a reservation for
a client. An example of passive online processing is overnight batch processing
of sales information received from local grocers by remote job entry at the
headquarters of a food chain. Reports based on information so processed can be
sent back to the grocers to help them decide what foods to order, what foods
to put on sale, and so on.

Active online processing may be subdivided into two parts: processing that does
not require any updating of the database (**non-modifying**) and processing that
does (**modifying**). A query to an existing database or processing of scientific input
data are examples of non-modifying processing. Functional online real-time
(OLRT) systems dedicated to process control or transaction processing in banking
or reservations are examples of processing that modifies the database. Modification
is also required in some general-purpose online computing, such as when a
manager or production engineer wants to know the effect of a certain parameter
change. **Time-sharing**, which is sharing a computer with other users (although
the speed of response may give one the illusion of being the sole user), is becoming
an increasingly popular mode of remote processing in the business sector.

Figure 6.1 illustrates the relationship of the modes of remote processing
discussed in this section.

Why remote processing?

Remote processing is a time saver. It allows a person to input data for computer
processing without having to go to the location of the CPU. Sometimes, a company
uses remote processing to an external source to supplement its own processing
capability, taking advantage of the storage capacity, specialized databases, or other
processing services offered by the source. An additional reason to combine remote
with local processing is to cushion surges in processing demand. When
professional personnel and corporate management want the computational power
of a large computer but need it only intermittently, remote processing may be
the most cost-effective answer.

Other firms choose remote processing as an alternative to developing an in-
house computing facility. They save space, equipment, and personnel resources

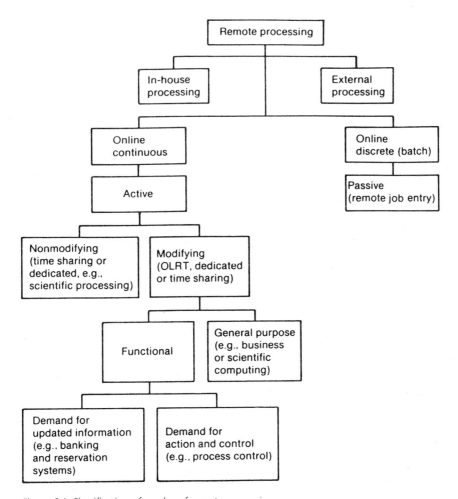

Figure 6.1 *Classification of modes of remote processing*

that would otherwise have to be allocated to a computer centre. Still other firms utilize remote processing as an interim solution to their processing needs while developing an in-house processing capability.

Selection of an external remote processing service

Factors that should be considered when deciding whether external remote processing is advisable are listed in Table 6.1. Turnaround time, for example, may be critical, so benchmarks should test the response time of prospective suppliers during both supplier and user peak periods, as well as during hours with normal workloads. Teleprocessing costs may also be decisive. Pricing is usually based

Table 6.1 *Factors to be considered in deciding on external remote processing*

Type of assistance needed:
  Hardware
  Software
    Operating systems, DBMSs, etc.
    Applications packages
  Support
Financial payoff
Remote processing performance:
  Turnaround and response time
  Error rates and accuracy
Effect on credibility and public relations when work is not done in-house
In-house knowledge and experience with remote processing
Experience to be gained by contact with outside firm
Telecommunications problems
Possible loss of control over data
Possible need to submit to outside standards
Added vendor contacts and hassles
Human factor considerations
Organizational impact

---

on transmission costs plus computing costs (per unit of connect time or per unit of computing time).

Most supplier firms have elaborate pricing algorithms that vary as much as 200 per cent. These algorithms are based on type of use and length of job. Adjustments may be made for guaranteed minimum usage, and discounts given according to number of terminals or other considerations. Charges may drop 20 per cent by simply mentioning a competitor. To help users understand pricing algorithms, many suppliers provide users with accounting reports so that expensive jobs can be identified. Often, by redesigning the jobs or rescheduling them to non-peak periods, users can cut processing costs.

A decision to contract for remote processing with an external source should be based on a cost–benefits analysis, and care should be taken in selecting the supplier of this computing service. Over time, increases in transmission costs or changes in volume of service may reduce the economic viability of remote processing. Therefore, a financial review of remote processing should be periodically conducted.

Consultants

Few firms can afford to staff their companies with experts in all technical fields. As a result, they face problems from time to time that no employee within the firm is qualified or competent to handle. The expertise of a **consultant** is invaluable when in-house experience is lacking. What is more, consultants can bring an independent viewpoint to problem solving. They often serve as mediators in internal politics and act as spark plugs to get projects moving.

In the field of computing, the need for consultants is accentuated by the fast pace of technological development. The typical computer processing department is struggling to fill backlogged user demands. There is no time for internal staff to develop expertise in such technical areas as micro to mainframe links, local area networks, office automation, telecommunications, information systems architectures, or general systems integration. Just to keep abreast of vendor trends in both hardware and software may require outside help. According to one observer the computer industry has been characterized by phenomenal change, and change creates uncertainty, and uncertainty creates the demand for consultants.

Even large firms with a wide range of specialists on the payroll often employ consultants. The need may arise because in-house personnel have ongoing commitments and do not have time to devote to new projects. Sometimes, a company wants the services of someone experienced in the problem at hand. For example, in applications development, a consultant who has had practical experience designing a similar system for another firm can be an invaluable member of a project team. Sometimes, the technicians a firm wants to hire are unavailable in the marketplace. Sometimes, a consultant rather than a full-time specialist is preferred because the latter's wage demands would distort the organization's wage and salary plan and create wage inequities.

An important advantage of consultants is that they are not a party to the internal power struggles within a firm and so can be more objective when seeking problem solutions. Their jobs and future promotions are not jeopardized by any recommendations they make. And not being bound to firm traditions or precedents, they should be able to evaluate vendors and systems without bias.

The outside consultant, on the other hand, will not be acquainted with the personalities in the firm and will not understand how departments interact or how the firm functions. Recommendations made without taking time to gain familiarity with the firm's unique environment may prove inappropriate. What is more, the presence of a consultant may be viewed as an intrusion and hamper smooth working relationships. The large hourly salary of the consultant may be resented by in-house staff. In addition, ruffled feelings may arise from the fact that advice received from internal staff members may have been ignored by top management while the same advice is accepted from the consultant. The question of security also arises. Should sensitive data be exposed to consultants who have not demonstrated loyalty to a firm? The possibility exists that the information the consultant learns about the business might later be sold to competitors.

The need for an outside opinion can arise in all phases of development and operations. For example, consultants often participate in feasibility studies, decisions of resource acquisition, systems specifications and the design of new systems. They may be hired to set standards, to establish privacy and security procedures, to help select personnel, or to run training programmes. They have even been known to function as project managers for short-term, highly technical development projects. Managerial consultants may also help organize departments, assist in planning, or devise strategies to reduce resistance to change.

The broad range and critical nature of these activities require that consultants be selected with care, with their qualifications and reputations carefully screened.

Selection

When searching for consultants, a good starting point is to ask professional associates to make recommendations based on their past experiences with consultants. Corporate executives may ask contacts at conferences or industry meetings to provide names of consultants with whom they have had successful dealings in the past. In addition, many professional organizations compile consulting lists. In the United States, the Independent Computer Consultants Association in St Louis has a listing of more than 1,600 member firms representing more than 4,000 independent consultants. Other lists of consultants may be obtained from organizations such as:

The Association of Professional Computer Consultants
The Association of Independent Computer Specialists
The British Computer Society
The Computer Services Association

These above listed are English organizations but many countries have similar professional bodies that compile lists of consultants. Many consultants advertise in newspapers and professional journals. Academia is another mine for consultants.

Unfortunately, no official body regulates or certifies consultants, so the selection of a suitable candidate can be a risky proposition. Here are some guidelines that should help narrow the field and control the consultant's work:

- Examine the consultant's personal and corporate background through reference checks and financial reviews.
- Draw up a detailed written project plan and schedule for the work the consultant is to do. Make sure that the consultant understands the assignment and can demonstrate competence in this area of work.
- Build checkpoints or milestones into the project.
- Conduct regular review meetings between milestones.
- Thoroughly test the work of the consultant.

These recommendations are basic hiring and project management techniques.

Consultants may be hired by the hour or by the job. Rates are high. Well-known consultants command £5,000 to £10,000 per day, plus expenses. Consulting firms may charge from £75 to £200 per hour: independents command fees that range from £40 per hour to the rates cited earlier for superstars. Nevertheless, most firms feel the money is well spent. Surprisingly, consulting firms find their clients mainly among successful companies rather than companies in trouble. A characteristic of growing, profitable organizations seems to be the ability of recognize corporate limitations. These companies are willing and able to spend money to hire outside consultants for the assistance they need.

Future trends

The fast pace of technological advance in the computer industry suggests that consulting work should continue to be plentiful in the near future. As in the past, corporations will undoubtedly call upon the services of consultants in order to keep up to date regarding developments in the computing field. However, many observers suggest that the more important role of consultants in the future will be to help corporations manage their information resources in order to gain a competitive edge. For example, customers who have installed personal computers, local area networks and telecommunications equipment will want to learn how best to integrate such technology in order to meet business objectives, information no single vendor or technician can provide. Consultants will be valued for their computer knowledge *plus* their business expertise.

Vendors

Vendors are often an underutilized source of technical expertise. Unlike consultants, vendors have a bias in favour of their own products, but this bias does not necessarily preclude sound advice on equipment and systems. (A company would, however, be wise to check the literature and other users for corroborative opinion.)

Vendors can often provide technical information on controls, security, and even installation of equipment. For example, when a computer centre is being planned, vendors frequently furnish an installation expert to help design the layout. The expert may supply tables and charts on clearances and power needs and even provide templates and sample layout diagrams. For microcomputers, many computer stores today offer a range of services, from maintenance and support to seminars and consulting. A store that sells both hardware and software may be in a better position to know what is wrong and how to solve the problem than either hardware or software vendors, who tend to waste time blaming one another when systems fail. A classic example of vendor assistance with systems design was IBM's contribution to the first commercial airline reservation system for American Airlines.

Vendors commonly provide documentation and training on systems they supply. One vendor specializes in training programmes featuring management games played at a country club, with golf interspersed between work sessions.

This is good publicity for the vendor, while informative and fun for the trainee. Vendors often keep clients informed regarding industry scuttlebutt as well, such as who is in the job market and what new products are being launched.

Of course, not all vendors perform such roles, but many do offer valuable counsel. Establishing good rapport with vendors can speed up delivery dates of equipment, even result in visits by the vendor's analysts and engineers. Without doubt, most vendor representatives are knowledgeable in their respective fields, well supported by their companies, carefully trained and well rehearsed. That they can be smooth talkers and high-pressure salespeople should come as no surprise. It is up to computer departments to be just as well prepared, know what questions to ask and review responses critically, compensating for bias.

Sometimes, a vendor representative responsible for equipment maintenance is assigned to a given firm and is on site daily. Such individuals become well acquainted with the staff and problems of the computer department and often act as informal consultants. On occasion, they take sides in disputes. Vendor representatives have even been known to appeal to corporate management to reverse computer department decisions and to win. Vendors have clout and sometimes use it.

Facilities management

Facilities management (FM) is the use of an independent service organization to operate and manage the contracting firm's own computer processing installation. Firms assign some or all of their computing to FM corporations for a variety of reasons. Some lack the technical personnel needed to run their computer processing centres. Others do not want responsibility for operating computing equipment. Still others utilize facilities management because their firm's own computer department has been so badly mismanaged (dissatisfied users, missed deadlines, poorly utilized equipment, frequent time and cost overruns) that it must be reorganized, rebuilt, and restaffed. In the interim, the FM company is given responsibility for the centre. Some firms also decide on a long-term facilities management contract because they believe that their centres will be better managed under FM than by in-house staff.

Advantages and disadvantages

Few firms can match FM corporations in the quality of their computing staff. This is one reason why companies turn to FM for computing assistance. Good salaries and challenging work attract highly qualified personnel to FM. Computer professionals are drawn by the range of experience that they can gain when employed by an FM firm, experience that helps them move quickly along their chosen career paths. Experts in fields such as teleprocessing, numerical control and planning that use linear programming or simulation are also attracted to FM because they are able to concentrate on their specialities full-time in an FM job. In other firms, demand for their expertise might be limited, resulting in work assignments outside their fields of expertise.

Under facilities management, a computer centre can often be operated more economically than when managed by a corporation's own computing staff, partly because FM firms buy in quantity lots and obtain bigger discounts from vendors than do other firms. The highly trained professionals who work for FM companies also get better efficiency, reliabilty and utilization from computer resources than the average employee in a computer processing centre. What's more, FM employees can redesign systems, reorganize and eliminate redundancies to achieve better performance in client firms without being encumbered by obligations to individuals or power blocks within that firm.

With FM, however, interface problems are compounded because computing is no longer organizationally in-house. The user must now interact with computer personnel whose primary loyalty lies with the FM company. New liaison procedures must be established, and new boundaries of authority and responsibility have to be defined between information users and FM personnel. Though obligations of the FM corporation should be detailed in the contract (see Table 6.2 for a list of subjects to be included in FM contracts), it takes time to develop smooth working relationships when an FM firm takes over management of a firm's computer centre. Considerable disagreement between information users and FM staff regarding performance under FM may surface as well, for evaluation of performance can be a highly subjective judgement. In such cases, relations are bound to be strained.

Another disadvantage of FM is that users lose control over their data and worry about privacy and security, particularly when the FM company is also servicing a competitor. (FM companies must guard against legal violations in such cases.) User flexibility is lost as well. And how can clients ensure that FM employees are motivated to act in the client's best interest? Designing contract incentives can challenge a client's lawyer.

Table 6.2 *Subjects for inclusion in facilities management contracts*

Duration of contract	Standards
Availability of personnel	Input requirements
Availability of expertise	Documentation scope
Lines of reporting for personnel	Output portfolio and schedule
Liaison	Priorities
Ownership of equipment	Changes
Ownership of software	Payments
Security	Limitation and liabilities
Privacy of data	Right to audit FM firm's operations
Property interests	Contract termination procedures
Applications portfolio	Scope and level of effort of FM personnel
Extension of applications	and contracting firm

When negotiating for FM services, the length of the contract period will depend on what type of service is required. Activities that have a long period of gestation, such as development of integrated systems or training programmes, cannot be undertaken when the FM contract is short-term. (An FM company may prefer to omit training, since lack of training may extend the company's need for FM and hence create a dependency on FM.) A long contract period, however, may so entrench FM that it is hard for the client to take back management responsibility for processing. Most firms do plan to manage their computer departments eventually, and they try to estimate the length of time needed to develop the technical expertise to do so, signing an FM contract for this interim period only. Indeed, many client firms find reliance on FM insulting to corporate management and believe their own personnel will be more responsive to internal processing needs than will FM staff. A compromise strategy is to take a short-term contract with an option to renew.

Cost

Cost of FM will depend on the size of the computer processing configuration to be managed, scope of processing activities of the client firm, level of performance to be achieved and ownership conditions. Contract length is also a factor (most run two to six years). The contract awarded Bunker Ramo by the National Association of Security Dealers (US) to run the nationwide stock market quotations and trading for over-the-counter securities is one example of what facilities management costs: $10.5 million (at 1980 prices) for a three-year contract. Though this figure may seem high, many firms find that FM is less expensive than the cost of developing equivalent in-house expertise and capability.

Cost-plus contracts are sometimes negotiated for facilities management. The problem is defining the 'plus' component.

Variations

FM contracts are based on user needs. Although most facilities management means processing is on the client's hardware, some FM firms will also contract for services on their own equipment. (One-third of a major FM corporation's 90 client firms, for example, use the FM company's hardware.) Advantages to the client include freeing equipment and personnel for other activities, and the creation of backup. Security and transportation are major problems in this arrangement.

Another variation is a contractual agreement whereby the FM company selects equipment, installs it, and makes it operational, providing the client with a **turnkey system**. The client takes possession and manages processing once all problems associated with systems development, database implementation, programming, testing and conversion have been resolved. This concept is popular in the Middle East, where technical expertise is in short supply but companies don't want foreigners responsible for daily operations.

Table 6.3 *Services offered by a service bureau*

Contribute to one or more stages of development	Storage capacity
	Facilities management
Provide specialized database	Capacity for excess workload
Prepare firm's database or assist in data conversion	Unexpected
	Seasonal
Prepare data for ongoing database	Growth
Provide programs	Handle processing when firm lacks:
Standard functional programs (e.g., accounting)	Capital for hardware acquisition
	Space
Programs for decision support systems	Personnel
	Time
Industry-specialized programs	Processing capacity
Customized programs	Miscellaneous
Process data in a variety of modes	Data collection
Batch	Output delivery
Interactive batch	Consulting
Online	
Online real-time	

Service bureaux

Service bureaux can provide equipment, software, or personnel to clients according to their needs. For example, the firm under contract to the service bureau may have its own computer department but lack hardware or programs for specialized computations, such as linear programming. Perhaps more data storage capacity is needed for a prediction model. Perhaps a special compiler (like SIMSCRIPT) is required for a simulation run. The firm will contract with a service bureau for hardware/software access of this nature to supplement in-house resources.

Some bureaux provide access to specialized databases, such as the full text of court decisions or updated daily lists of stock market transactions. One American service bureau has a database of extracts from Securities and Exchange Commission filings in the United States from over 12,000 publicly held companies; another has data on the Japanese economy, including a macro model and forecasts. Service bureaux can also prepare data, assist in data collection, consult and even contract facilities management. A sample list of service bureau offerings appears in Table 6.3.

Why service bureaux?

Many of the advantages of facilities management apply to service bureaux as well. Service bureaux can attract highly qualified personnel and specialists and can therefore operate at a higher level of efficiency and professionalism than the average firm. They can also operate at lower cost, taking advantage of economies of scale. For example, program development is less costly when shared by a large base of users. Because of this base, service bureaux can also maintain large computer installations, develop extensive databases and offer all modes of processing (batch, interactive batch, online and online real-time). Firms that utilize service bureaux may not have the in-house capability of performing needed activities or may find it more economical to use a service bureau than to gear up for the activity. Even well-known large firms, including Boeing, Chase Manhattan, Control Data, GE, GTE, Lockheed, New York Times, Time Inc. and Xerox Corporation are service bureau customers. In some cases, these same firms sell services to others and buy services concurrently (for example, Boeing and Control Data).

Selection

A firm considering the option of a service bureau should first examine the economic feasibility of handling the activity in-house, then contact a number of service bureaux and compare their offerings, because service bureaux differ in their fee structures. Some charge a flat rate. Others base fees on the amount of resources used, how they are used and for what applications. Before a service bureau contract is signed, costs should also be compared with other alternatives (for example, facilities management or acquisition of minis and software packages).

But cost of services should not be the only criterion for selection of a service bureau. Table 6.4 lists other factors that should be considered.

The challenge facing service bureaux

The availability of inexpensive microcomputers has enabled many firms to keep

Table 6.4 *Factors to be considered in service bureau selection*

Services offered	Hardware configuration
Reputation of service bureau	Arrangements for data transfer
Years of operation	Time involved
Experience with firm's industry	Convenience
Competence of personnel	Frequency
References	Availability for access
Financial stability	Benchmark results
Promptness record	Backup facilities
Quality of service	Pricing algorithms
Errors	Normal load
Reruns	Offload
Integrity	Reruns
Security and privacy record	Liability and damage conditions
Software portfolio	Discontinuation conditions
Compatibility	

work in-house that was formally contracted to service bureaux. The bureaux have also lost clients because the cost of software is down. Many companies can afford to purchase all of the programs they need, so software availability is no longer a major service bureau attraction.

With revenue dropping, service bureaux are consolidating and redefining their role. Some industry observers predict that the field will be narrowed in the 1990s to a few gigantic superbureaux that emphasize information management instead of processing. These bureaux will offer services such as time-sharing, on-site microcomputers, and turnkey systems. They will help set up information centres and increase installation support and education. More emphasis may be placed on software-related consulting services. The companies may download software to customer microcomputers or act as distributors of small software developers. Electronic data interchange, the linking of buyers and suppliers, is a technology that may open new markets for service bureaux. Artificial intelligence and voice recognition may lead service bureaux in still other directions.

Change in the service bureau industry is nothing new. The industry today is radically different in appearance from that of the 1960s, when service bureaux were primarily hardware vendors. The industry has survived by meeting the evolving needs of clients, providing services that users have been unable to develop for themselves.

Computer utilities

A **computer utility** is a source of remote processing, selling computer time and services. Utilities offer unique processing features that distinguish them from service bureaux and other remote processing suppliers. Instead of contracting with a client for a specific service, time-sharing is available at any time, for as long as requested, to any user who can pay for it. The computer utility resembles an electric utility in so far as computing power, like electric power, is continuously offered and able to handle fluctuations of demand. This requires a grid or network, so that computing power can be accessed from a distant site if regional facilities are overloaded.

Figure 6.2 shows a sample utility configuration. Individual customers at home or business may be serviced by a utility node supported by a variety of resources (software, databases, and computers), as illustrated. The node may draw on computing power from other nodes for special services or during peak periods of demand. Compatibility of hardware, software, and interfaces is therefore needed. Telecommunications and protocols to link utility nodes are also required.

Public fears over data security and privacy issues may slow public acceptance and use of utilities. Will proprietary data be safe from unauthorized intrusion when processed by a distant utility? Will linked utility databases infringe upon individual privacy rights? How utilities should be regulated is also an unresolved question. The social implications of computer networks need to be addressed now

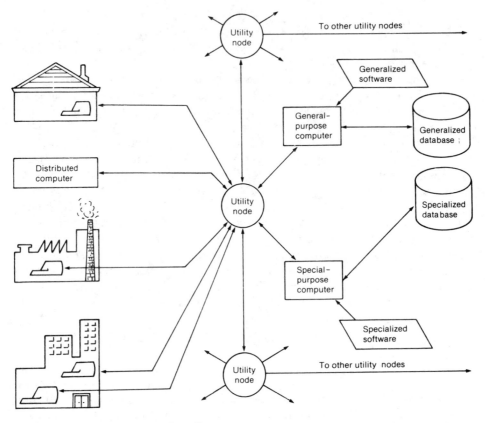

Figure 6.2 *Sample configuration of a utility*

by computer specialists, political theorists and social scientists. The growth of utilities as a sector of the computer services industry will depend, to a large extent, on government legislation affecting network regulation and control.

Summing up

This chapter describes segments of the computing service industry. Both consultants and vendors offer professional services based on their technical knowledge and experience. Consultants are more objective, have a broader base of experience and wider range of knowledge; but the services of vendors are usually free and, within narrow parameters, equally professional. Another difference between the two is that consultants may be hired to give advice to

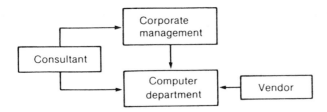

Figure 6.3 *Relationship of consultants and vendors to the client*

corporate management or the computer department, whereas vendors counsel mainly the latter and have a bias in favour of their own products, a difference illustrated in Figure 6.3.

Facilities management is useful when a firm owns equipment but does not wish to operate it. The firm may have had a bad experience with ineffectual internal management of computing in the past, or the shortage of qualified candidates means personnel capable of managing high technology cannot be hired. FM can be a short- or long-term solution to computing problems for small and medium-sized companies. Large firms are usually able to attract or generate the management necessary for their computing operations and so use FM less frequently.

Remote processing, service bureaux, and utilities may be contracted for external processing. Remote processing is appropriate for firms that want access to hardware, software, or databases not available in-house, or that have occasional demand for a powerful computer. Remote job entry is also an alternative for firms that want to gain experience in computer processing before setting up an in-house processing facilitiy. Many small and medium-sized firms that want a full range of computer services are attracted to service bureaux.

Two other sources of professional assistance not discussed in the chapter deserve mention. One is auditors, whose functions are described in Chapter 9. The other is software houses, sellers of standard packages, which can also develop customized software and will, if paid, provide programmers and analysts to assist in software implementations, including documentation.

Table 6.5 summarizes, by source, professional services available to computer departments.

In selecting a supplier for computing services, cost−benefit studies should be conducted and bids from more than one vendor received, because pricing and services vary considerably. Alternatives should also be periodically re-evaluated, since costs and benefits may change in time. For example, the availability of low-cost microcomputers means that many of the applications formerly contracted to outside service companies can now be done more cheaply in-house by many corporations.

Table 6.5 *Professional services available to computing departments by source*

Source	Management consultants	Computer consultants	Auditors	Vendors	Facilities management	Software houses	Service bureaus	Utilities
Planning for computing	X	X		X	X		X	
Organization of computer department	X	X					X	
Phases of development		X	X		X		X	X
Standards		X	X		X	X	X	
Program implementation				X	X	X	X	
Control systems design		X	X	X	X		X	
Audit of efficiency and performance		X						
Hiring of computer personnel		X		X				
Training		X		X	X	X	X	
Planning for change	X	X		X	X			
Selection of computing resources		X					X	
Operations					X		X	X

Case study: Barcelona '92: the Olympic Games

Responsibility for organizing the information technology infrastructure for the 1992 summer Olympic Games fell under the jurisdiction of The Organizational Olympic Committee of Barcelona '92 (COOB '92). The philosophy adopted by the committee was to decentralize the system as much as possible. They designed a system configuration that revolved around IBM mainframes loosely connected with approximately 3,600 PS/2s located throughout the city of Barcelona. A local area network operated autonomously in each stadium, but data was sent to central mainframes for processing.

Software applications for the Games were divided into four major categories:

- Management of total operations.
- Calculation and management of events.
- Management of city resources to support the Olympic Family (including athletes, journalists, invited personalities, committee members, and so on).
- Systems for internal use of COOB '92.

Contracts for development of these applications were awarded to Sema Group PLC, Electronic Data Systems Corp., Entel, Calcul i Gestio and Apple Computer Inc.

A number of factors contributed to the complexity of the design of this infrastructure. For example, the Games had a fixed starting date. All systems had to work perfectly on day one. Furthermore, the buildings in which the PCs, telephones, photocopiers and walkie-talkies were to be installed were only available two or three days before opening ceremonies. Because of this last-minute installation, testing was limited to parts and components. No time was available for total system testing or fine-tuning. A breakdown in telecommunications or information systems would potentially be visible to 300 million people, the worldwide audience of the Games.

Source: Enrique San Juan. 'Barcelona '92: the technological games', *Datamation*, vol. 36, no. 13 (1 July 1990), pp. 107–8.

Questions

1 Over time, information technology has moved forward. A main objective of the Olympic committee was to take advantage of improvements and advances in this technology. How should Olympic committees plan the information infrastructure? Who should be the decisions makers? What qualifications should they have?

2 Would you describe the information infrastructure designed by COOB '92 as remote processing? Explain.

3 If you had been a member of COOB '92, what use would you have made of the expertise of:
(a) Consultants?
(b) Vendors?
How would you decide which consultants, which vendors, to call upon?

4 The software applications of the Games were remotely connected to IBM's in-house data centre in Barcelona, called the IBM Calculations Centre, which was set up just before the Games began. But IBM engineers cooperated in software development and the company allowed contractors to test their software on IBM equipment. Would you describe the agreement with IBM as FM? Why? What reasons do you think led COOB '92 to discard the idea of setting up its own centralized computer processing centre?

5 As a COOB '92 committee member, would you see a possible role for service bureaux in the information infrastructure of the Games? What role?

6 How might a computer utility serve the Games?

Case study: Consultants for British parcel delivery

Securicor Express, Britain's second largest overnight private parcel delivery service, has a fleet of 4,500 trucks and a network of 120 branches in the United Kingdom. Each week, 1.3 million packages are handled by the company. In order to speed package processing, meet the demands of an expanding workload and gain an advantage over package-delivery competitors, Securicor recently restructured its operations. Consultants were hired to help determine what systems the company would need to meet the challenges of the 1990s.

A major decision Securicor faced was whether to adopt the single entry form of documentation used by Federal Express or retain its traditional multiple-entry document setup. Should package documentation be attached to the package in a pouch, or be marked with a unique identifier and address, with documentation travelling separately as in the past?

Source: Peter Judge. 'IT delivers at Securicor', *Datamation*, vol. 36, no. 7 (1 April 1990), pp. 100.1–.3.

Questions

1 The consultants first favoured a switch to single entry documentation. How do you think the consultants reached that decision?

2 On learning of this single entry documentation recommendation, business managers said, 'Hold on. Let's check with customers.' After a four-month survey of 1,000 customers, the consultants recommended that Securicor stick with its multiple entry scheme. Why do you suppose the consultants changed their opinion in this matter? What does this example tell you about the role of consultants versus the role of business managers in solving a specific business problem?

3 Securicor also vetoed the advice of consultants to base branch systems on OS/2s. One reason was that OS/2 represented advanced technology not even available in 1988 when this advice was given. Do you think this example is typical — that consultants are more willing to gamble on advanced information technology than business managers? Explain. Why bother to hire consultants if their advice is not going to be followed?

4 When Securicor decided on a fourth-generation language (4GL) solution for a working prototype of a branch computer system, a consultant suggested circulating the specifications among a wide range of 4GL suppliers. According to Roger Teal, Securicor Group IT director, the suppliers were then asked to develop a prototype operating system free of charge. 'I thought it was damn cheeky', said Teal. 'But to my surprise, a number of suppliers came back very quickly.'

What knowledge did the consultant have that Teal lacked in this instance? How was that knowledge acquired? Why do you suppose that Teal was unaware that suppliers might contribute in this manner?

5 If you had been a member of Securicor's board of directors, would you have favoured the hiring of consultants in the business overhaul? How would you have chosen which consultants to hire?

Case study: FM for Mothercare

Mothercare, a subsidiary of Storehouse, decided in 1989 to replace its central IBM 3090 150E mainframe with two IBM AS/400 computers to serve a distributed network environment.

Management wanted the switchover to be completed in little more than a year. Because this tight schedule would strain the organization — a strain compounded by the fact that a second project, the installation of approximately a thousand new point-of-sale terminals in its 256 stores, would be run concurrently — Mothercare decided to farm out the running of the 3090 to an FM company. Another reason for the FM decision was budgetary: management believed that FM would cut staff costs.

Hoskyns won the £4.5 million, two-year FM contract after agreeing to take on any staff Mothercare did not want to retain. (The new AS/400s would require a smaller operations staff than the 3090; packaged software would eliminate the need for Mothercare's software development staff.) Twenty-seven members of Mothercare's staff became employees of Hoskyns and the 3090 was physically moved from Mothercare's Watford head office to a Hoskyn's site at Vauxhall in London.

The new AS/400 network will be run in-house. As Richard Granville, Mothercare's commercial director, explained, 'I don't think Hoskyns could run it cheaper than we could.'

Source: Tim Ring. 'Mothercare: choosing an FM solution', *Which Computer*, vol. 13, no. 9 (September 1990), pp. 50–52.

Questions

1 What benefits will Mothercare receive by using FM to help in the transition from its outdated computer system to more modern technology?

2 Mothercare rejected an FM proposal for a five-year contract, preferring a maximum of two years. Give reasons why you think Mothercare favoured the relatively short Hoskyns two-year deal?

3 Why do you think Mothercare stipulated that Hoskyns physically remove the 3090 mainframe from its head office in Watford?

4 British Home Stores (BHS), another Storehouse subsidiary, considered but rejected FM. Like Mothercare, BHS was upgrading its mainframe, but felt that it could manage the transition with in-house staff because the system was basically up to date. Writer Tim Ring says, 'The message from Storehouse seems to be that FM is appropriate for a company such as Mothercare with older technology which could be run more cheaply by an outside agency. Companies with more modern systems can more readily trust their in-house IT department to run it cost effectively.' Do you agree with Ring's interpretation of 'the message from Storehouse?' Comment. What other reasons might lead one branch of a company to choose FM, another to reject FM?

Key words

Active online processing	Facilities management (FM)	Professional services
Batch processing	Modifying	Remote processing
Computer utility	Non-modifying	Service bureaux
Consultants	Passive online processing	Time-sharing
Continuous processing		Turnkey system
		Vendors

Discussion questions

1 How can consultants be used by
   (a) Computer executives?
   (b) Steering committees?
   (c) Top management?
   (d) Managers of information users?
   (e) Project managers?
   (f) Planning personnel?
2 What are the problems and limitations of engaging a consultant? How can these be minimized?
3 What are the advantages of using a computer consultant? What environmental conditions must be created to maximize these advantages?
4 If you were top management, would you hire a computer consultant if you had a computer technician with equivalent experience and knowledge of your staff? Why or why not?
5 A consultant is a highly paid outsider and is therefore respected. An in-house expert is relatively underpaid and much less respected. Do you agree? Comment.
6 What are the advantages of contracting software development to a consultant or software house, as opposed to developing the software in-house? Would there be a difference in:
   (a) Documentation?
   (b) Run efficiency?
   (c) Maintainability?
   (d) Reliability?
7 Would you use vendors as sources of information to help with recruiting, training and design; or as a sounding board on future developments? Why?
8 Comment on the statement: In dealing with FM, a lawyer is needed to protect the contracting firm's interests.
9 Do you believe that FM hinders the building of in-house processing capability? Comment.
10 List arguments for and against FM for the following businesses:
   (a) Department store in a middle-sized town.
   (b) Warehouse of shoes.
   (c) Pharmacy chain of 20 stores.
   (d) Hospital with 450 beds.
   (e) University with 7,000 full-time students.
   (f) Racetrack.
   (g) Stock broker.
   (h) Restaurant.
   (i) Grocery chain of 25 stores.
11 Is remote processing appropriate for firms or departments that have

specialized tasks using special programming languages or databases? Comment.

12 Is remote processing appropriate to supplement centralized processing for intermittent and one-shot jobs? Comment.

13 Compare the difference between online real-time and time-sharing service for a manufacturing business.

14 How does the interactive capability of time-sharing affect a user in business? Which type of use will be most affected?

15 Compare the advantages and disadvantages of time-sharing from a commercial outside source with time-sharing in-house.

16 Can remote processing be used profitably for testing programs? What limitations exist?

17 What are the advantages and pitfalls of using a service bureau? Under what circumstances would you recommend such use?

18 Why might management choose an external computing service instead of developing an in-house processing capability?

19 Under what conditions might a firm decide to use:
(a) A service bureau?
(b) A computer utility?
(c) In-house computing?
Identify the problems and pitfalls of each.

20 What future do you foresee for remote processing, utilities, and service bureaux?

21 Should the sale of computer services, like the sale of electricity, be regulated by government? Explain.

22 Comment on the following statement: The problem of privacy and security is difficult to control with time-sharing, a service bureau, or a utility, and the problems will get worse in the future, not better.

Bibliography

Ardle, Jack M. 'What do you do after choosing a data processing consultant?', *Office*, vol. 99, no. 6 (June 1984), pp. 63–4.

Fersko-Weiss, Henry. 'Managing your computer consultant', *Personal Computing*, vol. 10, no. 1 (January 1986), pp. 75–85.

Gable, G. 'Consultant engagement for computer system selection', *Information and Management*, vol. 20 (1991), pp. 83–92.

Healy, Paul. 'Good advice, bad advice', *Which Computer?*, vol. 14, no. 6 (June 1991), pp. 76–88.

Kahin, B. 'The software patent crisis', *Technology Review*, vol. 93, no. 3 (April 1990), pp. 52–8.

Kirkpatrick, David. 'Why not farm out your computing', *Fortune*, vol. 124, no. 7 (23 September 1991), pp. 103–12.

Koenig, Michael E.D. 'Information services and downstream productivity', in Martha

E. Williams (ed.), *Annual Review of Information Science and Technology*, vol. 25 (1990), pp. 55–86.

Meiklejohn, I. 'Making the Euro-cap fit', *Management Today* (December 1989), pp. 117–18.

von Simon, Ernest M. 'The centrally decentralized IS organization', *Harvard Business Review*, vol. 68, no. 4 (July–August 1990), pp. 158–62.

Ring, Tom. 'Who's in charge?', *Which Computer?*, vol. 13, no. 9 (September 1990), pp. 40–6.

Wittenberg, Aviwah. 'France's age of reason', *International Management* (September 1990), pp. 52–5.

PART TWO
Control of processing

The purpose of devoting a separate part of this book to control is to emphasize the importance of preventing errors and of protecting information from unauthorized access or illicit use in the business world today. Clearly, the need for control and security of business data predates the use of computers. But the speed of computer transactions and the volume of confidential data processed by computers means that inadequate controls can lead to problems of a much higher magnitude than in the past. Consider, for example, the large sums of money being transferred daily with electronic fund transfer (EFT) and the scope for embezzlement if EFT security can be breached.

Chapter 7 describes where control mechanisms should be located to monitor systems for human and machine error. Solutions to common problems are suggested.

Privacy and security issues are the subject of Chapter 8. Layers of protection are recommended, including access restrictions to computer resources, processing controls, physical safeguards and organizational policies to discourage employee malfeasance.

Finally, Chapter 9 discusses how computer centres evaluate their own performance. Evaluation criteria and methods of collecting data on performance are outlined. Operations that need evaluation are also identified. The chapter closes with a discussion of computer audits by individuals not employed by the computer facility so that a measure of objectivity in evaluating operations can be obtained. The role of auditors in controlling controls is also explained.

7 Quality control

Sign on computer centre wall: 'Mistakes made while you wait.'

Never before in history has it been possible to make so many mistakes in so short a period. Because of the rapidity of computer calculations and the repetitious nature of computer operations, undetected errors compound at an alarming rate. Some errors are built into systems by poor design. Some result from programming mistakes. But many are procedural mistakes or the result of careless machine operation, such as the use of an outdated code, the wrong input tape, or incorrect output distribution.

The determination of technical control measures to ensure accuracy, timeliness and completeness of data is generally the responsibility of information technology (IT) personnel. However, management needs to identify which data needs protection and to specify standards of control after weighing monetary costs of control measures against the risk of inadvertent errors and security violations. The cost of delays and inconvenience to employees from controls must also be considered. For example, companies can go too far with controls, causing production to fall off because access to computers is made difficult for bona fide users or because procedures impede performance.

This chapter will describe how information systems should be monitored for human and machine error. Figure 7.1 shows where controls are necessary during processing. Potential threats to data quality and privacy at each location (circle) will be discussed, countermeasures to these threats will be suggested, and the personnel responsible for control will be identified. Systems security and the prevention of unauthorized access or illicit use of information are touched on briefly in this chapter. They will be discussed in depth in Chapter 8.

Control locations

Control of procedure and code manuals (Circle 1)

In information processing, codes often replace the natural language and represent values of a data element. For example, an employee code such as an identification number may be used instead of an employee name in processing personnel records. Table 7.1 summarizes common sources of error when using code and procedure manuals and suggests control solutions. In many firms, the database

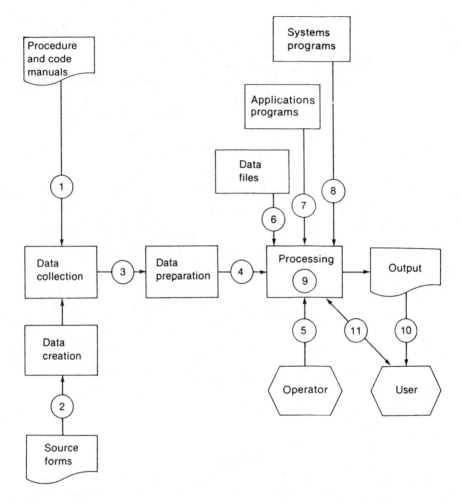

Figure 7.1 *Quality control locations (circles) during information processing*

administrator (DBA) or someone on the DBA's staff is responsible for establishing codes at the request of users and for coordinating assignment of codes so that redundant coding schemes do not occur. Publication, maintenance and distribution of uniform code manuals are also delegated to this individual. Procedure manuals are the responsibility of management.

Users provide feedback to computing personnel regarding the effectiveness of procedures and codes. They may also initiate changes when the manuals prove unsatisfactory. In this way, users contribute to control over procedures and codes.

Table 7.1 *Control of manuals*

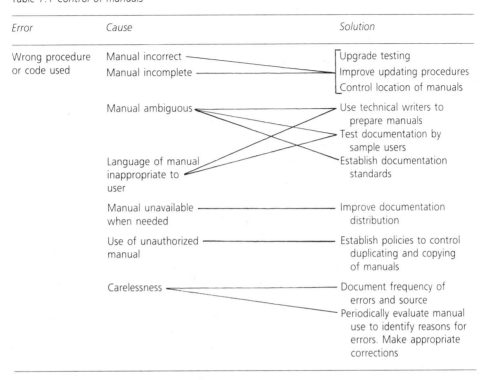

Error	Cause	Solution
Wrong procedure or code used	Manual incorrect Manual incomplete	Upgrade testing Improve updating procedures Control location of manuals
	Manual ambiguous Language of manual inappropriate to user	Use technical writers to prepare manuals Test documentation by sample users Establish documentation standards
	Manual unavailable when needed	Improve documentation distribution
	Use of unauthorized manual	Establish policies to control duplicating and copying of manuals
	Carelessness	Document frequency of errors and source Periodically evaluate manual use to identify reasons for errors. Make appropriate corrections

Form control (2)

A common method of collecting data for an information processing system is through the use of forms. A well-designed form helps to ensure that collected data are error free. For example, banks usually provide customers with deposit slips that have the name, address and customer account number preprinted on them so that only spaces for date and amount need to be filled. This **turnaround document** reduces the possibility of input errors entering the bank's processing system. (When customers write their own account numbers, they frequently interchange digits.) Other examples of turnaround documents are the tear-off sections of utility and credit card bills that accompany bill payment, and preprinted complaint forms that come with mail-order merchandise.

Error-free data collection may be impossible, but errors can be minimized by complying with the following principles of **form design**:

- Instructions should be easy to understand.
- Input codes (if used) should be unique and unambiguous.

- Adequate space, without crowding, should be allowed for completing information.
- Questions should be sequenced to avoid confusion and should be worded unambiguously.
- Lines for typed answers should conform to typewriter spacing.
- Vertical alignment on forms to be typewritten should enable clerks to use tabs.
- Larger spaces should be provided for handwritten data than for typewritten data.
- Only variable values should be requested.
- No information should be lost when the form is filed or bound.

In addition, the colour of forms should be chosen for emphasis and ease of reading. (Light brown and light green print have been found empirically to be easy on the eye.) Some forms are printed on paper with shaded horizontal stripes to facilitate reading across columns of data without drifting of sight. The grouping of related data items on forms and spacing between data groups contribute to the ease with which forms can be read and collected information interpreted. These measures also facilitate accurate conversion when data on forms are readied by operators for the computer.

The importance of careful form design and pretesting cannot be overemphasized. Here is an example of how poor sequencing of questions and inadequate form directions resulted in the collection of incorrect data. One firm's application asked for name, address, birthdate, father's name and date of high school graduation, in that order. Many applicants filled the form with their father's date of graduation, whereas the information desired was the applicant's own high school graduation date. Had the form been pretested by sample users, this sequencing problem might have been identified and, consequently, the order of the questions changed before the form was put into use.

The entry of numbers on forms is also a frequent source of errors. For example, handwritten ones and sevens often look alike. The use of boxes on forms for numerical data seems to encourage the user to write numbers legibly. IT personnel commonly use the European convention of placing a dash on the stem of a seven (7) to distinguish it from a one. They also place a dash on the Z (Z) so it won't be mistaken for a two, and a slash through the zero (Ø) to distinguish it from the letter O.

Date entries, such as 3/1/52, can also cause problems of interpretation because the data convention in some firms and countries is month/day/year and, in others, day/month/year. For this reason, forms with labelled boxes for the entry of dates are advisable.

However, there still remains the possibility that 'Mo', meaning Monday, might be filled in as day of birth instead of the desired numerical date. One way to avoid the latter problem is to supplement form instructions with sample correct and incorrect responses.

Month	Day	Year

Another form variation is a series of boxes that users check to indicate a condition. For example:

Marital status	1	2	3		4
	☐	☐	☐		☐
	Single	Married	Divorced	Other, specify _____	

Input boxes are also used on forms that can be read by special machines, although the boxes may then have to be marked by a special pencil. This technique, called **mark-sensing**, reduces processing time and inaccuracies in processing, since data need not be manually converted into a machine-readable format.

Table 7.2 summarizes frequent causes of errors in filling out forms, and possible control solutions.

Data collection (3)

Data collection is not only the source of many careless errors but also the focus of much criminal activity. For example, in the United States a Blue Cross/Blue Shield claims examiner mailed forms to relatives who filled them in with real names and policy numbers to defraud the system of £72,000. In another recorded case of fraud, eleven employees of the Los Angeles County Department of Social Services issued cheques to themselves, using terminated welfare accounts. Other cases of manipulation of input data include:

- The arrest of four individuals by City of London police for suspected ATM fraud, after finding 1,864 cash cards in their possession.
- The theft of approximately £60,000 from a bank account, using the magnetic ink character recognition (MICR) number found on a discarded deposit slip.
- A conspiracy between an accounting clerk and a grocer resulting in a theft of more than £68,000 over the years by issuing false invoices for undelivered food.

Inadvertent errors can be equally harmful to an organization. In one firm, the code for equipment costing £12,000 was erroneously used to code the price of 50 manuals on that equipment. This mistake resulted in an inflated inventory value of £560,000.

Table 7.2 *Form control*

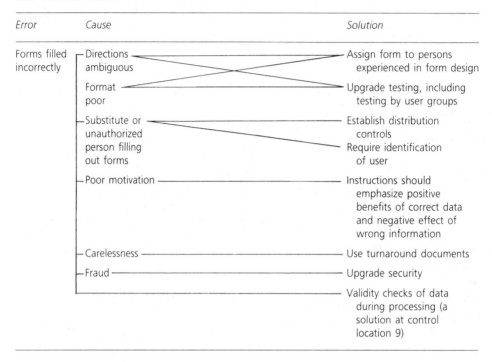

Error	Cause	Solution
Forms filled incorrectly	Directions ambiguous	Assign form to persons experienced in form design
	Format poor	Upgrade testing, including testing by user groups
	Substitute or unauthorized person filling out forms	Establish distribution controls
		Require identification of user
	Poor motivation	Instructions should emphasize positive benefits of correct data and negative effect of wrong information
	Carelessness	Use turnaround documents
	Fraud	Upgrade security
		Validity checks of data during processing (a solution at control location 9)

Table 7.3 summarizes common errors in data collection and suggests possible control solutions.

Data preparation (4)

Errors in data preparation occur when data are incorrectly converted into machine-readable form. Control is exercised by the department responsible for the data preparation. Recommended control measures are summarized in Table 7.4.

Ways to detect errors and procedures to correct mistakes are not all that is needed. The source of the errors should be traced and procedures amended so that the same errors do not recur.

Operations (5)

Employees can be trained in emergency procedures should flood, earthquake, fire or an explosion interrupt operations. Although damage may be minimized as a result of such training, equipment may be destroyed and data lost in such disasters. To safeguard the information function against such adversity, **backup** is needed. That is, duplicate data files should be stored in a secure vault at another

Table 7.3 *Data collection control*

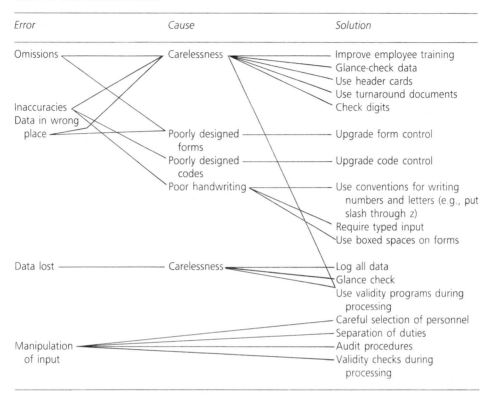

Error	Cause	Solution
Omissions	Carelessness	Improve employee training
		Glance-check data
		Use header cards
		Use turnaround documents
Inaccuracies		Check digits
Data in wrong place	Poorly designed forms	Upgrade form control
	Poorly designed codes	Upgrade code control
	Poor handwriting	Use conventions for writing numbers and letters (e.g., put slash through z)
		Require typed input
		Use boxed spaces on forms
Data lost	Carelessness	Log all data
		Glance check
		Use validity programs during processing
		Careful selection of personnel
		Separation of duties
Manipulation of input		Audit procedures
		Validity checks during processing

location, and backup processing facilities at a distant computer centre should be available and tested for restart and recovery. Backup is also good insurance against intentional errors or wilful damage, such as sabotage. Indeed, incidents of sabotage to computer equipment and data files have increased in recent years, particularly in industries engaged in research in politically sensitive areas such as nuclear energy or chemicals that might be used in warfare.

In handling sensitive information, the following basic operating precautions are recommended. Two operators should always be present. Work schedules should be changed frequently so that no single operator handles the same programs over a long period of time. No employees should be assigned processing tasks when a conflict of interest might arise. (For example, bank employees should not handle programming that will affect their own accounts.) In addition, proof of authorization and sign in/sign out controls for handling sensitive files should be initiated. Finally, neither programmers nor analysts should be assigned routine operating tasks.

Many controls are needed to prevent errors or intrusion during data preparation and operations, because information systems are especially vulnerable during

Table 7.4 *Data preparation errors and solutions*

Error	Cause	Solution
Incorrect data	Poorly written data entry instructions	Upgrade procedures manual, include visual aids
	Hardware error	Proper maintenance
	Carelessness	Supervise data entry
		Periodically evaluate work of data entry clerks and operators
		Use check digits
Handling errors (Tapes or disks misplaced, put out of order, damaged, or duplicated inadvertently)	Carelessness	Glance check
		Validity programs
		Upgrade employee selection and training
	Poor procedure	Upgrade procedure testing
		Log data

these activities. Most problems at this stage can be traced to lax procedures and careless operators. And these incidents can be costly indeed. For example, the running of an accounts payable program using an outdated price list cost one firm £56,000. In another expensive mistake, a bank employee fed a printout of sensitive data on depositors into a shredder with the line of print parallel to the blades instead of at right angles. As a result, strips of readable confidential data were thrown in the trash where they were spotted, retrieved, and peddled at a local bar by a drifter. The cost to the bank? Reward money for return of the strips and an incalculable loss of customer confidence.

More stringent control procedures could also have prevented the following incident. A hotel mixed address tapes, sending to vendors, instead of to past guests, letters explaining recent hotel renovations and urging them to return. Instead of goodwill, the hotel received irate calls from vendors whose spouses were citing the letters as evidence of their infidelity.

Failure to test control procedures produced this fiasco: when a fire broke out in a computer centre, employees discovered that narrow doors barred passage of fire-extinguishing equipment. But who was to blame when a corrosive leak in an air-conditioning system destroyed a computer several floors below?

It simply isn't practical to devise control methods for all possible threats to an information system. Controls are costly, and too many controls can impede operations. The controls summarized in Table 7.5 are those most frequently adopted for operations.

Table 7.5 *Control of operations*

Error	Cause	Solution
Incorrect operation	Poor instructions	Upgrade personnel selection, training, and procedure testing
	Carelessness	Check data file labels
Machine breakdown	Poor maintenance	Upgrade maintenance
		Upgrade testing
		Upgrade personnel selection
	Careless operators	Upgrade training
	Act of nature (flood, storm)	Backup equipment
		Shutdown devices
	Fire	Emergency training
		Heat and smoke alarm
		Fire extinguishers
		Panic switches
Fraudulent operation	Sabotage	Intrusion detectors
		Police patrol
	Desire for personal gain	At least two people on duty
		Steel or steel mesh on windows and doors
		Control physical access
		Control access to files
		Remove conflict of interest
		Vary work schedules
		Strict supervision
		Upgrade personnel selection
		Bond personnel
Data not processed on time	Documents lost or misrouted	Establish documentation procedures (logging, checking record totals, etc.)

Data files (6)

If data files are centrally stored, a librarian generally is assigned responsibility for control. Otherwise, the owner of the data is responsible for their security.

Cited in computer literature are numerous cases of errors and fraud relating to data files. Stolen programs have been held for ransom. Disgruntled employees have maliciously scratched or destroyed tapes. A product support engineer, fired for non-performance, was caught downloading proprietary software of the Woolongong Group, her former employer, onto her home computer. She was able to do so because her secret password and privileges had not been invalidated. In another organization, data files were damaged when an employee moved files to storage. He wedged the vault open but forgot to remove the wedge after the

Table 7.6 *Data file controls*

Error	Cause	Solution
Warped cards, dirty tapes or disks	Poor physical storage	Control storage humidity 'Clean room' conditions Special cabinets Periodic cleaning
	Lack of clearly defined responsibility for data files	Centralize storage under a librarian
	Inadequate procedures	Upgrade storage procedures
Destruction of files	Natural disaster	Special vaults Backup data
	Theft, fraud, or sabotage	Control access to files: Data librarian Lock words Control labels

move was complete. Although the vault was fireproof, a fire swept through the open door and destroyed hundreds of the tapes.

In most cases, destruction of data files can be attributed to lax security. In addition, they can be damaged by humidity, dust or contaminants during storage. Table 7.6 summarizes the types of control needed to protect data files.

Programming controls (7, 8)

Many mistakes in computerized systems can be attributed to faulty programming. One bank, for example, lost £170,000 by paying customers interest on 31-day months. A hyphen omitted from a programming card caused an American rocket being tested to head for Rio. It had to be destroyed mid-flight at a loss of £10,000,000. Unintentional errors may result from an incorrect algorithm, erroneous programming logic, or a cause as minor as one out-of-sequence programming statement. Training, care, strict adherence to standard programming procedures and proper documentation during systems development are necessary to minimize such problems.

The controls summarized in Table 7.7 should trace inadvertent errors and also help prevent fraud. Control measures should be initiated and enforced by computing personnel responsible for systems analysis and programming. Unfortunately, programming fraud is difficult to detect, and the crimes themselves are often quite ingenious. The first US federal prosecution of computer crime in 1966 was against a bank programmer who programmed the system to omit his name

Table 7.7 *Programming controls*

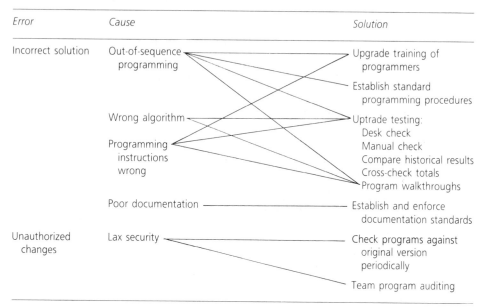

Error	Cause	Solution
Incorrect solution	Out-of-sequence programming	Upgrade training of programmers
		Establish standard programming procedures
	Wrong algorithm	Uptrade testing: Desk check
	Programming instructions wrong	Manual check Compare historical results Cross-check totals Program walkthroughs
	Poor documentation	Establish and enforce documentation standards
Unauthorized changes	Lax security	Check programs against original version periodically
		Team program auditing

from a list generated daily of overdrawn accounts. He withdrew large sums of money before being caught. Control measures, however, did not bring about his downfall. The overdrafts were detected when the computer broke down and the bank had to revert to manual processing.

Another US programmer assessed a 10-cent service charge to each customer and put the amounts in a dummy account under the name of Zwicke. By chance, a public relations gimmick unmasked the bogus Zwicke. The fraud was discovered when it was decided to award a bonus to the first and last name on the firm's alphabetical list of customers.

Nibble theft, stealing small amounts of money over a period of time, is more difficult to detect than **bite-size fraud**, the embezzlement of large sums. The latter can be uncovered by auditing and checking for unreasonable values or control totals. But no matter how well designed the controls, someone will think up a new technique for cheating the system. Constant vigilance is required.

Processing (9)

At the time of processing, many errors in data preparation that pass Controls 2, 3 and 4 can be caught by the computer itself, using stored **validation rules**. These rules, determined by management and information users, need to be specified with care. Underspecification may lead to undetected errors, causing the system to produce unreliable information. On the other hand, overspecification adds unnecessarily to processing costs.

Validation tests include checks for completeness, format, range, reasonableness, consistency, sequence, transaction count and recalculation of check digits. Some errors will still escape detection, such as data entry mistakes that fall within allowable ranges. But validation programs will help pinpoint invalid data resulting from:

- Entry error by data collector.
- Misinterpretation of documentation during input preparation.
- Coding errors.
- Operator errors in data conversion (largest single cause of input error).
- Errors in data transmission or data handling (for example, lost data or incorrect sequencing).

In the following sections, common validation rules and methods will be described.

Completeness
A validation rule for **completeness** requires that all characters be expressed before processing takes place in data that have a prescribed length, such as nine digits for a US social security number. Completeness checks are necessary only when missing data will affect results, so completeness requirements should be carefully specified. For example, it would be necessary to halt processing of an order with a truncated product number or one with quantity blank, whereas the order could probably be filled if the client's middle initial were absent or if a digit were omitted from the client's phone number.

Format
Permuted characters can be specified in validation programs and the data checked against these predetermined rules. For example, a validation program can be written to identify as an error an alphabetic character in a dollar data field or numeric data in names. The check can divide the **format** into subfields. An address may be assigned numeric fields for house number, alphabetic blocks for street and city, and an alphanumeric field for postal code.

Range
A check rule may state that data entry is limited to predetermined values or a range of values. If M and F are used as sex codes, only these two characters would be valid in the sex code field. Any other letter or number would be listed as an error. Similarly, a **range of values** could be specified. If a firm's minimum wage per hour rate was £3 and the maximum £30, the computer could be programmed to identify as invalid any data with values under or over these amounts, errors called definite or **fatal errors**. The computer might also be programmed to identify possible or **suspected errors**, data near the limits of acceptable values. For example,

if few employees earned over £25, a listing of employees in the $\geq £25 - \leq £30$ range could be provided for recheck. The validation rule would be:

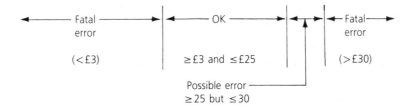

Fatal errors identified by the validation program would have to be traced and corrected. The data would then be reprocessed. Possible errors are checked and corrected, if necessary. An overriding code will permit processing of suspect data that proves valid.

Reasonableness
In any given situation, a number of checks for **reasonableness** can be postulated. Date of employment cannot predate a worker's birth, a probationary student cannot graduate with honours, and so forth. The cost of processing such checks must be weighted against losses (monetary and credibility) should errors pass undetected. Such decisions require management's judgement.

Consistency
One way to check data values is to compare the same raw data collected from two or more sources. Another way is to generate values of data elements from input and then match these generated values with keyed values for the same data elements. The latter method is used, for example, to check totals. If the information in Table 7.8 were keyed, a computer validity program could add £53.20, £32.80 and £39.90 in Batch 1 and match the total with the batch total £125.90 entered as input. Or each invoice total could be calculated by computer (price times quantity) and the product compared to the figure listed in the value column. Any discrepancy would be identified on an error listing. Most frequently, invalid data is a mistake in keying the input.

A **hash total** entered as input is also a useful check for **consistency**. All the data in one transaction are totalled, even though the units are not the same. The computer then totals the 'hash' independently (320 + 16 + 3.20 + 53.20 in the first transaction in Table 7.8) and compares the total with the keyed hash total of 392.40. Since many transactions involve 80 to 100 characters, the hash total is an important validity check.

Duplicate processing is another method of checking for consistency. One firm needing to determine a coefficient to two decimal places (from complex calculations for the allocation of over £4 million) used both COBOL and FORTRAN to make the calculations. Because of the large amount of money involved, it was helpful

Table 7.8 *Transaction data*

	Invoice number	Quantity (units)	Price (£)	Value (£)	Batch total (£)	Hash total
Batch 1	320	16	3.20	53.20		392.40
	321	8	4.10	32.80		365.90
	323	21	1.90	39.90	125.90	511.70
Batch 2	324	25	4,00	100.00		363.00
	325	31	4.20	130.20		490,40
	326	9	5.80	52.20		393.00
	327	5	6.10	30.50	312.90	681.60
				438.80	438.80	

to compare calculations made by the two compilers, which differed in rounding and truncation rules.

Sequence
In Table 7.8, Invoice 322 is missing. A validity test for **sequencing** would identify this situation. The document may have been mislaid or lost, in which case corrective action (such as recollection of the data) would take place. Often, an explanation will be found, such as a cancelled order. In processing payrolls, logs are kept of cheques damaged, destroyed by the printer, or left blank — a record that is searched when a sequence validity test flags an error.

Transaction count
When a given number of transactions are to be processed, this total is entered as input. The transactions are again counted during processing. An invalid state will be identified if the totals do not match. **Transaction counts** will alert operators to a lost document, records stuck to one another, or possibly even multiple processing of the same transaction.

Self-checking codes
A **self-checking code** is sometimes used to check for transposition of data or data entry errors, situations that often occur in data elements consisting of a long string of digits. This code, called a **check digit**, is calculated by a prescribed set of rules based on the value of the digits in the number and their locational relationships. The code is then added to the data element number and recalculated every time that data element is processed. If the recalculated value does not coincide with the original check digit, an error is identified.

   Modulus 10 is one technique for calculating a check digit. In this technique, the position of digits in a number is significant. Digits in odd positions (such as first, third, fifth, etc.) are added for a subtotal. Digits in even positions are multiplied by two, and the digits in the products added together for a second subtotal. The subtotals are then added and divided by 10. The number that must be added to the remainder to make it divisible by 10 is the check digit.

For the number 142796539, the check digit, according to these rules, is 2. To demonstrate the derivation of the check digit, the number will be aligned in two rows, digits in odd positions separated from digits in even positions. The calculations are then performed as follows:

	Multiplied by 2	Subtotal of digits in row
1 2 9 5 9	No	1 + 2 + 9 + 5 + 9 = 26
4 7 6 3	Yes	8 + (1 + 4) + (1 + 2) + 6 = 22
		Total = 48

Remainder when total is divided by 10 = 8
Number to be added to remainder to equal 10 = 2
New check digit = 2

New number = 1427965392

To test the working of the check digit, study the following example in which the value of one digit is changed.

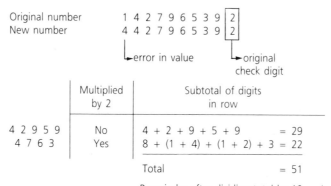

Original number   1 4 2 7 9 6 5 3 9 $\boxed{2}$
New number   4 4 2 7 9 6 5 3 9 $\boxed{2}$

error in value   original check digit

	Multiplied by 2	Subtotal of digits in row
4 2 9 5 9	No	4 + 2 + 9 + 5 + 9 = 29
4 7 6 3	Yes	8 + (1 + 4) + (1 + 2) + 3 = 22
		Total = 51

Remainder after dividing total by 10 = 1
Number to be added to remainder to equal 10 = 9
New check digit = 9
Original check digit = 2

The new check digit does not equal the original check digit. Therefore, an error exists. In the next example, two adjacent digits are transposed:

Original number   1 4 2 7 9 6 5 3 9 2
New number   (4 1) 2 7 9 6 5 3 9 2 ← check digit

↳ error from single transposition

	Multiplied by 2	Subtotal of digits in row	
4 2 9 5 9	No	4 + 2 + 9 + 5 + 9	= 29
1 7 6 3	Yes	2 + (1 + 4) + (1 + 2) + 6	= 16
		Total	= 45

Remainder after dividing total by 10 = 5
Number to be added to remainder to equal 10 = 5
New check digit = 5
Original check digit = 2

The new check digit does not equal the original check digit. Therefore, an error exists.

The problem with Modulus 10 is that double transposition can take place without affecting the check digit (for instance, 5431 transposed as 3154). **Modulus 11**, another method of calculating a check digit, overcomes this problem. In Modulus 11, each digit in the value of the data element is assigned a separate weight, such as numbers in an ascending or descending scale. Each digit is then multiplied by its corresponding weighted value, and the products are totalled. The number that must be added to this total to make it divisible by 11 is the check digit. All types of transposition (double, triple and so forth) and data entry errors are caught by this technique.

The use of a check digit has disadvantages. It adds to the length of numbers and increases data preparation effort, the time required for processing and storage space requirements. The longer number is also harder to remember. But when reliability is important and the number is repeatedly used in processing, detection of errors may be worth the inconvenience and cost. Self-checking codes are commonly the last digit in identification numbers for employees, vendors, customers, accounts and parts. Their use will identify posting of transactions to wrong accounts.

Other processing controls, the responsibility of computing personnel, are summarized in Table 7.9.

Output controls (10)

Output is the product of all input and processing. If proper control is exercised during both of these operational phases, the output should be free of error. But most firms add output controls in an information system's design to cross-check for errors that may have slipped past input and processing controls. Responsibility for these is divided between computing personnel responsible for output production and management using the output. Output controls are summarized in Table 7.10.

Table 7.9 *Processing controls*

Error	Cause	Solution
Records lost	Carelessness	Validity checks
		Upgrade training of personnel
		Log jobs
Use of incorrect file	Carelessness	Use standard labels for all files
		Use program to automatically generate updated data
Lack of necessary supplies	Carelessness	Upgrade planning and inventory control

Table 7.10 *Output control*

Error	Cause	Solution
Inaccurate output	Processing errors	Audits
		Validation programs
		Interfile comparison
		Defer large-volume printing until proof data checked
		Sample check of output with corresponding input
	Operation error	Sight check
Incomplete output	Operation or processing error	Check page counts
		Check control totals for each process or report

Many output mistakes can be caught by cursory sight checks. For example, a payroll run of paycheques issued without decimal points could be easily spotted by an alert operator, since the amounts would be unreasonable. In addition, many of the validation programs used for input can be run to control output.

Teleprocessing (11)

Access controls and the use of cryptography protocols (described in Chapter 8) are methods of protecting data during teleprocessing. **Parity checks** facilitate error detection. A bit of data is added to each set of bits representing a character so that the total number of 1 bits is odd (for an odd parity check) or even (even parity check). Upon receipt of the transmission, the bits are added and compared to the parity rule. When an error is detected, a signal is sent for retransmission of the data.

Checking for the use of a prescribed pattern of ones and zeros to represent characters is another method of tracing errors. Automatic checking of prescribed patterns can make this a self-checking code. This raises costs, however, since additional check bits must be transmitted and processed.

Fortunately, improved technology (such as large-scale integrated circuitry) is reducing the error rate in communications systems and is improving reliability.

Control in a microcomputer environment

The controls discussed in this chapter are appropriate for microcomputers as well as for business environments in which large computers predominate. However, responsibility for quality control varies in these two situations. Computer professionals generally install and monitor controls for mainframes and minis; the user is usually responsible for quality control in a microcomputer environment. Another difference is that much attention is placed on quality control at processing centres under the jurisdiction of computing professionals, whereas the micro-computer user often treats quality control casually. Indeed, many persons who use micros in their jobs have no training or knowledge regarding the management of computer resources. As a result, productivity using a micro may be poor, processing costs may be high, and micro output may be faulty.

One of the major problems facing businesses today is how to ensure quality at distributed processing nodes. Inaccurate, unreliable information generated by micros because quality controls are lacking can affect the work not only of individuals at the node but of the entire company. For example, the faulty information may be included in reports that are subsequently used as a data source for the work of other departments and thus pollute the company's data stream. The danger of such pollution is magnified with micro—mainframe intercommunication.

There is no easy solution to the problem. Rigid quality control administered by computer professionals undermines one of the major benefits of microcomputer use: user independence. But without such controls, how can a corporation be sure that its employees are using valid data and programs that actually do what they are supposed to do? One answer is to train micro users in the control measures outlined in this chapter and to motivate them to adhere to corporate standards for quality control. The subject of quality control at distributed nodes is of great concern to the computing profession at the present time because of the recent proliferation in microcomputer use.

Summing up

This chapter examines controls for documentation, forms, data collection, data preparation, operations, data files, programming, processing, output and teleprocessing. Deciding how much control is necessary is a management dilemma. Too much control is costly: it can impede work and affect morale. Too little control permits inaccuracies and security infractions, reducing the usefulness of systems.

The importance of carefully designed controls cannot be overstressed. Most readers will have personally experienced the frustration of trying to correct a billing error resulting from inadequate control procedures. Indeed, a major source of public distrust of computers can be traced to such experiences and the feeling of consumers that they are being victimized by computer systems. The reputation of a firm generally depends on the quality of its customer service. Inadequate controls over computerized information can lead to a decrease in clients, a decline in profits and a loss of goodwill.

Control measures should be planned, implemented, tested and evaluated during the development of information systems. Adding controls at a later date is both expensive and disruptive. This is especially true of online and real-time systems. This chapter has focused on batch systems, but the need for controls applies to all modes of operation. And quality controls are appropriate for all types of computers, from micros to mainframes.

Chapter 8 will discuss systems security, a subject closely related to quality control.

Case study: **Check digit on book numbers**

When publishers and book distributors began using computers in order processing and inventory control in the late 1960s, it became evident that unique identification numbers were needed for books. Several international conferences addressed the problem, and alternative numbering systems were proposed. The system chosen, the international standard book number (ISBN), is a ten-digit number with four parts consisting of a group identifier (national, geographic or other grouping of publishers), publisher's prefix, title identifier and check digit.

The check digit is used to detect errors in book numbers when processing orders. A calculation based on the other nine digits of the book number, using Modulus 11, is performed by the computer to check whether numbers have been transposed or miscopied, the source of the majority of ordering errors. Use of the check digit guards against more than 99 per cent of these errors.

Here is an example of how the ISBN check digit was calculated for Hussain and Hussain, *Information Systems for Business*.

ISBN number	0	1	3	4	6	3	6	4	7
ISBN weights	10	9	8	7	6	5	4	3	2
Weighted values	0	9	24	28	36	15	24	12	14

(ISBN digits
multiplied by
ISBN weight)

Weighted total (sum of weighted
values) = 162
Number added to make total divisible
by 11 = 3
Check digit = 3
ISBN number = 0-13-463647-3

If the check digit had been calculated as 10, an X would have been used instead of the number, since only one character is assigned to the check digit. ISBN 0-256-02121-X, for James

A. O'Brien's text *Computers in Business Management: An Introduction* (1979), fits this pattern.

Questions

1 What types of errors in placing orders will not be caught by the ISBN check digit? Which types of errors will be caught? Explain why.
2 Figure out the rules of Modulus 11 from this example. State the rules.
3 What do you suppose were some of the difficulties encountered in getting approval of an international publishing check digit standard in the United Kingdom and in different countries around the world?
4 What are the benefits of an international book standard?

Case study: Electronic trading system fails at the London Stock Exchange

A 1986 crash at the London Stock Exchange was not caused by the falling price of stocks. It was the crash of an electronic trading system — consisting of five networked IBM PC ATs with an additional AT network controller — designed to handle options. (An option gives the holder the right to deal in a share at a future date at today's prices.) The failure of the system caused the exchange to halt options trading for a day in order to clear up the backlog left by the crash.

The purpose of the system is to match buyers and sellers, an activity previously carried out using a mainframe-based batch system at the London Options Clearing House. The crash occurred on the first day that the new system was in operation. Its cause? A hardware fault in one of the terminals locked up the network. Many brokers blamed the failure on inadequate testing: conversion to the new system took place after only three days of a parallel run. Another criticism heard at the exchange was that the system lacked a backup facility, although one had originally been specified.

Questions

1 Who was responsible for this failure? Should or could a failure such as this one have been anticipated? By whom?
2 What type of testing should have taken place? If a system passes all tests, does that guarantee that no failure will ever take place? Explain.
3 Would periodic testing of the system be disruptive? How? Would you recommend such testing? Why?
4 How would you organize an official inquiry into the reasons why the system collapsed? Whom would you appoint to conduct the inquiry? What resources would you allocate to the inquiry? What constraints (on funding and time) would you impose?

Case study: Fly-by-wire system reliability

The European A320 Airbus, like many other modern aircraft, depends on fly-by-wire systems. The pilots' control over wings and tailplane do not depend on mechanical linkages. Instead, 'a pilots' analogue control movements on the joystick or control column are converted to digital pulses which in turn drive servo motors and other power systems that move the ailerons, rudder and elevators'. That is to say, the physical link that used to connect the pilot with control surfaces has been replaced by onboard computers that interpret control movements and then activate changes in the position of wing and tail parts.

During the 1980s, the UH–60 Blackhawk, a utility helicopter that utilizes fly-by-wire technology to control the main rotor and tail rotor, was investigated by the US Air Force after several machines either spun out of control or nose-dived into the ground. The cause of the mysterious crashes was found to be inadequate shielding of some of the logic modules of the onboard computer. As a result, microwave and other radio transmissions could affect the computer, causing it to send erroneous signals to the helicopter's hydraulic system. This explained the uncontrollable nose-dives.
Source: Tom Forester and Perry Morrison, *Computer Ethics*, Cambridge, Mass.: The MIT Press, 1990, p. 68.

Questions

1 What caused the unreliable fly-by-wire system of the Blackhawk? What control measures should have been in place to prevent the uncontrollable nose-dives? Who was responsible for these accidents?

2 For public safety, should fly-by-wire systems be outlawed? Comment.

3 Why can't we build computer systems with the same inherent reliability as bridges and buildings?

4 If computer system reliability is defined as the probability that a given system will not fail during a given period of operation under given conditions, can any system be guaranteed for reliability? What problems may arise that will make a 'reliable' system unreliable?

5 Why are complex computer systems so unreliable? Should we entrust responsibility for complex activities, such as the control of a nuclear power station, to computer systems that are less than totally reliable?

6 What steps would you recommend to improve computer system reliability?

Key words

Backup
Bite-size fraud
Check digit
Completeness
Consistency
Duplicate processing
Fatal errors
Form design

Format
Hash total
Mark-sensing
Modulus 10
Modulus 11
Nibble theft
Parity checks
Range of values

Reasonableness
Self-checking codes
Sequencing
Suspected errors
Transaction count
Turnaround document
Validation rules

Discussion questions

1 What are some of the common causes of errors in computer systems? Classify them in terms of:
   (*a*) Source.
   (*b*) Motivation.
   (*c*) Importance.
   (*d*) Difficulty to trace.

(*e*) Difficulty to correct.
2 Identify control locations where measures should be taken to ensure security of data. Explain what measures you would require and why.
3 How can careless errors be reduced?
4 What are the need and significance of editing and validation? At what point in processing should they be performed? What resources are necessary?
5 Can the following errors be caught by validation? In each case, state the validation rule.
   (*a*) £93A2.4.
   (*b*) DR. HUSS3IN.
   (*c*) £3 2.64.
   (*d*) WAGE £1686 per hour.
   (*e*) Account number incorrect.
   (*f*) Age incorrect by one year.
   (*g*) Age incorrect by 100 years.
6 When should a file be verified? Must all the contents be verified in each verification run?
7 Explain six validation rules for data.
8 What are common causes for invalid data?
9 How does quality control in a distributed processing environment where microcomputers are in use differ from control of centralized processing?
10 Comment on the statement: A computer system adds to the probability of errors, fraud and destruction of data and information.
11 Comment on the statement: Computers never make mistakes. People do.
12 Can error-free data be guaranteed? Can error-free results be guaranteed? Explain your answers.
13 Suggest ways to reduce the introduction of programming errors.
14 What measures can be taken to protect against the introduction of errors during operations?

Bibliography

Cashmore, Carol and Richard Lyall. *Business Information*, Hemel Hempstead: Prentice Hall, 1988, pp. 235–55.
Darst, Don. 'Balancing productivity and quality', *Datamation*, vol. 36, no. 18 (15 September 1990), pp. 117–19.
Duncan, Mark. 'Quality: toward a definition', *System Development*, vol. 10, no. 10 (October 1990), pp. 7–8.
Dunn, Robert. 'SQA: a management perspective', *American Programmer*, vol. 3, no. 11 (November 1990), pp. 21–5.
Glass, R.L. 'Quality measurement: two very different ways', *Systems Development*, vol. 10, no. 6 (June 1990), pp. 9–10.

Huh, Y.U., F.R. Keller, T.C. Redman and A.R. Watkins. 'Data quality', *Information and Software Technology*, vol. 38, no. 8 (October 1990), pp. 559–606.

Johnson, James R. 'Hallmark's unique approach to quality', *Datamation*, vol. 36, no. 4 (15 February 1990), pp. 119–28.

Madsen, W. 'The role of quality assurance managers as epidemiologists', *Quality Data Processing*, vol. 4 (April 1990), pp. 29–30.

Misvanks. 'Integrity analysis', *Information and Software Technology*, vol. 30, no. 10 (December 1988), pp. 595–611.

Oppenheim, Charles. 'Should information providers be liable for the information they provide?', *Advanced Information Report* (January 1991), pp. 1–4.

Perry, William E. 'Quality in MIS: misunderstood, misapplied, often missing', *American Programmer*, vol. 3, no. 11 (November 1990), pp. 12–16.

Yellin, Robert. 'Pinpointing production turnover problems', *Datacenter Manager*, vol. 2, no. 2 (March/April 1990), pp. 8–10.

8 Privacy and security

Every new technology carries with it an opportunity to invent a new crime.
Laurence Urgenson

Most commercial, industrial and financial organizations process and transmit proprietary and sensitive information in the course of their daily activities. Protecting privacy and securing data from criminal access is a major concern. Equipment, software, manuals, forms and other components of computer systems are also vulnerable to wilful damage and theft.

This chapter examines the issue of privacy and outlines security measures that help safeguard the security not only of data but of all computing resources. Recovery following natural disasters is also discussed. Management's responsibility in planning and implementing security is presented, and the question 'How much security is essential?' is addressed.

Privacy

Issues of privacy

In modern society, data of a personal nature is collected by most business units. For example:

- Employers keep personnel records that include data on the address, age, education, work experience, salary, dependents, sick leave, capabilities and job performance of employees.
- Information on the status of customer accounts, including history of account ageing, payment record, and personal credit data, is kept in the files of organizations involved in sales.
- Patient information on health history, allergies, disabilities and prescribed medications is located in the files of physicians.
- Insurance companies store information on the number and cost of vehicles, types, accident record and claims of clients.
- Banks keep records of loans, savings, deposits and withdrawals of account holders.

This list could go on and on. Just about every salient fact about every individual is in a computer file somewhere.

Although record-keeping has always been a part of organized society, the amount of data collected in the past was constrained. Because of access and storage problems and the inability to integrate and correlate data with speed, it was impractical to develop large databases prior to electronic processing. Nowadays, the ability of computers to process, store and retrieve vast quantities of data at high speeds has led to the collection of pools of data that constitute comprehensive personal dossiers. The data need not be centralized in a single, all-inclusive data bank. With the technology of linked databases and telecommunications networks, bank records can be integrated with medical records, employment records can be linked with government records, and so on.

Few people want the intimate details of their private lives in the public domain. They believe that they have a right to privacy, including the right to control the collection, dissemination and use of information of a personal nature. They recognize that their human rights and freedoms may be infringed when governments and other organizations have unrestricted files of personal data, for such files can be used for purposes of social control through surveillance. For example, a file listing an individual's race might be used to limit opportunity; a file listing political affiliation might be used to encourage conformity.

Concern for the 'dignity and worth of the human person' underlies the historical and philosophical origins of claims to personal privacy. Some countries, like Germany, have constitutional underpinnings for the right to privacy. Most others rely on their legislators to study privacy concerns, develop codes of fair information practices and pass laws to protect citizens from the misuse of personal data. In the United Kingdom, for example, a Data Protection Act 1984 regulates automatic processing of personal data. (See Figure 8.1 for the data protection principles that the British Act upholds.) A register of data users who hold personal data is mandated by the Act and a registrar is given powers to enforce compliance with the Act's provisions. A Data Protection Tribunal composed of barristers, advocates or solicitors to represent the interests of data users and data subjects is mandated to hear appeals against rulings of the registrar. Further appeals on points of law may be made to the courts.

Public pressure on the House of Commons for data privacy legislation was not the main impetus for passage of the UK Data Protection Act: the thrust for implementation was the need to conform to European standards on databases and data flows. Ministers feared that failure to pass privacy legislation would be a stumbling block to trade. Within Europe, *Guidelines on the Protection and Privacy of Transborder Flows of Personal Data*, published by the OECD in 1980, contributed to awareness of privacy issues. All twenty-four OECD members, including the UK, subsequently adopted these guidelines. And, in 1985, the Council of Europe's *Convention for the Protection of Individuals with Regard to Automatic Processing of Personal Data* went into effect.

Not all countries with data privacy laws follow the same legislative model. For example, the Americans have no federal watchdog agency to protect privacy like the UK's Data Protection Tribunal, and federal privacy law regulates only

DATA PROTECTION ACT 1984
THE PRINCIPLES
Personal data held by data users

1 The information to be contained in personal data shall be obtained, and personal data shall be processed, fairly and lawfully.
2 Personal data shall be held only for one or more specified and lawful pruposes.
3 Personal data held for any purpose or purposes shall not be used or disclosed in any manner incompatible with that purpose or those purposes.
4 Personal data held for any purpose or purposes shall be adequate, relevant and not excessive in relation to that purpose or those purposes.
5 Personal data shall be accurate and, where necessary, kept up to date.
6 Personal data held for any purpose or purposes shall not be kept for longer than is necessary for that purpose or those purposes.
7 An individual shall be entitled —
 (a) at reasonable intervals and without undue delay or expense —
   (i) to be informed by any data user whether he or she holds personal data of which that individual is the subject; and
   (ii) to access to any such data held by a data user; and
 (b) where appropriate, to have such data corrected or erased.

Personal data held by data users or in respect of which services are provided by persons carrying on computer bureaux

8 Appropriate security measures shall be taken against unauthorized access to, or alteration, disclosure or destruction of, personal data and against accidental loss or destruction of personal data.

Figure 8.1 *Principles of the UK Data Protection Act 1984*

government handling of personal data, not corporate data banks. Some countries allow their citizens to check the accuracy and relevance of personal data in police files, which British law does not. See Table 8.1 for a summary of privacy protection provisions in Germany, Sweden, France, Canada and the United States.

Unfortunately, the existence of a legal framework for privacy legislation does not ensure that the public is being adequately protected from privacy infringement. As stated by David Flaherty, author of *Protecting Privacy in Surveillance Societies*:

> It cannot be emphasized too strongly that the incentives for the government and the bureaucracy are in the direction of invading, or at least ignoring or neglecting, privacy interests rather than protecting them. Most measures that are perceived as 'necessary' to cope with a societal problem involve surveillance through data collection. Especially in difficult economic times, the predominant goals are to improve efficiency, to reduce fraud, to cut expenditures on programs and staff, and to step up monitoring of the target population. (Flaherty, 1989, p. 382)

A universal trait of data protection has been lax enforcement of legal provisions for audits and inspections. Complaints of misuse of or inaccurate data are common in all countries with privacy legislation. In England, Community Charge officers are being investigated for failure to comply with the Data Protection Act on

Table 8.1 Models for protecting privacy

	Germany	Sweden	Canada	France	USA
Act	Federal Data Protection Act 1977	Data Act 1973, twice amended	Privacy Act 1982. Coupled with Access to Information law in one bill. Strengthens privacy provisions of Canadian Human Rights Act 1977	Law of Informatics and Freedoms 1978	Privacy Act 1974
Purpose	To 'ensure against the misuse of personal data during storage, communication, modification and erasure (data processing) and thereby to prevent harm to any personal interests of the person concerned that warrant protection'	To prevent undue encroachment on individual privacy. Requires registration and licence of databases with personal information	To regulate collection and use of personal information by the federal government. Includes principles of fair information practices	To protect data, with expanded coverage to a broad range of societal issues, with separate subcommissions on freedom to work, research and statistics, local government and technology and security	To place limits on government surveillance. Defines code of fair information practices for the collection and handling of personal data by agencies of the federal government
Organizational model	Bundestag selects a Data Protection Commissioner with advisory responsibilities to: 1 Assist in developing new data protection laws 2 Modify existing laws 3 Establish guidelines for data protection 4 Advise on policy implications for surveillance of different legislative proposals	Creates Data Inspection Board to control collection and dissemination of personal data, regulate data usages and enforce system of responsible keepers for computerized data banks. Law establishes detailed set of duties for data keepers	Creates Office of the Privacy Commissioner. Commissioner is Officer of Parliament. Acts as ombudsman	Creates the National Commission on Informatics and Freedoms to implement law. Commission authorizes information systems and has 13 regulatory duties, including issuing deliberations, setting standards or issuing rules on security, making recommendations such as on right of access, carrying out inspections, and reporting offences	Requires that reports on new or altered information systems be submitted to Congress and the Office of Management and Budget, and the publication of these reports in summary form in the Federal Registrar. Responsibility for implementing fair information practices widely diffused

Table 8.1 (*continued*)

	Germany	Sweden	Canada	France	USA
Powers of intervention	No authority for binding instructions if law is infringed, but can submit formal complaint to the competent body	Series of penalties and damages for breach of statute. But both government and legislature retain power to create data banks exempt from the Board's supervision	Commissioner has powers of investigation and auditing, but role is advisory. Overseeing is secondary. Law makes each government institution responsible for administration of Privacy Act within the organization	Statutory burden on those being regulated to cooperate with Commission. Penal sanctions can be imposed for those who hinder the Commission's activities or refuse to supply information	Includes criminal sanctions for wilful disclosures of personal data or wilfully maintaining a record system without meeting public notice requirements. Enforcement left to officers in government agencies and individuals who can bring lawsuit to redress a grievance
Special features	Eleven states have counterparts of federal Data Protection Commissioner's office. States are mainly responsible for data privacy in education, health and police whereas the federal focus is security, defence, insurance and social security	Mandatory licensing system for information systems. In amended law licensing requirements were modified to reduce bureaucratic burden and cost of data protection	Direct relationship between Commission and legislature through a standing committee of Parliament. Individual or privacy commission may appeal to the Federal Court-Trial Division following complaint to commissioner. Potential to reach Supreme Court of Canada. First time a country has linked laws on freedom of information and data protection in coherent manner	Part-time commissioners, many of whom are senior members of state bodies such as the administrative courts. Most are politicians with experience in government work but lacking technical competence	No privacy protection commission at the federal level. Dependence on litigation for enforcement

Model effectiveness	Federal Commissioner's advisory function well developed, but there is a risk that advice will be ignored. lack of regulatory power for specific sensitive surveillance practices. Law needs strengthening	Sweden already is more of a surveillance society than western counterparts, which reduces scope of privacy in individual relations with the state	Data protection system suited to a federal state. Main problem: lack of implementation	Ineffective commission, bogged down in paperwork, weak leadership, inexperienced staff. Commission neglects audits, investigation of complaints and meaningful public relations. Commission highly politicized, unwilling to confront government on surveillance practices	Overseeing Privacy Act left to Office of Management and Budget which assigns low priority to this duty. Congressional committee overseeing has been limited and episodic. Loopholes in law, like 'routine use' provision that allows fair use provisions to be bypassed. Yet progress is being made. Latest example: passage of the Computer Matching and Privacy Protection Act 1988

Source: David Flaherty, *Protecting Privacy in Surveillance societies.* Chapel Hill, NC: University of North Carolina Press, 1989.

Community Charge registration forms. More than 125 local councils are asking unwarranted personal questions on the forms, such as the relationships between people living at the same address, dates of birth and educational details. And government leaflets have failed to tell Scottish Community Charge payers how personal data will be collected and compiled from confidential sources to form the Community Charge register. It is not enough simply to pass privacy protection laws: those charged with implementation must make the laws work.

Many westerners see the protection of privacy as a major societal issue of the 1990s. The problem is to allow organizations to collect and process personal data when they have a legitimate need to do so while at the same time protecting privacy.

Privacy in business

Every business with computerized files stores data on its employees and clients, often sensitive data of a personal nature, such as financial data, health status and work evaluations. Business managers have an obligation to ensure that such data are accurate, updated, secret and used for restricted purposes. Indeed, all of the data protection principles listed in Figure 8.1 should be adopted by business as good practice, even when not mandated by law.

Data accuracy

Unfortunately, many businesses have lax data protection policies. Data accuracy, for example, may not be a priority unless accuracy is crucial to operations. To illustrate, a birth certificate is not required when applying for a bank loan or credit card since approval does not depend on the applicant's exact age. Yet a birth date mistake in bank records is important if that mistake is passed on to another organization where an accurate birth date is vital.

Most database administrators claim that they have no obligation to determine the accuracy of information that they receive from others. This is the position of TRW Information Service, a company that sells thirty-five million credit reports each year to twenty-four thousand subscribers in the United States. Each month TRW receives computer tapes from thousands of companies containing the status of their customer accounts. TRW computers then lift, organize and store information from the tapes so that credit history can be supplied to TRW clients making credit checks. This service could not be provided if TRW were forced to check the accuracy of data elements on each tape. (It should be noted, however, that the company tries to ensure the accuracy of its files.)

Inaccuracy of files is not a trivial problem. Each year some 350,000 people register formal complaints about mistakes in TRW reports and about 100,000 of these result in change to information stored in TRW computers. How many incorrect entries are never noticed, never corrected? A business with personal data on file that are inaccurate may be responsible for:

1 Customer inconvenience and frustration. For example, a billing error may take numerous telephone calls and letters to correct.
2 The denial of goods and services to which individuals are entitled. For example, a car loan may be denied on the basis of inaccurate credit information.
3 The ruin of reputations and disruption of lives. For example, a mistake in an evaluation rating may cost a worker a deserved promotion.

One way to reduce errors in data banks is to allow individuals the right to inspect personal records and to challenge mistakes that they find. However, there is no way for the challenger to know whether mistakes were circulated prior to correction and, if so, what other databases contain the error. This explains why civil libertarians are concerned with the growth of computerized data banks and the unmonitored exchange of data.

Unfair use of personal data

Most people want control over the collection and use of personal data. They view secret files as a threat to individual freedom, and want limits placed on data collection to prevent organizations from gathering data that has no relevance to their legitimate needs. They favour *fair use* policies: for example, corporate policy stating that only personal data relevant to an organization's mission can be collected; that an individual's consent is required before stored personal data is passed from one data bank to another.

Personal information has a market value. For example, merchants can determine from such information where to direct their advertising. The can draw up lists of persons who like the outdoors, to whom camping equipment might appeal, or lists of Cadillac owners, who might be attracted to diamond jewellery. By gaining access to a data bank of personal information, a mailing list of prospective customers could be prepared. Would this activity constitute an invasion of privacy?

A fair-use restriction gives individuals the right to participate in this decision. **Fair use** means that consent must be obtained before personal data in a data bank are shared with others. After all, data pools are attractive targets for all types of groups. Consider how a thief might value information regarding who goes camping weekends or who likes diamond jewellery.

Fair use has gatekeeping ramifications as well. **Gatekeeping** is restricted access to services, privileges, benefits or opportunities. An example of gatekeeping is the point-scoring method used by many credit agencies to determine whether an individual is a good credit risk based on age, salary, duration of employment and so forth. In this case, gatekeeping serves a legitimate business interest; but gatekeeping can also be used to discriminate in ways that to most people would seem unfair. For example, suppose that doctors refused to treat all patients (and their families) whose names appeared in the database of malpractice claimants. Also, suppose that real estate agents used their church membership databases to grant or deny rental requests.

Computer processing facilitates gatekeeping just as it does the exchange of personal data. As stated by the US Privacy Protection Study Commission (1977):

> The ability to search through hundreds of thousands, or even millions, of records to identify individuals with particular characteristics of interest is at once the most important gain and the most important source of potential harm stemming from the automation of large-scale personal data record-keeping systems.

Guidelines for businesses

Most business managers today are becoming sensitive to the public's concern over privacy. The following guidelines are ways to ensure that individual rights are respected when personal data are collected, maintained and used in the course of daily operations:

1 *Store only essential data*. Purge irrelevant and outdated information. This will not only reduce the danger of privacy invasion but will also diminish the information glut which plagues many firms, thereby lowering storage costs.
2 *Improve the security of data*. Periodically review and update physical safeguards and carefully screen personnel. Many computer systems in use today were designed before widespread concern over privacy issues and hence lack adequate data protection.
3 *Identify which data elements are sensitive*. Add data descriptions to these elements so they can be easily extracted from the data stream for control inspections and correction. Require management approval when use of these elements is extended to new applications.
4 *Adopt as policy that personal data should be complete, accurate and timely*. This requirement is good business, irrespective of privacy ramifications. One reason why it is difficult to isolate and assess the cost of privacy measures is that all sound information processing and control practices also serve the interests of privacy.
5 *Appoint an officer* to plan security and privacy measures, coordinate privacy policies with legal requirements and oversee privacy policy implementation.
6 *Establish procedures to implement notification and challenge rights*. Authorization forms for consent of use or release of information may be required.

Appeal routines should be established. In many cases, procedures can be automated.

7 *Anticipate privacy legislation.* Design new information systems to report on sensitive data and to log and monitor use of the data: such controls will likely become law in the future. (Some privacy laws are already on the statute books, although they are not as comprehensive as many citizens would like.) Privacy features can be added to a system under development at low marginal cost, whereas adding them after a system is operational involves expensive redesign.

Cost of privacy

Two types of expenditures are involved when implementing corporate privacy policies: one-time development costs and recurring operational disbursements.

Development costs include analysis and design of procedures for privacy protection and the acquisition of equipment and software dedicated to that purpose. The main component of operations is salaries, primarily for clerks handling notification, access, challenge, correction and erasures. The cost of a manager's time to monitor procedures and standards and to resolve disputes should be added to this category, as should fees paid for legal advice. Other operational costs are for computer time, data storage, data transmission, rental or maintenance of security equipment and supplies. Operational costs peak after passage of privacy legislation, when many people exercise new rights of access and challenge and then stabilize at a lower level.

One problem in determining costs is that so many implementation strategies exist for privacy policies. Some companies require written consent from each data subject for each application. Others use a single release for all applications. If companies discontinue (or do not initiate) applications because of privacy considerations, should operational costs include estimates for degraded service?

Cost allocation is a problem when practices that affect privacy also serve other business interests. For example, security measures that protect personal data reduce the danger of lost records, guard trade secrets and circumvent sabotage of facilities. How can the cost of privacy policies be isolated from security costs?

Robert Goldstein has developed a model to simulate cost components and total costs, given different assumptions of privacy protection requirements and different management strategies. Goldstein's model is based on the premise that privacy costs do not come 'out of the blue' but rather arise in response to various events. Each time one of these events occurs, certain actions are taken to comply with privacy regulations. These actions consume resources and, hence, generate costs. The model includes twenty-two events and nineteen requirements (laws are represented as sets of requirements) and can calculate a potential of 7,500 different actions from the eighteen most useful combinations of strategy variables. In spite of the complexity of this model, however, the costs produced will not be accurate figures for any given organization because of the many unproven assumptions on which the model is based. The model's usefulness is for comparing relative costs of various strategies and for identifying variable relationships and assumptions.

Security

To ensure privacy of information, computer systems must be secure. That is, data must be protected against unauthorized modification, capture, destruction or disclosure. Personal data are not the only vulnerable data. Confidential data on market strategies and product development must be kept from the eyes of competitors. The large sums of money transferred daily by electronic fund transfer must be protected against theft. The very volume of business information processed by computers today means that the rewards for industrial espionage and fraud are of a much higher magnitude than in the past and are still increasing.

Records must also be protected from accidents and natural disasters. For example, a breakdown in the air-conditioning system may cause a computer to overheat, resulting in loss of computing capabilities. Fire, floods, hurricanes, even a heavy snowfall causing a roof to collapse, can cause destruction of data and valuable equipment.

The **security** measures described in the following sections are designed to guard information systems from all of the above threats. The measures can be envisioned as providing layers of protection, as shown in Figure 8.2. Some controls guard against infiltration for purposes of data manipulation, alteration of computer programs, pillage or unauthorized use of the computer itself. Other measures guard the physical plant, monitor operations and telecommunications and regulate personnel. Since control of inadvertent errors was the subject of Chapter 7, this chapter will focus on protection against calamities and criminal acts.

Plant security

Many protective measures can be incorporated in the construction or renovation of buildings to protect a computer from unlawful intrusion, sabotage or destructive acts of nature such as fire, floods or earthquakes: for example, locks and window grills, alarms and panic buttons, smoke detectors, earthquake-proof foundations and automatic fire extinguishers. (The fire extinguishers should be gas extinguishers, not water. Water can be almost as destructive as fire to electronic equipment, particularly to magnetic storage.)

Terminal use controls

Controlling the access to terminals is a common method of guarding a system from illicit use. When all terminals are located in the computer centre, closing the centre to unauthorized personnel will provide one method of access control.

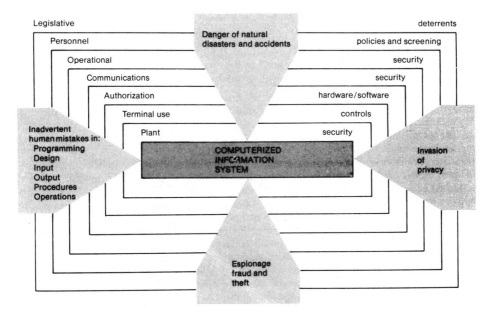

Figure 8.2 *Layers of control*

Badge systems, physical barriers (locked doors, window bars, electric fences), a buffer zone, guard dogs and security check stations are procedures common to restricted areas of manufacturing plants and government installations where work with secret or classified materials takes place. A vault for storage of files and programs and a librarian responsible for their checkout provide additional control.

With online systems using telecommunications, security is a greater problem, since stringent **access controls** to terminals may not exist at remote sites. The computer itself must, therefore, ascertain the identity of persons who wish to log on and must determine whether they are entitled to use the system. Identification can be based on:

- What the user has, such as an ID card or key.
- Who the user is, as determined by some biometric measure or physical characteristic.
- What the user knows, such as a password.

Keys and cards

Locks on terminals that require a **key** before they can be operated are one way to restrict access to a computer. Another way is to require users to carry a **card** identifier that is inserted in a card reader when they want to use the computer.

A microprocessor in the reader makes an accept or reject decision based on the card.

Many types of card system are on the market. Some use plastic cards, similar to credit cards, with a strip of magnetically encoded data on the front or back. Some have a core of magnetized spots of encoded data. Proximity cards contain electronic circuitry sandwiched in the card; the reader for this card must include a transmitter and receiver. Optical cards encode data as a pattern of light spots that can be 'read' or illuminated by specific light sources, such as infrared. In addition, there are smart ID cards that have an integrated circuit chip embedded in the plastic. The chip has both coded memory, where personal identification codes can be stored, and microprocessor intelligence.

The disadvantage of both keys and cards is that they can be lost, stolen or counterfeited. In other words, their possession does not absolutely identify the holder as an authorized system user. For this reason, the use of passwords is often an added security feature of key and card systems.

Biometric systems

Some terminal control systems base identification on the physical attributes of system users. For example, an electronic scan may be made of the hand of the person requesting terminal access. This scan is then measured and compared by computer to scans previously made of authorized system users and stored in the computer's memory. Only a positive match will permit system access.

Fingerprints or palm prints can likewise be used to identify bona fide system users. Such security systems use electro-optical recognition and file matching of fingerprint or palm print minutiae. Signature verification of the person wishing to log onto the computer is yet another security option. Such systems are based on the dynamics of pen motion related to time when the signer writes with a wired pen or on a sensitized pad. A biometric system can also be based on voiceprints. In this case, a voice profile of each authorized user is recorded as an analog signal, then converted into digital from which a set of measurements are derived that identify the voice pattern of each speaker. Again, identification depends on matching: the voice pattern of the person wishing computer access is compared with voice profiles in computer memory.

Biometric control systems, of special interest to defence industries and the police, have been under development for many years. Although technological breakthroughs that enable discrimination of complex patterns have been made recently, pattern recognition systems are still not problem free. Many have difficulty recognizing patterns under less than optimal conditions. For example, a blister, inflammation, cut, even sweat on hands, can interfere with a fingerprint match. Health or mood that changes one's voice can prevent a voiceprint match. A combination of devices, such as voice plus hand analyzers, might ensure positive identification; but such equipment is too expensive at the present time to be cost effective for most operations in business.

Passwords

The use of **passwords** is one of the more popular methods of restricting terminal access. One example of a password system is the required use of a personal identification number to gain access to an automated teller machine at a bank.

The problem with passwords is that they are subject to careless handling by users. Some users write the code on a sheet of paper that they carry in their wallet, or they tape the paper to the terminal itself. When given a choice, users frequently select a password that they can easily remember, such as their birth date, house number or names of pets, wives or children. Top of the list in Britain seems to be 'Fred', 'God', 'Pass' and 'Genius'.

Someone determined to access the computer will make guesses, trying such obvious passwords first. Even passwords as complex as algebraic transformations of a random number generated by the computer have been broken with the assistance of readily available microcomputers. Of course, the longer a password is in use, the greater the likelihood of its being compromised.

One-time passwords are a viable alternative. But systems of this nature are difficult to administer. First of all, each authorized user must be given a list of randomly selected passwords. Then there must be agreement on the method of selecting the next valid password from the list, a method that is synchronized between computer and user. Finally, storage of the list must be secure, a challenge when portable terminals are used by personnel in remote sites where security may be lax.

Recently, a number of password systems have been put on the market that generate a new password unique to each user each time access is attempted. This is done with a central intelligent controller at the host site and a random **password generator** for each user. Typically, the system works as follows. To gain mainframe access, the user enters his or her name (or ID code) on a terminal keyboard. The computer responds with a 'challenge number'. This is input to the user's password generator. By applying a cryptographic algorithm and a secret key (a set of data unique to each password generator) to this challenge 'seed', a one-time password is generated. The user then enters this password into the computer. The central controller simultaneously calculates the correct password and will grant access if a match occurs.

Such password management systems are difficult to compromise, because passwords are constantly changed. Only a short period of time is allowed for entry of the correct password. Furthermore, the control system is protocol dependent. This compounds the problems of a person trying to breach the system in a network having a variety of protocols. The advantage to the user is that the password generator is portable, usually a handheld device, and easy to use.

In recent years, much publicity has been given to **hackers**, usually youths, who often derive malicious pleasure in circumventing computer access controls. Figure 8.3 shows damage that hackers have caused by secretly inserting spurious software in information systems.

Only a few lines of secretly inserted code by a hacker can cause problems to computer uses. When buried in complex programs, the secret instructions are virtually invisible even to expert programmers.

1 A software 'worm' inserted by a hacker can alter a system's fundamental operations by deleting specific portions of a computer's memory.
2 Another software demon, called a 'virus', destroys stored files. In one case on record, Dick Streeter's screen went blank as he was transferring a free program from a computer bulletin board into his machine. Then the following message appeared: 'Art, arf. Got You.' Nearly 900 accounting, word processing and game files that were stored in Streeter's machine were erased.
3 A 'trapdoor', collects users' passwords as they log on, giving the hacker an updated list of access codes. This technique was used to gain unauthorized access to hospital records at Manhattan's Memorial Sloan–Kettering Cancer Center.

4 Secret software may be inserted in computer files to interrupt operations, erase files, or cause equipment to fail, called a 'logic bomb'. At the Los Angeles Department of Water and Power, a logic bomb froze the utility's internal files at a preassigned time, bringing work to a standstill.

The results of a recent poll conducted in the UK by Gallup for *Which Computer?* show that three-quarters of the computer security managers surveyed have no policy for the protection of their data. Indeed, a majority do not think hacking is a major problem in the UK, although they acknowledge that their companies are open to attack. Nevertheless, a majority back anti-hacking and virus-writing legislation, mainly in the hope that legislation will deter perpetrators. Only a minority cite company losses as a reason for making hacking an offence.

No one knows how much hackers cost UK business. An amount frequently quoted is £400 million a year, though how this figure has been derived is never made clear.

Figure 8.3 *Hackers 'pranks'*

Authorization controls

In addition to the identification systems outlined in the preceding sections, control systems can be installed to verify whether a user is authorized to access files and databases, and to ascertain what type of access is permitted (read, write or update).

Data directory
A computer can be programmed to reference a stored **data directory security matrix** to determine the security code needed to access specific data elements in files before processing a user's job. When the user lacks the proper security clearance, access will be denied. In a similar manner, the computer might be programmed to reference a table that specifies the type of access permitted or the time of day when access is permitted.

The data elements accessible from each terminal can likewise be regulated. For example, according to a programmed rule, the terminal in the database administrator's office might be the only terminal permitted access to all files and programs and the only terminal with access to the security matrix itself. A sample printout from an access directory, sorted by user identification number, is shown in Table 8.2.

Table 8.2 *Access directory*

User identification: *076–835–5623*				
Access limitation: *13 hours (of CPU time for current fiscal year)*				
Account Number: *AS5842*				
Data elements	Type of access	Security level	Terminal number	Time lock
Customer number	Read	10	04	08.00–17.00
Invoice number	Read	10	04	08.00–17.00
Cash receipt	Read/write	12	06	08.00–12.00

Assigning access levels to individuals within an organization can be a difficult task. Information is power, and the right to access it is a status symbol. Employees may vie for clearance even when they do not require such clearance for their jobs. Managers should recognize that security measures designed to protect confidential data and valuable computing resources may antagonize loyal employees. It is important that the need for security be understood by workers and that security controls be administered with tact.

Security kernel

Unfortunately, the use of a security matrix does not provide foolproof security. In a multiuser system, data in a file can be raided by installing a 'Trojan horse' program. Figure 8.4 shows how this is done. Although the data directory does not authorize Brown to access File A, confidential data from that file is copied into another file that Brown is entitled to access, on the direction of a secret program, thereby circumventing system security.

The concept of a **security kernel** addresses the Trojan horse issue. A kernel is a hardware/software mechanism that implements a **reference monitor**, a systems component that checks each reference by a subject (user or program) to each object (file, device or program) and determines whether the access is valid according to the system's security policy. Figure 8.5 shows how Brown is foiled by a reference monitor in his attempt to raid File A.

A security kernel represents new technology still in the developmental stage. Although a number of projects have attempted to demonstrate the practicality of this security approach, results thus far have been mixed.

Virtual machine

An entirely different approach to security in a multiuser environment is a **virtual machine**. With this systems structure, each user loads and runs his or her own copy of an operating system. In effect, this isolates one user from another although they use the same physical machine, because each virtual machine can be operated

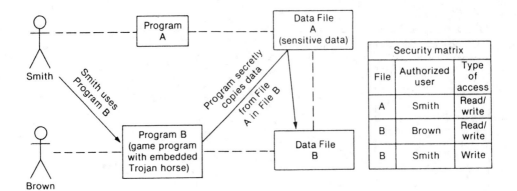

Suppose that Smith has read/write access to sensitive data in File A. Brown, who wishes access to that file but lacks the necessary clearance, first gains legitimate access to the computer and creates File B, giving himself read/write access and also setting the access control list to allow programs executed on Smith's behalf to write into it. (Smith is not told of this situation.)

Now Brown writes a program that Smith is likely to use, such as a game program. This program has secret embedded instructions (the Trojan horse) that tell the computer to copy data from File A and to write the data in File B when Smith plays the game. (The Trojan horse program is designed so that it can detect when Smith is the user.) The security matrix does not prevent this raid, since Smith has authorized access to File A.

Figure 8.4 *Raiding files: a Trojan horse program*

at a separate security level. With a virtual memory structure, several user programs can reside in computer memory simultaneously without interference.

Communications security

Computer processing is today closely linked with telecommunications, which allows the transference of computer data between remote points. Protecting the confidentiality of this data at the initiating terminal, during transmission itself or when transmission is received, has required the development of sophisticated security techniques. For example, a **handshake**, a predetermined signal that the computer must recognize before initiating transmission, is one way to control communications. This prevents individuals from masquerading, pretending to be legitimate users of the system. Most companies use **callback boxes** that phone would-be users at preauthorized numbers to verify the access request before allowing the user to log on. A hacker who has learned the handshake code would be denied access with such a system. Protocols, conventions, procedures for user identification (described earlier in this chapter) and dialogue termination also help maintain the confidentiality of data.

During transmission, messages are vulnerable to wiretapping, the electromagnetic pickup of messages on communication lines. This may be eavesdropping, passive listening or active wiretapping involving alteration of data, such as piggy-

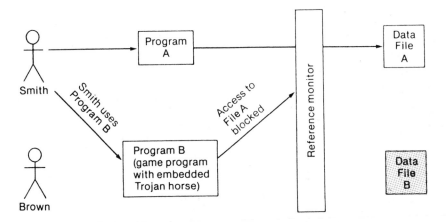

Suppose that there are two levels of security. One allows access to sensitive data (white) and one access to non-sensitive data only (grey). Suppose that the security monitor enforces the rule that states that a subject (a user or a program) cannot read a file at a higher security level nor can it write to a file at a lower security level.

Since Smith, Program A, and File A have the sensitive security rating, Smith can access File A. Brown, however, cannot. When Smith unkowingly triggers Brown's Trojan horse program, the program acquires his security rating. Nevertheless, the reference monitor blocks the computer from carrying out the raid instructions, because File B has a lower security rating than File A.

Figure 8.5 *How a reference monitor blocks a Trojan horse raid*

backing (the selective interception, modification or substitution of messages). Another type of infiltration is reading between the lines. An illicit user taps the computer when a bona fide user is connected to the system and is paying for computer time but is 'thinking', so the computer is idle. This and other uses of unauthorized time can be quite costly to a business firm.

One method of preventing message interception is to encode, or encrypt, data in order to render it incomprehensible or useless if intercepted. **Encryption**, from the Greek root 'crypt' meaning to hide, can be done by either transposition or substitution.

In transposition, characters are exchanged by a set of rules. For example, the third and fourth characters might be switched so that 5289 becomes 5298. In substitution, characters are replaced. The number 1 may become a 3, so that 514 reads 534. Or the substitution may be more complex. A specified number might be added to a digit, such as a 2 added to the third digit, making 514 read 516. Decryption restores the data to its original value. Although the principles of encryption are relatively simple, most schemas are highly complex. Understanding them may require mathematical knowledge and technical expertise.

An illustration of encryption appears in Figure 8.6. A key is used to code the message, a key that both sender and receiver possess. It could be a random-

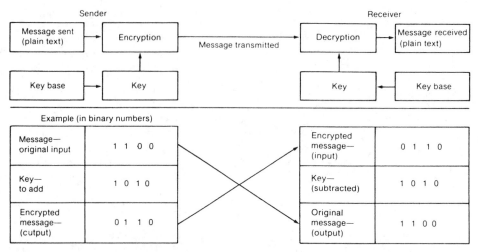

Figure 8.6 *Encrypting and decrypting data in teleprocessing*

number key or a key based on a formula or algorithm. As in all codes, the key must be difficult to break. Frequent changing of the key adds to the security of data, which explains why many systems have a key base with a large number of alternate keys.

In the past, the transportation of the encryption key to authorized users has been an Achilles' heel to systems security. An additional problem is that there sometimes is insufficient time to pass the key to a legitimate receiver. One solution is a multiple-access cipher in a public key cryptosystem. This system has two keys, an E public encryption key used by the sender, and a D secret decryption key used by the receiver. Each sender/receiver has a set of D and E keys. To code data to send to Firm X, for example, a business looks up Firm X's E key, published in a public directory, and then transmits a message in code over a public or insecure transmission line. Firm X alone has the secret D key for decryption. This system can be breached but not easily, since a tremendous number of computations would be needed to derive the secret of D. The code's security lies as much in the time required to crack the algorithm as in the computational complexity of the cipher, because the value of much data resides in timeliness. Often, there is no longer need for secrecy once a deal is made, the stock market closed, or a patent application is filed.

Cryptography, in effect, serves three purposes: identification (helps identify bona fide senders and receivers); control (prevents alteration of a message); and privacy (impedes eavesdropping). With the increased reliance of businesses on teleprocessing, much research has been done on cryptographic systems. But experts disagree about how secure even the most complex codes are. Some claim that persons bent on accessing encrypted data will be able to break all codes, using the power, speed and advanced technology of modern computers.

Operational security

Control measures to protect information systems during processing were discussed at length in Chapter 7. What needs to be emphasized here are general administrative strategies to protect the system as a whole. For example, empirical evidence shows that systems are particularly vulnerable to intrusion during conversion, after the new system has passed acceptance tests and is being readied for operations. Employees inexperienced with the new system are not alert to possible security infringements, while technicians, exhausted by the rigours of conversion, are often less attentive than usual. As a result, changes in procedures, data and programs may be introduced without notice. Experience has shown that it is advisable to intensify security during conversion.

During daily operations, a careful check of logs, utilization reports and irregular behaviour should be the norm. Most companies schedule periodic audits as well. (For more audits, see Chapter 9.) Some firms hire private detectives to oversee security, although this can have an adverse effect on employee morale. There are even reported cases of companies hiring individuals on parole for programming fraud on the premise that someone who knows how to break the system also knows how to prevent security violations.

But even the best security cannot prevent natural disasters, and determined malefactors have circumvented controls too often for any guarantee of a given system's immunity to attack. Insurance will compensate for monetary losses in some cases, but an essential part of operational security is planning for **recovery** of what is lost (data, programs or hardware) and for placing the system speedily back in operation. This is a manager's responsibility. Many vendors supply customers with manuals, including checklists, to assist in reconstruction planning.

In order to plan what procedures should be implemented following a disaster or system collapse, management must:

1 Determine the minimum resource configuration needed to resume operations.
2 Identify which computer records are vital.
3 Establish job priorities. (Given reduced capacity, which jobs should be run? What turnaround times are crucial?)
4 Assign recovery responsibility. (Who has the authority to mobilize organizational resources and rule on conflicts of interest during recovery?)

An alternative processing site should also be planned in case the computer facility is extensively damaged. Since a backup computer in the same building might also be destroyed in the same disaster, a distant secondary facility is advisable, although this adds communication difficulties to problems of recovery. Firms with distributed processing generally can function when one network link is broken. Firms with centralized computing will require this secondary facility.

One solution is to join a mutual backup consortium or to make a mutual assistance arrangement with another firm. Each firm agrees to carry an extra workload (a third shift, perhaps) should a partner be in need. In such cases, problems of systems compatibility need to be resolved and backup files for the alternative site must be maintained.

Some auditors recommend, as part of regular auditing procedures, surprise tests to check the effectiveness of disaster planning. Certainly, planning for systems breakdown should take place in all firms, and employees should be informed what actions to take in emergencies. A simple memo may suffice or detailed handbooks may be necessary, depending on the nature or complexity of the business.

Personnel safeguards

One might expect that external threats to security would be a firm's major concern, but many studies show that users and computer personnel within an organization are more likely to breach security than outsiders. Security may be breached by terminal operators, programmers, computer operators, even vice presidents. Motives for criminal acts can be attributed to ego (the desire to demonstrate individual superiority over the system), revenge, financial gain, irrational behaviour and zealous adherence to a cause. When screening applicants, assigning duties and supervising operations, managers should be cognizant of their vulnerability to internal security violations.

One well-known organizational principle that serves security is **separation of responsibility**: no employee should perform all the steps in a single transaction. For example, record-keeping should be separated from the physical custodianship of records.

Computer systems can be divided into five basic functions:

- Programming and systems development.
- Handling input media.
- Operation of data processing equipment.
- Documentation and file library.
- Distribution of output.

It is advisable that the work assignment of no employee cross these functional lines. Separation of responsibility serves as a deterrent to crime, because a given job must pass through many hands, which facilitates many independent checks for accuracy and possible fraud. Although separation may not be feasible in small organizations because the limited number of employees means a single individual may have to perform many jobs, the principle should be followed whenever possible.

Security can also be promoted by rotating the duties and responsibilities of employees, by unannounced audits, by establishing a climate of honesty, and by close observation of disgruntled employees. Giving publicity to security measures may serve as a deterrent to attempted systems intrusions. Employees should be trained in security risks and procedures. In addition, the appropriateness, adequacy and readiness of emergency planning should be periodically tested by drills. Many security officers state that the installation of security devices, such as alarms and detectors, is not the hard part of their jobs. What is difficult is motivating employees to be alert and sensitive to security issues.

Security in a microcomputer environment

Even though microcomputer systems process less volume of information than mainframes, they too must be protected from accidental or intentional data loss. Most of the measures described in this chapter for guarding the privacy of data and ensuring systems security are as appropriate in a microcomputer environment as in a computer centre housing minis and mainframes.

However, a number of factors do contribute to unique problems in administering a microcomputer security programme. For example, many micro users have limited computing experience and, unlike IT professionals, are not aware of or alert to possible security infractions. Contingency planning is frequently ignored, regular backup procedures are lacking, provisions for audit trails are uncommon, and few local networks monitor network activity. Unfortunately, the current generation of micro hardware and software does not support effective security for the most part. The low cost of micro systems, in effect, limits the amount of system resources devoted to security. What's more, microcomputer hardware seems to present a temptation to thieves, while software theft for personal use on other machines is a common problem.

One solution to the security of micros is the use of Bernoulli drives. These have removable cartridges that can store an entire database and the source code that generates that data. After use, the disks can be secured under lock and key. Passwords and encryption are two other protective measures frequently used with microcomputer systems. Ironically, one of the principal reasons for the spread of micros — to let more people benefit from computer capabilities — is the very advantage that creates so many security problems.

Who is responsible?

Figure 8.7 summarizes management's role in planning, implementing, monitoring and evaluating security measures. A firm's survival is at stake when losses must be absorbed due to sabotage or theft. Its reputation for quality service may be imperilled and years of accumulated goodwill endangered when security proves inadequate. Although IT personnel should participate in technical control decisions, corporate management has the responsibility to identify vital data, establish security points, outline security procedures, assign enforcement personnel, allocate needed resources and take corrective action when security is violated. Management is also responsible for training programmes to make employees sensitive to privacy and security issues. Clearly, all security measures adopted should be flexible, effective and enforceable.

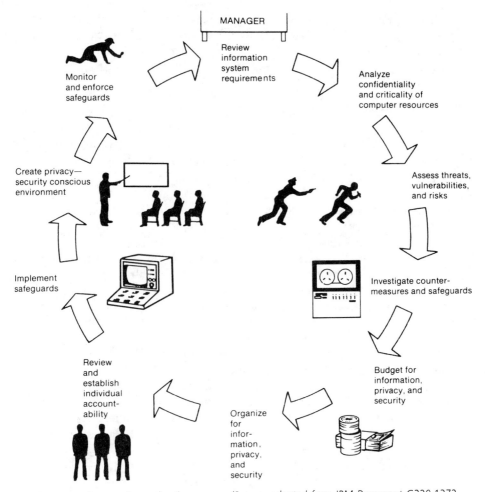

Figure 8.7 *Security overview and action process (Source: adapted from IBM Document G320-1372, 1974, pp. 42–3)*

How much security?

Security is costly. In addition to the expense of equipment and personnel to safeguard computing resources, other costs must be considered, such as employee dissatisfaction and loss of morale when security precautions delay or impede operations. In deciding how much security is needed, management should analyse **risk**. How exposed and vulnerable are the systems to physical damage, delayed processing, fraud, disclosure of data or physical threats? What threat scenarios are possible?

As illustrated in Figure 8.8, systems and user characteristics should be assessed

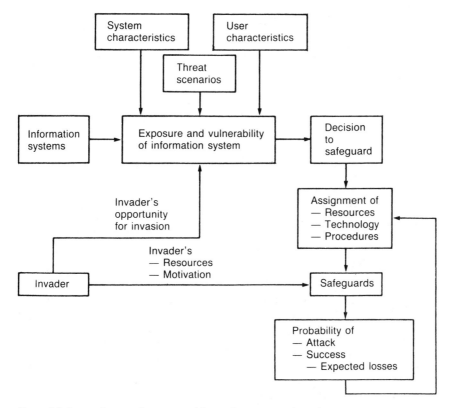

Figure 8.8 *Factors in assessing expected losses from systems intrusion*

when evaluating risk. Opportunities for systems invasion, motives of a possible invader, and resources that might be allocated to invasion should be considered. The resources available to deter or counter a security breach should also be appraised. The amount of security that should be given to systems should be based, in part, on evaluation of expected losses should the systems be breached. One way to calculate expected losses from intrusion is by application of the formula:

Expected loss = $L \times P_A \times P_B$

where

L = Potential loss.
P_A = Probability of attack.
P_B = Probability of success.

An insurance company or computer vendor can help management determine the value of L. Probability values are more difficult to obtain. Rather than attempting to assign a specific value (0.045 or even 0.05 may be of spurious accuracy), relative risk (high, medium or low) should first be determined and a numerical value assigned to each of these relative probabilities (for example, 0.8, 0.5 and 0.2, respectively). The risk costs can now be calculated according to the formula. For example:

Exposure	L	×	P_A	×	P_B	=	Expected loss
1	£500,000		1.0		0.2		£100,000
2	200,000		0.6		0.5		60,000
3	50,000		0.2		0.8		8,000
Total expected loss							£168,000

Loss is determined for each exposure; the sum of the expected losses is the total risk value to the system. If P_A and P_B are probabilities for the year, expected loss is £168,000 per year.

The application of this formula will help management determine whether the addition of security measures is worth the cost and where the greatest reduction of expected losses could occur by improving security.

The figures derived from the formula are approximations at best. We simply do not have the data to calculate reliable probabilities, because the computer industry is too new to have a long historical record of invasions on which to base probability assessments. Furthermore, firms are reluctant to publicize how their security has been breached lest their credibility suffer, so news of security invasions is seldom broadcast. This means data on security infractions are incomplete. More serious, persons who design security measures are not always aware of the tricks and techniques used by perpetrators of crime to break systems security and so cannot plan countermeasures.

Prosecution of computer-related crimes

A legal muddle exists in most countries with regard to computer-related crime. The fast pace of advance in information technology leaves legislators behind, struggling to define IT crime and enact legal remedies for individuals (or organizations) who want to stop unauthorized access of their computer files and deter malicious acts against their computer resources.

For example, take the issue of software theft. As recently as 1985, delegates to a UNESCO-WIPO conference in Geneva were unable to agree on the definition of software piracy, so came to no consensus about how to protect programs. Many countries have since enacted (or amended) copyright legislation to encompass computer software. Nevertheless, there remains opposition to US moves through GATT (General Agreement on Tariffs and Trades) to recognize such copyright protection. Brazil, Thailand and other Third World countries argue that copyrighted software would strengthen transnational computer companies and prevent underdeveloped nations from building up their own informatics industry.

Today, most computer crimes are prosecuted under laws written for other purposes. In the United Kingdom, a hacker who destroys information can be prosecuted under the Criminal Damage Act of 1971, or charged with 'abstracting' electricity under the Theft Act of 1968. In the United States, more than forty sections of the US Code can be cited to provide sanctions for computer-related criminal conduct. The challenge facing legislators throughout the world is to write comprehensive laws specifically against computer crime and to provide a legal framework for computerized business operations.

Summing up

Computer technology poses a threat to personal privacy because of the speed of processing, the collection of vast data banks, instantaneous retrieval capabilities and the worldwide network of data transmission through teleprocessing.

Privacy is closely linked to systems security. No one disputes that information systems must be guarded from unlawful intrusion, that human errors should be detected and that damage from natural disasters must be minimized. Management's dilemma is not whether security is needed but how much. Computer crime is increasing at an alarming rate. This can be attributed, in part, to the temptation arising from the large sums being transferred by electronic fund transfer and to the fact that more criminals are becoming knowledgeable about computer technology and equipped with computers to help them plan and execute their crimes. There are also individuals who are challenged simply to 'beat the system'. For example, an Oregon youth used a remote terminal to gain access to the computer of the Department of Motor Vehicles, then put the system into irreversible disarray just to illustrate its vulnerability.

According to commentators, crime figures are destined to rise unless the computer industry and organizations that use computers pay greater attention to security issues and devote more resources to the protection of information systems. All known protective mechanisms can be broken, given enough time, resources and ingenuity. Perhaps the major objective of security systems should be to make intrusion too expensive (in equipment costs and risk) and too time-consuming (in planning effort and time needed to actually breach safeguards) to make attempted violations worthwhile.

Risk analysis is one method of helping management determine which security strategies are most cost effective, given budgetary constraints. Systems security can·be provided by access controls, physical safeguards, personnel screening and policies, and operational controls as discussed in this chaper and in Chapter 7. Laws that act as a deterrent to computer crime also provide a measure of security.

Case study: **Stolen vehicle incident**

When the owner of a petrol station in Etampes, a small town near Paris, noticed that a customer's licence plate was taped together, he jotted down the plate number and notified the police, suspicious that the vehicle was stolen. After querying their 'stolen car' database and finding the motor car listed, the police dispatched a patrol car to intercept the vehicle, now stopped at a traffic light. The two plain clothes officers, one carrying a machine gun, the other a .357 magnum revolver, jumped out of their patrol car to arrest the driver. In the next few moments of confusion, the magnum revolver was fired, which pierced the windshield of the suspect car and wounded one of the three young Frenchmen inside. While an ambulance assisted the injured man, the two others were handcuffed and questioned.

Upon investigation, it was found that the motor car had been purchased ten days before by one of the occupants of the suspect car. Though it was true that the vehicle had once been stolen, the missing report was three years old. In the meantime, the vehicle had been recovered by the insurance company, sold to a second-hand car dealer, then legally resold to one of the men involved in the incident. Failure to update police files was the cause of this 'mishap'.

Source: Tom Forester and Perry Morrison, *Computer Ethics*, Cambridge, Mass.: The MIT Press, 1990, p. 88.

Questions

1 Discuss the premise that databases and computer-based information affect the quality of our lives. How does this police incident illustrate the premise?
2 Who gave the police the right to collect information on stolen vehicles? Should citizens have the right to inspect police databases to check for the accuracy of information stored therein? What would be the cost? Who should pay? How would such inspection affect police work?
3 How does this incident illustrate the conflict that exists between a citizen's right to privacy and the role of the police in modern society? What balance between individual rights and police powers do you favour? What measures would you recommend to foster this balance?
4 Does this incident alarm you? Why? Who should shoulder responsibility for the incident? How could the 'mishap' have been prevented?

Case study: **German hacker invades US defence files**

Suspicion that someone was engaged in electronic espionage at the Lawrence Berkeley Laboratory was aroused when Clifford Stoll, manager of a multiuser computer system at the laboratory, noticed a 75 cent accounting discrepancy. Eighteen months of detective work followed in which Stoll cooperated with law enforcement agencies to track down a hacker who used the 75 cents worth of unauthorized time — a hacker subsequently arrested by German authorities under suspicion of espionage.

Stoll was able to monitor the hacker's activities and observe that he methodically invaded files in some three dozen US military complexes to sift out information on defence topics. But the hacker's identity remained a mystery until a trap, a fictitious file on the Strategic Defense Initiative, was inserted by Stoll in his lab's computer. The hacker, whose interest was piqued when he spotted the file, stayed online reading and copying the file long enough to be traced. German police believe they have cracked a major computer spy ring that has been selling sensitive military, nuclear and space research information to the Soviets.

Source: Karen Fitzgerald, 'The quest for intruder-proof computer systems', *IEEE Spectrum*, vol. 24, no. 8 (1989), pp. 22–6.

Questions

1 What types of processing control alerted authorities to a possible intruder in this case? Was it merely chance that the intrusion was noticed? Was it good systems design or well-controlled operations?

2 What types of system control would you recommend to prevent further intrusions of this nature?

3 Some people argue that mistakes and crime by employees account for most monetary losses due to compromised computer data. They believe publicity on cases such as this one obscures this fact, and argue that more resources should be put into internal policies

to prevent such losses than into preventing attacks from outside. Comment.

4 This hacker rifled through US military files from the comfort of his German home a continent away. What new dangers to systems security does advanced telecommunications technology pose?

5 Is a computer detective the best strategy for tracking down computer error and system intrusions? Should computer security personnel be employed to 'break' systems in order to discover their weaknesses? Discuss.

6 Suppose that you are responsible for computer security at the Lawrence Berkeley Laboratory. How would you calculate the risk of system intrusion? The cost of breached security? How much would you spend to prevent future violations of systems security?

7 Can business managers benefit from the experience at military installations regarding systems security? Explain.

Case study: **Buying the silence of computer criminals**

The Computer Industry Research Unit in the United Kingdom reports that the practice of offering amnesties to people who break into their computers and steal funds is widespread. Rather than prosecute, the corporations keep silent on the crimes if part of the money is returned and the swindler reveals how the fraud was carried out. Employers fear that business might be lost if customers learn that their computer security is flawed.

In one such case, a programmer who illegally diverted £8 million to a Swiss bank account gave back £7 million in return for a non-disclosure agreement protecting him from prosecution. According to a member of Scotland Yard's computer fraud squad, employers who make such agreements may end up in court them-

selves, prosecuted for perverting the course of justice.

Source: Lindsay Nicolle and Tony Collins, 'The computer fraud conspiracy of silence', *The Independent* (19 June 1989), p. 18.

Questions

1 In your view, is it ethical for an employer to sign an non-disclosure agreement with a computer criminal? Explain your position.

2 Some company directors argue that a police investigation of a security breach may disrupt the day-to-day running of their company, and they fear that the police will be unable to cope with the complexity of their computer systems. Some directors fear that they may lose their job if shareholders learn of the

crime. Some believe that learning how the fraud was committed is more important than punishing the culprit. If you were chairman of the board, how would you respond to these arguments?

3 According to computer experts, the scale of computer crime cannot be known with any certainty because companies are reluctant to discuss security breaches. What are the ramifications of silence in such matters?

4 In a police exercise named Comcheck in the City of London, financial institutions were asked to track the number of unauthorized log-ons over the Easter bank holiday. Many banks had no security checks in place so could not tell if their networks had been penetrated. Some had to produce special software to take part in the exercise. Do you think financial institutions in your country are as lax in their computer security? Why? Who is responsible? What measures can be taken to reduce financial losses through unauthorized system access?

5 Are security controls that work well in the United Kingdom transferable to businesses in other countries? Suggest scenarios where such security measures might be effective. Suggest measures that might not be effective in other societies, explaining why.

Key words

Access controls
Accuracy
Biometric control
  systems
Callback box
Card
Data directory security
  matrix
Encryption

Fair use
Gatekeeping
Hackers
Handshake
Key
Password generator
Passwords
Privacy

Recovery
Reference monitor
Risk
Security
Security kernel
Separation of
  responsibility
Virtual machine

Discussion questions

1 Comment on the statement: A computer system adds significantly to the probability of errors, fraud and destruction of data and information.
2 Describe types of crimes perpetrated against computerized systems.
3 Describe five situations in which personal identification might be required before access to a computer is granted. In each case, which of the following methods would you recommend?
   (*a*) ID card.
   (*b*) Password.
   (*c*) Signature identification.
   (*d*) Hand form identification.
   (*e*) Voice identification.
   (*f*) Handprint identification.

4 Why is privacy of data important to business clients and customers? What other segments in business are affected and why? How can each privacy problem be successfully approached?

5 How can the conflict between need for data privacy and need for data access be resolved? What trade-offs can be made?

6 If you were the head of an organization not bound by a privacy code, would you institute privacy measures? What measures? What obligation do you believe private organizations have regarding the privacy of client records?

7 Who should decide what information is sensitive and must not be collected because it violates the privacy of individuals?

8 Should the verification of the accuracy of data files be mandatory? What are the advantages and disadvantages of such a requirement?

9 What is meant by the term *gatekeeping*? Is gatekeeping in the interests of business? Explain your answer.

10 What is a password? Do password systems guarantee the security of data? What are some of the pitfalls?

11 How does a password generator work?

12 Give two examples of unexpected results that might be produced because of:
(*a*) Malfunction.
(*b*) Mistakes.
(*c*) Fraud.
(*d*) Theft.
(*e*) Sabotage.
How might security be improved to prevent incorrect results caused by each of the above?

13 What are some common abuses of computerized information systems? How can these abuses be prevented?

14 Has your privacy been invaded by business computers? How can such invasion of privacy be prevented?

15 Can a computer system ever be completely secure? What are the trade-offs in costs? What are the social and non-monetary costs?

16 Identify control points where measures should be taken to ensure security of data. Explain what measures you would require and why.

17 What should be management's role in planning systems security?

18 What makes particular industries more vulnerable to security violations than the average? What makes a particular firm within an industry more vulnerable than others? How can this vulnerability be reduced, if not eliminated?

19 What would you do if you suspected a fellow employee of being a computer criminal? Should your action depend on your industry? Would your action differ if you were working in a:
(*a*) Bank?

    (*b*) Retail store?
    (*c*) Multinational firm?
    (*d*) Insurance company?
20 Are laws in your country adequate for detecting, discouraging and punishing:
    (*a*) Computer crime?
    (*b*) Privacy violations?
    Discuss.
21 Is the cost of privacy excessive? How can a firm decide what security precautions to ensure privacy are worth the cost?
22 Explain the concept of a security kernel.
23 How does data encryption add to systems security? What is the purpose of encrypting data if coding schemes can be broken?
24 Describe controls that can protect a computing facility from natural disasters, such as earthquakes, floods, fire or lightning.

Bibliography

Cashmore, Carol and Richard Lyall. *Business Information,* Hemel Hempstead: Prentice Hall, 1988, pp. 256–69.

Chen, Christopher D. 'Computer crime and the Computer Fraud and Abuse Act of 1986', *Computer Law Journal,* vol. 9, no. 1 (Winter 1990), pp. 71–86.

Flaherty, David. *Protecting Privacy in Surveillance Societies,* Chapel Hill, NC: The University of North Carolina Press, 1989.

Forester, Tom and Perry Morrison. *Computer Ethics,* Cambridge, Mass.: The MIT Press, 1990.

Hafner, Katie and John Markoff. *Cyberpunk: Outlaws and hackers on the computer frontier,* Hemel Hempstead: Simon & Schuster, 1991.

Highland, Harold Joseph. 'Random bits and bytes', *Computers and Security,* vol. 10, no. 1 (1991), pp. 4–16.

Hruska, Jan. 'Computer viruses', *Information Age,* vol. 12, no. 2 (April 1990), pp. 100–8.

Hurford, Chris. 'Computer fraud — the UK experience', *Computer Bulletin Series III* (May 1989), pp. 19–20.

Lobel, Jerome. 'Managing information security in the space age', *Information Age,* vol. 11, no. 4 (October 1989), pp. 195–98.

Peuckett, Heribert. 'Enhancing the security of network systems', *Siemens Review, H & D Special* (Spring 1991), pp. 19–22.

Price, Wyn. 'Data security', *The Computer Bulletin,* vol. 2, no. 9 (September 1990), pp. 10–11.

Sacco, Vincent F. and Elia Zureik. 'Correlates of computer misuse: data from a self-reporting sample', *Behaviour and Information Technology,* vol. 9, no. 5 (1990), pp. 353–69.

Sizer, Richard and John Clark. 'Computer security — a pragmatic approach for managers', *Information Age,* vol. 11, no. 2 (April 1989), pp. 88–98.

Stuart, Rob, Christina Mitchell and Keith Jackson. 'How to stop computer fraud', *Which Computer?*, vol. 12, no. 10 (October 1989), pp. 30–46.

'The eye of the beholder', *The Economist*, vol. 319, no. 7705 (4 May 1991), pp. 21–3.

US Privacy Protection Study Commission, *Final Report* (1977).

von Solms, R., J.H.P. Eloff and S.H. von Solms. 'Computer security management: a framework for effective management involvement', *Information Age*, vol. 12, no. 4 (October 1990), pp. 217–22.

Yovel, Shlomo. 'On viruses and top managers', *Information Age*, vol. 11, no. 4 (October 1969), pp. 202–4.

9 Performance evaluation and auditing

The perfect computer has been developed.
You just feed in your problems — and they
never come out again.
Al Goodman

In order to ensure quality computing, the performance of an information systems (IS) department should be regularly evaluated. This evaluation, called **computer performance evaluation** (also known as 'computer performance management' and 'computer performance monitoring'), consists of a comparison of actual performance with desired performance in resource utilization, operations and service, as shown in Figure 9.1. When performance fails to measure up to prescribed standards, corrective action followed by re-evaluation is required. A satisfactory performance evaluation indicates no immediate need for change but is no grounds for complacency. Computing is not a static field. New technology, an altered business climate, increased load, a change in users, demand for new applications, or delays in new systems development can suddenly turn contented clients into frustrated information users. For this reason, evaluations should be scheduled at regular intervals so that systems weaknesses can be identified and rectified before they become chronic. Evaluation should also be initiated whenever problems arise.

Performance evaluation is, in effect, a control mechanism. Surprisingly, many IS departments that design and maintain financial and performance reporting systems for the organizations they serve treat performance evaluation of their own operations casually. This occurs even though improved computing performance would have a multiplier effect, enhancing the performance of other departments in turn. After all, an information system is a service function that exists to better the effectiveness of a firm's line functions. Systems are installed because they promise to deliver benefits that equal or exceed their cost. It follows, therefore, that any gain in the effectiveness of the information function would be magnified for the organization as a whole.

There are also financial reasons to focus on improved performance of computer operations. IS departments consume from 1 to 5 per cent of the revenue generated

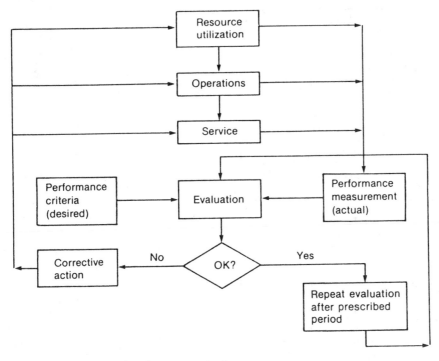

Figure 9.1 *The process of performance evaluation*

by most manufacturing concerns. As much as 20 per cent of operating costs can be attributed to information systems in service organizations and public agencies that deal in information. What company would not welcome a way to reduce such expenditures? Performance evaluations lead to cost savings by identifying computing inefficiencies and tracking the results of corrective action.

This chapter describes the mechanisms of performance evaluation. First, critical performance variables that need to be evaluated are identified, and then evaluation criteria are described. This is followed by a discussion of how performance data are collected, measured and analyzed. Finally, corrective action and evaluation of the evaluation process itself are considered. Sections in this chapter correspond to steps in the evaluation process as shown in Figure 9.2. Personnel, timing and evaluation tools and techniques will be discussed at each step when relevant.

Auditing is yet another level of control. This chapter also describes the function of auditors and examines approaches to computer auditing. No attempt is made in this chapter to explain in detail the technical aspects of auditing — auditors require professional training — but the scope of an auditor's control over comput-ing is discussed at length. Sections are also devoted to the role of auditors in the development of new information systems and to auditing benefits and problems.

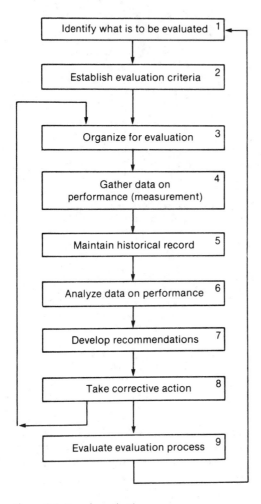

Figure 9.2 *Steps in evaluation*

Identify what is to be evaluated

In computing, four areas comprise keys to performance:

- Financial management — management of the financial resources allocated to the information systems function.
- Applications management — control and reporting of the design, implementation, and maintenance of applications sytems.
- Productivity/operations management — availability and utilization of computers.

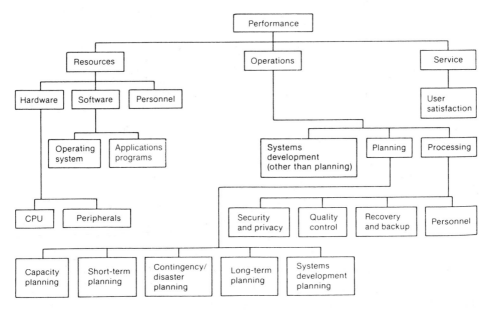

Figure 9.3 *Performance components to be evaluated*

- Human resource management — productivity of personnel assigned to information systems.

An organization that wants to improve its information function should collect performance variables in each of these four areas of analysis. The problem is to decide exactly which variables to collect and how to organize collected data for evaluation. Should data be gathered on expenditures by object of expense (salaries, supplies, and services)? By activity? By the cost to run, maintain and enhance applications programs? By customer? What aspects of production should be measured? On-time/in-budget delivery of systems? Resource consumption? Is an analysis of human productivity needed in order to evaluate performance, or would a study of the distribution of the workload and skill improvements through training suffice?

In deciding what performance variables to monitor and evaluate, corporate management, information users, planning groups, data administrators and IT personnel should all have a voice. They should also participate in discussions of what performance objectives should be. Figure 9.3 shows commonly evaluated components of the information systems function. (Usually, the evaluation of daily operations is distinct from the evaluation of systems development. Many firms consider planning so important that separate evaluations are held for capacity planning, contingency planning, long- and short-term planning and systems development planning.)

Establish evaluation criteria

Efficiency of operations and effectiveness of product are basic evaluation criteria. Historically, information systems departments have focused on the computing process to ensure a high ratio of output to input (efficiency). Today, however, more emphasis is placed on effectiveness of the information function. The real issue, according to many corporate managers, is what level of service is being provided to computer users by the information systems department.

Let us now turn to a discussion of evaluation criteria in the two categories of efficiency and effectiveness.

Efficiency

Efficiency (η), a concept used in production management, is the ratio of output (O) to input (I) as expressed in the formula $\eta = O/I$. Unfortunately, the benefit of output in computing cannot always be calculated in tangible units. How can one measure the monetary value of a timely report, accuracy, or the absence of fraud? By keeping input constant, however, a change in output can be noted: if output increases, efficiency is increased; if output decreases, efficiency is decreased. Efficiency is generally measured in terms of throughput, productivity, resource utilization and costs.

Throughput
The design of equipment, in part, determines computer **throughput**, the amount of work that can be performed during a given period of time. Throughput is advertised, known to the buyer at the time of purchase. Central processing unit (CPU) throughput may be measured in thousands of operations per second (KOPS) or millions of instructions per second (MIPS). Unfortunately, these measurements are not as standardized as horsepower or kilowatt hours, so one cannot always compare the throughput of computers sold by different vendors.

CPU throughput, however, is rarely the prime processing constraint. Rather, efficiency is limited by peripheral devices used in pre- and postprocessing, such as optical recognition equipment, printers, bursters and routing equipment. Such peripheral devices advertise throughput as a selling feature so that competing models can be compared by the buyer. When sales claims prove unsubstantiated, the vendor can be held accountable, provided that a well-written, detailed, legally binding contract has been signed.

Productivity
Productivity is the term usually applied to throughput performance of personnel — that is, the quantity of work produced by an individual in a unit of time. For example, the efficiency of data entry operators can be evaluated by comparing number of keystrokes per hour with standard tables. Lines of code (LOC) per

programmer-day can measure a programmer's productivity. Other common productivity measures are documentation pages per documenter-month, cost per defect, CPU hours per programmer-month, and test cases developed and executed per programmer-month.

The problem is that the measurement of productivity in such work units can be misleading. For example, LOC is biased in favour of programmers who do not optimize their codes. This measure also penalizes high-level languages, making it harder to compare productivity between programmers. Many traditional productivity measures do not take program complexity, correctness, or reliability into account, nor whether the software is structured or not. They make little allowance for the program's size, for the organization of the programming team, or for the programmer's experience. Furthermore, some standard productivity measures are founded on unproven assumptions. As a result, the quantity of a programmer's work is somewhat discredited as a productivity measure. Many companies are in search of new ways to evaluate productivity.

One new technique that is currently attracting attention is function-point measurement, a method of characterizing the size and complexity of applications based on the amount of function delivered to the users. This method, under study at IBM, attempts to quantify the cost per function and assign a benefit to the function. Halstead metrics, another new technique, counts the number of action statements (operators) and data elements (operands) in a program. It has been demonstrated that the sum of the number of operators and operands is correlated with the error rate and productivity of a program.

Unfortunately, flaws and errors in programs often take a long time to surface. A programmer who is rewarded for high productivity based on a measure such as lines of code may be writing software that requires excessive maintenance.

Utilization
Another gauge of efficiency is **utilization**, the ratio of what is used to what is available. Unused capacity is a waste of resources; however, a high utilization value may indicate that bottlenecks in processing will occur in the near future. The same utilization data that are studied during performance evaluations can be used for capacity planning and scheduling as well.

Cost
Efficiency is increased when **cost**, with constant output, drops. One way to evaluate performance is by comparing budgeted with actual expenditures and reviewing trends in cost indexes:

$$\text{Material cost index} = \frac{\text{Cost of materials}}{\text{Total cost of computing centre}}$$

$$\text{Personnel cost index} = \frac{\text{Cost of personnel}}{\text{Total cost of computing centre}}$$

$$\text{Software maintenance index} = \frac{\text{Cost of maintenance (software)}}{\text{Total cost of computing centre}}$$

In computing, inefficiency can often be traced to waste of materials (tapes, paper) and run time. Habits of waste frequently develop when user departments do not pay for computing services and computer time is not constrained. By charging for services, costs may be lowered dramatically — an example of a budgetary policy that may affect performance efficiency.

Effectiveness

Effectiveness evaluation is based on the objectives of the information function. An effective system is one that satisfies the expectations of users. When effectiveness is under study, the following questions are asked: Are user needs being met by the IS department? Does the output produced by applications programs meet user requirements? Are systems user friendly? Are users satisfied with their information systems?

When an organization focuses on effectiveness, the emphasis shifts from the technical aspects of information production to the problems that the computer can solve. Information specialists take on a business orientation, working closely with users and corporate management to ensure that information strategies fully support business plans. Performance is measured in terms of systems availability, information quality, timeliness, accuracy and reliability, since user satisfaction is based on these criteria.

Availability
Machine **availability** may be measured as the percentage of time that equipment is in service. A company with three shifts that has half an hour daily downtime (for breakdowns or maintenance) has an availability index of roughly 98 per cent (23.5/24). As downtime is reduced, systems effectiveness will increase. The problem with this index is that if the half-hour downtime remains fixed but the denominator changes, the index changes although the machine is no less available from the operational point of view. For example, if the half-hour downtime occurs during operations when the machine is utilized only 12 hours instead of 24, the index is roughly 96 per cent (11.5/12) although no change has taken place in machine availability because of downtime. (Restrictions on availability as a result of priority scheduling or overloading is a separate problem of scheduling and capacity planning.)

One can also evaluate availability in absolute terms. If a job requires 300 minutes of machine time on a specific date, is that 300 minutes available when needed?

Quality
Quantitive measures of **quality** are difficult to formulate, but one can identify costs associated with quality. For example, prevention cost is a measure of the

money spent to prevent errors or do the job right the first time. Appraisal costs include the money spent for reviewing and testing systems to see that they meet systems requirements. Failure costs are those associated with defective systems. Evaluation teams should study these figures as they look for ways to help improve the information function.

Generally, quality is measured in terms of user satisfaction. Factors that will influence this satisfaction are:

- Ease of use of computer systems and software.
- Security and confidentiality of data.
- Technical support given users by computer specialists.
- Completeness, readability, and organization of documentation.
- User confidence that state-of-the-art technology is being applied.
- Ease with which systems can be maintained and upgraded.
- Portability and reusability.
- Ease with which a system can be audited and tested.

Timeliness

There are really three measures for **timeliness**: turnaround time, response time and schedule adherence. **Turnaround time** is the period of time between job submission to the IS department and the return of output. This is usually a measure for batch work and will be measured in hours or days. **Response time** is a way of measuring the timeliness of interactive online activities and will typically be measured in fractions of a second. **Schedule adherence** refers to the ability of a computing facility to process applications on time and to deliver new systems that are under development when promised.

Other ways to evaluate timeliness would be to study waiting time, length of queue, number of days projects are delayed and backlogs. It is often better to have ten projects that are each delayed one day than to have one project ten days late.

Accuracy

Accuracy can be defined as the absence of error. But what constitutes an error? When a calculated value is 1.962256, one can truncate the number to 1.96 when the unit is dollars and cents but not when 1.962256 represents millions of dollars. A misspelled name on the mailing list for an advertising circular would be regrettable but not crucial. But suppose the misspelling were the name of the chairman of the board in a firm's annual report?

These examples illustrate that accuracy must be carefully defined when evaluating systems effectiveness. The permissible magnitude of error should be established, rate of acceptable error defined (for example, one in 1 million calculations), and error limits set in absolute terms (for example, number of allowable errors per month). Degree of accuracy should be set not only for computer processing but for peripherals, telecommunications and data entry as well.

Since errors usually result in reruns, rerun data are one way to measure performance accuracy.

Reliability

Reliability is an elusive concept although many formulas have been published to measure it. The problem is that too many variables in reliability calculations cannot be precisely measured. The relative importance of these variables in contributing to **systems reliability** is also difficult to impute. For example, what role do sickness, absenteeism, turnover, training and operator motivation play in systems reliability? Should reliability be based on the effort, cost or time required to keep a system operational?

Software reliability (a function of the complexity of the software, the competence of programmers, and viability of a given development approach) is also difficult to assess. The problem of identifying software errors compounds the difficulty of measuring systems effectiveness in terms of reliability. Systems may appear to function smoothly but be producing inaccurate output due to inherent, undetected software errors.

Users are generally interested not in a technical measure of reliability (involving statistics and probability theory) but rather in availability. They want to know whether they can count on the computer being operational when they need to use it.

Conflicts between evaluation criteria

Before concluding this section, a word should be said about the interrelationships that exist between performance criteria. In many cases, a high evaluation rating for one criterion precludes a high rating for another. For example, lowering response time may raise costs, and vice versa. Suppose the response time–cost curve for a given firm is as illustrated in Figure 9.4, with OC an acceptable response time according to management and OD an acceptable cost. Compromise is necessary since they yield different points on the curve. That is, both performance objectives cannot be met at the same time. At point E, for example, the cost corresponds to DD′, but the response time OF corresponding to FF′ is slower than CC′. At Point B, the response time corresponds to CC′, but the cost AA′ is higher than DD′. One of the two variables has to give, or both may be compromised somewhat to fall within Points E and B on the curve. This means either a slower response time or higher cost than desired by management.

The same type of conflict may exist between other variables, such as quality and cost, or quality and timeliness, as shown:

$$\text{Quality control} \rightarrow \left. \begin{array}{l} \text{Quality} \uparrow \rightarrow \quad \text{Desirable} \\ \text{Costs} \uparrow \rightarrow \quad \text{Undesirable} \end{array} \right\} \text{Conflict}$$

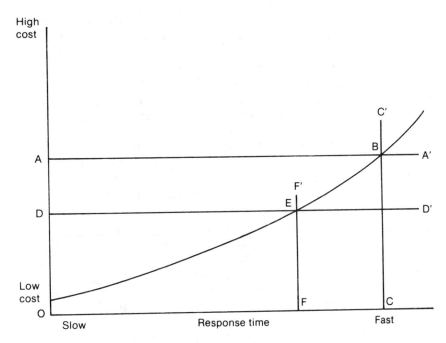

Figure 9.4 *Response time–cost curve*

Quality control → Quality ↑ → Desirable ⎫
Timeliness ↓ → Undesirable ⎭ Conflict

Key:
→ = leads to
↑ = increase
↓ = decrease

Indeed, more than two criteria may be in opposition in a given situation. Management must then search for a satisfactory or acceptable mix of controllable factors and set performance standards that minimize the effect of conflicts. This is not an easy task.

Organize for evaluation

Who evaluates the performance of an IS department? Often, a staff member in the department is assigned the task, someone who is technically competent and also knowledgeable regarding organizational policies and procedures. Sometimes, more objectivity is sought. A person within the organization but working in another department — with no role in daily computer operations — will be given the responsibility of evaluating the information function. Still other firms hire a consultant to evaluate performance. For large organizations with complex information systems, an evaluation team may be required.

Performance evaluation should be a regularly scheduled activity. The staff member responsible for evaluation should be appointed, a budget for evaluation activities drawn up, and the purpose and scope of the evaluation publicized. Evaluations should be conducted openly, not secretly, with the evaluator and evaluation results known to workers. Employees can be helpful to evaluators in identifying and diagnosing poor performance, and their cooperation is needed when corrective producedures are initiated.

The frequency of evaluations will vary from one firm to another. Many organizations require the submission of monthly performance reports organized around financial management, applications management, productivity/operations management and human resource management for study by the individual (or team) charged with performance evaluation. The reports may subsequently be reviewed at meetings with the IS department head and staff.

Not all companies require such a rigid evaluation structure. Most corporate managers weigh the cost of evaluation effort, computer time, and organizational disruption against the potential costs of unidentified inefficiency and ineffectiveness. They then schedule evaluations accordingly.

Gather data on performance (measurement)

Once performance criteria are specified and variables identified, data on the values of variables must be collected for analysis. This can be done by logging, using monitors, or canvassing users, as illustrated in Figure 9.5.

Logs

In many computer centres, manual **logs** are kept by operators. These logs are a source of information when evaluating performance. For example, data on the length of downtime for maintenance might be determined from an operator's log.

One disadvantage of such log use is that drawing information from a log is time consuming: a simple calculation, such as percentage of jobs delivered on schedule, requires someone to search logs for relevant data. And human error is always possible in the calculation itself. Job accounting programs can replace manually collected statistics in some areas, but cost again is a factor, albeit much less so.

Monitors

Computer performance can also be measured using hardware and software monitors (see Figure 9.6).

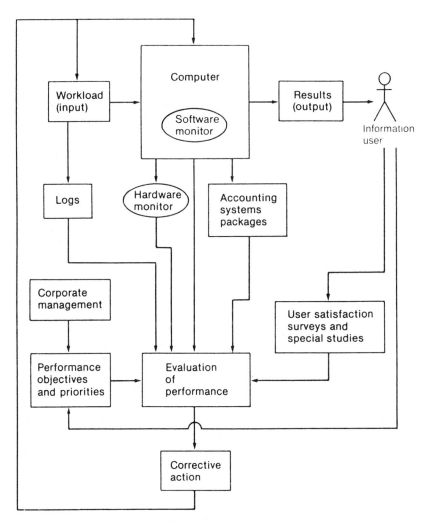

Figure 9.5 *Sources of data for performance evaluation*

Hardware monitors, equipment with sensors in input and output channels, record desired data on instrument panels or on tape for later analysis. An **accumulating monitor** is a counter used in simple computational environments. It might be used to count the number of jobs completed in a given time period, for example. A **logical monitor** is essentially a minicomputer used in more complex processing, such as multiprogramming. Both types of hardware monitors are suitable for collecting utilization statistics and data on component conflicts — data needed for capacity planning.

A wide variety of counting measures are possible using hardware monitors. The monitors can accurately report data on short-term activities and measure

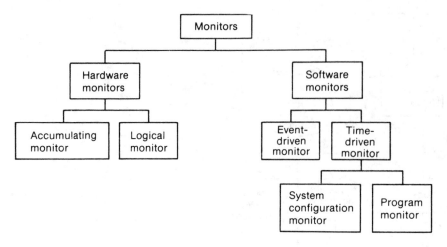

Figure 9.6 *Types of monitors*

systems overhead. However, hardware monitors are costly, have a long setup time, and require skilled personnel to operate. Probes and connections can be accidentally dislodged, damaged, or incorrectly connected, resulting in false data.

A **software monitor** is an application program that is part of the operating system or stored internally. The software contains a data collector that takes time counts and gathers data by reading internal tables, status registers, memory maps, operating system control blocks, and so on. Then an analyzer/reporter reads the data and reduces, orders, groups, summarizes and computes values of interest. Finally, the information is displayed in a logical manner. Sometimes, output is printed in hard copy; sometimes, it is displayed on a terminal screen.

Software monitors are of two types. An **event-driven monitor** interacts with the operating system's interrupt-handling mechanism and can monitor almost every occurrence of the event being studied. A **time-driven monitor** is a periodic sampling system activated at user-specified intervals. It is subdivided into system configuration monitors (which generate information on system components) and program monitors.

Software monitors can generate utilization figures, as hardware monitors do, and can also report on the performance of systems and applications programs. They are easy to use, low in cost and allow flexibility in choosing options for data collection. However, the monitors may not be able to monitor concurrent events. The cost of CPU and storage overhead is also a disadvantage. In addition, these monitors generally have low priority for CPU access, and the software must be reprogrammed when changes are made to operating systems.

User surveys

Data on user satisfaction with the performance of information systems can be collected in **user surveys** using questionnaires and interviews. The problem is designing relevant questions and framing them in a manner so that they are not misunderstood and resisted. In addition, the respondent must be motivated to reply candidly. Questions should be non-threatening and neutral, so that there are no implicit 'right' answers. Otherwise, respondents will distort their replies for self-protection. That is, respondents must perceive their work environment as one in which they will not be penalized for making critical responses.

Questions might be asked on the following topics:

- Timeliness of operations and reports.
- Validity and completeness of reports.
- Achievement of predetermined acceptable levels of operations.
- Frequency of errors.
- Response time to meet users' requests.
- Protection of privacy.
- Data and systems security.
- Systems reliability.
- Achievement of long-range goals.
- Degree of incorporation of latest technology.
- Training availability and effectiveness.
- Quality of output and service.
- Lines of communication with IT personnel.

This list is essentially a restatement of efficiency and effectiveness criteria described earlier in the chapter. Sample questions that might be used in evaluating systems performance appear in Figure 9.7. It is helpful if questionnaires are designed so answers can be mark-sensed or read by optical scanning equipment. A terminal might also be used, with answers collected by one-stroke responses or by touch-sensitive screens.

Maintain historical record

When evaluating performance data, it is useful to compare current performance with records from the past. For this reason, historical records need to be maintained. Performance data stored in a data bank should help with longitudinal analysis, setting standards, identifying performance trends and calculating moving averages.

1 Please express your overall satisfaction with the service you receive from the computer centre.
   - ☐   Very good
   - ☐   Good
   - ☐   Fair
   - ☐   Poor
   - ☐   Very poor

2 For Report #20 (Cost Distribution by Department), please express your satisfaction in each of the areas listed on a scale of 1 to 10. (Low satisfaction would be indicated by a 1; high satisfaction by a 10.)

	For cost analysis	For fund management	For cost estimation	For decision making
Format				
Content				
Amount of detail				
Timeliness				
Overall rating				

3 How do you evaluate the charging policies for service at the data centre?
   - ☐   Very reasonable
   - ☐   Reasonable
   - ☐   Unreasonable
   - ☐   Outrageous

4 Please express how charging policies affect your use of the computer centre.
   - ☐   No effect
   - ☐   Discourage use
   - ☐   Encourage use

5 Which of the following charging policies would you consider reasonable?
   - ☐   Service at no cost
   - ☐   Service at marginal cost
   - ☐   Service at full cost
   - ☐   Service at a cost that is competitive with external computing facilities.

* These respresentative questions are drawn from a survey to show how questions might be formatted. They are only sample questions, however, and the survey is by no means complete.

Figure 9.7 *Questions from user satisfaction survey**

Analyze data on performance

Without analysis of collected performance data, the collection effort is wasted. Yet, too often, sheaves of performance data are stacked on an evaluator's desk

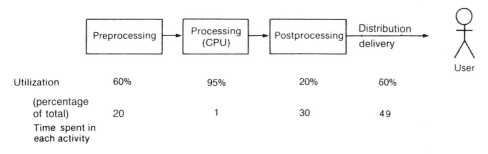

| Preprocessing | Processing (CPU) | Postprocessing | Distribution delivery | User |

Utilization	60%	95%	20%	60%
(percentage of total)	20	1	30	49
Time spent in each activity				

Figure 9.8 *Data on performance for analysis of CPU utilization*

waiting for analysis that never takes place. Time must be set aside to review and interpret data.

Analysis usually starts with a glance-check at data to see if the values of variables are reasonable. This may be followed by a trend analysis and a check to see how performance measures up to local, national and industrial standards.

For example, let us look at the sample figures on CPU utilization listed in Figure 9.8. If the 95 per cent were for three shifts, excluding preventive maintenance (often 5 per cent), the computer would be running near full capacity. The person evaluating these figures would recognize that the figures indicate a need for system expansion or the acquisition of a larger system.

The 60 per cent utilization figure for preprocessing and 20 per cent for postprocessing is within an acceptable performance range. (The person who evaluates these figures should be well informed on standard performance statistics.) However, these figures may hide bottlenecks at specific equipment, so disaggregated data should be collected — for example, utilization statistics on all channel ports as well as utilization figures for tapes, disks and other input/output devices. The 49 per cent figure for distribution activities in this sample is high compared with other computer systems. The evaluator would recognize this to be one area of performance that could be upgraded if delivery procedures were changed.

Develop recommendations and take corrective action

On the basis of data analysis, evaluators should formulate a set of recommendations to improve performance, supported by reviews and reports. A sample listing of what should be included in these documents appears in Table 9.1.

Recommendations for corrective action may include changes in resource usage, new procedures and techniques, revised user interfaces, or perhaps alteration

Table 9.1 *Reviews, reports and recommendations by performance evaluators*

Reviews	Reports	Recommendations
Service levels	Exceptional	Cost-effective innovations
Priorities	Summary	Technical
Workloads	Technical	Organizational
Forecasts of:	Financial	Corrective actions to
Resource needs		improve performance
Personnel		
Acceptance levels		
Relevance and obsoleteness		
Cost effectiveness		

of the firm's planning process. The aim of corrective action should be not merely to bring performance to targeted levels but to raise it to higher standards.

Recommendations for action to correct an unacceptable service level situation are not the sole responsibility of the evaluator. In most companies, managers meet with information users and IT personnel to consider evaluation reports and to devise strategies to improve the information function. Various tools and techniques may be called into play to help determine what changes to make. For example, job accounting packages, benchmarks, or modelling and simulation might be used to experiment with changes to the equipment configuration, the schedule, software, or any number of other variables that affect performance. The responsibility for selecting what performance improvements to make and how to implement these improvements rests with management following recommendation of technical personnel.

Evaluate evaluation process

A final responsibility of the evaluator is to evaluate the evaluation process itself. That is, problems in planning, organizing and implementing the evaluation should be identified, changes in the basic premises or philosophy of evaluation suggested (if any are needed), and tools and techniques for future evaluations recommended. Such an evaluation is particularly important following a computer centre performance evaluation, because firms are still learning how to conduct such evaluations. The speed with which technological advances take place in computing also complicates the evaluator's role, because new models of equipment and new applications of software are continually being introduced.

Auditing

In addition to evaluation by an evaluations committee, most firms appoint an **internal auditor** to provide an additional level of control. This employee will be

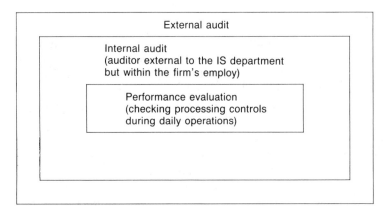

Figure 9.9 *Layers of control*

knowledgeable about computer systems but not involved with daily operations of the IS department. An **external auditor** from outside the organization may add one more level of control by auditing the internal auditor's report. (Figure 9.9 shows the relationship between performance evaluations, internal and external audits.) To preserve the objectivity and independence of auditors, they commonly report directly to a senior executive such as the firm's financial vice president. It is management's responsibility to evaluate a computer centre's exposure, the potential magnitude of loss and the probability of systems intrusion when deciding the depth of coverage and frequency of audits.

The function of an **auditor** is two-fold:

1 To ensure that controls to protect corporate resources are in place.
2 To ensure that transactions are processed according to desired procedures and decision rules.

Traditionally, the primary focus of an auditor was hard-copy audit trails and accounts and financial records prepared by hand under the jurisdiction of a firm's comptroller or financial officer. Nowadays, sales, accounts receivable and payable, payroll and inventory are all processed by computers. As a result, computing skill, in addition to accounting expertise, is required to monitor modern record-keeping systems. Furthermore, the auditor's job is complicated by that fact that error-free transactions processed by computer depend on procedures, standards, decision rules and security that are embodied in the design of computer systems. For this reason, auditors generally participate in the development of new systems to make sure that adequate controls are part of the system's design. They also oversee development to be sure that the new system can be audited. Still another way in which the auditor's role has changed is that data, manuals, software, peripherals and processors have been added to the list of corporate resources that need to be audited.

Approaches to auditing

There are two main approaches to auditing computer-based applications: auditing around and auditing through the computer.

When **auditing around the computer**, output is checked for a given input. It is assumed that if input is correct and reflected in the output, then the processing itself is also correct. Hence, the audit does not check computer processing directly. This type of audit uses traditional auditing methods and techniques, tracing who did what, when and in what sequence.

The problem with this approach is that processing errors may exist even though no errors are apparent when checking output against input. For example, there might be compensatory processing errors that do not show in the output. Unfortunately, computer calculations provide few intermediate results for auditors to check processing accuracy by traditional trailing methods.

To check both input and process, **audits through the computer** can be made. This auditing approach may use test data, auditor-prepared programs, auditor-software packages, or special-purpose audit programming languages. The logic of an applications program may also be reviewed.

Use of test data

An auditor may design and process sample transactions using test data in order to see how the system handles different transactions and whether programmed controls are part of the system. In other words, the accuracy of the computer program itself in performing calculations is examined and operating procedures used by the firm are checked for consistency with corporate policies. Auditors search for extreme conditions, out-of-sequence data, out-of-balance batches and so forth, the types of error frequently found when testing applications programs.

Auditor-prepared programs

In this approach, specially written programs prepared by the auditors are used to check specific conditions and to identify situations that need further study and analysis. The programs also spot check for unauthorized manipulations by programmers and operators, and provide listings of 'before' and 'after' changes which facilitate auditing.

Auditor-software packages

Standard auditing programs can be purchased. These are not as specialized as programs written by auditors for a specific information system but they are cheaper and easy to use.

Audit programming languages

Special programming languages can be used to generate output needed by auditors. System 2170, for example, developed by the accounting firm Peat,

Marwick and Mitchell, is a language that can be learned in about one week and has twenty-one audit commands.

Review of logic
The logic of an applications program can be reviewed to determine whether the program functions as purported.

Unfortunately, through-the-computer auditing can create problems when used on real-time systems. Unless extreme care is taken and expensive precautions are adopted, sample data can get mixed with the live data stream. One solution is to create a representative set of data for the company and to use it for auditing independently of the live data system. This approach is referred to as the **mini-company approach**.

It is beyond the scope of this text to explain auditing techniques of computer systems in greater detail. What needs to be stressed here is that auditors today use computers when auditing information systems. Unfortunately, current computer audit techniques are not as advanced as the technology being audited and the computer profession shows no sign of slowing its pace to wait until auditors catch up.

Scope of auditing

What should be audited? Attention is focused on the adequacy of controls in the following areas:

- Budgeting and finance.
- New systems development.
- Applications.
- Operations.
- Data security and privacy.
- Recovery.

An auditor uses many of the same criteria to evaluate the efficiency and effectiveness of information processing in each of these areas that IT professionals use during performance evaluation discussed earlier in this chapter. However, an auditor's perspective may differ. For example, both analysts and auditors are concerned with error rates, but an auditor may focus on the total monetary value of errors rather than the frequency of errors per se. Auditors are also much less worried about user satisfaction than in ensuring that expenditures fall within allocated amounts. Whereas computer personnel use monitors to identify specific problems that need correction, auditors search for weaknesses, test extreme values, and may attempt to break a system to test its limits. Indeed, a major responsibility of auditors is to evaluate the adequacy and sufficiency of systems not only for normal and peak workloads but for projected needs. In identifying

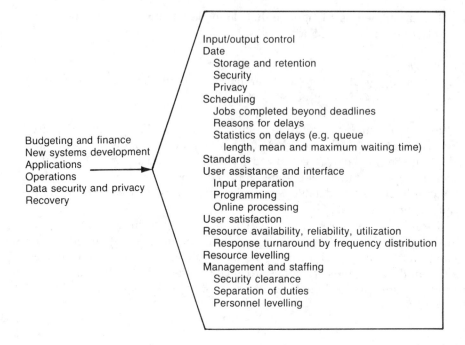

Budgeting and finance
New systems development
Applications ———————▶
Operations
Data security and privacy
Recovery

Input/output control
Date
   Storage and retention
   Security
   Privacy
Scheduling
   Jobs completed beyond deadlines
   Reasons for delays
   Statistics on delays (e.g. queue
     length, mean and maximum waiting time)
Standards
User assistance and interface
   Input preparation
   Programming
   Online processing
User satisfaction
Resource availability, reliability, utilization
   Response turnaround by frequency distribution
Resource levelling
Management and staffing
   Security clearance
   Separation of duties
   Personnel levelling

Figure 9.10 *Auditing concerns*

areas where demand will exceed capacity in the future, the auditor's report is a valuable tool in long-range planning.

Each of the auditing concerns, listed in Figure 9.10, consists of numerous subsets of activities. This figure shows a blow-up of one subset: activities that are evaluated by auditors with regard to operations. Some of the information that the auditor requires is provided by operating systems. In-house programs can also be written to collect the needed data. Auditors will have to examine logs and records to gather needed data as well.

To give an example, analysis of delays will include examination of statistics on average delay time, maximum delay time, average length of queue, maximum length of queue, and so forth — data than can be collected by monitors. But to find reasons for delays, the auditor will have to examine the workflow from input submission, input preparation, preprocessing (for example, validation of data), processing and postprocessing to distribution. Unless the cause is traced corrective action cannot be taken and the purpose of the audit will be defeated.

The auditor should also be concerned with output of the computer centre. It is possible that needed information is not being generated, that two reports might be more efficiently combined into one, or that certain reports have outlived their usefulness. A questionnaire, such as the one presented in Table 9.2, might be

Table 9.2 *User questionnaire on reports*

---

1 How useful do you consider this report?
2 How often do you use this report?
3 How many persons in your department use this report? How and why (briefly)?
4 How much of the data in this report do you use?
5 Can this report be:
   (a) Subsumed in another report?
   (b) Eliminated?
6 If this report were eliminated, would you easily find equivalent information elsewhere?
7 How do you store this report?
8 How long do you keep this report?
9 Is the report timely (available when needed)?
10 Is the report used for the following?
   (a) Reference.
   (b) Action and decision making.
   (c) Exceptional reporting.
   (d) Planning.
   (e) Control.
   (f) Operations.
   (g) Analysis.
11 Do you consider the mode of processing satisfactory? Which mode would you prefer? Why?
12 Is the report likely to be useful to you in the future? For how long?

---

circulated to users to ascertain the value of given reports. The answers might lead to report alternatives not previously considered. Perhaps the responses of users will lead auditors to conclude that the expense of space, equipment, utilities, insurance and security to store reports is more costly than the value of report retention. Or that the storage media should be changed to computer output on microfilm for more efficient storage and retrieval.

After one serious breakdown at a computer centre, which resulted in an entire week of processing being lost, an auditor questioned users and found that 34 per cent missed a report and complained, 24 per cent missed a report but did not complain, and 42 per cent were not even aware of reports not processed. This analysis led to the cancelling of many superfluous reports. Another auditor determined that information included in a regularly scheduled report could be generated as efficiently at one-third the cost if produced on a 'need to know' basis on a terminal. Such examples illustrate that an auditor can help identify systems weaknesses that may slip past users or computer centre personnel. Figure 9.11 shows some details that auditors examine — in this case, the audit is of an off-site storage facility of computer tapes.

Cost

Audits are expensive, and with each new advance in information technology, the cost of maintaining an audit program is rising. This increasing **cost** reflects escalating salaries, training, use of hardware and software to monitor performance,

To help explain what an auditor does, here are some of the review activities that take place when an audit is conducted of an off-site facility for the storage of computer tapes:

1 An inventory is made of the off-site facility. The physical count of the tapes is matched with the log kept at the main computer centre that lists tapes in storage.
2 Government and corporate retention standards are examined to see if the standard need to be updated. Then a check is made of ways in which standards are enforced.
3 The physical security of the tapes is evaluated. Fire alarms are tested. Temperature and humidity controls are examined. Questions such as the following are addressed: Is access restricted? How? What security measures are in place?
4 A disaster may be simulated to test whether tapes stored at the off-site facility are adequate for recovery of the main computer centre. Or specific applications may be tested to see if the use of off-site data would be sufficient to restore operations from a specific point in time.
5 Delivery procedures to off-site storage are checked. Are back-up tapes delivered to storage on holidays? What security measures are in force during transit?
6 Older files are examined to make sure that data can still be read on them.
7 Tape reel labels are sampled to be sure that they correctly identify data on the tape.
8 The method by which tapes are arranged in storage is studied. Is the method efficient? Can a specific tape be quickly located?
9 Procedures for requesting a tape in storage are reviewed. Who has authority to access tape?
10 Responsibility for the off-site facility is evaluated. Who is accountable? What supervisory structure is in existence?

Figure 9.11 *Auditing off-site storage*

maintenance of logs and other control documents, and computer time to collect and process audit data that may be available only in electronic form. It also reflects management's increasing commitment to the establishment and maintenance of quality control systems.

The frequency of audits is another cost factor. Although there is no rule of thumb regarding frequency, regularly scheduled audits and surprise audits are indeed the norm, and they may be called for when problems arise that require thorough, objective analysis. Also, the cost of disruption must be considered when users and overburdened technicians are interrupted from their usual tasks to participate in interviews and to provide audit assistance.

In spite of these costs, many executives would not consider managing a firm without audits. As the primary benefits that their corporations derive, they cite reduced operational errors and omissions, reduced criminal loss/exposure, better control over inefficiency and overruns, and increased user confidence and satisfaction.

Summing up

Performance objectives are set by corporate management. To make sure that an information systems department meets performance objectives, periodic

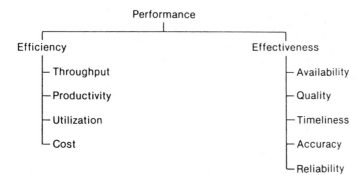

Figure 9.12 *Components of performance*

evaluations should be scheduled; they should also be triggered when problems arise.

Evaluation begins by identifying what is to be evaluated and setting evaluation criteria. The number and nature of evaluation criteria will vary from firm to firm and depend on managerial preference and processing maturity. In most organizations, both efficiency of operations and systems effectiveness are evaluated. Figure 9.12 lists common evaluation criteria in each of these two categories.

An information systems department can run efficiently, yet still be ineffective, and vice versa. For example, the process of generating information may cost little and optimize resource use, yet deliver output that fails to meet user needs. On the other hand, the department may provide quality information that improves the productivity of employees throughout the organization, yet take so much computer time to generate this information that the cost of the output is more than its value. The difference between efficiency and effectiveness as performance measures is illustrated in Figure 9.13.

Once performance criteria have been established, performance data in these areas are collected. The data are gathered primarily by logs, user questionnaires or interviews, and hardware and software monitors. It is the responsibility of the evaluator to study performance data in order to identify performance weaknesses and to report these weaknesses to management. The evaluator should also propose recommendations to improve the information function in accordance with processing objectives. Recommendations should also be solicited by management from users and IT personnel. Which recommendations are adopted is a management decision. The implementaiton of accepted recommendations also rests with management.

The evaluation process should itself be evaluated. A report listing problems and mistakes as well as successful strategies of evaluation will be useful when the evaluation cycle is repeated. The evaluation process should be periodically scheduled and should also be initiated when major performance problems arise.

Evaluation, as described in this chapter, is one level of performance control.

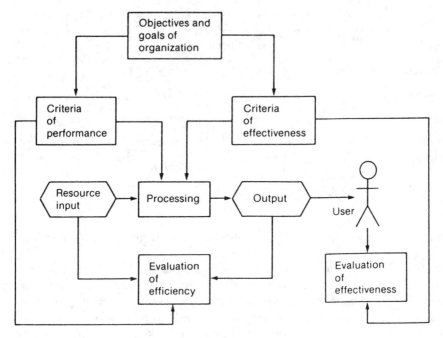

Figure 9.13 *Efficiency and effectiveness evaluation*

A second level of control is provided by an internal auditor, who periodically reviews processing and the effectiveness of designed controls. To bring a measure of objectivity to the audit and to ensure the auditor's independence, the auditor should not be a member of the computer staff. Instead, it is recommended that the internal auditor report directly to a corporation executive, such as the vice president of finance, whose authority parallels that of the vice president to whom the computer centre director reports. An external auditor hired from outside the organization can provide a third level of control.

Auditors examine both micro and macro controls. They review and control components of the systems, such as administrative procedures regarding input and output, and applications controls, such as audit trails. (These are micro controls.) Auditors also evaluate the system as a whole, looking into contingency and disaster planning and separation of duties (macro controls).

A computer centre can be characterized as a 'high payoff' audit area because of the concentration of records and activities to be audited. Furthermore, computer centres have a record of poor control, with many past operational and developmental disasters. It is in a manager's interest to see that audits take place, if only for self-protection, because responsibility for systems security and error-free computing is ultimately management's.

Auditors of computerized information systems need more than accounting skills and auditing experience. They must be knowledgeable about computer systems, especially the implementation of databases, documentation, data security and recovery. In addition, programming skills are needed, not only to check the decision rules incorporated in a program but also because computer programs are used in the audits themselves. (COBOL is the language most commonly employed in business programs and audits.) Audit programs can control calculations, comparisons, and verifications; perform intermediary operations, such as sampling and extractions; and also perform the functions of monitors, collecting data on operations.

Unfortunately, auditing techniques have failed to keep pace with advances in computer technology. Computer input, for example, is the source of many inadvertent errors and the point where theft and fraud are often attempted. In order to design input control strategies, computer scientists have spent many years analyzing the source and nature of errors and intrusions during input. Today, however, chips to receive voice input are being developed that will require controls quite different from those used for card or terminal input. In all probability, by the time adequate controls for the chips have been designed and implemented, the technology will have changed once again. This lag is one of the major problems facing the computer industry and auditors today.

Case study: System to warn of runway incursions

Norden Systems, Inc., is developing an information system called RIM (Runway Incursion Management) to help controllers manage the movement of aircraft and vehicles at airports. RIM analyzes data from ASDE-3, a high-resolution ground-mapping radar system that gives controllers a traffic picture of runways and taxiways, then predicts and gives aural and visual warnings of possible conflicts. For example, the system warns controllers when aircraft are moving toward a hazard. In addition, algorithms have been developed to detect:

- Two aircraft on the same runway.
- Planes crossing runways, landing, or taking off on an intersecting path that could lead to collision.
- An aircraft taking off on an inactive runway or in the wrong direction.

Source: Bruce D. Nordwall, 'Norden develops system to warn controllers of runway incursions', *Aviation Week and Space Technology*, vol. 30, no. 22 (29 May 1989), p. 28.

Questions

1 You are responsible for the control tower of a major international airport that has installed ASDE-3 and RIM.
   (a) Would you evaluate whether the dollar resources allocated to RIM are worth the benefits of the system? If so, how?
   (b) Would you evaluate the efficiency and effectiveness of RIM? If so, how?
   (c) Would you evaluate the impact of this information system on the availability and utilization of control tower computers? If so, how?
   (d) Would you evaluate the productivity of

controllers who use the information provided by RIM? If so, how?

2 How would you decide what performance variables of RIM to evaluate on a regular basis?

3 How often would you evaluate the performance of RIM? Control tower operations? Explain.

Case study: Cautionary tales of performance failure

Stories about information system failures abound. Here are some examples.

■ A New Zealand schoolboy slipped the cardboard from a lollipop packet in a deposit envelope, inserted the envelope into a United Building Society ATM, and punched a $1 million deposit which was credited to his account.

■ British hackers allegedly erased traffic violations from the records of people willing to pay £100 per erasure at the Driver and Vehicle Licensing Centre in Swansea, South Wales.

■ The Flight Processing System at the National Air Traffic Services' Oceanic Centre at Prestwick, Scotland, a system to control the bulk of trans-Atlantic flights, 'crashed' nine times during the early months of 1987. In one instance, controllers were forced to call nearby air traffic control centres by telephone to find out which aircraft were still supposedly under their control.

■ NASA observation satellites used during the 1970s and 1980s rejected the ozone readings they were registering at the time as spurious because they were so low. The deviations from established, normal levels were so extreme that the readings were discounted. When British scientists, using ground-based instruments, reported a decline in ozone levels, NASA reprocessed its data and confirmed the British findings.

■ In a simulated flight, an F-16 fighter using an inertial guidance system became inverted whenever the plane crossed the equator.

■ A man undergoing microwave arthritis therapy was killed when the therapy programmed his pacemaker.

Source: Tom Forrester and Perry Morrison, *Computer Ethics*, Cambridge, Mass.: The MIT Press, 1990, p. 190.

Questions

1 You are responsible for evaluating each of the above information systems. For each system, assume that this is a routine evaluation taking place four months after development, testing and implementation. In addition, no system breakdowns have yet occurred.
   (a) What performance variables would you evaluate for each system? Why?
   (b) How would you gather data for evaluation?
   (c) Who would you include in the evaluation team? Explain the reasons for your choice.

2 Now let us assume the above breakdowns occur soon after this routine evaluation in which no major problems were identified.
   (a) Is the evaluation team responsible for these breakdowns? How could these breakdowns happen if the systems had been tested following development? If the systems were operating satisfactorily until the breakdown?
   (b) What areas of performance failed in each of the above examples? Could these breakdowns have been prevented if the evaluation process had been more thorough? How?

3 How can nine system failures at Prestwick over

a period of a few months be explained? What types of problems do these breakdowns suggest? How might the director of the air traffic centre correct these problems?

4 How could an evaluation of the evaluation process following each of these breakdowns help prevent similar breakdowns in the future?

Case study: **High-performance computing in Australia**

Data centres in Australia have earned a reputation for high-performance computing. It is not uncommon for a company to modify its software to squeeze out extra performance, as did Westpac, a Sydney bank, which took apart and rebuilt its IBM MVS operating system and TSO teleprocessing software, resulting in 50 per cent more performance than IBM thought possible.

This do-it-yourself approach seems to be the key to productivity at Australian information centres, in part an operational practicality because of the country's remote location and small population. The cost of importing new machines is high and consultants and technical support centres are limited. A telephone call for help abroad is unlikely to solve a mysterious system crash without a long delay because of time zone differences.

As a result, Australians have developed a high degree of self-sufficiency. Impetus for fine-tuning systems can also be attributed to limited budgets, exchange rate variations, transport charges and import duties which make it impractical to replace old systems.

Source: Tony Healy, 'Impressive performance', *Datamation,* vol. 35, no. 19 (1 October 1989), pp. 72.9–72.10.

Questions

1 What factors contribute to Australia's aggressive attitude to improving standard systems? Does this attitude exist in your country? If so, why? If not why not?

2 Why does a do-it-yourself approach help boost productivity? What are the limitations of this approach?

3 A survey of 221 IBM large-systems users found that Australian computer sites worry less about operating system complexity than users elsewhere. 'That shows Australians are not scared of the complexities, that they know their way around the operating system', says Alan Hansell, a Sydney-based industry specialist. Does this survey result help explain the high performance of Australian systems?

4 The above survey also found that Australians give more attention to information systems planning than elsewhere. Why do you suppose this is true? How does planning relate to high performance?

5 Is Australia's experience in information system productivity transferable to other countries? If yes, how? If not, why not?

Key words

Accumulating monitor	Auditing around the computer	Computer performance evaluation
Accuracy	Auditor	Cost
Audits through the computer	Availability	Effectiveness

Efficiency	Productivity	Throughput
Event-driven monitor	Quality	Time-driven monitor
External auditor	Reliability	Timeliness
Hardware monitor	Resource utilization	Turnaround time
Internal auditor	Response time	User survey
Log	Schedule adherence	Utilization
Logical monitor	Software monitor	
Mini-company	Software reliability	
approach	Systems reliability	

Discussion questions

1. What is necessary to initiate a program of performance evaluation for an information systems department?
2. Comment on the following statement: Mathematical formulas and models are not useful when evaluating performance in a computer centre.
3. Performance appraisal of a computing activity is highly subjective. It should be conducted by a psychologist or sociologist rather than a computer scientist. Comment.
4. How is the performance evaluation of computing in a bank different from a similar evaluation in:
   (a) A manufacturing business?
   (b) A wholesale firm having a large warehouse?
   (c) A large office?
5. What is a monitor? What are the functions of monitors?
6. How can an information system's components, such as hardware, software and procedures, be evaluated separately? Is such evaluation desirable?
7. When should evaluation take place? Who should be responsible?
8. What is the difference between the efficiency and effectiveness of an information system? How can they be evaluated?
9. What are the steps in the evaluation process?
10. Describe four common efficiency criteria.
11. What is the difference between the following effectiveness measures?
    (a) Availability and timeliness.
    (b) Quality and accuracy.
    (c) Completeness and correctness.
12. Can a conflict exist between performance criteria? Explain.
13. What is the difference between hardware and software monitors?
14. Comment on the statement: Operational efficiency should be given priority over systems effectiveness.
15. Should computer operations be audited? If so, at what level or levels?

16. Consider a manufacturing plant with 1,200 employees and a computer system employing 30 people that processes 15 main applications.
    (a) What level or levels should be audited?
    (b) Would you recommend an internal auditor, an external auditor, or both?
    (c) Would you also recommend internal control by the computer centre itself?
17. When is an external auditor advisable?
18. In what ways do internal auditors, external auditors, and control personnel within a computing centre complement or overlap one another?
19. What are the differences between auditing a computer application and a non-computer application?
20. How can an auditor help prevent:
    (a) Input errors?
    (b) Design errors?
    (c) Computer fraud through unauthorized modification of a program?
    (d) Theft of computer time?
    (e) Theft of a data tape?
    (f) Unauthorized access to a database through a terminal?
    (g) Theft of manuals?
    (h) Dishonest computer operation?
    (i) Dishonest management?
21. How can an auditor help a firm recover from natural disasters or fire?
22. Do computers make internal controls easier or more difficult? How?
23. Do computers aid auditors or make their jobs more difficult? How?
24. How does one compensate for the fact that an audit trail is not available in a computer system?
25. How could audit requirements be incorporated in the design of an accounting-oriented information subsystem?
26. How can an auditor defeat collusion among computer centre staff? What types of clues might there be to such collusion?
27. Is it possible to overaudit? How could one detect an overaudit and prevent it from happening again?

Exercises

1. Two programmers, A and B, have each completed programs of equal complexity. Statistics on their performance are:

	A	B
Lines of code	3,200	2,800
Number of output reports	5	4

Time taken (units of time)	6	5
Language used	PASCAL	FORTRAN
Response time	12	13

If you were manager, how would you evaluate each programmer on a scale of 1 to 5 (1 is lowest)? Explain the reasons for your evaluation.

2. Two CPUs are being operated in your shop. Which has a better performance, X or Y? Explain.

	X	Y
Cache memory	256K	512K
CPU cycle time	0.3 microseconds	0.2 microseconds
CPU memory	8 megabytes	10 megabytes
I/O channels	8	12
I/O channels at 3 megabytes	2	1
Manufacturer	A	B

Bibliography

Davis, Arthur G. 'Moving towards high quality and productivity', *Manufacturing Systems*, vol. 8, no. 3 (March 1990), pp. 54, 56.

Diebold, John. 'How computers and communications are boosting productivity: an analysis', *Siemens Review*, vol. 56, no. 1 (January/February 1989), pp. 4–9.

Duncan, Doris and Karl Chester. 'Productivity metrics for information technology', *Managing Information Resources in the 1990s*, Proceedings of the 1990 Information Resources Management Association International Conference. Harrisburg, Pa.: Idea Group Publishing (1990), pp. 38–43.

Flaherty, David F. *Protecting Privacy in Surveillance Societies: The Federal Republic of Germany, Sweden, France, Canada, and the United States*. Chapel Hill, NC: The University of North Carolina Press, 1989.

Gould, J.D., S.V. Boies, and Clayton Lewis. 'Enhancing computer applications', *Communications of the ACM*, vol. 34, no. 1 (January 1991), pp. 75–85.

Hinnant, D. 'Performance measures', *UNIX Review*, vol. 8, no. 12 (December 1990), pp. 34–40.

Kolodziej, S. 'Performance management and optimization: getting the most from what you got', *Computerworld*, vol. 24 (8 October 1990), pp. 80–8.

Kumar, Kuldeep. 'Post implementation evaluation of computer-based information systems: current practices', *Communications of the ACM*, vol. 33, no. 2 (February 1990), pp. 203–13.

Martin, Merle P. and William L. Fuerst. 'Effect of computer knowledge on user performance over time', *Information and Software Technology*, vol. 30, no. 9 (November 1988), pp. 561–7.

Perry, William E. 'Two (of many) problems in EDP auditing', *Journal of Accounting and EDP*, vol. 6 (Spring 1990), pp. 50–3.

Weill, Peter and Margrethe H. Olson. 'Managing investment in information technology: mini case examples and implications', *MIS Quarterly*, vol. 13, no. 1 (March 1989), pp. 3–18.

PART THREE
Management of processing

Part Three concerns the management of computer resources in daily operations. It focuses on the day-to-day responsibilities of a computer centre director and suggests ways to prepare employees in a firm for changes that occur when the role of computers is expanded.

Chapter 10 describes the flow of a job through computer processing, from scheduling to output control and distribution. When output proves unsatisfactory, systems modification may be required, a process also examined in the chapter. Chapter 11 introduces budgetary approaches, examining elements and cost trends in computing budgets and alternative revenue schemes. This chapter also suggests methods of controlling budgets so that discrepancies between budgeted and actual expenditures are minimized.

The need for standards in computing is examined in Chapter 12 and the role of a standards committee in setting standards is examined. In addition, industry, national, regional, and international sources of standards are described.

The last chapter in this part, Chapter 13, deals with managing resistance to change. In this case, change means the introduction of new computerized systems in a given firm. Strategies to foster positive employee attitudes toward computers are suggested.

10 Processing and systems maintenance

Leave room in the system for the feedback of experience to redesign the system itself.
Max Ways

If an applications package is purchased or custom-developed for a microcomputer system, the user will store the program until it is needed, then load it into a micro for use. IT staff will typically have no responsibility for processing the application unless the user asks for assistance because the program fails to work or the microcomputer itself breaks down. However, the processing of software purchased or developed in-house for large computer systems falls under the jurisdiction of the IS department. Computer operators will be on duty at the time the job is run to oversee processing, perform manual operating tasks (such as loading peripherals), and troubleshoot if a processing malfunction occurs. Throughout processing, controls ensure the efficiency and effectiveness of processing and protect the security of computing resources.

Once the user is satisfied with output, the processing responsibility of the computer department ends. But should output fail to meet user needs or departmental standards, corrections will have to be made. Often, operational personnel can identify the cause of errors, make the necessary adjustments and schedule a rerun. (Perhaps a peripheral device had an incorrect setting or the wrong output paper was used.) Sometimes, however, operators do not know how to correct the problem, or they lack the authorization to make necessary changes. In such cases, the job is sent to the group or department responsible for systems maintenance.

The first half of this chapter is on processing, the steps of which are shown in Figure 10.1. Topics discussed are scheduling, job run, output control and distribution, and production controls. Then the chapter addresses the issue of unsatisfactory output. Is hardware or software at fault? Does the system need modification or extensive redevelopment? Maintenance in both small and large systems environments will be considered.

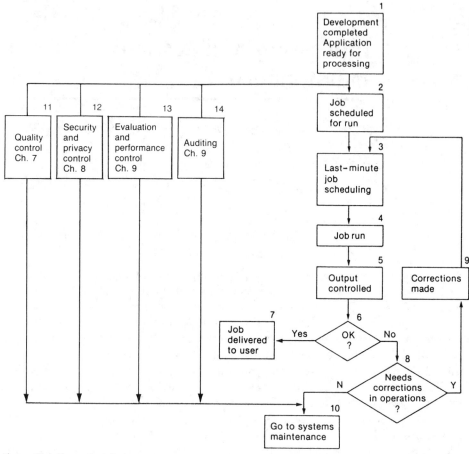

Figure 10.1 *Flow of a job through operations*

Processing

Scheduling (Boxes 2 and 3)

Ideally, there should be no constraints on processing. Run time should be available whenever needed. In practice, however, processing conflicts invariably arise in multiuser computer systems. (This explains in part, the appeal of microcomputers.) Demand Curve A in Figure 10.2, typical when a computer is a shared resource, shows that capacity is exceeded at certain hours of the day. In such situations, jobs must be staggered to equalize the workload, to flatten Curve A to Curve B. (Curve C, with demand consistently higher than capacity, shows bad forecasting and poor capacity planning.)

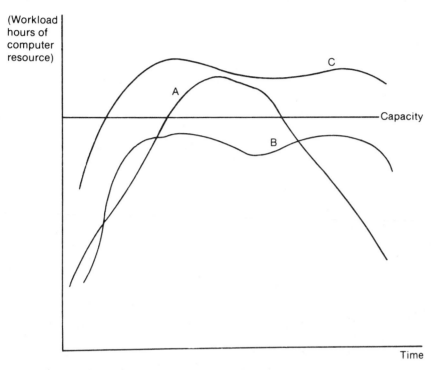

Figure 10.2 *Different patterns of processing demand*

Online real-time uses are controlled by internal computer scheduling mechanisms, while multiuser batch processing is regulated by a **master schedule**. Most firms form a **user committee** to establish scheduling procedures, guidelines and priorities, although the actual scheduling will be delegated to someone in operations, such as a **schedule officer** or production manager.

Scheduling is not as easy as it may seem. Problems generally arise because of limited resources. Some computers are peripheral-bound, with the speed of processing restrained by an input reader, printer, or other peripheral, causing jobs to backlog. Processing demand is often unpredictable, with unexpected peaks of demand. The availability of resources can be difficult to forecast as well. For example, delivery of new equipment may fall behind schedule, or a breakdown may wreak havoc with the master schedule. When users are competing for computer time, tensions can build and tempers flare.

A master schedule includes batch jobs that are processed on a regular basis. Because the volume of input for such a job and the length of time required for processing are generally known, as is the time that the job will be submitted for processing, the job can be scheduled well in advance. For example, if payroll is regularly received by operations at 12 noon the last working day of the month,

Table 10.1 *Data on four jobs competing for priority scheduling*

Job	Processing time required (units of time)	Arrival	Due date Target	Due date Deadline	Priority class (1 = urgent)
A	3	09.00	Monday	Tuesday	1
B	5	09.15	Monday	Monday	1
C	1	09.10	Tuesday	Thursday	4
D	4	09.20	Wednesday	Friday	3

payroll processing can be blocked on the master schedule weeks, even months, ahead.

Not all batch jobs processed on a regular basis need to be as rigidly scheduled as payroll. Many weekly or monthly reports can be placed on the master schedule wherever there are open time blocks, as long as they are scheduled within a given time period (for instance, within the last week of the month). Other blocks of time can be allocated to regular users on the master schedule. Secretaries may be given one hour of processing time mornings and afternoons, for instance, and programmers assigned two hours daily.

Many jobs received by a computer centre, however, cannot be planned in advance, so day-to-day scheduling within the master schedule framework is also needed. Perhaps the need for a special report arises during a bargaining session with union representatives; perhaps last-minute information is required to complete a sales bid; perhaps a programmer needs extra run time to meet a deadline. Maybe a user has forgotten to request computer time in advance; maybe the master schedule has been thrown out of kilter because a job scheduled months ahead is not ready for processing. A crisis atmosphere always seems to pervade computer centres when it comes to scheduling.

To illustrate the dilemma of a schedule officer, let us consider the problem of deciding how to schedule the four jobs listed in Table 10.1. One **scheduling algorithm** is *first come, first served*, also called first in, first out (FIFO), an algorthim used in inventory control. Another option is *least processing time first*. This is a very common decision rule when the amount of processing time required for some jobs is much less than for others. The rationale behind this algorithm is that users demanding only a second or fraction of a second of scarce processing time should be given priority over a single user wanting to 'hog' the computer.

Yet another scheduling possibility is to give priority to the job that has the *least slack time* between target date and deadline. Sometimes the job with the *earliest target date* (or *earliest deadline date*) is processed first. Using still another decision rule, scheduling can be based on urgency. Each job is assigned a numerical rating according to its urgency as assessed by the user, a rating that is reviewed by the

Table 10.2 *Criteria used for scheduling jobs in Table 10.1*

First come, first served	Least processing time first	Least slack time first	Earliest target date first	Earliest deadline date first	Highest- priority classification first
A	C	B	A or B	B	A or B
C	A	A		A	
B	D	C or D	C	C	D
D	B		D	D	C

schedule officer or user committee. According to the priority rule, jobs classified as 1 in Table 10.1 would be run before the jobs with a 2 rating, 2s would be run before jobs with a 3 classification, and so on.

In Table 10.2, priorities are assigned to each of the jobs listed in Table 10.1, using a variety of decision rules. Note that processing order is not always clear-cut, since some of the decision rules result in ties. In such cases, more than one rule has to be applied.

Table 10.2 lists only four jobs competing for processing time. In reality, scheduling is far more complex. Hundreds of jobs need to be scheduled per day in large computer centres, and scheduling algorithm possibilities are not limited to the six used in the table. Jobs might be processed on a round-robin basis. Priority might be based on length of wait, elapsed time from request to deadline, processing cost, status of user, length of advance notice to computer centre, or any number of factors.

Scheduling algorithms can be categorized as either *user oriented* or *computer centre oriented*: some stress service while others minimize cost or optimize use of computing resources. In most computer centres, the user committee weighs the value and effectiveness of possible algorithms, decides what performance criteria are important to the computer centre, and ranks the relative importance of selected criteria. (Table 10.3 lists performance criteria that are commonly used to evaluate scheduling algorithms.)

Once the priority rules are established, software internal to the operating system of the computer can help with the scheduling, or software packages can be purchased so that scheduling can take place automatically within parameters defined by the committee. Such software can be overridden manually, enabling an operator to interrupt and change priorities when special circumstances arise. Although guidelines for scheduling are the responsibility of the user committee, authority is generally delegated to the schedule officer to make on-the-spot decisions when conflicts or problems arise.

Users should be informed of the decision rules on which scheduling is based and have access to processing schedules. Since the master schedule is prepared

Table 10.3 *Performance criteria used in scheduling*

Category	Criteria
User oriented	Minimum mean job lateness (completion time minus due time). Minimum mean job throughtime (job completion time minus job arrival time). Maximum mean earliness (amount of time job completed before deadline).
Computer centre oriented	Maximum mean throughput (number of jobs processed in a fixed time period). Minimum number of jobs waiting to be processed. Maximum percentage of resource utilization. Minimum total processing cost.

Source: Howard Schaeffer, *Data Center Operations* (Englewood Cliffs, N.J: Prentice Hall, 1989), pp. 238–9.

weeks or months in advance, it can be distributed in hard copy. The updated daily schedule should be available on a need-to-know basis at a conveniently located console or terminal, so that users can keep track of the status of their jobs. Many systems provide enhancements to this status output. For example, users may be able to interrogate the system for processing information, such as estimated time a given job run will start or reasons why a job is being delayed.

Job run (4)

Once scheduled, a job is run. Assuming that the operator's manual (written as part of systems documentation) is complete, that the operations staff is well trained, and that hardware and software are well maintained, the **job run** should be problem free. Before processing begins, pertinent data and relevant programs are assembled, and the computer and needed peripherals are assigned to the job. Job control (operational parameters) can be automated, manual, or a combination of the two, depending on the sophistication of the computer centre. The sequence of run activities is illustrated in Figure 10.3.

Most systems require operators to fill out a number of forms when jobs are run. Some are checklists describing what steps to take, how and when. Others are control forms used to log operations and collect processing data. Table 10.4 is a list of common processing forms. Run information that is collected on the forms is later used by performance evaluators and auditors and may be referenced by analysts when seeking the solution to processing problems.

The list in Table 10.4 is not all-inclusive. Many firms have supplemental forms to collect processing data for unique needs. Unfortunately, forms tend to proliferate. Management should recognize the cost involved in designing and

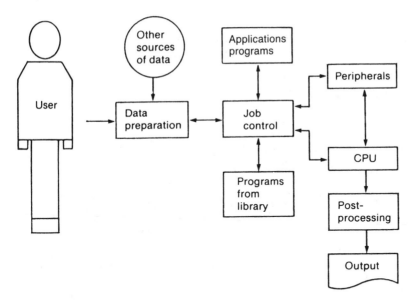

Figure 10.3 *Job run sequence*

implementing forms and in training personnel in their use. Storage of information and forms is also expensive. The need for new forms should be carefully reviewed by management, form design should be assigned to professionals, and strict control should be exercised by evaluators and auditors over each form used. Consolidation and elimination of forms without a loss of processing efficiency and effectiveness should be the goal.

In addition to forms, processing reports assist in control of operations. Some can be generated by the operating system. Others are prepared by IT staff. These should include information on scheduling, work flow, job execution, downtime,

Table 10.4 *Forms used in processing*

Batch ticket	Output distribution log
Computer problem log	Problem statement log
Data conversion instructions	Production control log
Data preparation instructions	Program maintenance instructions
Data validation instructions	Request form for computing services
Distribution control sheet	Routing tickets
Input data log sheet	Shift turnover log sheet
Job control instructions	Software problem report
Job monitoring log	Storage maintenance instructions
Job scheduling instructions	Usage log sheet
Job setup sheet	

resource utilization, and the status of workstations. Like forms, reports have a tendency to multiply. They should be subject to the same stringent standards as forms, so that only needed information is processed.

Output control and distribution (5 and 7)

In the batch mode, **output control** following a job run consists of checking to see that output specifications formulated during development and listed in systems documentation are met. Some controls, such as accuracy or completeness validation, can be exercised by software. The scrutiny of operators is also invaluable because their eyes can readily spot many errors, such as wrong format or size of a report, incorrect number of copies, or faulty packaging.

An example of a costly error that could have been avoided by an attentive operator was the mailing of 14,000 duplicate grade reports to a single individual, Mr L.C. Abel, the first name on a list of students at a university. A programming error caused the output to be a repetition of Mr Abel's grade report instead of a report for each of the 14,000 students on the list. A simple glance at the output by an operator or control clerk would have caught the mistake and saved the university embarrassment and the expense of materials, labour and postage for the mailing. Numerous anecdotes of a similar nature surface in computer literature. Humorous to the reader but not to those involved, these anecdotes demonstrate the importance of output control in batch processing. Many computer centres give an internal control clerk the responsibility of checking all output.

Output distribution is an additional responsibility of IT personnel in batch systems. Delay in a user's receipt of a run can often be traced to inefficient distribution procedures rather than to an overloaded computer. Since privacy of output is valued as highly as timeliness by many users, both security of output and speed should be priorities in delivery systems.

Online output is not reviewed by IT personnel, since processed results are delivered directly to the user. Although software will monitor and control processing to some extent, checking to ensure that output satisfies run specifications is the responsibility of the user.

Production control

In batch processing, a **production manager** supervises and controls processing activities from scheduling through output distribution to a satisfied customer. The manager also oversees most phases of online processing, though the user will control online input and output.

The following fall under the production manager's jurisdiction:

- Input/output (batch).
- Processing.

- Data.
- Privacy.
- Security.
- Costs.
- Documentation.
- Library.
- Supplies.

Table 10.5 *Responsibilities of a computer librarian*

Safekeep resources (data, programs and documentation) and backup
Ensure resources are updated
Control access to resources to authorized personnel
Maintain resources in usable condition
Record errors and malfunctions experienced by users of library resources
Charge, discharge and log resource use
Keep statistics on library uses

Library

A computer centre **library** is the repository of data, programs and documentation. Although security measures are the responsibility of management, a librarian must enforce these measures so that stored materials are protected, and must control access to the resources to bona fide users only.

One of the librarian's primary duties is guarding resources from fraudulent use. Badges, logging and checkout systems can be used to keep resources from the hands of unauthorized users. A need-to-know policy might restrict individuals to certain resources. For example, an analyst might be permitted to withdraw documentation and programs, but not the operator's manual. In theory, the analyst would then lack the operational know-how to run equipment, which would prevent illicit processing. Restrictive policies may not be practical in small organizations where a single employee wears many hats; but in large firms, a need-to-know policy is a useful control.

Table 10.5 summarizes the control responsibilities of a computer librarian.

Supplies

Control of supplies in a computer centre is similar to inventory control of supplies in other departments. The computer, however, can resolve shortages of printed header forms if headers are in computer programs and a multifount printer is available for printing needed forms.

Security must be tight for many computer supplies, such as unprinted payroll checks or stock certificates. These must be counted upon receipt, tallied when printed, and a careful log kept of any damaged or destroyed during operations.

Unsatisfactory output (6, 8, and 9)

Thus far in this chapter, we have assumed that output meets specifications. Not all jobs pass output control successfully, however. Many need to be rerun because of hardware failure (central processing unit or peripheral breakdown), software problems (bugs, such as mistakes in programming logic), input errors, operator blunders, inadequate documentation, faulty procedures, or lack of controls. Sometimes the environment can be blamed, such as when electrical power is lost. To trace what is the matter or why output fails to meet specifications is not always easy, particularly when a combination of circumstances is responsible for errors. Also, to isolate the problem, make corrections, then repeat processing can be an expensive proposition, raising the question: should users be assessed the cost of finding problem solutions and charged for reruns?

Charging users the cost of **reprocessing** when they are at fault has advantages. Too often, users are careless in their input preparation and shift the responsibility for finding errors to IT personnel instead of controlling input before a job is submitted for processing. For example, a receptionist in one user department was responsible for data preparation in free moments when the phone was not ringing or clients were not at the desk. The need for job reruns dropped significantly when a charge system for reruns was initiated. To avoid payment, the department hired a trained data entry clerk and took control measures to ensure that input was correct prior to submission.

User responsibility for errors is not always so clear-cut, however. Should users be charged for program errors caused by inadequate user specifications or for errors traced to poor documentation? It would certainly be unfair to charge users for equipment breakdown or operator mistakes.

Since computer centres usually absorb the cost of most reruns, it is in their interest to plan strategies that minimize the need for and cost of reprocessing. Stringent operating controls are advisable. The establishment of procedures for failure diagnosis and failure recovery is useful. For example, careful analysis of rerun trends may help identify causes. One firm found that the rush during peak periods of demand reduced operator efficiency. By scheduling new jobs in off-hours, when personnel had more time for handling and troubleshooting unfamiliar reports, the number of reruns dropped.

Preventive maintenance of equipment is a necessity. When hardware design or hardware manufacture causes a recurring problem, some firms prod the vendor into corrective action by complaining to a person one step higher in the vendor's organizational hierarchy each time the problem arises.

Each firm has a unique environment, so measures taken to ensure satisfactory output will vary from firm to firm. But all firms should make a determined effort to find ways to reduce the need for reruns.

Sometimes, error correction requires the expertise of a computer specialist. Hardware may need repair; perhaps the software requires modification or redevelopment. This chapter closes with a look at the problems of systems maintenance.

Systems maintenance (10)

Hardware breakdown

Although hardware is becoming increasingly reliable, computer systems do malfunction on occasion. To minimize downtime, a corporation has the following options:

1 *Internal service.* A **service department** to maintain hardware can be set up within the company. Some companies even offer repair service to other computer owners outside of their organization. Only organizations with many computers choose this option.
2 *Manufacturer's fixed fee.* A **manufacturer's maintenance agreement** may be signed. For a fixed monthly fee, the manufacturer agrees to repair most equipment malfunctions during specified hours of the day.
3 *Time and materials charges.* Equipment can be serviced by the manufacturer under a time and materials arrangement. That is, a charge will be made for each service call.
4 *Third-party service.* Maintenance can be contracted to a **third party maintenance** firm. This arrangement resembles a manufacturer's maintenance agreement but generally costs 10–25 per cent less. For large customers, spare parts are commonly stocked at the site by third-party providers, which helps speed repairs.
5 *Combining service systems.* A **hybrid maintenance system** is also possible. A maintenance contract may be signed for major problems, but a company may rely on self-maintenance for minor ones. For example, they may stock replacement parts, such as logic boards and keyboards. Some hardware manufacturers provide customers with self-help maintenance manuals and supplement this instruction with a technical answering service.

Much of the growth in the third-party maintenance market can be attributed to this service arrangement's popularity with microcomputer owners. In fact, some PC dealers offer service contracts with third-party companies instead of doing repairs themselves. Individuals who own microcomputers like the fact that many third-party companies pick up machines that are out of order; others will accept defective machines through the mail. A corporation with many microcomputers purchased from different manufacturers may find that only an independent maintenance company can service their whole product line. And only a national service company can easily contract for maintenance when a corporation has microcomputers in offices scattered throughout a wide geographical area. (A typical micro system needs repair once or twice a year, at the minimum. Disk drives and printers cause the most problems.)

Negotiating a maintenance agreement is generally advisable when deciding to acquire a new system. The quality and quantity of maintenance personnel should be a major consideration. Check references. Find out how many different sites are serviced by the company, also the number of service people available. Ask what happens when service is requested during off-hours. Is backup support offered? What is the company's relationship to manufacturers? How about spare parts? Does the maintenance agreement allow relocation of equipment without the vendor's consent? Be sure to examine the contract agreement carefully to determine exactly what is covered. Customers can protect themselves by explicitly spelling out service requirements in maintenance contracts.

Software maintenance

The failure of output to meet user needs may lie with software. In such cases, software maintenance is required. The term *software maintenance* is used to describe any work done on an existing system or program. Many other terms are used in computer literature as synonyms, including program maintenance, systems maintenance, production monitoring and control, systems control, systems tuning and even postimplementation development. What is important, is not the name but the maintenance function. There are four types:

- **Corrective maintenance** occurs when a program is not meeting the requirements in the original specifications: for example, the correction of latent software design errors or program bugs.
- **Adaptive maintenance** means that software is altered to meet changing external requirements: for example, updating in response to changed environmental conditions such as new government regulations.
- **Upgrading** is needed when changes in hardware, software, or protocols — for example, a new operating system — necessitate program modifications.
- **Enhancement** takes place when user specifications themselves change, requiring corresponding changes in programs and systems design.

Maintenance is costly. It is estimated that maintenance work constitutes more than half of the work of the typical IS department, that 50 per cent of information processing budgets are allocated to maintenance, and that more than $30 billion is spent on maintenance annually worldwide. The problem is not always the nature of software but current programming practices and the tools that programmers use. Many experts believe that more effort should be spent during systems development to make software reliable and modifiable. They stress the need for improved modification techniques as well. For example, a methodology is needed that permits code reuse without risk and the separate storage of unique and reusable code so that each can be maintained independently.

Many corporations are replacing software that has 'aged'. One reason is that old software systems are written in languages that are no longer commonly used by today's programmers, such as assembly language. The software may use outdated programming and design practices, factors that complicate maintenance. Programs may have been extensively 'patched', with changes poorly documented, or they may have been increased in size beyond what their structure was originally designed to bear. Few people who worked on the original systems may be available to answer questions or explain how the programs work. One might compare an old system to an old car that becomes increasingly unreliable and costly to maintain with age. Besides, most users (like car owners) want the latest technology. They favour the use of software that takes advantage of streamlined facilities and standard routines. They may even choose to redevelop software before the replacement of old systems can be economically justified.

Maintenance/redevelopment life cycle

Every firm needs a maintenance policy and procedures to identify maintenance problems and their solutions. A committee generally decides when maintenance or redevelopment is needed. In general, maintenance is defined as a change that affects few users and does not require much effort or many resources (not more than two weeks of a programmer's time, for example). Redevelopment, on the other hand, requires a major allocation of resources and personnel.

Figure 10.4 illustrates that the **maintenance/redevelopment life cycle** is similar to that of in-house systems development. First, the need for maintenance or redevelopment is identified. When change is under consideration, users should participate in discussions to ensure that proposed modifications meet their needs and that the final system will be accepted. When analysts are new to the organization and unfamiliar with the software that requires maintenance or redevelopment, the user can often save time for maintenance personnel by explaining how the system works and what problems to expect.

A feasibility assessment should be the next stage of the life cycle, including a cost estimate of the effort required to complete the change. Following management approval of the maintenance/redevelopment project, the job is scheduled and assigned to maintenance personnel. Once changes have been made, the modified software is tested to verify that it performs as expected. When both users and manager approve the test results, documentation must be completed, and the old software is replaced with the modified software.

Even routine maintenance should not skip steps in the development cycle. Too often, stages (such as need specification or testing) are omitted because of time pressures. This can lead to monumental blunders, such as the error mentioned earlier: Mr Abel's receipt of 14,000 duplicate grade reports. This happened because a programmer changed statement numbers when patching a program. Figure 10.5 shows the original statement numbers (to the left of each box) and modified numbers (to the right). Since the 'GO TO 10' statement was unaltered but the

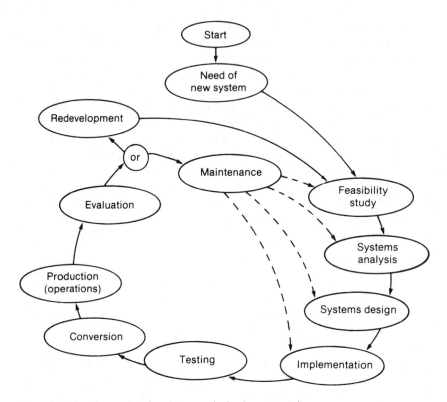

Figure 10.4 *Development and maintenance/redevelopment cycle*

statement numbers had been changed, the program skipped 'Read grade data on next student'. In this case, the maintenance programmer omitted an important step: testing. Output controls also proved inadequate; a supervisor should have caught the error. Mistakes of this nature can be expensive, disruptive, and ruin a firm's credibility.

The control principles outlined in Chapters 7 to 9 apply to software maintenance as well as to systems development and daily operations. The privacy of data needs to be protected, computing resources should be kept secure, and the performance of individuals working on maintenance should be monitored and periodically evaluated to ensure quality work within budgetary constraints.

What triggers software maintenance?
The impetus for software modification may come from a number of factors:

1 *Error in output*. Debugging a program during a new system's development can never reveal the absence of errors, only their presence. Many design errors are not revealed until the program has been in use for some time.

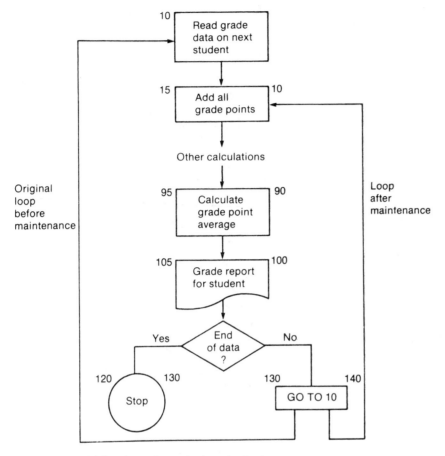

Figure 10.5 *Partial flowchart of a carelessly maintained program*

When a previously working system ceases to function, emergency maintenance is called for.

2 *External environment*. New laws and changed government regulations are two common reasons why systems must be modified. Also, competitors may so alter market conditions that systems redesign must be initiated. When regular changes in the external environment are anticipated, such as revision of tax rates, flexible programs can be written that make modification part of routine maintenance.

3 *User management*. Systems modification is sometimes triggered by a change in management. A different style of decision making may lead to the need for a different threshold of information (level of information detail). Or management may simply learn to use information systems more effectively. An increased awareness of a system's potential often causes

management to place increased demands on the system. Policies of an organization may change, requiring new methods for calculations, such as new depreciation methods. Or frequent errors and inconsistencies resulting from poor systems specification, bad design, or hasty and incomplete testing may become apparent to management when the system is put into operation. User management may also have a wish list of features to be added to the system when finances permit.

4 *IT personnel*. Systems generally require modification when new equipment is acquired. IT personnel will alert management of the need for such modification. For example, more secondary storage would allow a larger database, and increased processing would be feasible. Technological advance in the computer industry is swift-paced. Organizations adopting new technology or merely expanding their systems with more sophisticated computers will find that their information systems need modification.

Once systems are operational, analysts may detect errors resulting from poor design and implementatgion or invalid assumptions, errors that contribute to processing inefficiency or reduce systems effectiveness. Computer personnel, like users, may also have a wish list not included in the original development because the design was frozen or because development resources were lacking at the time. The list might include reorganization of data, new output form design, or even new programming solutions. Generally, these ideas were conceived and documented during development. Once the system is made operational, the suggestions are renewed and re-evaluated.

Software maintenance management

Companies that rely on information technology all need to plan for software maintenance and to manage and control the process. **Maintenance management** entails a number of considerations.

Personnel
In spite of the large share of the information processing budget that is consumed by software maintenance, few companies are making a serious effort to reduce maintenance. It has earned the reputation of a second-class job and is typically delegated to junior programmers and programming trainees, not to the qualified senior-level programmers and analysts whose skills are often needed. Surveys reveal that maintenance work has only one-half to two-thirds of the motivating potential of other programming/analysis work and that the job is regarded as non-creative and non-challenging. Persons assigned to maintenance tasks seldom receive status or professional recognition for their contributions. One indication of this fact is that few companies have even established the job classification of maintenance analyst or maintenance manager. Indeed, of all IT personnel, the

systems maintenance person is most prone to unhappiness and turnover.

A computer director might improve systems maintenance productivity by:

- Hiring persons with a flair for detective work and a preference for systems maintenance over other analysis/programming tasks.
- Enhancing maintenance jobs so that the motivational level and work status are comparable to new systems development.

Since the first suggestion is impractical because of the lack of candidates, let us focus on the second. Five variables (or job dimensions) typically motivate data processing personnel: skill variety, task identity, task significance, autonomy, and feedback from the job. The job of management in organizing systems maintenance is to design the work to enhance as many of these dimensions as possible.

For example, maintenance jobs may be rotated so that individuals work with a variety of software instead of specializing in one system. This will promote skill variety required by the job. Management should reward quality work, perhaps with monetary compensation. A career track should allow for professional advancement. Maintenance analysts and programmers should be challenged to apply new technology to their jobs and to try new maintenance methodologies. Chapter 4, which dealt with IT staffing, discussed still other ways to motivate data processing personnel.

Software maintenance contract

Software maintenance is not always in-house maintenance. A company may enter into a licence agreement for a software product, including maintenance. Key provisions of the contract that will affect cost are:

- User responsibility for escalation of charges.
- Overtime and travelling charge.
- Unsupported services or extras.
- Response time to maintenance requests.
- On- or off-site maintenance.
- Termination rights by user.
- Payment terms.
- User rights to source code.

Chargeback policies

The way in which maintenance costs are assessed and charged to users can be a source of ill feeling. If systems modifications are performed without charge by a computer centre, users may be tempted to demand more maintenance than necessary. Users may also fail to include maintainability in their specifications for custom software or to approve maintenance features in the design of new systems because of their added cost.

On the other hand, a fair assessment of charges is difficult in an integrated system in which more than one user benefits from maintenance. Questions also arise about where the fault lies when maintenance is required: Are maintenance costs because of technical problems the responsibility of users? Is it fair to charge users for program modifications that are needed because the computer centre installs a new operating system or institutes new procedures?

Computer centres vary in their charge structures. (See Chapter 11 for more on this subject.) A decision regarding which structure to adopt is the responsibility of corporate management.

Microcomputer software maintenance

Software for microcomputer users is often purchased as a package. In this context, **microcomputer maintenance** may be little more than showing the user how the system works and providing help when the user is unable to understand terminal messages or generate expected output.

Microcomputer users may also write their own programs. The development of non-procedural languages, such as query languages, report generators, and very high-level programming languages, means that users now have tools that allow them to construct their own systems. Sometimes, users wish to modify packages that they have purchased as well.

To give these users maintenance assistance, many firms have established **information centres** staffed by IT professionals, a subject discussed in Chapter 2. One role of the centre may be to train users in program modification techniques. For example, centre personnel may give courses on a particular fourth-generation language. After teaching how to write software using that language, they might then ask: 'Suppose the conditions of your original problem change?' By doing exercises in rewriting code, users will gain maintenance experience and, in the process, will learn ways to write programs so that they can be more easily maintained.

Maintenance priorities

Usually, a committee composed of the database administrator, an auditor and users' representatives assigns priorities to maintenance requests and reconciles conflicts between user departments, settling jurisdictional problems of maintenance when they arise. Ideally, maintenance priorities should be decided on the basis of benefits—cost and benefits—performance ratios. The availability of personnel is, of course, an important consideration. Since most analysts and programmers prefer systems development, personnel with the skills and interest in maintaining old systems may be in short supply. Some firms base maintenance priority on the worst-first rule, clearly a subjective judgement. Too often, the assignment of priorities is based on corporate politics (for example, preference given to the boss or to the person who shouts the loudest and longest), not on economic or technological grounds.

Table 10.6 *Responsibilities for operations in batch and interactive environments*

Function	Responsibility	
	Batch environment	*Interactive online environment*
Determination of priorities	User committee	User committee
Scheduling algorithm and procedure determination	User committee	User committee
Scheduling jobs	Job scheduling software or production staff	Job scheduling software
Preparing input	User or data entry staff	User of data entry staff
Running jobs	Production staff	Computer (automatic)
Postprocessing	Production staff	User
Check output	User or control staff	User
Output distribution	Production staff	Job dispatch software

Summing up

Processing begins with scheduling and input preparation. Jobs must be run, their output checked and results delivered to users. Responsibility for these operations differs in a batch environment from responsibility in an interactive online environment, as shown in Table 10.6.

When output proves unsatisfactory, the problem must be identified. If it is a minor operational error, the correction can be made by operating personnel and the job rescheduled. When major hardware or software problems arise, maintenance personnel will have to be called in. Equipment may have to be repaired or the software modified or redeveloped. Software maintenance and redevelopment should follow the systems development life cycle illustrated in Figure 10.4.

Control over maintenance activities is exceedingly important, since statistics show that security violations often occur during maintenance procedures. There is also a tendency to cut corners in maintenance work to get to more exciting projects. Control procedures should ensure that one job is completed before the next is begun.

Maintenance is very costly and takes a large share of effort, compared to the effort spent in the initial development of information systems. Managers should recognize the strong correlation between high standards in the original development process and low maintenance. To reduce the need for maintenance, systems developers should plan ahead for equipment and software compatibility, test thoroughly for systems weaknesses and maintain high standards of documentation so that the effort needed for future maintenance is minimized.

One major problem of software maintenance management is finding and retaining personnel with the skill and patience needed to trace errors and weaknesses of programs. Correcting, testing, and documenting changes is often less interesting work, from an analyst's point of view, than attacking a new project. The need for maintenance often results from inadequate documentation, bad design, and unrealistic procedures. Senior programmers and analysts, who should be engaged in maintenance because of their experience and skill, generally shun maintenance duties.

Job enlargement, giving analysts maintenance responsibilities in addition to other duties, is one solution to this problem. Rotation has advantages as well, for a pool of maintenance analysts provides systems backup and brings a variety of approaches and fresh solutions to maintenance problems.

Case study: Videotex health system in Brazil

Since 1987, a videotext-based network, designed to improve communication and interaction among health workers, has been in operation in São Paulo, Brazil. The system is used to report cases of infectious diseases, to transmit laboratory test results, to request supplies, to schedule consultations in referral hospitals, to access statistical health information, and to communicate with senior health officials about technical and administrative issues. The only equipment required is telephone lines and inexpensive MSX-compatible microcomputers rented from the local state telephone company to serve as videotex terminals. The system provides electronic mail service and enables users to transmit collected data to, and consult information in, databases of São Paulo's Secretariat of Health. Non-specialized users can learn to operate the system in only two hours.

Originally a pilot project involving forty health units, the videotex system has now been extended to eighteen divisions of the Secretariat, to regional administrative offices of the city of São Paulo, to fifty-eight primary care facilities, and to hospitals, laboratories and supply units. Expansion in the future is expected in response to user demands. There is general agreement about present and potential benefits of the system. In addition, the system is low cost (terminal rental is about US $15 a month and telephone line charges are reasonable) and users like the ease with which the technology can be mastered.

Source: Ilana Fogelman and Eduardo O.C. Chaves, 'User-friendly videotex', *World Health* (August–September 1989), pp. 14–15.

Questions

1 Did the designers of the São Paulo health system have to consider scheduling issues? Explain.

2 A coordinating team of four people, two physicians and two videotex technicians administer the São Paulo health network. What duties do you think are assigned to them?

3 Give examples of problems that might arise with this health system that would require software maintenance.

4 Suppose this health system is to be expanded. What types of expansion would be classified as maintenance? As redevelopment? Given the simple infrastructure of the health system, will it be necessary to follow the maintenance/redevelopment life cycle? Explain.

Case study: **Survey finds severe maintenance problems**

According to survey results released by the Quality Assurance Institute in 1986, the software maintenance problem within large data centres has yet to be solved. Here are some of the highlights of the survey, which polled thirty-seven Fortune 500 companies.

- In the companies surveyed, maintenance backlogs ranged from two to sixty months. The average was twenty-three months.
- Expenditures for maintenance ranged from 10 per cent to 90 per cent of information processing budgets. The average was 51 per cent.
- Nearly 80 per cent of the respondents had systems with logic that could only be understood by specific individuals. This prevented rotating maintenance responsibility among IT personnel.
- Formal methods for deciding when to rewrite programs existed in less that 15 per cent of the companies surveyed. That older systems conform to the same programming standards as newly developed systems was required in 16 per cent of the firms.

- In all but 5 per cent of the firms surveyed, it was acknowledged that a programmer working on new systems development had a more prestigious position than one assigned to maintenance.

Source: John Gallant, 'Survey finds maintenance problem still escalating', *Computerworld*, vol. 20, no. 4 (27 January 1986), p. 31.

Questions

1 Why do analysts have trouble understanding the logic of a system? What is the solution?

2 Why should a company have formal methods for deciding when to rewrite programs?

3 The survey reveals that programmers working on new systems have a more prestigious position that programmers working on maintenance. Should this difference exist? Does it benefit the firm? Explain.

4 Are you surprised at the results of the survey? Appalled? Explain.

5 What conclusions do you draw from the survey?

Key words

Adaptive maintenance
Corrective maintenance
Enhancement
Hybrid maintenance
    system
Information centres
Job run
Library
Maintenance
    management

Maintenance/
    redevelopment life
    cycle
Manufacturer's
    maintenance
    agreement
Master schedule
Microcomputer
    maintenance
Output control

Output distribution
Production manager
Reprocessing
Schedule officer
Scheduling algorithm
Service department
Third-party
    maintenance
Upgrading
User committee

Discussion questions

1. A computer centre is like a firm: it has to produce a product (information). It needs resources (hardware and software) and raw materials (data) for production. It requires specialized and professional labour. It must price and market its product, and it must control costs. Comment.

2. Why is the scheduling at a computer centre different from scheduling bus routes, police on patrol duty, or jobs on a factory lathe?

3. What are the differences in operations in a batch mode compared with online processing?

4. Why is forecasting of demand and supply of computing resources different from the forecasting done by wholesalers or retailers?

5. How would you organize rerun problem analysis and correction activities?

6. Who should receive control reports on:
   (a) Input?
   (b) Output?
   (c) Library?
   The production officer? Someone independent of the computer centre?

7. Describe the role of a computer librarian.

8. What service options are available to companies in the event of hardware malfunction or breakdown?

9. What is systems maintenance? What is systems redevelopment? How are they related?

10. Give some examples of systems maintenance. In each case, explain how maintenance was triggered.

11. Can decision rules or standards be developed for determining when maintenance must be performed, or will maintenance decisions always be subjective?

12. Who should make a maintenance or redevelopment decision? Should the process be formalized?

13. Why is it difficult to pinpoint the reasons for and costs of maintenance?

14. Why is maintenance:
    (a) Costly?
    (b) Important?
    (c) Difficult?
    (d) Unpopular?

15. Should users be charged for systems maintenance, or should maintenance be part of the overhead of the data processing department? Justify your position.

16. How does maintenance in a microcomputer environment differ from maintenance for mainframes?

17. How long can the life of an information system be extended by modification and redevelopment? How can the cost-effectiveness of these activities be determined?
18. What are the role and the importance of maintenance programmers?

Bibliography

Balakrishnan, Prabha. 'A survey on software needs of user organisations vis-á-vis in-house development', *Dataquest* (India) (June 1991), pp. 21—4.

Bohlin, Ron and Christopher Hoenig. 'Wringing value from old systems', *Datamation*, vol. 35, no. 16 (15 August 1989), pp. 57—60.

Butler, J. 'Salvaging existing systems', *Systems Development*, vol. 10, no. 6 (June 1990), pp. 6—8.

Cox, H. Keith. 'Strategic program maintenance', *Systems Builder*, vol. 3, no. 3 (June—July 1990), pp. 40—3.

Fisher, Sharon. 'Streamlining network memory', *Datamation*, vol. 35, no. 16 (15 August 1989), pp. 55—6.

Gandhi, Parvin. 'Maintenance is not just after sales service', *Dataquest* (India) (June 1991), pp. 111—14.

Moad, J. 'Maintaining the competitive edge', *Datamation*, vol. 36, no. 4 (15 February 1990), pp. 61—72.

Ricketts, John. 'Information systems renovation', in A.M. Jenkins, H.S. Siegle, W. Wojtkowski and W.G. Wojtkowski (eds), *Research Issues in Information Systems — an agenda for the 1990s*. Dubuque, Ia: Wm. C. Brown, 1990, pp. 193—216.

Rombach, H.D. 'Software reuse: a key to the maintenance problem', *Information and Software Technology*, vol. 33, no. 7 (July 1991), pp. 643—742.

Swanson, E. Burton and Cynthia Mathis Beath. 'Departmentalization in software development and maintenance', *Communications of the ACM*, vol. 33, no. 6 (June 1990), pp. 658—67.

Zvegintzov, Nicholas. 'Glue: software that sticks software together', *Software News*, vol. 8, no. 8 (August 1990), pp. 9—11.

11 **Budgeting for computer processing**

More people should learn to tell their dollars where to go instead of asking them where they went.
Roger Babson

This chapter deals with budgeting of recurring and operational expenditures in an information systems (IS) department. Discussed are approaches to budgeting, elements of the IS budget, problems in costing and pricing computer services, and control measures to keep actual computing expenditures in line with budgeted figures.

Approaches to budgeting

Three **approaches to computer budgeting** are possible. The IS head can (1) ask for needed resources, (2) be told the amount to be allocated, or (3) negotiate a budget based on changing demands and priorities from one year to the next.

In the early days of computing, an 'asking budget' was common. Since corporate executives had neither background in computing nor experience managing computer centres, computer departments would present a list of needs, which would then be budgeted if the firm had sufficient monetary resources. This method of funding was not very satisfactory, because it encouraged computer managers to overstate basic requirements while it denied top management the type of budgetary control commonly exercised over other departments within the organization.

The opposite extreme, a 'telling budget', occurs when top management makes all decisions on spending for computer processing. This method may not provide sufficient resources for efficient computing. Should funding be generous, panic spending may result to prevent budget cuts the following year.

Although dialogues may take place between top management and technical personnel when both asking and telling budgets are being formulated, a negotiated budget based on periodic re-evaluation of hardware/software requirements and operational costs is most responsive to IS departmental needs and managerial constraints. This latter method of budget preparation is better able to take into consideration the difficulty of making estimates and projections in the field of computing, and it allows for periodic reassessment of budgets. It also allows for fluctuation in computing expenses and changes in priorities (for example, a large budget one year for acquisitions, the next for development expenditures). A disadvantage is that top management and the IS head must spend a great deal of time and effort in budget preparation. But the time is well spent if it contributes to efficient utilization of information processing resources.

Elements of a budget

Table 11.1, an example of **object class accounting**, lists elements to be found in IS budgets and shows what percentage of the total IS budget is allocated to each element, based on US industry figures. Some of the elements are fixed costs. Others are line items that vary according to load. For instance, if the computer

Table 11.1 *Elements of an EDP budget*

	Category	Costs
40.7%	Technologies ■ Hardware ■ Software ■ Communications	Computer and peripherals (purchase, lease, or rent costs) Overtime charges Maintenance Application systems Operating systems Teleprocessing monitors Packages Equipment (modems, concentrators, voice) Maintenance, insurance, and taxes Line charges
41.3%	Salaries	Wages and overtime Benefits (taxes, insurance, vacations, education, etc.)
10.1%	Overheads	Tapes, list, microfilm Forms, cards, stock paper, binders Office supplies Travel, conventions, and conference costs Printing, postage Utilities Journals Education for personnel Hiring, firing, and moving expenses
7.9%	Outside services	Outside services (time-sharing, consulting contract programming, etc.)

Note: Percentage values are for Fortune 1,000 sites in the United States.
Source: Ralph Carlyle, 'Recovery', *Datamation*, vol. 36, no. 7 (April 1, 1990), pp. 35–9.

is fully saturated during normal hours, extra hours of work will involve overtime pay, a variable cost.

The biggest budget category is personnel, partly because computer personnel are a scarce resource and premium salaries have to be paid to attract and retain experienced staff. This helps explain why IS salary expenditures may be higher than in other departments of the firm. Education may also be a costly IS line item. Many firms sponsor in-house educational programmes to train needed analysts, programmers, data specialists, and operators or give employees subsidies to work towards a degree in outside classes.

When preparing an IS budget, estimating hardware expenditures is sometimes difficult because costs fluctuate from one year to the next. A new model that incorporates new features may be considerably more costly than older models on the market. Or a dramatic drop in price may occur due to competitive pressures and savings resulting from innovative applications of technology. The final price will also depend on the type of financing decision reached (rent, purchase, lease) and negotiations over discounts, trade-ins, lease time, service contracts, and so on. Sometimes, budgeted hardware is not delivered when anticipated, because manufacturers do not release new models when expected or they may fall behind in delivery schedules. In such cases, the expenditure may fall in the next fiscal year instead.

A measure of uncertainty is involved when budgeting for software as well. Software purchased with hardware may not fulfil needs. One firm, for example, spent over £300,000 to develop a FORTRAN and COBOL compiler more appropriate to its command-and-control system than the compiler that was supplied. Whether supplementary packaged software will be available is also uncertain. On the other hand, estimating costs for in-house applications development (the alternative to a package) is an inexact art at best. The time required and corporate resources that will have to be assigned to the project are hard to predict: systems development projects are well known for cost overruns.

Development does not appear as a separate cost item in Table 11.1, because the salaries of programmers, analysts and technicians appear under personnel expenses in object class accounting. Equipment and purchased software used in development are charged to the year that the expenditure was incurred or amortized. One cannot easily ascertain the cost of a project or isolate the expense of project implementation when spending is reported by object of expense.

In **expenditure accounting**, on the other hand, an effort is made to assign a cost to information processing activities. Typically, four main activities are identified:

- Development
- Maintenance
- Production
- Administration.

Table 11.2 shows the percentage of an IS budget that should be spent on each

Table 11.2 *Expenditures by activity, as percentage of total data processing spending*

Activity	Percent of budget	
Development	0–20% ⎫	
Maintenance	10–20 ⎬	1:1
Production	40–60 ⎫	
Administration	5–20 ⎬	1:2½

of these categories, according to some computer specialists. In practice, many companies spend a higher percentage of effort on maintenance than is listed in the table. This often can be attributed, in part, to a few culprit application systems that consume a disproportionate share of maintenance effort and should probably be replaced. (By one rule of thumb, 20 per cent of software generally requires 80 per cent of the maintenance effort.)

Software enhancement in this table is categorized as a development activity, not maintenance. (In Chapter 10, we considered enhancement an integral part of maintenance.) The problem of definitions limits the usefulness of the table. For example, many organizations charge feasibility studies to IS overhead (administration) instead of listing them as an expense of development. The lack of standard definitions for terms such as maintenance and development hampers information exchange and dialogue in the computing field.

Another problem with Table 11.2 is that the activity labels themselves are somewhat misleading. For example, many hidden or indirect costs of project development are not generally included in the development category. These include the cost of data management or statistical packages ostensibly provided free by manufacturers when equipment is acquired but actually included in the rental, lease, or purchase price.

Problems in reporting personnel costs may also lead to inaccurate reporting of development expenditures. In a given project, development effort is not spent in discrete units nor is effort distributed evenly throughout the period of development. Figure 11.1 shows how the need for analysts and programmers changes as development progresses. Of course, this pattern may vary, depending on the nature of a specific project, but the figure does illustrate that it would be incorrect to charge a project for full-time services of analysts or programmers throughout development. Most companies plan so that personnel can work on more than one project simultaneously. They schedule development so that the peak demand for the services of an analyst or programmer in one project coincides with troughs of demand in another. Also, maintenance, documentation and redevelopment tasks can be assigned during periods when the services of programmers and analysts are not needed for development work.

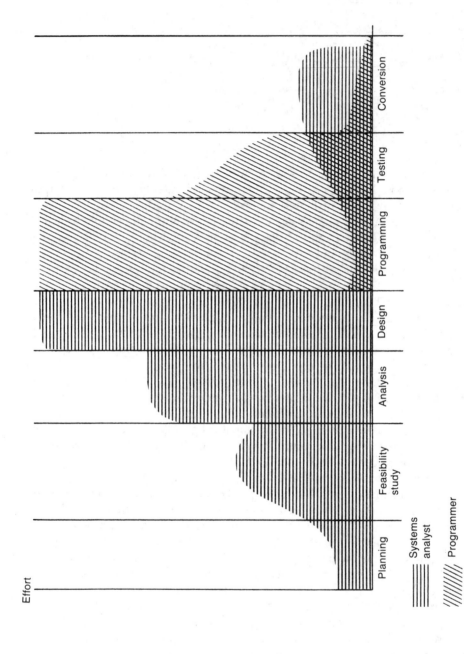

Figure 11.1 *Effort distribution of analyst and programmer during systems development*

Costing and pricing concerns

Cost trends

Although comparing surveys based on diverse industry samples, different methods of off-loading computing costs to the end-user, and different assumptions regarding cost categories, is difficult, **cost trends** for components of IS budgets are, nevertheless, apparent. Unit costs of mainframe computers are dropping. But total equipment expenditures in many firms are on the rise, since there is a demand for more powerful central processing units (CPUs) and for more sophisticated peripherals. For example, clients today demand intelligent terminals, and they want colour and graphic capabilities, voice synthesizers, attached printers and connections to retrieval units with access to large databases. The budget category of data communications (local networks, private branch exchanges and other connection schemes) shows strong growth as users move to connect the many stand-alone systems they have installed in recent years.

All the same, the budget slice allocated to hardware is still smaller than formerly, because other cost components are making proportionately greater demands on budgetary resources. Also, the total pie is getting larger every year, which means that the increase in equipment expenditures can be absorbed without requiring a larger slice of the total information budget. (Although growth in information processing spending was erratic in the late 1980s, US IS budgets grew from 4 to 8 per cent yearly despite a recession causing decline or stagnation of many sectors of the economy.)

Personnel costs, the biggest budget category, typically consume 40–50 per cent of a user's total IS budget. With the increased importance of information technology, staff size continues to grow. Exact numbers are hard to come by because many persons formerly employed by the computer centre for data entry, operations and analysis are now on user department payrolls. That is, the growing popularity of distributed data processing has shifted computer specialists to user departments. So it can be misleading to look only at IS departmental budgets to determine IT personnel costs, or, for that matter, other IT costs. Currently the IS budget accounts for only some 50–60 per cent of total IT spending. For example, software development costs may be buried in the budgets of distributed processing nodes and the cost of teleprocessing, software packages, minicomputers, small business systems and educational services may be found in end-user budgets.

Planning an operational budget

The **one-year operating budget** of an IS department should implement strategic and long-range information processing objectives. To make the translation from long-range plans to an annual budget, the IS head must first:

- Review ongoing activities and long-range information processing plans.

- Select projects for the coming year that can be implemented within budgetary constraints and will help fulfil information processing goals.

Then, a one-year data processing operational plan is prepared. This plan should identify the application systems agenda, including ongoing applications, maintenance of existing systems, enhancements and new systems development. Services and support for this applications agenda should be described; that is, plans for disaster preparedness, security, and control should be detailed. Finally, the IS head must outline resource requirements for implementing both applications and services, including hardware, software, staffing, environmental facilities, supplies, administration, outside services (consulting, time-sharing, service bureau), and training.

Actual budget preparation begins when costs are estimated in each resource category for each application project and for each service and support function. Then, estimates similar to those in Table 11.3 are inserted in budget worksheets. (Instead of filling out a paper worksheet, spreadsheet software may be used.) Last year's actual expenditures provide a basis for projecting ongoing costs for the coming year. Past experience, feasibility studies, historical records and reports can help the budgeters estimate new-project expenditures.

Expenditure analysis

Corporate executives, who ultimately approve or reject information processing budgets, want to know whether too many or too few corporate resources are devoted to information technology and whether the money is spent on the right things. Commonly 1 to 7 per cent of total corporate revenues is spent on information processing. Wide variations from this norm exist among industries and even within specific industries. For example, capital-intensive heavy industries and small firms spend less than companies that want to be on the leading edge of technology.

An organization that establishes a database of financial information on the information processing function, including historical data for comparative purposes, can perform an analysis of expenditures with the help of data management systems such as popular spreadsheet programs. For example, using cost figures collected by project or product, by user area, and by activity, the ratio between development and operations might be ascertained. Line cost ratios, such as the relationship of IS administrative costs to total expenses, might also be determined. Financial analysis tools can help senior management develop a model for **expenditure analysis** to fit the unique needs of the corporate environment. Such tools facilitate cost control and help managers make cost projections for the future.

Revenues

Information processing budgets must deal with constraints on **funding**, a very

Table 11.3 Simulation of a budget (£000)

	Fiscal year 1988				Fiscal year 1989				Fiscal year 1990			
	1st Qtr	2nd Qtr	3rd Qtr	4th Qtr	1st Qtr	2nd Qtr	3rd Qtr	4th Qtr	1st Qtr	2nd Qtr	3rd Qtr	4th Qtr
Revenues	£11,617	£13,233	£13,013	£14,211	£14,913	£15,023	£18,397	£15,968	£17,787	£18,470	£16,842	£19,727
Cost of sales	5,095	5,747	5,595	6,355	6,541	6,202	8,306	6,259	7,257	7,314	6,880	8,822
Net revenue	6,522	7,486	7,418	7,856	8,372	8,822	10,091	9,709	10,530	11,156	9,962	10,905
Selling and administrative expenses	2,323	2,647	2,603	2,842	2,983	3,005	3,679	3,194	3,557	3,694	3,368	3,945
Other overhead	1,452	1,654	1,627	1,776	1,864	1,878	2,300	1,996	2,223	2,309	2,105	2,466
Net profit	£ 2,746	£ 3,185	£ 3,188	£ 3,237	£ 3,525	£ 3,939	£ 4,112	£ 4,519	£ 4,749	£ 5,153	£ 4,488	£ 4,494
Percentage of revenues	23.6	24.1	24.5	22.8	23.6	26.2	22.4	28.3	26.7	27.9	26.7	22.8

controversial aspect of computer management. Many firms assign computing costs to overheads and do not charge internal user departments. Others develop formulas so that departments can be charged for computing services. These two approaches will be discussed next.

Overhead accounting
In the early days of computing, potential users were sceptical about the benefits of electronic processing and needed an incentive to switch from traditional manual processing methods to IS. Management in many corporations decided to offer free computer services to user departments to help reduce resistance to the new technology. The expense of computing was charged to overheads. Although users were not required to pay for computer runs, they generally received notification of the financial value of their share of computer time. This often had the salutary effect of reducing wastage of computer resources, because users tried to use the computer efficiently once they were aware of the cost.

The problem with **overhead accounting** was that demand soon outstripped available overhead resources in most organizations. In order to generate income to expand computing facilities, many organizations switched to chargeback systems. Nevertheless, some companies today still retain their IS departments as part of corporate overheads for the following reasons:

- Overhead accounting has organizational and accounting simplicity.
- The overhead system places responsibility for information processing costs in the IS department.
- The IS department should account for its funds in a straightforward manner. Costs should not get buried under other department budgets. This helps restrain ungoverned growth of the information processing function.
- The corporate controller feels that better control over all department expenditures can be exercised under overhead accounting.
- The IS department might experience a sharp drop in requested service from user departments during periods of economic stress. Budgeting stability is important because of the long lead time required for systems development and because budgetary continuity is needed to plan for the acquisition (or enhancement) of hardware/software resources.

Chargeback systems
One of the main advantages of charging user departments for computing services is that users are not likely to consume computing resources on projects that do not demand information processing. Furthermore, they will cooperate with computer personnel in the development of efficient and effective applications in order to minimize processing costs. With competing demands on departmental budgets, efforts will be made to prevent the wasteful use of processing time. Other advantages of a **chargeback system** include:

- Top management receives information on how IS services are used by different departments within the organization.
- All of the expenditures of departments (including IS expenditures) are known. This helps management evaluate the efficiency and capability of departments.
- Economic data are available to help management make a decision whether to centralize or decentralize processing.
- Revenues can be generated to finance growth in the information processing function.

For chargeback systems, the problem is how to establish an equitable rate structure. What happens when a department in need of electronic processing cannot afford to pay for computing services? Should selected users be subsidized? Partial costing is one answer. For example, development costs might be assigned to computer overheads, with users charged only for operational costs. Integrated applications also raise questions. How does one assess individual departments for shared resources? Maintenance poses another dilemma. Some firms assign it to the IS department. Others, to discourage unnecessary maintenance, charge users. What happens when input data are collected by one department for use by others? Practices vary, but many firms compensate the data collector to ensure quality collection and input preparation on schedule.

Few companies have computing-charge formulas that generate profit, although they may seek external jobs to spread overhead costs. It is common for IS departments to bear a portion of computing costs or to draw from the firm's reserve funds when computing costs do not balance revenues. Figure 11.2 is an example of one firm's chargeback structure. Of course, many other schemes are also feasible.

Rates

Rate structures can range from a fixed flat fee per department per month/quarter for computing services to charges based on formulas for milliseconds of computer time, input read, lines printed, units of data stored, or other such services. During the 1970s, users were commonly charged for the CPU cycles they consumed. This proved to be a reasonably equitable form of accounting, since the CPU was the largest cost component in processing departments at that time.

In recent years, the cost characteristics of computing have changed. Improved database management technology now allows users to store vast databases. Computer centres have actually become data storage centres. According to surveys conducted by IBM and other disk manufacturers, data storage requirements in the average processing centre have grown an average of 40 per cent to 60 per cent per year since the mid-1970s. At the same time, network technology has allowed the migration of input/output functions to users at remote locations, and CPUs have been put on the market with increasingly fast processing speeds. These

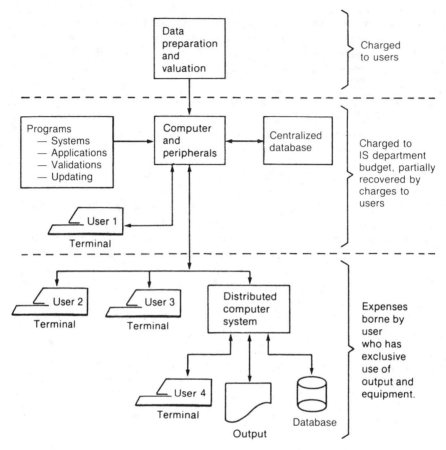

Figure 11.2 *Who pays for what? Sample chargeback structure*

factors have led to the consideration of new rate structures for processing-chargeback systems.

For example, some computer centres total network-associated costs, then divide this figure by the number of terminals using the network, to determine a network subscription fee. For some, rate structures for mainframe processing are based on the type of information processed. 'Survival information' — information required for the long-term operation of a company — being most important, is charged the highest rate. Project information — that which loses its value after a period of time and is, hence, less important — is assessed at a lower rate. Still another rate structure used by some centres is to charge for data storage. The assumption here is that users with large databases consume more computing resources than users with small databases.

When determining rate structures, some firms run simulation programs to see how different rates affect revenues, and they establish highly complex chargeback schemes. Others engage in a long period of trial and error before management is satisfied with pricing. Since firms differ in their equipment configurations, stages of growth, levels of sophistication and intensity of computer use, it is not surprising that rate structures vary widely.

Rate structures can do more than simply provide revenues. They can encourage efficient utilization of resources, for example, by charging low rates for night processing, surcharges for rush jobs. They can also be used to support corporate policy. An example of the latter would be setting teleprocessing charges artificially low to encourage the switch from centralized to decentralized processing.

A major problem in pricing computer services is that there is no market mechanism to help corporate management assess the value of information, no competitive structure to regulate charges. In the manufacture of an automobile, costs must be kept low so models will sell. Information is a product too, but the market doesn't provide cost guidelines such as for manufactured goods. What's more, since computing rate structures may be set to reflect corporate policy, pricing of services can be totally unrealistic from a strictly economic viewpoint.

One control that pressures IS departments to be competitive in service and price is to allow user departments the option of going outside the firm to have their jobs processed by a computer service bureau. This forces the in-house computer centre to root out inefficiency and keep rates low. Many firms also allow processing departments to take on external jobs when they have excess capacity, to sell their services on the open market like a utility. Both practices introduce market mechanisms in rate setting.

A great deal of controversy surrounds rate setting in the field of computing. Philosophical differences exist over such questions as: Should computing be a service or a profit maker? Should computer departments have a monopoly, or should users be allowed to process jobs on the outside? Should rates be set to foster centralization or decentralization? Whatever structure is chosen, it should meet two accounting goals: equitability and simplicity. Procedures for reviewing rates should also be established. A firm's environment will change in time, as will, perhaps, management's viewpoint. The rate structure adopted today may be totally inappropriate in the future.

Control of operational expenditures

Once an IS budget has been formulated, approved, and implemented, it becomes the responsibility of the IS head to keep expenditures within targeted amounts. For **control of expenditures**, the manager needs to receive from staff members periodic financial reports on work in progress. Then expenditures are reviewed and compared to costs that were estimated at the time the budget was drawn up. Figure 11.3 is an example of how costs might be analyzed. In this graph, the absolute values of salaries (budgeted and actual) are plotted; but percentage values or variances might be used instead.

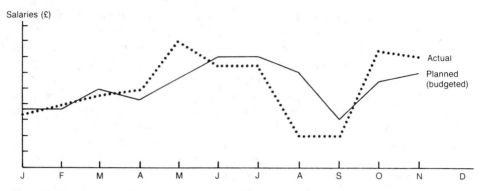

Figure 11.3 *Comparison of budgeted and actual salaries, by month*

After studying the graph, the IS head should try to ascertain reasons why actual expenditures deviate from budgeted amounts. Perhaps a delay from August to October in a planned subsystem explains why expenditures were lower than expected in August and higher than anticipated in October. Perhaps November was a month with high overtime.

Similar graphs might be prepared for other expenditures (for example, teleprocessing or software) or for costs by function (such as data entry or maintenance). Sometimes, reasons for variances can be determined by using control software provided by manufacturers at the time of equipment purchase or programs bought from software houses or developed in-house. Finance and accounting staffs can often help explain reasons for discrepancies. Auditors and consultants can also provide insights.

When variances pinpoint a problem, the IS head must take corrective action. Examples of such actions are file consolidation, simplification of procedures, or the revamping of rate structures to give users incentives to save. To collect and analyze control data and then to plan changes in operations involve a cost in staff time (and possibly computer time) that should be recognized. But most large installations and those that find that planned budgets deviate greatly from actual expenditures justify this expense by the savings generated when problems are identified and measures taken to improve operating efficiency.

Control data should also be used to identify mistakes made in planning the budget. For example, when **feedback data** on budget overruns, in a systems development project, are sent to the development team, the team can analyze whether faulty procedures were used in formulation of the budget or whether incorrect budget assumptions were made. The team can then make recommendations to future development teams that may help avoid a repetition of budgeting errors. This feedback cycle is illustrated in Figure 11.4.

By analyzing overrun data, one firm learned that changes in user specifications during development were the main cause of overruns. Overruns in future projects

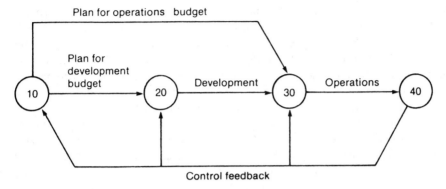

Figure 11.4 *Control feedback for operations budget*

were brought under control by setting a freeze date after which no respecifications were permitted. In another firm, an improved salary structure to attract and retrain competent personnel proved the solution to time overruns attributed to high programmer turnover. In both these examples, the corrective action was a policy decision requiring intervention by top management. But many problems can be resolved by changing the assumptions and priorities of budget planners or by measures that fall within the jurisdiction of computing departments.

Summing up

In general computer budgets are on the rise in spite of the slowdown of growth in the information processing industry as a whole. A noticeable trend is that the hardware and supplies costs as percentages of the budget have dropped, whereas communications, software packages, conferences and training are today costing proportionately more than in the 1980s.

The annual information processing budget will incorporate ongoing activities and new projects that are in keeping with the company's long-range management information systems (MIS) plan. The operations budget can be prepared from monthly financial reports of the past year, with the addition of known or estimated increases such as planned or negotiated salary increases or price escalations in goods or services. Effective budgeting is an iterative activity. The first version of the budget may prove untenable because it is not affordable. Budgets have to be reconciled with financial reality and other resource constraints.

Computing was originally conceived as a service, charged to overhead at no cost to user departments. This helped reduce employee resistance to computer use and fostered centralization of computing resources. Once demand started to outstrip resources and users were willing to pay for services rendered, chargeback structures developed. This has encouraged more efficient use of resources and helped finance the expansion of computing facilities. However, other problems have arisen, such as how to set equitable rates for all users.

Both development and operational expenditures should be periodically reviewed, and deviations from the budget should be analyzed. The budget itself may prove unrealistic, in which case the assumptions and priorities of the budget planners should be studied, the errors identified, and recommendations made to future budget planners so that mistakes won't be repeated. In other cases, corrective action (such as new budgetary controls) may bring expenditures in line.

Budgets should be viewed as guidelines to management preferences and constraints, not as something to 'beat'. IS budgeting is similar in principle to budgeting in other departments within a firm, although line items differ.

Case study: IT for the insurance industry

In the late 1980s, the European insurance industry increased its investment in information technology (IT) in order to brace itself for stiffer competition in the post-1992 unified market. The focus was on the development of electronic data interchange (EDI) networks to link insurance salespeople in retail outlets to client databases, and to distribute comparative information on life, non-life and reinsurance policy options. With more than 30,000 retail outlets selling insurance in the United Kingdom alone, administrative costs to provide policy information to outlets has been costly in the past. It is expected that networks will reduce sales costs by providing brokers and financial institutions with access to information stored in insurance company mainframes, such as details on insurance contracts and premiums.

However, investment in information technology requires a major financial commitment on the part of insurers. For example, the European Reinsurance and Insurance Network, an EDI service on the continent, charges a one-time membership in the region of £240,000 per company. As IT becomes increasingly important in selling policies, many smaller insurance companies are forming alliances or merging with others to gain more investment clout. Major insurers are currently investing about 2 per cent of their annual gross premium income on IT.

Source: John Lamb, 'Insurers rewrite IS policies', *Datamation*, vol. 36, no. 17 (1 September 1990), pp. 109–12.

Questions

1 Prior to economic unity in Europe, regulations prohibited insurance companies from setting up branches in neighbouring countries. A single European market will place 4,000 insurance companies in competition for the business of 325 million customers. Suppose you are on the board of directors of an insurance company in this market. Will you recommend increased expenditures in information technology? Why? In what areas?

2 What approach to budgeting will you favour for IT in your insurance company? An 'asking', 'telling', or negotiated budget? Explain.

3 How would you assess the value of an EDI service to your company?

4 How can network linkage give an insurance company a competitive edge?

5 One observer of the insurance industry cites management technophobia with regard to information systems. How would you, as IS department head in an insurance company, convince corporate management to budget a larger share of corporate revenues to information technology?

Case study: Getting a grip on IT spending at Midland Bank

Is our data centre cost effective and productive? How does our IT spending compare to other banks? Ron Price pondered these questions as he reviewed the £380 million IT budget under his control as group IT director at London's Midland Bank. For answers, he turned to Compass Holding BD, a firm that measures actual costs and benefits of data centre production for clients by collecting and analyzing production data at 900 measurement points, including capacity and load statistics, financial information and staff information. The client then receives a detailed report which itemizes every operation and cost, including such information as 'cost per million instructions per second, response time at the terminal, cost per unit stored and cost per line printed'. Overall results are also reported on a Compass diagram representing IS performance in absolute terms and relative to peer companies.

With this report as a guide to prune and reshape operations, Price rebuilt Midland's information processing, reducing the number of the bank's data centres, IT staff and support vendors. 'Since 1987 (and measured in 1987 terms) we've cut 22.3 per cent of our cost, 25 per cent of our work force and achieved a threefold improvement in throughput — that is, in actual measurable work done', says Price.

Source: Ralph Carlyle, 'Getting a grip on costs', *Datamation*, vol. 36, no. 4 (15 July 1990), pp. 20–3.

Questions

1 A number of companies are on the market that provide comparative metrics like Compass. Most evaluate the cost of a client's data centres and rank the client within its industry category. Why would such information be useful to an IS director? To corporate management?

2 How could a report like the one Compass prepared for Midland Bank help a company decide:
   (a) Chargeback policies for data centres?
   (b) Whether to buy or rent computers?
   (c) Whether to transfer computer operations to a service company or computer utility?

3 Why do many firms turn to companies like Compass to evaluate IS operations? Why not rely on the evaluation of internal IS staff, computer vendors, or consultants?

4 Many IS executives are apathetic about the services offered by firms like Compass. Why?

5 How can a performance evaluation report contribute to the preparation of an IS budget?

Key words

Approaches to computer budgeting	Cost trends	Funding
Chargeback system	Expenditure accounting	Object class accounting
Control of expenditures	Expenditure analysis	One-year operating budget
	Feedback data	Overhead accounting
		Rate structures

Discussion questions

1 How does the preparation of a budget for IS differ from budget preparation for other departments in a firm?

2 What elements of IS budgets are unstable and unpredictable? How can uncertainties be eliminated or reduced?

3 Is budget preparation in a distributed environment easier and more responsive to needs than budget preparation in a centralized environment? Explain.

4 Should the IS budget be developed bottom-up or top-down? Why?

5 Why is the revenue of an IS department hard to estimate?

6 What is an equitable way to charge for computing services? What are the advantages and limitations of alternative charge systems?

7 Should the budget for IS be zero-based budgeting, or would you recommend some other approach, such as an incremental cost approach? Justify your choice.

8 Which IS costs do you think should be charged to overheads? Why?

9 An IS budget often has overruns. Why? How can overruns be controlled?

10 How can software costs be controlled?

11 What are the cost trends in computing? To what factors do you attribute them? Are the trends irreversible?

12 Why is it difficult, using standard costing methods, to cost each application and each job in an IS department?

13 How can the high personnel costs in computing be reduced?

14 How can developmental costs be reduced without affecting quality?

15 How is an annual operating budget prepared?

16 Should a firm actively solicit processing jobs (inside or outside of the organization) to reduce overheads? Will this reduce quality of service?

17 What are the advantages and disadvantages of overhead accounting?

18 How might the rate structure of an IS department be used to promote corporate policy? Give examples.

Bibliography

Boddie, John. 'Cost/benefit analysis — the sordid truth', *Tech Exec*, vol. 4, no. 4 (April 1990), pp. 14, 56.

Carlyle, R. 'Recovery', *Datamation*, vol. 36, no. 7 (1 April 1991), pp. 34–47.

Cohen, Fred. 'A cost analysis of typical computer viruses and defenses', *Computers and Security*, vol. 10, no. 3 (1991), pp. 239–49.

Earl, Michael J. *Management Strategies for Information Technology*. Hemel Hempstead: Prentice Hall, 1989, pp. 158–91.

Ewusi-Mersah, K. 'Evaluating information systems projects: a perspective of cost–benefit analyses', *Information Systems*, vol. 14, no. 3 (1989), pp. 205–17.

Hamlet, John, Steve Culliford and David Pollock. 'To buy or not to buy', *Which Computer?* vol. 13, no. 7 (July 1990), pp. 42–59.

Loew, Gary Wayne. 'Budgeting: a top-down, bottom-up, top-down process'. *Small Systems World*, vol. 13, no. 2 (February 1985), pp. 26–8.

Pliskin, Nava. 'Design of charging mechanisms according to the interaction between information technology type and diffusion lifecycle phase', *Data Base*, vol. 21, nos 2 and 3 (Fall 1990), pp. 30–40.

Sassone, Peter G. and A. Perry Schwartz. 'Cost-justifying OA', *Datamation*, vol. 32, no. 4 (15 February 1986), pp. 83–8.

Silk, David. 'Managing IS benefits for the 1990s', *Journal of Information Technology*, vol. 5 (1990), pp. 185–90.

12 Standards

If you think of 'standardization' as the best that you know today, but which is to be improved tomorrow — you get somewhere.
Henry Ford

When measuring weights, time or distance, we adhere to standards — such as 16 ounces to a pound, 60 minutes to an hour or 3 feet to a yard. We expect a dozen eggs to a carton, eight hours to a workday, eleven players in a cricket team and a holiday on Christmas Day. These are standards we all unconsciously acknowledge. **Standards** are accepted authorities or established measures for operations, behaviour or performance.

In the field of computing, standards are needed in programming languages, operating systems, electromechanical devices such as disks, printed circuit boards, chips and wafers, database design, communications protocols, documentation, program development and testing methodology, data element representation — the list could go on and on. Without such standards, programs cannot be transferred from one computer to another. Computer customers cannot incorporate hardware and software marketed by different manufacturers into a single computer system. The interchange of information among computer users and computer professionals is hampered. Technological progress is slowed because competing computer manufacturers tie up critical resources by duplicating product development instead of building on past work.

The computer industry has been criticized for its lack of commitment to standardization. Many computer vendors favour proprietary systems rather than standardized ones in order to lock their customers into brand loyalty. Some entrepreneurs, in search of profits, hope to make their own proprietary systems the world's standard, as IBM has done so successfully in the past. Perhaps the high-tech slump of the 1980s was due, in part, to customer unwillingness to invest in new system components unable to communicate with the old.

Computer standards are the subject of this chapter. The evolution of computer processing standards will be discussed first, followed by an explanation of how computer vendors and computer users create, implement, review and enforce computing standards within their own organizations. A section on standards for documentation is included to illustrate problems in setting standards and the benefits that can be derived from them. The chapter closes with a look at the role played by industry, professional bodies and both national and international organizations in the establishment of standards for the computer industry.

Evolution of standards

When computers were first introduced, no generally accepted guidelines existed for writing programs, designing forms or processing output. In order to use software, the premises of the programmer had to be accepted. As a result:

> Patterns of behaviour arose which, with sanction of time ... became standards accepted by the bulk of programmers.
>
> Eventually somebody discovered that we were de facto using standards, but that they weren't written down and given formal blessing. So the scribes got to work, created standards committees, and offered long careers to their members. (Sanders, 1978)

Critics charge that much of the inefficiency, duplication and incompatibility found in the computer industry can be traced to this slapdash approach to the development of standards in the early days of computing. Today, computer professionals are far more aware of the need for standards, and a large number of groups (described later in this chapter) are making a concerted effort to develop standards for the industry. For example, we could not have plug-compatible systems, common today, without standards.

Types of standards

Standards can be classified as reactive, a response to a problem or situation; progressive, providing a framework for operations; or retrospective, based on historical data and experience. Within a single installation, even within a single stage of processing, all three types of standards may coexist.

A standard may be a constraint, such as a rule that limits 'GO TO' statements in programming. It might be a procedure: for example, time sheets, work targets and formal employee evaluation sessions for appraising employee performance. It might be a technical specification, such as networking protocols that allow telex and teletex terminals to exchange written messages. It might be merely a list of terms, definitions or symbols. Some standards are strictly local standards. These may be nothing more than work guidelines, or they may be mandatory to provide management with a measure of control over performance. Other standards may be formulated by national committees of computer professionals. Whether or not an individual firm complies with such standards is usually voluntary.

Clearly, not all computer facilities will operate under an identical set of standards. Yet, a common core of standards, with unique variations to fit local needs, is common. A description of this core would require more pages than have

Table 12.1 *File specification standard (data required in each file)*

File name	Record data for each:
File label	Record name
File number	Record code
Summary file description	Record description
Source of file	Record size
Disposition data	Record content for each:
Blocking factor	Element name
Prepared (initially) by	Element number
Revised by	Element size (in 8-bit bytes)

been allocated to standards in this text. In this chapter, we give only two samples, Tables 12.1 and 12.2. The first is an example of a standard for file specification; the second is a standard format to report the findings of a feasibility study.

Figure 12.1 identifies areas of computing that benefit from standards and illustrates the concept that standards in one area should mesh with standards in other functional areas. A three-dimensional figure would be an even better representation, since standards in non-bordering activities in the figure should also be coordinated.

Standards committee

In a firm that has a computer facility, the responsibility for establishing computing standards for the organization is commonly delegated to a committee. This **standards committee** should be a standing committee, not a special ad hoc assignment, because continual creation, revision and updating of standards will be required as the firm expands, products change or new technology is introduced. In addition to drawing up standards, the committee should assist management in explaining the need for standards to employees and in motivating employees to follow standards adopted by the firm. Standards should be viewed as helpful discipline, not resented, ignored or bypassed.

Membership in the standards committee should be drawn from upper levels of management in the functional areas served by the firm's computers and should include both information users and technical personnel. Sometimes, outside consultants are also members of the committee.

The first job of the committee is to develop standards that govern the formulation of standards. That is, the structure, modularization and contents of standards manuals need to be decided. The format has to be designed, standards for indexing and cross-referencing have to be approved and conventions for writing standards must be established. Once this groundwork has been laid, the computing standards themselves can be created and documented in the manuals.

Table 12.2 *Standard for analyst findings in feasibility study*

Timing:	Part of feasibility study
Preparation:	By senior analyst assigned to project
Content:	**1** Detailed and summary costs in work-hours and dollars for:

1 Detailed and summary costs in work-hours and dollars for:
    Development of system
    Annual operation of system
2 Non-monetary cost of system for:
    Development
    Operations
3 Listing of system benefits:
    Tangible
    Intangible
4 Estimated duration of project with probability associations
5 Anticipated problems of development
6 Evaluation of and comments on:
    Data on which estimates are based
    Any further investigation warranted
7 Recommendations, if any

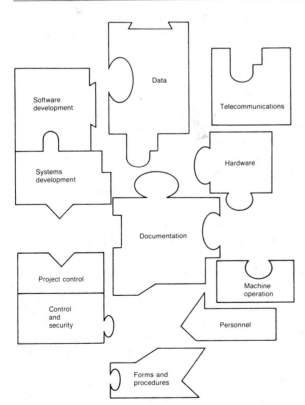

Figure 12.1 *Sets of standards for computing*

Generally, implementation, maintenance and operational control of standards are delegated by the committee to a part- or full-time **standards officer**. By one rule of thumb, one employee-week per year is required to create and maintain standards for each standard area. Some firms partially automate the control of standards. For example, a manufacturing firm may establish time and cost standards for given tasks, then monitor these tasks by computer through a badge or terminal check-in, check-out process. When operations consistently deviate from a prescribed standard, the standard is automatically revised or a computer report is sent to the standards officer, who then reviews the work. This review may lead to changed procedures, a reprimand to employees or a recommendation to the standards committee that certain standards be revised.

Setting standards

In firms with a standards committee and a standards officer, the formulation and evaluation of new standards typically follow the flowchart in Figure 12.2. The standards committee receives input from information users, computing staff and consultants when new standards are under consideration. Once a new standard has been formulated, approved and put into operation, a formal evaluation is made of that standard by the standards officer and IT staff to ensure that it is effective and that employees are using the standard in their work. When problems are observed, the committee should be notified so that the standard can be reconsidered. All standards should be periodically evaluated, even though they have been effective in the past. The environment of the firm may change over time so that old standards may no longer be appropriate.

To be sure, not all firms are organized in the same manner. In some firms, managers establish and implement standards in their areas of responsibility; other firms have no formal modus operandi for adopting standards. More and more firms are forming standards committees, however, because experience has proven their value.

The network diagram in Figure 12.3 shows the activities associated with the development of standards. First, the area where standards are lacking must be identified (Activity 5–10). Then management should approve the purpose and potential scope of the new standards (10–20) before they are actually developed. This approval helps control the number of new standards that are introduced (systems should not become encumbered with needless standards) and focuses the attention of the committee on management priorities. In general, priority is given to standards that affect accuracy (as in data preparation), promote communication (as in documentation) or show immediate returns in terms of efficiency (as in programming).

Ideas about what the standards should encompass are next solicited from personnel in the functional areas for which standards are being developed (20–30). Since cooperation is essential if standards are to serve their purpose, employees

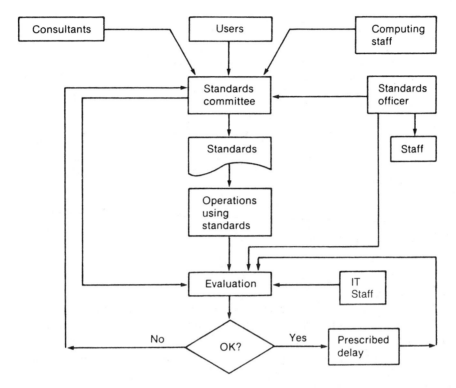

Figure 12.2 *Organization for setting and evaluating standards*

should have a voice in standards formulation. Often, the very process of assisting in the development of standards makes employees aware of the need for, and value of, standards. They then willingly follow standards in their work. A draft of the new standards is then prepared (20–30) and tested (30–40). If satisfactory, the standards are introduced (40–80), monitors are set in place for their enforcement (40–60), and employees are trained in their use (40–50). Periodically, the standards should be evaluated. If unsatisfactory, they should be modified or withdrawn (80–90).

Example: Setting documentation standards

Documentation is an activity that is generally unpopular at computer facilities but is essential to communication and systems continuation. Many tales are told in computer literature of systems having to be redeveloped because an analyst or programmer resigned without leaving adequate documentation for successors to maintain the existing system. Only by setting standards for documentation and enforcing them can such problems be avoided.

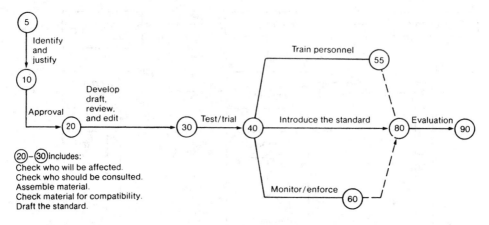

Figure 12.3 *Activities relating to standards formulation*

A standards committee, assigned the task of developing documentation standards, has to decide how to structure documentation and what level of detail is needed. Modular documentation is generally favoured at medium- and large-sized computer installations. That is, four manuals are typically designed to include all of the documentation on operations for the computer centre. These manuals include a:

- Systems manual, with general information on the system and its objectives.
- Programmer's manual, containing descriptions of programs.
- Operator's manual, giving directions for running programs.
- User's manual, detailing procedures for use of the system, including data flow diagrams, decision tables and program descriptions written in terms that users understand.

This division allows groups with differing needs to have simultaneous access to documentation information.

Next, the material to be contained in each manual is prescribed by the standards committee. (This task is sometimes delegated to the development team.) Usually, each manual is designed to contain abstract, detailed and summary documentation.

The level of detail of the standards for documentation may include symbol shapes for flowcharts. Because of the inaccuracies that can result in reading and interpreting alphanumeric data and codes, documentation standards generally include character shape specifications as well. (The lookalikes 5 and S sometimes cause confusion, as do the letter I and numeral 1, or the letter O and numeral 0.)

Another detail that may be addressed when setting the documentation standards is paragraph structure. Some installations require that the main paragraphs in manuals be headed by sequential decimal codes to identify topics and subtopics.

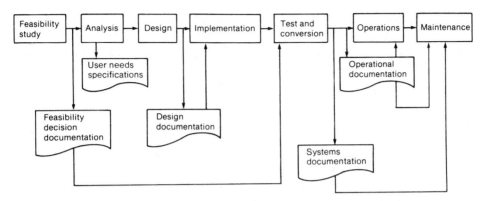

Figure 12.4 *Documentation at different stages of development*

Other organizations do not prescribe paragraph structure, the premise being that such a standard inhibits creativity, lowers morale and causes problems in enforcement.

A standard on the timing of documentation may be set. For example, completion of documentation may be required one month after a job is operational or six weeks after acceptance testing. Figure 12.4 shows a documentation standard that prescribes progressive documentation after milestones in the development process. According to this standard, documentation prepared following the feasibility study is used in testing to ensure that the expectations of the system are fulfilled; design documentation is used during implementation; and the final documentations (operational and system) serve as the basis for operations and maintenance.

Few standards committees have the competence to set standards for all functional areas of an installation, so they delegate this responsibility to others. The problem is deciding who should set, evaluate and implement standards. Formulation of documentation standards might be delegated to an analyst, programmer, user or outside consultant. Perhaps documentation will be automated with a computer program, such as AUTOFLOW in flowcharting. (In effect, the programmer who writes such software sets documentation standards.) A decision must be made regarding who should evaluate and test documentation, take custody of manuals, assign and control manual access, and be responsible for updating and revisions. Generally, the committee (or person) that writes documentation standards also makes such decisions.

Programmers and systems analysts generally dislike documentation, because it is a tedious and time-consuming task. They often argue that they are too busy or that documentation should wait until the system stabilizes. Since systems are constantly redesigned, such stabilization rarely occurs; documentation may be indefinitely postponed. Some companies will contract for systems development at a 20 per cent reduction in cost if no documentation is required. Acceptance of such a proposition is penny-wise and pound-foolish because documentation is too important to be compromised in this manner. A major responsibility of a standards committee is to educate both employees and management regarding the importance of documentation standards. For example, in pointing out their value, the committee should stress that documentation standards:

- Ensure that all commitments and expectations are on record.
- Help initiate and train newcomers to the system.
- Provide information needed to change the system should the environment or management's needs alter.
- Prevent systems dislocation and cost that might otherwise occur if knowledge of the system were centred in a few individuals who might resign, relocate or be subsequently reassigned to other duties.
- Facilitate routine evaluation, auditing and control.

An equally strong case could be made regarding the importance of standards for all of the components of an information system. It is obvious that no firm can permit secretaries to organize unique filing systems or allow programmers to use unique symbol sets. The problem is recognizing the fine line between standards that promote productivity and those that stifle creativity. The objective should be a set of standards that facilitate communication, control and compatibility — standards that promote efficiency and effectiveness in operations and are recognized by employees as doing so.

Cost and benefits of standards

In assessing the **cost** of standards, the salary of the standards officer, committee time and secretarial expenses in drafting, typing, editing and reviewing/updating standards should be calculated. Also included are the expense of testing standards and the costs associated with enforcement of standards and training employees in their use. In addition, the cost of conformity and reduction of choices should be considered, though the latter is particularly difficult to quantify.

Benefits, in addition to those discussed earlier in the section on documentation, include:

- Better communication.
- Improved utilization of computing resources.
- Portability of data, procedures, equipment, software, personnel and sometimes even subsystems or entire systems.
- Greater ease and speed in maintaining programs and systems at lower cost.
- Improved planning, control and security.

External sources of standards

Thus far in this chapter, we have discussed standards developed in-house. In deciding what standards are appropriate, a standards committee can benefit from the experience of other organizations with a similar environment or turn for guidance to books and manuals devoted to the subject of standards. It can also adopt standards set by committees formed by industry representatives or by professional groups. In addition, many standards recommendations come from national institutes, government and international bodies. The advantage of adopting standards set externally is that compatibility with the operations and products of other firms may result.

This chapter closes with a look at national groups and international organizations having an interest in computer standards.

Industry standards

One example of an industry standard is the magnetic ink character found on the base of cheques, a coding standard adopted by the banking industry in many countries to facilitate computerized processing of banking transactions. Use of this code speeds processing because cheques can pass through a machine that reads the data, then sorts and routes the cheques according to the preprinted magnetic ink block codes.

Another industry standard familiar to most readers is the Universal Product Code (UPC) found in retailing. This standard was developed by the Symbol Standardization Subcommittee of the Uniform Grocery Product Code Council Inc. to speed grocery checkouts. Scanning equipment reads the product identification code, which is fed to a computer to ascertain retail price.

Sometimes, industry representatives will agree on technical standards for new products. For example, in the 1980s, a standard was reached in the electronics industry in the United States for wiring office machines together. Usually, such agreements require the backing of a major company. When small firms attempted to get a standard accepted for the size of disk memories for microcomputers, the attempt failed.

National standards organizations

At the national level, you will find private sector organizations and governmental bodies with an interest in computing standards. An example of the former is ASC X3, the Accredited Standards Committee for Information Processing Systems, one of the subcommittees of the American National Standards Institute (ANSI). The work of X3 occurs in seven main categories of technical committees:

recognition, media, language, documentation, data representation, communication and systems engineering. An example of the latter is the Canadian Standards Association (CSA) which operates in conjunction with provincial and national governments of Canada to develop and test standards that will ensure product quality and consumer safety. The technical committees that actually write the standards are volunteers drawn from consumers, manufacturers, government, labour and consultants. Of particular interest to the IT community are the electrical/electronics programme which deals with the performance of electrical products, and the communications/information programme which deals with telecommunications, computers, office products and electromagnetic interference.

The Deutsches Institut für Normung e.V (DIN) is Germany's major standards organization. DIN, which plays an active role in the international arena to ensure that German products are used and accepted internationally, has no machinery to require that its standards be followed, relying instead on the technical excellence of its standards to win converts. The Association Française de Normalisation (AFNOR) is the national public body in charge of standards for France. Although founded as a private organization, AFNOR has been entrusted by the French government with the development of mandatory standards and control of the use of the NF label — a trademark that shows compliance with a French national standard. The organization also represents France at international meetings.

The British Standards Institute (BSI) is a voluntary organization with membership open to interested parties who fund the organization and derive revenues from the sale of standards developed by its technical committees. BSI owns and operates a test house and administers the BSI Quality Assurance Programme, giving compliance marks to products and services that meet BSI standards for quality.

The Japanese Industrial Standards Committee (JISC) has no true parallel in Europe, since it seems to have a special relationship with the government and with major manufacturers. Since standards in Japan are used as a marketing weapon, a major goal of the JISC is to develop standards that will allow Japanese industry to compete internationally in the IT and telecommunications industries. A major function of the committee is to monitor standards-developing activities of other countries and engage in bilateral and multilateral talks with representatives of these standards organizations.

Although countries differ in the structure of their national standards organizations, all have them. In general, voluntary organizations are concerned with creating and maintaining professional and manufacturing standards, while governmental bodies focus on standards that affect the public good.

Regional standards organizations

Two European regional standards bodies at work in the field of information technology are Comité Européen de Normalisation (CEN), formed in 1957 with the inception of the Common Market with members drawn from national standards organizations, and Comité Européen de Normalisation Electrotechnique (CENELEC). Although these two groups are voluntary standards organizations, they are under contract to develop technical standards for the European Community, which pays 70 per cent of their support. At present, CEN/CENELEC are ploughing through more than 3,000 work items that will affect areas such as programming languages, office document architectures, interfaces for operating systems, applications portability, telecommunications and so on, with a target date of January 1993 for completed standards. Following acceptance, the proposed standards will be the basis for certification, testing and quality assessment for IT products sold on the European market. (Figure 12.5 lists sample ENVs (European pre-standards) issued by CEN/CENELEC. The next step is adoption by member EC countries and the discontinuation of conflicting national standards.)

CEN has a subordinate body, CENCER, to issue certificates of conformance to CEN standards and to certify test houses. Should CEN succeed in compiling a regionally accepted list of test houses, the organization will become a major adjudicator of standards for the IT industry, not only in Europe but worldwide as well.

International standards organizations

The **International Standards Organization (ISO)** is one of the principal international bodies concerned with computer standards. This is a private body affiliated with the United Nations, its membership drawn from most of the countries in the world. In the ISO, the most important technical committee is TC97 (Computers and Information Processing), which is organized into sub-committees, many of which are further subdivided into working groups. Figure 12.6 shows the wide range of topics under consideration by the subcommittees. Figure 12.7 describes one of the projects of the ISO, network standards.

Other international organizations with an interest in computer standards include the International Electrotechnical Commission, the Consultative Committee on International Telephone and Telegraph, the European Computer Manufacturers Association, the International Federation for Information Processing and the Organization of Economic Cooperation and Development.

Summing up

According to many experts, incompatibility of computer systems is a major problem in the computer industry. Standards are the answer.

Formulation of standards within a firm may be the responsibility of a standards committee, a standards officer, or both. Industry and professional groups and both national and international organizations also contribute to computing standards.

The term *standard* has a slightly different meaning at each of these levels. For

- LAN — Provision of the OSI connection-mode transport service on a CSMA/CD single LAN (Connection service multiple access — collision detection)
- LAN — Provision of the OSI connection-mode transport service on a CSMA/CD LAN in a single or multiple LAN configuration
- LAN — Provision of the OSI connection-mode transport service in an end system on a CSMA/CD LAN
- Packet-Switched Data Networks — permanent access: OSI connection-mode transport service over either the OSI connection-mode network service or the T70 Case
- Packet-Switched Data Network (PSDN) — switched access
- Digital Data Circuit (CSDN): Provision of the OSI connection-mode transport and the OSI connection-mode network service (CO–NS)
- CSDN–CO–NS Circuit-switched data network, connection oriented network service — permanent and switched access
- Information systems interconnection: Local area networks provision of the OSI connection-mode transport service using connectionless-mode network service in an end system on a token-ring single LAN
- Information systems interconnection: local area network provision of the OSI connection-mode transport service and the OSI connectionless-mode network service in an end system on a token-ring LAN in a single or multiple configuration

Figure 12.5 *Sample European Pre-Standards issued by CEN/CENLEC*

in-house operations, firms develop procedures or guidelines that they call standards, such as standards for documentation. Businesses may sign an agreement to adopt a common method of operations, creating standards such as UPC. Sometimes, a manufacturer's product becomes a de facto standard; other companies design their product lines with the same or compatible specifications. (For example, Sony's $3\frac{1}{2}$-inch microfloppy may become an industry standard.) Industries, standards institutes, governments and international bodies develop standards of a different nature. They concentrate on technical descriptions, rules for programming languages and definitions of terms that will promote the interface of systems components, common measurements and communication between persons working in the computer field.

In each of these cases, the nature of the standard, the procedure for setting the standard and the obligation of individuals (or corporations) to follow the standard differ. But all standards have two common goals:

- To promote communication so that groups within and between firms can integrate operations and compare results.
- To contribute to productivity by providing guidelines for products or operations.

Perhaps too many groups compete with one another today in the setting of standards. Some critics suggest that there should be a way of selecting the best organizations and people to work on needed standards. Another problem is motivating individuals and corporations to follow standards, since conformity

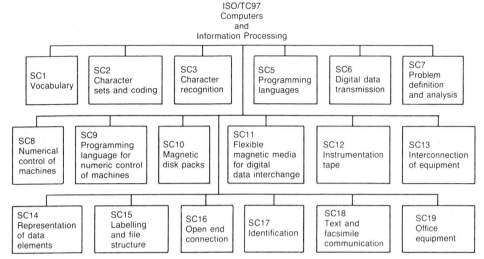

Figure 12.6 *Topics under consideration by subcommittees of the International Standards Organization, Technical Committee 97*

A special committee of the International Standards Organization (ISO) was chartered in 1977 to devise communication standards for network equipment. The result is the Open System Interconnection (OSI) Reference Model which identifies seven layers in network architecture, defines the function of each layer, and sets guidelines for connectivity at each level for those who design and manufacture network equipment.

OSI levels of architecture are as follows:

1 *Physical*. Concerns transmission of an unstructured bit stream over physical media (twisted wire, cable, microwave, fibre optics and satellite).
2 *Data link*. Concerns preparation of data into strings of characters and readiness for transmission across physical links. Addresses issues like framing data, packaging, batching, protocols which decide message size, error control and flow control.
3 *Network*. Concerns switching technologies used to connect systems and issues of security, privacy and collision.
4 *Transport*. Concerns route data will take between two end points and provides for recovery and flow control.

5 *Session*. Concerns control structure for communications between applications (dialogue management) as well as management and termination of connections.
6 *Presentation*. Concerns protocol conversion when data representation (syntax) differs among network nodes.
7 *Application*. Concerns assess to the OSI environment by users for distributed information services such as teleshopping, electronic mail, telebanking, and so on.

Only the first three layers of the ISO/OSI model have been implemented. The other layers are in various stages of definition and implementation. In contrast, IBM's competing architecture, systems network architecture (SNA) is fully implemented, tested and in widespread use. But IBM has agreed in a court settlement with European countries to accept the ISO/OSI model and make some of its equipment compatible with the model.

In all likelihood, SNA and ISO/OSI will continue to compete in the years ahead. We may never reduce telecommunications architecture to a single standard.

Figure 12.7 *Network standards*

and discipline are not popular concepts. There is also a cost to standards: staffing, training, implementation and updating. But most computer professionals recognize that standards are a prerequisite to orderly, efficient and effective growth of information processing.

Case study: Open systems

Most computer users favour open systems architecture that allows them to mix and match system components from a number of different manufacturers; to illustrate, a microcomputer built by Bull connected to an Olivetti printer. But compatible hardware does not entirely solve the problem. Differences in operating systems, commands, screen layout and procedures can impede the portability of software applications across multiple hardware systems.

Unix, an operating system developed at Bell Laboratories which helped popularize the idea of open systems, allows a computer user to take software written for one brand of equipment and run it on another. By 1993, Unix will be the software core for an estimated 19 per cent of the worldwide systems market. The French government uses Unix for home terminals linked to the telephone system and there are sixty French Unix suppliers. All major Brazilian manufacturers have or plan Unix-based systems, although the country has restrictive policies about the import of most foreign hardware/ software. The largest Unix market is currently in the United States. However, sales for Unix-based products are growing in Europe as trade barriers drop and a single pan-European market is forged. *Source:* Kirtimaya Varma, 'International Unix', *Computers Today*, vol. 5, no. 57 (November 1989), pp. 38–42.

Questions
1 How will the manufacture of computer systems based on open systems standards contribute to an 'open Europe'?
2 Japanese computer manufacturers sell more than 50 per cent of their products in the local market and export the rest. How will the concept of open systems contribute to their computer industry?
3 How can open systems standards facilitate alliances and mergers of small computer companies? Will such alliances affect the computer user? The computer industry worldwide? How?
4 In Europe, the open systems movement is spearheaded by the public sector as well as the scientific and engineering communities. For example, most computer-aided design and manufacturing hardware has Unix operating systems. Give probable reasons for this.

Case study: Standards for electronic data preparation and transfer

In the mid-1980s, the US Department of Defense (DoD) decided to ask contractors to replace the paper manuals of engineering drawings and technical information used to support new ships, aircraft and weapons with digital computer-readable documentation. (More than a million pages of information telling how to operate, maintain and procure spare parts accompany a single aircraft: a destroyer takes about 27 tons of documentation to sea.) Before implementing this move to digital technology, however, standards had to be set for the preparation and transfer of this electronic documentation, because the major defence contractors had diverse computer systems for design, engineering, manufacturing and document preparation. Today, contractors wanting to do business with the DoD must conform to the standards of Cals (Computer-aided Acquisition and Logistics Support).

Large companies worldwide, such as automotive and electronic companies, are interested in the Cals programme. They, too, want a fast, reliable data exchange mechanism with suppliers: for example, the ability to tap computer databases of contractors regarding component specifications in order to speed the design and manufacture of products. The problem is that manufacturers and suppliers seldom have compatible hardware and software. Cals is addressing this problem, at work on a universal translator for product information — work that has captured the imagination of manufacturers the world over. A universal translator will allow a complete definition of a component part to be transferred from one computer to another of a different make.

The International Standards Organization (ISO) is coordinating an effort to develop an international standard for the exchange of product data as well. A first draft was published in 1989 and rejected.

Source: Di Palframan, 'Greater savings on paper with new data translator', *Management Today* (November 1990), p. 134.

Questions

1 Why was it necessary for the DoD to develop standards for electronic transfer of data in order to implement its switch from paper documentation on ships, aircraft and weapons to computer-readable documentation?

2 Who benefits from this switch? How? Who is hurt?

3 Why would companies outside the United States be interested in the Cals philosophy?

4 What makes it easier for the DoD to develop standards for the preparation and transfer of electronic data than for the ISO to do likewise?

5 Who do you think might oppose an ISO standard for the exchange of product data? Why? What factors might be slowing the development of this standard?

Case study: **Telecommunications standards for Europe**

In Europe, public monopolies — the post, telephone and telegraph authorities (PTTs) — have a stranglehold over telecommunications equipment and services. Although the technology of ISDN (Integrated Services Digital Network) is in use, each European PTT uses its own definition of ISDN, causing telecommunications systems across national boundaries to be incompatible.

The European Commission, in the belief that telecommunications is the basic business infrastructure of the future, is trying to build a single European market in communications products and services. The task is the contemporary equivalent to building a railway network across Europe in the early nineteenth century. Market liberalization is required, the breaking of PTT monopolies and deregulation of telecommunications. The European Commission is setting rules under which private service operators can gain open access to public networks.

The Commission has the power to issue telecommunications directives without going through the long process of consulting member states, and has done so, a tactic that has provoked fierce criticism. However, member states generally approve the Commission's aims, though they dislike the Commission's style.

Source: 'Moves to break monopolies' stranglehold', *Financial Times* (19 July 1989), section 3, p. 12.

Questions

1 The Commission argues that rules are needed to ensure that PTTs do not abuse their power and pass technical standards that will prevent private operators from using public networks. Britain argues that the rules threaten to suffocate deregulation of telecommunications. Which position do you take? Explain your views.

2 Telecommunications industry deregulation is being pursued at different speeds in Great Britain, Germany, France and Italy. Why?

3 'The telecommunications industry will have a deep and pervasive influence on post-1992 business.' Comment.

4 Why do you suppose the European Community has given the Commission the unusual and controversial power to issue laws on public service monopolies without going through the normal process of consulting member states?

5 How will managers of business corporations, especially multinational corporations, be affected by open communications networks?

Key words

Benefits (of IT)
Costs (of IT)
Documentation
Industry standards

Industrial Standards
   Organization
National Standards
   Organization

Standards (for IT)
Standards committee
Standards officer

Discussion questions

1 Standards are expensive to institute, difficult to enforce, unpopular with users and cause disruption when they are implemented. Comment.

2 At what stage of the development of an information system should one start thinking of standards? Why?

3 Who should initiate standards for a computer centre: someone within the computer centre, someone within the organization but in another department, or an outside consultant? Explain.

4 Comment on the following statement: The benefits of standards are largely intangible. Does it matter that a cost–benefit ratio for standards cannot be calculated?

5 How can one determine whether expenses for a standards programme are justifiable?

6 How do standards depend upon:
(*a*) Size of computing centre?
(*b*) Complexity of applications portfolio?
(*c*) Number of users?
(*d*) Industry?
(*e*) Clients?
(*f*) Maturity of computing centre?

(g) Computer executive?

7 Do we need standards for standards? Do we need to control standards? Explain.

8 Under what circumstances would a firm adopt local standards that differ from standards adopted by:
   (a) The firm's own computer centre?
   (b) The industry the firm represents?
   (c) National standards organizations?
   (d) International standards organizations?

9 Under what circumstances should standards be mandated by:
   (a) The industry of the firm?
   (b) National standards organizations?
   (c) Regional standards organizations?
   (d) International standards organizations?

10 Who should be responsible for the enforcement of standards? Should this be an ongoing responsibility, should spot checks be the norm, or should controls wait until something goes wrong?

11 Explain how standards help to:
   (a) Avoid disasters.
   (b) Improve performance.
   (c) Control operations.
   (d) Assist in employee training.
   (e) Contribute to good working habits.

12 Should we have standards for:
   (a) Performance?
   (b) Procedures?
   (c) Design?
   Are these areas too intangible and variable to be standardized?

13 Describe the Standards Organization in your:
   (a) Country.
   (b) Region.

14 Can standards act, in effect, as a non-tariff barrier to trade? Explain.

Bibliography

Berlack, H.R. 'How not to write commercial standards', *Computer*, vol. 23, no. 5 (May 1990), pp. 79–81.

Blyth, David, Cornelia Boldyreff, Clive Ruggles and Nik Tetteh-Lartey. 'The case for formal methods in standards', *IEEE Software*, vol. 7, no. 1 (September 1990), pp. 65–7.

Bugod, Julian. 'DISC — an update', *Computer Bulletin*, Series 2, vol. 2, part 9 (November 1990).

Cargill, Carl. *Information Technology Standardization*, Bedford, Mass.: Digital Press, 1989.

Evan, P. 'How can professional standards be set and maintained?', *Computers and Security*, vol. 9, no. 4 (June 1990), pp. 113–16.

Frenkel, Karen. 'The politics of standards and the EC', *Communications of the ACM*, vol. 33, no. 7 (July 1990), pp. 40–51.

Homer, Steve. 'Setting standards in Europe', *Computers and Security*, vol. 9, no. 4 (1990), pp. 295–300.

Karten, Naomi. 'Standards for user-driven applications development', *Journal of Information Systems Management*, vol. 8, no. 3 (Summer 1991), pp. 60–2.

Moad, Jeff. 'The standards process breaks down', *Datamation*, vol. 36, no. 18 (15 September 1990), pp. 24–32.

Sanders, Norman. *A Manager's Guide to Profitable Computers*, Manchester: AMACOM, 1978, pp. 120–1.

Tillman, M.A. and David Yen. 'SNA and ISO: three strategies of interconnection', *Communications of the ACM*, vol. 33, no. 2 (February 1990), pp. 214–24.

Zeitler, Eddie L. 'Developing standards for protecting electronic financial data', *Bank Administration*, vol. 62, no. 10 (October 1986), pp. 38, 40.

13 Managing resistance to change

More than machinery, we need humanity.
Charlie Chaplin, in the film *Modern Times*

Over four hundred years ago, Machiavelli observed:

> It must be considered that there is nothing more difficult to carry out, nor more doubtful of success, nor more dangerous to handle, than to initiate a new order of things. For the reformer has enemies in all those who profit by the old order, and only lukewarm defenders in all those who could profit by the new order. This lukewarmness arises partly from fear of their adversaries, who have the laws in their favor, and partly from the incredulity of mankind, who do not truly believe in anything new until they have had an actual experience of it. (Machiavelli, 1952, pp. 49–50)

Resistance to a new order has not lessened in this century. Indeed, the pace of the technological revolution has heightened fears that humans are becoming subservient to machines and stiffened resistance to technology that threatens to disrupt the status quo. This threat is perceived in information systems that incorporate advances in process control, microtechnology, teleprocessing, robotics, graphics, voice recognition, distributed processing and word processing.

Implementation of **change** in computing does not require the guile of a Machiavelli. But implementers do need to identify and analyze why employees oppose innovations and to develop strategies to promote acceptance of change. Figure 13.1 is an overview of the stages in the management of change. These stages will be discussed in the following sections of this chapter.

Detecting resistance to a computer environment

A drop in production, failure to meet deadlines, absenteeism, mounting employee turnover, complaints and low morale, and a reluctance to learn new job skills are all symptoms of employee resistance to change. What makes human resistance to computers different from the antagonism felt towards other machines (an antagonism that has existed since the industrial revolution) is that software adds a new dimension to the conflict. Today, as shown in Figure 13.2, one must add human–software interface (B) and human–machine–software interface (D) to the problem of human–machine interaction (C).

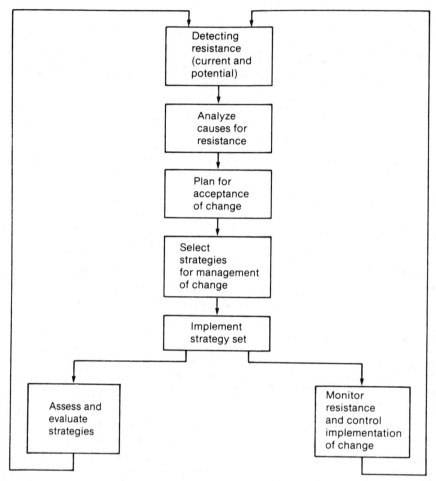

Figure 13.1 *Stages in the management of change*

Human factors, sometimes referred to as **human engineering** or **ergonomics**, is a field in which human–machine interrelationships are studied. European research tends to focus on physiological considerations, such as fatigue when operating machines, breathing rates and pupil size, whereas the American emphasis is more on psychological factors. On both sides of the Atlantic, recommendations for improving the computing environment can sometimes seem quite mundane: for example, that workstations be comfortable and pleasing, since the arrangement of furniture and workspace around a terminal can affect user morale and an inconvenient layout may contribute to employee errors. The size of terminal keys, angle of the screen, flicker and colour of displays are all factors that may affect production.

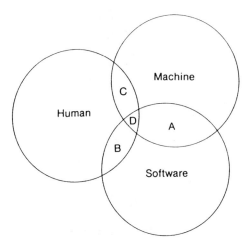

Area A = Machine–software interface.
Area B = Human–software interface.
Area C = Human–machine interface.
Area D = Human–machine–software interface.

Figure 13.2 *Relationship between humans, machines and software*

When designing electronic information processing equipment and developing software, many human engineering problems arise from the fact that users have a wide range of background knowledge and experience. For example, the same hardware devices may have to serve clerks (who use terminals primarily as input devices), professionals (analysts and programmers), managers (whose interest is primarily output) and specialists (such as product designers using computer-aided design). Non-professionals often have difficulty communicating with a computer. They may require interactive and conversational modes or special training materials and documentation in order to take full advantage of the potential of computers in problem solving. Users with a computing background, on the other hand, will have less need for special user-friendly features and may even prefer a 'bare-bones' system (for example, a minimum of menus and help routines). Unfortunately, many systems designers do not recognize the existence of individuals who see broad patterns and total pictures rather than well-bounded problems as they do, so they fail to incorporate features appropriate to all classes of users in the systems that they develop.

Growing recognition of the importance of human factors should help correct this shortcoming. The literature on human factors is, indeed, quite extensive. Management should follow research in this field because no computerized information system can achieve its full potential as a tool in management decision making when aspects of human engineering are ignored.

Figure 13.3 summarizes relationships in a computer environment. Human–machine relationships exist between the computer and management/clients.

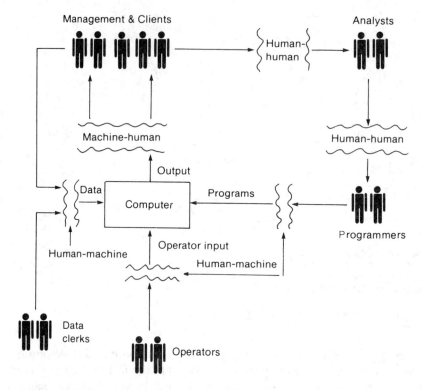

Figure 13.3 *Computer-human interaction*

Human–human interchange takes place between management, computer personnel and clients. This figure illustrates why information systems should not be categorized as machine systems or even as machine-dominated systems, since humans have a role in all aspects of processing. Because humans specify the need for information, design and implement systems, write programs, provide input, operate and monitor equipment and use output, a climate receptive to the change is vital when new information technology is being introduced to an organization. Without human cooperation, the new technology will fail to live up to its productivity potential.

Why resistance?

That employees resist change should come as no surprise to business managers, since this phenomenon has been well documented. For example, the Hawthorne Study at Western Electric in the late 1920s noted that factory conditions or salaries alone did not explain worker attitudes. Actions perceived as a threat to job security triggered a strong emotional response. According to the literature of operations research and management science, a similar negative reaction to change occurred at managerial levels when mathematical and statistical methods of decision making were first introduced.

Resistance to computers can be found at all levels of an organization. Employees at operational levels, such as assembly-line workers and technicians, may be as disturbed by disruption of the status quo as managers in the upper echelons of the company. People are creatures of habit and become upset when new technology jars their sense of control or disturbs their sense of purpose. They fear the change that the new technology will impose on their lives. Procedures may be altered, jobs may gain or lose status and totally new relationships may have to be forged as departments are restructured in accordance with the expanded role of computers. Employees wonder how the technology will affect their jobs, their security, their authority, their access to information, their interaction with co-workers, and their values. They know that they may have to learn new job skills and that information technology can lead to job displacement and unemployment. Concerns such as these lead to resistance. Persons who see their power base eroding will, in self-interest, scheme to defeat the new technology. (On the other hand, employees who feel they will have an opportunity to attain privileged status because of their expertise in computers favour the introduction of information systems.)

Resistance to computer technology at managerial levels can often be traced to managers feeling that they are being hemmed in by information technology, that their choices are restricted because computer systems seem to centralize important decision making. Some local managers resent having daily goals defined, the action to achieve these goals specified and performance evaluated by what they perceive as an impersonal machine. Computer systems may also provide data that managers prefer to suppress and may reveal staff incompetence. For example, a report by one company comparing monthly sales showed a correlation between low performance and the deer-hunting season. Foremen lax in controlling unexcused absences of hunters were easily identified.

Perhaps the main reason managers oppose information systems is that computers alter the decision-making process. Decisions in a computerized environment are largely based on data provided by systems and supplemented by human judgement and experience. This method of decision making requires a different type of conceptual thinking than intuitive decision making, common in the past. Many managers find their old style of reaching decisions under attack and yet are unable to adjust to decision making that utilizes the new technology. Reasons for resistance are summarized in Table 13.1.

Although resistance generally has adverse effects, not all resistance is bad. If management examines the objections of employees and improves proposed systems by listening to constructive criticism, resistance can serve a useful purpose. Perhaps technicians have not paid enough attention to human needs in designing the work environment. Perhaps the stress has been on technology,

Table 13.1 *Effects of new technology on employees' reasons for resistance*

Reason for resistance \ Level primarily affected →	Operating personnel	Operating management	Middle management	Top management
Loss of status	XX	X		
Economic insecurity	XX			
Interpersonal relationships altered	X	X	X	X
Change in job content	XX	X	X	
Change in decision-making approach		X	X	X
Loss of power		X	X	
Uncertainty/ unfamiliarity/ misinformation	XX	X	X	X

Key X = Some affect; XX = Strong affect

ignoring the human—machine interface on which success of new systems depends. Careful assessment of employee objections may help avert costly flops. Those who assume that all resistance is the grumbling of malcontents do their firm a disservice.

Tolerance to change depends on a number of variables. Some commentators suggest that resistance is greater among older employees with a long record of service to a company than among younger workers, and is more likely among those with limited education and little background in computers. Resistance is generally proportional to the number of persons involved in the change and also increases as the rate of change increases. Rapid change has been known to produce dysfunctional behaviour such as alienation, withdrawal, apathy and depression, but even controlled change can lead to emotional stress and illness.

This phenomenon has been studied by psychologists T.S. and T.H. Holmes, who devised a system of scoring events in a person's life according to the amount of trauma they produce. For example, points are given for divorce, birth of a child, vacations and a death in the family. It is significant that changes in employment, such as altered hours of work (20 points), new duties (29) or a loss of a job (47), represent 20 per cent of the list and have high score values. According to the Holmeses, a score of 200 at any given time is so disruptive that an individual is susceptible to disease or illness. Clearly, changed work conditions as a result of the introduction of an information system would score highly under this system, explaining the behaviour of some individuals when their departments are computerized.

Planning for attitude change

Once resistance is identified, plans to change employee attitudes need to be made. Planning for change should resemble the planning of a project. That is, once the need for change is identified, strategies to implement the change should be developed, responsibilities for this implementation assigned and a schedule for implementation adopted.

Often, a systems analyst is the change agent. But firms that have little experience in the management of change may hire a technical consultant to effect the change. The change agent should be technically competent and skilled in communication and procedural skills. The individual should also have expertise in human–machine interaction and human performance technology. In addition, knowledge about the integration of human factors with instructional technology is important, and the person should be schooled in industrial and organization psychology. The function of the change agent is to recommend policies that will smooth transition to new technology and to devise ways to alter the behaviour and attitude of employees resisting change.

Skilled change agents know that employees must be made aware of a proposed change and have time to grapple with what the change means to them. Initial confusion, a lack of understanding of the ramifications of change, should not be misinterpreted as resistance. To avoid the heated, emotion-charged environment that accompanies sudden change, employees should be told early in a new system's development the reasons why new technology is being introduced and what will happen as a result. They will then have time to reflect on the change and will be able to evaluate the pros and cons of the project with greater objectivity. Given a period of adjustment, affected employees will have time to learn new job skills or to seek alternative employment. Firms can help smooth adjustment by providing in-house retraining and by offering the option of early retirement or severance pay to affected personnel.

Experienced change agents also recognize that an individual's assessment of new technology may be mixed, fluctuating between positive and negative emotional and intellectual judgements. At one moment, hope that work in a computerized environment will lead to professional advancement may dominate; at another, deep-felt anxiety about job displacement or unemployment may surface. The best expediters of technological change are adroit in accentuating positive reactions to the new technology. They know that when positive perceptions predominate, commitment to change will follow.

Initial commitment may be ephemeral, turning to pessimism when bugs in the new technology surface. It is the responsibility of the change agent to encourage employees to discuss systems faults so that bugs can be identified and efforts made to correct them. Often, the information obtained from disgruntled employees can be used to fine-tune the new system and, as a result, win back their support. The highest form of commitment occurs when employees, believing that the new technology is worthwhile, contribute to the design of new procedures or the moulding of the technology for their own purposes.

There is a cycle in an individual's attitude toward change, as depicted in Figure 13.4, that a change agent hopes to influence. Each person's emotional response to change is preconditioned by background, education and past experience with change (Box 1). Emotional responses lead to attitudes (3) that affect whether the impact of innovation at work will be perceived as beneficial or as a threat (4). This perception, in turn, influences whether change will be accepted or opposed (5) and the degree of willing participation in the implementation of the change (6). This experience becomes part of the employee's background (1), conditioning future reaction to change.

The change agent hopes, by handling change in an equitable and humane manner (2), to interject new experience or knowledge into this cycle and reinforce positive responses to change. The employee's attitude towards change hopefully will be favourably altered, with resistance to change diminished in the future.

Behaviour alteration strategies

Two approaches to behaviour alteration are possible when employees resist change: a **participative change**, which originates from within the individual, and a **directive change**, a response to management initiatives.

A participative change starts with new knowledge (formal education, self-instruction or observation). This knowledge kindles new attitudes that, in turn, affect behaviour — first individual, then group behaviour. Such change can be nurtured by the environment. For example, time off may be given to employees for class attendance or a bonus offered for joining educational programmes.

A directive change is one imposed by management. Policies are formulated that require alteration of group behaviour, which then modifies the knowledge and attitudes of individuals. For example, participation at orientation sessions may be compulsory, or employees may be told their jobs are in jeopardy if new job skills are not learned. A change in attitude can also be fostered by involving employees in systems development projects. Resisters can be co-opted, given an active role in identifying problems and planning solutions. Generally, individuals thus involved begin to see computers as valuable business aids and their fears of a machine takeover fade.

Which of the two approaches to change, participative or directive, works best in an information processing environment? Generally, a participative change is most desirable. Self-motivated employees tend to imbue others with their enthusiasm and their willingness to try new ideas often serves as a catalyst to

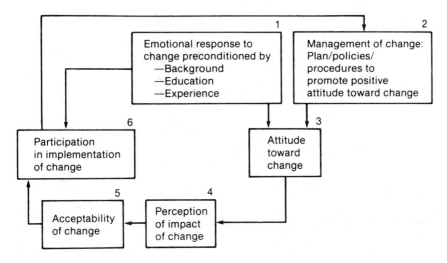

Figure 13.4 *Cycle in attitude towards change*

a change in attitude of co-workers. The approach is also more appealing because it is open and democratic.

But when no employees voluntarily engage in activities that will transform behaviour, management must implement strategies to encourage a positive attitude towards change even when these strategies smack of rigidity, formality and bureaucratic authoritarianism. Time may also be a factor mandating the directive approach, since participative change is generally a slower process.

Figure 13.5 shows that the impetus for change comes from opposite directions in participative and directive change. That is, a participative change begins with the acquisition of knowledge and an attitude adjustment of individuals leading to altered group behaviour. A directive change alters group behaviour first in the expectation that the attitudes and knowledge of individuals will be changed accordingly.

Strategies to promote acceptance of change

Since every firm has a unique environment, appropriate techniques to promote acceptance of change and to ease the throes of conversion to new systems will vary from one organization to another. Common techniques to facilitate technological assimilation include:

- Conduct a pilot study to determine impact of change.
- Assign responsibility for change to upper-level managers who possess the organizational power to legitimize change and assign agents to implement change.

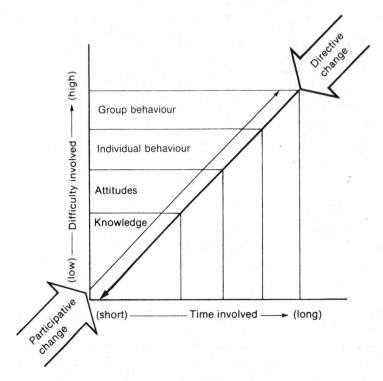

Figure 13.5 *Participative and directive changes (Source: adapted from Paul Hersey and K.H. Bianchard, Management of Organizational Behavior: Utilizing human resources, Englewood Cliffs, NJ: Prentice Hall, 1972, pp. 281–2)*

- Identify individuals in the organization who must learn new behaviours, skills or knowledge because of the change.
- Institute educational programmes to provide employees with needed behaviours, skills and knowledge.
- Involve employees in the development of new systems.
- Open up lines of communication between employees and management. For example, provide forums where employees can voice their concerns about new technologies.
- Publicize information regarding systems changes.
- Pace conversion to allow a readjustment period to new systems.
- Implement new systems in modules.
- Alter job titles to reflect increased responsibility.
- Reward ideas that will improve throughput.
- Document standards so that new procedures are easy to learn and reference.
- Clearly establish in advance the demarcations of authority that will exist following changeover.

- Upgrade the work environment following change, incorporating recommendations of human factor studies.
- Show sympathy and be receptive to complaints following conversion.
- Conduct orientation sessions.
- Arrange job transfers.
- Call a hiring freeze until all displaced personnel are reassigned.
- Provide job counselling.
- Offer separation pay.
- Organize group therapy.
- Initiate morale-boosting activities, such as a company newsletter and parties.

The key to success with these techniques lies in management's ability to demonstrate support and sympathy for employees adversely affected by the change and to show understanding when the disruption and dislocation caused by change produce anxiety and tension even among those not directly involved in the conversion. Management's skill in handling interpersonal relationships largely determines whether a firm can absorb technological advances in the field of computing.

Here is an example of what can happen when the introduction of new technology takes place without explaining the implications of the change to employees. One firm developing a computerized information system announced that installation would involve a reduction in the number of employees, but failed to identify which individuals would be displaced. Fearing loss of work, 40 per cent of the company resigned to seek secure employment. Many who left the firm were in positions that would have been unaffected by the change, and others left whose skills were vitally needed to run the new system. At a time when competent employees were sorely needed, the firm lost some of its best workers and was left with deadwood, persons with poor qualifications and hence little job mobility, to handle systems conversion.

Resistance among computer professionals

Before concluding this chapter, one other source of resistance should be discussed. Employees with no background in computing are not the only ones in a firm to resist the fast pace of information technology. Information technology professionals, like non-technical workers, fear unemployment and powerlessness as advances in computer technology foster change in their work assignments.

For example, end-user computing and distributed data processing, which transfer responsibility to users for the operation and administration of computing resources, are often viewed with alarm by computer personnel. (End-user computing and distributed data processing are treated at length in Chapter 2.) Computer specialists claim that unauthorized and incompatible files will spring up, security will be lax and applications will be ineffective and inefficient, all of

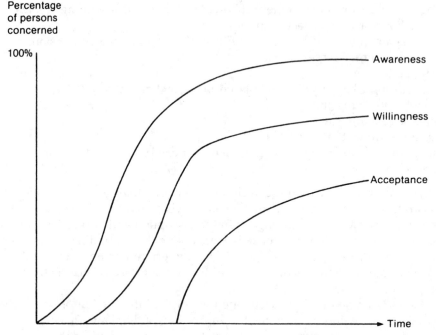

Percentage
of persons
concerned

Note: The shapes of the curves (the starting point, slope gradient, and time horizon) will vary
with
(a) The complexity of technological change being implemented.
(b) Education, training and communication (will especially affect awareness curve).
(c) Strategies of change (will affect willingness and acceptance curves).

Figure 13.6 *Responses to change over time*

which they will be blamed for. The realization that other employees can now
interact with computers without the intermediary of the computer centre is
evidence that computing is no longer an exclusive club, that status and power
have been lost. This helps explain some of the resistance to information technology
that is found within the computer profession itself.

The same types of strategies are needed to promote acceptance of change in
computer departments as in other departments of the firm. In general, resistance
is short lived once IT people realize that their jobs are not in jeopardy and that
computing advances relieve them of many of the tedious duties associated with
processing, freeing them for more challenging, exciting systems work.

Summing up

In computing, information systems are commonly redeveloped every four to six
years. New systems may affect the firm's organizational structure and require

the forging of new interpersonal relationships among technical personnel, information users, data providers and clients. Resistance is an inevitable part of the change process. To prevent escalation of costs, disrupted production schedules and lowered morale, change must be carefully planned, implemented and controlled.

Management of change is more than merely supporting and sympathizing with workers adversely affected by new systems. Change agents should take an active role in systems development to ensure that human factors are incorporated in the design and implementation of proposed systems. They must help establish a work environment receptive to change, ready to 'change with change so that when change comes, there will be no change' (advice given to a patrician uncle at a time when Garibaldi's armies were overthrowing the old Sicilian order in Giuseppe Lampedusa, *The Leopard*).

Figure 13.6 illustrates how people respond to change over time in terms of awareness, willingness and acceptance. Management can alter the starting point and gradient of the slopes of the curves by policies that create an atmosphere fostering change. The object of managing change is to shift the curves upward and to the left: that is, to increase awareness, willingness and acceptance, and to reduce the time it takes for employees to demonstrate these attributes. Orientation sessions, retraining programmes and modular conversion are examples of techniques that predispose employees to acceptance of technological innovations in computing. A major goal of these and other change strategies is to humanize computer systems, to make them friendlier and easy to use, and to ensure that no employee perceives computers as an economic or social threat.

Case study: IT for London's money markets

Can London retain its position as a financial centre in the 1990s? Lowered trade barriers and the removal of restrictive regulatory and fiscal restraints in Europe mean that London's dominant role in international banking and money markets is no longer assured. Paris, in particular, is competing to become the business hub of the new Europe.

The problem for the City is that money market institutions have been slow to embrace information technology. For example, the settlement system used by sterling money markets depends on a messenger carrying relevant pieces of paper from the seller institution to the buyer. After a review of the documents to ensure that the transaction information is correct, the buyer writes a cheque which the messenger delivers

back to the seller. This paper stream floods the streets of London, representing transactions worth as much as 10 billion pounds in a single hour.

Messengers also hand-deliver bearer bonds. Surprisingly, few bonds (or messengers) are reported missing, though recently an estate agent spotted £4 million of lost bearer bonds on the pavement. In contrast, Paris uses an electronic register, SICOVAM, for bearer certificates, eliminating some 2,500 tons of paper. The system cuts transaction costs by an estimated four-fifths. (London Clear, a project to replace messengers with a computer system, floundered in the City over the set-up cost (£16 million) and ongoing tariff (£4.25 per transaction)).

London's equity market also relies on paper-based settlement, though without hand-delivery. Two weeks for paper processing, known as the Account, are built into the system. International investors prefer 'cash against delivery (CAD)' systems; that is, speedy electronic payment and transfer of securities. Paris is close to CAD across its money markets, a competitive advantage.

Failure to implement information technology in the City can be attributed, in part, to the fact that the reputation and profits of some companies are based on mastery of the paper maze. They have been unwilling to participate in a cooperative effort to revamp business processes unless given 'compensatory advantages'. In addition, some companies fear that information technology will benefit only their bigger rivals. Others fear that IT might be used by banks, or the Stock Exchange, or the government, to extend their control. In a climate of suspicion and bargaining for advantage, as many as sixty proposals for new money market systems have been advanced. It is not surprising that the City continues to operate much as it did in the nineteenth century.

Source: David Morton, 'Why the Bank is banging heads', *Management Today* (April 1990), pp. 75–8.

Questions

1 How does this case illustrate resistance to change? Do you think such resistance is characteristic of English institutions? Why or why not?
2 Can the City retain its position as the world's largest foreign exchange trading city, as the home of some 520 foreign banks, as dominant in the Eurobond market, without embracing information technology? Explain your position.
3 Why do you think Paris is moving faster than London in its development of electronic 'cash against delivery' systems?
4 The Bank of England has announced that it will go ahead with an alternative system to the London Clear project and will develop a central depository and computerized book-entry transfer system for the wholesale money markets. Why do you think that the Bank has decided to take this role? Do you agree with this role? Explain.
5 You are appointed as a member of a team to develop an alternative system for London Clear. Your responsibility is to recommend ways to gain the support of institutions for whom the system is being designed. What would you recommend?

Case study: Underwriters resist

An insurance company with eighteen branches has recently acquired a computer system for insurance policy processing. Managers at the decentralized branches have discretion over the system's implementation and use. Some have required underwriters to adopt the new system. Others are letting employees convert to the system at their own pace. Whereas the effects of computerization for policies in personal lines have been positive, the new system has disturbed the delicate balance of work practices of commercial lines, resulting in conflict and stress. Here are sample comments that illustrate negative attitudes to the new system.

> Underwriters stopped using the system. They just wasted too much time, too much bother, and they especially stopped using the system when they were under a lot of pressure. When they had to get a lot of work out in a short period of time, they just bypassed the whole thing.

> I prefer to do the work manually. Even the documentation — I just put a note in the file

saying: 'The system was down. Had to paper-document.'

Our manager didn't even use the computer. In fact, he asked for it to be taken out. He didn't even want it.

Even the way you had to enter data was unfriendly, because you had to convert yeses and nos into 1s and 2s and year 1 was really year 0. All these things went against your normal train of thought. So that made it difficult.

We tried to ask for one documentation screen, just give us one blank screen. And we'll put all the documentation in it. That couldn't be done without restructuring the entire system.

For an underwriter, it was very difficult to use the system because we were still using paper as three-quarters of the file and a computer for a quarter of it. It almost included double work.

They originally designed the system to have a seven-second response time between when you keyed in the information and when you got the information back. There are times of heavy usage that it takes minutes to get a response and then the system becomes totally ineffective. . . . If people have to wait, they are frustrated and say, 'to hell with it'.

Source: T. Hirscheim and M. Newman, 'Informa-tion systems and user resistance: theory and practice', *The Computer Journal*, vol. 31, no. 5 (1988), pp. 398–406. Quotes taken from or adapted from this article.

Questions

1 Draw some conclusions about the way in which this insurance system was designed from these comments.
2 For each comment, discuss the following:
   (a) The complaint of the underwriter.
   (b) Where the fault lies, assuming the complaint is valid.
   (c) Steps that can be taken to resolve the complaint.
   (d) Measures management might have taken to prevent a complaint of this nature.
3 What lessons can be learned from the above comments? Are the lessons to be learned unique to insurance systems or could they be applied to other disciplines? Explain.
4 Perhaps most underwriters like the systems and these complaints are atypical. How could management determine overall employee satis-faction with this system?
5 'The development and implementation of computer-based information systems is a type of major organizational change. Only those development strategies which view such change in terms of social and political processes are likely to prove satisfactory.' Comment.

Case study: Downsizing at Britannia Airways

Britannia Airways, Britain's second biggest airline, has recently moved its computer processing from mainframe towards minicomputers and desktop PCs. For ten years, Britannia's mainframe-base engineering system has kept track of stock parts and logged all activities associated with company aircraft. But a system review team in 1990 which studied cost drivers — the financial infrastructure systems, the scheduling and crewing system, and the engineering system — decided that all the solutions could run in a more flexible mini environment at reduced cost. (Ernst and Young, an American consulting firm, claims that processing power on a mainframe is five times more than on a mini, fifty times more than on a microcomputer.) This led to the decision to downsize. In addition to installing minis, the company is planning to add hundreds of PCs. The change, says Peter Buckingham, Britannia's systems director, will give the company a new outlook.

Source: 'Britannia Airways: a case study', *Which Computer*, vol. 14, no. 2 (February 1991), pp. 47–8.

Questions

1 Describe changes that will occur in the Britannia organization as a result of this downsizing.
2 Would you expect resistance to these changes within the company? By whom? Why?
3 If you were a Britannia manager, how would you introduce this change to your department?

How would you identify resistance to the changes? What measures would you take to alter resistance behaviour?

4 According to Mr Buckingham, 'Everything has a finite life. I think people understand that more easily with hardware, but applications tend to get held onto, and that is when people can get themselves into problems. They wait too long and that is when the transition becomes painful.' Explain in greater detail Mr Buckingham's point of view. Give examples of the type of problems he is referring to. Do you agree with Mr Buckingham that periodic change is necessary? Explain.

5 Mr Buckingham does not recommend downsizing under all circumstances. 'It's a mistake to start with the answer', he says. 'If you go through the process of identifying business needs, and what systems are needed to support them, it will lead you to the answer.' Comment.

Key words

Change	Human engineering	Participative change
Directive change	Human factors	Resistance
Ergonomics		

Discussion questions

1 Resistance to change resulting from the introduction of computer technology is not unusual and should be expected when implementing new information systems. Comment.
2 In a computing environment, resistance may occur not only when a change is first introduced but throughout the life of a system. Comment, and explain the reasons why.
3 Will the same types of resistance to computer applications be found in a bank, manufacturing plant, government office, warehouse and retail outlet? Explain.
4 Will resistance differ in:
   (*a*) Old and young employees?

(*b*) Skilled and unskilled workers?
(*c*) Management and workers?
(*d*) Top management and operational management?
(*e*) Small and large organizations?
Explain.

5 A project that will displace 30 employees is kept secret until it is ready to be implemented. Comment on the ethical implications of such a strategy.

6 How is the management of change in a computer environment different from change in another technological environment, such as factory automation? Will resistance be of a different nature and magnitude?

7 How should strategies of change differ in the following situations?
(*a*) Implementation of a functional application.
(*b*) Implementation of an integrated system.
(*c*) Implementation of computer-aided design.
(*d*) Implementation of computer-assisted manufacturing.
(*e*) Implementation of a database management system.
(*f*) Implementation of a network application.
(*g*) Implementation of a distributed processing environment.
(*h*) A change from decentralized to centralized computing.

8 Under what circumstances would you approach human resistance on an individual level rather than a group level?

9 Is the problem of management of change in computer systems going to become easier because of experience or harder because systems are becoming more complex? Explain.

10 In the future, we may have:
(*a*) Automated offices.
(*b*) Home computers connected to offices, with work done at home.
(*c*) Robot-driven factories.
(*d*) Cashless businesses and teleshopping.
(*e*) Telemail and telenewspapers.
(*f*) A wired city.
(*g*) Intelligent management information systems with artificial intelligence capabilities.
In each of these cases, what unique problems of resistance should be expected? How would you plan to minimize adverse human factor effects?

11 Where should responsibility for human factors lie? With the vendor, analyst or users?

12 What variables are important in anticipating, measuring and dealing with resistance to organizational change?

13 Why do some computer professionals resist advances in information technology?

Bibliography

Cashmore, Carol and Richard Lyall. *Business Information*, Hemel Hempstead: Prentice Hall, 1988, pp. 270–86.

'Change management in information systems', *I/S Analyzer*, vol. 28, no. 8 (August 1990), p. 17.

Earl, Michael J. *Management Strategies for Information Technology*, Hemel Hempstead: Prentice Hall, 1989, pp. 192–213.

Godnig, E.G., J.S. Hocunda and R.I. Charleston. 'How to enhance visual comfort using computers', *Computers and Visual Stress*, Seacoast Information Services Inc., 1990, p. 108.

Gunton, Tony. *End User Focus*, Hemel Hempstead: Prentice Hall, 1988.

'Helping others become comfortable with technology', *I/S Analyzer*, vol. 6, no. 8 (August 1988), p. 16.

Hirschheim, R. and M. Newman. 'Information systems and user acceptance: theory and practice', *The Computer Journal*, vol. 31, no. 5 (1988), pp. 398–408.

Machiavelli, Niccolò. *The Prince*, translated by Luigi Rice, revised by E.R.P. Vincent, New York: New American Library, 1952.

Molich, R. and J. Nielsen. 'Improving a human–computer dialogue', *Communications of the ACM*, vol. 33, no. 3 (March 1991), pp. 338–48.

Ray, Nina A. and R.P. Minch. 'Computer anxiety and alienation: towards a definitive and parsimonious measure', *Human Factors*, vol. 32, no. 4 (August 1990), pp. 479–91.

Sankar, Yassin. *Management of Technological Change*, New York: John Wiley, 1991.

Westerman, John and Pauline Donoghue. *Managing the Human Resource*, Hemel Hempstead: Prentice Hall, 1989.

PART FOUR
Looking to the future

In this final section of the book, we discuss the impact of information systems on managers today, then look ahead to some of the political issues and technical advances of information technology that will affect the conduct of business tomorrow.

Chapter 14 talks about ways computers have changed management decision making, job responsibility and span of control. We also address the subject of IT as a competitive weapon and talk about personnel issues arising from computerization.

Chapter 15 looks at the problems of developing an information infrastructure and pool of computer expertise in the developing nations of the world. Do governments in advanced countries and western business managers have an obligation to transfer IT to the Third World? The chapter also discusses the issue of transborder data flow and how political restrictions on this flow can affect the world economy.

The final chapter of the book, Chapter 16, looks at future directions in computing and ways advanced IT technology will affect managerial decision making and business operations. Will society benefit from a telematic future? The views of optimists and pessimists are presented.

14 Impact of information systems on management

The purpose of computing is insight, not numbers.
Richard Hamming

Information technology is changing the nature of work at all organizational levels, from the factory floor to the board room. In this chapter we focus on the impact of computers on management: that is, how information systems are changing the way in which decisions are made, altering work and the span of a manager's control and challenging top-level management to use information technology as a **competitive weapon**.

Changes in decision making

With the emergence of business computing in the 1950s, many observers predicted that computers would be the managers of the future. This has not happened. Managers continue to be indispensable, particularly at higher managerial levels. What has changed is the **decision-making process** because of the ability of computers to process and deliver information to managers on which decision making is based.

To illustrate, most managers today receive computerized reports on the status of work for which they are responsible: for example, reports on production quotas, orders, inventory levels, sales targets, accounts payable, and so on. The type of report, the amount of detail, the time horizon of the data, the degree of data aggregation and the source of data input are tailored to the manager's position in the organizational hierarch. If the manager is at the operational level, the report will probably contain details of work in progress, such as sales per representative, quantity and cash value of each product sold, or cost figures for each unit in production in order to answer the question 'what is?'. Middle managers responsible for control are more likely to receive summarized data, figures on branch or division performance. The reports may compare current data with historical data, or current data with planning projections in order to identify discrepancies that call for corrective action. Computerized reports designed for top level managers concerned with strategic planning will contain operational figures for

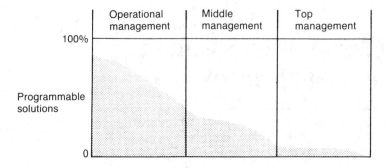

Figure 14.1 *Current problem-solving effort by computer, relative to programmable solutions possible with current technology*

the organization as a whole and will try to answer 'what if?' questions. Without doubt, computers provide today's managers with more information, more timely information and better quality of information on which to base decision making than in the past.

In addition, solutions to many managerial problems can now be programmed. Although the actual percentage of programmed versus non-programmed decision making varies from one industry to another, somewhere between 30 and 80 per cent of all decisions at operational and middle-management levels are programmable or semi-programmable given the current state of the art, especially in areas such as accounting, finance and manufacturing. (Figure 14.1 approximates current computer problem-solving effort in relation to decisions that could be programmed. The figure shows that managers do not take full advantage of the capabilities of present-day information technology.)

For upper management fewer decisions are programmable, because many problems at this level are ill-structured (often called **wicked problems**), complex in nature, with variables that cannot easily be quantified. Personnel decisions fall into this category. So do decisions regarding goals and policies. Top management's business acumen in promoting innovation, motivating the workforce and resolving disputes cannot be programmed. Indeed, there are many areas of business decision making that may never be automated. (The management functions where computers have thus far had little impact appears in Table 14.1.)

Nevertheless, many of the decisions of high-level managers are based on operational and control information generated by computer. In addition, the use of computerized planning and control models is becoming more common. Computer **decision support systems (DSS)** are of particular value in finding solutions to semi-structured problems — problems for which the solution requires managerial judgement and subjective analysis of information derived from a large number of, or complex, computations. For such problems, the manager plus the system can provide a more effective solution than either alone.

Table 14.1 *Impact of IT on functions of corporate management as of 1990*

Areas of impact ↓	Top management	Middle management	Operational management
Identify areas for use of IT	Little	Little	High
Analyse potential IT areas	None	Some	High
Decision to develop			
■ complex solutions	High	Little	Little
■ functional solutions	None	Little	High
Develop solutions	Little	Some	High
Implement functional solutions	None	Little	High
Implement DSS (Decision Support System) and EIS (Executive Support System)	High	High	Little
Evaluate solutions			
■ functional	None	Little	High
■ DSS/EIS	High	High	Little
Overcome resistance	High	Some	Some
Project Management	Little	Little	High

Suppose a sales representative receives an order for a product to be delivered in four months' time. The order is passed to the production department where a computerized order processing system — a conventional management information system (MIS) — reports that the order cannot be filled in the time specified given the production schedule.

Instead of rejecting the order out-of-hand, the production manager uses a DSS to evaluate the consequences of refusing the order. A query language with a database management system (DBMS) is used to check the customer's record. Does the product that the customer wants to order have a generous mark-up? Is the customer a regular who places orders of high monetary value? The answers that the system supplies to these and similar questions will help the production manager to decide whether refusal of the order will represent considerable loss of profit to the firm and jeopardize future orders.

If the customer is worth pursuing, the manager will consider options other than rejection. For example, a scheduling model of the DSS might be employed to determine if the order of another, less important customer, could be delayed, thus opening a slot in the production schedule. A production spreadsheet program might be used to examine the price of overtime, subcontracting parts or substitute components to fill the order. A cost–benefit model might be used to determine the effect of a lower profit margin or loss of goodwill. Various combinations of options might be entered as parameters of a simulation model to determine possible strategies. The decision of whether to accept or reject the order will ultimately be the production manager's, but the information provided by the DSS will contribute to this decision.

On the market today are hundreds of business-oriented packages that may be incorporated in a DSS. These include packages for general ledger, billing, invoicing, cost—benefit analysis, investment analysis, insurance, manpower planning, mailing, order transaction, payroll, auditing, inventory management, shareholder accounting, cheque processing, tax calculation and so on.

Programs packaged exclusively for decision support are also available off-the-shelf.

DSS executive software, designed to coordinate and monitor all software in a DSS system, is a sample DSS package. This software acts, in effect, like an operating system. For example, when processing in a remote mode or when the DSS accesses remote databases, the DSS executive software will coordinate and control the teleprocessing software.

Financial modelling language (FML) is another type of DSS package. FML consists of programs for financial forecasting, budgeting and management science computations. Most FMLs include the following capabilities:

- Financial ratio analysis.
- Statistical analysis.
- Return on investment (ROI) analysis.
- Forecasting and sensitivity analysis.
- What-if analysis.
- Graphics.

Sometimes, general purpose software, such as word processing, data management, communications, spreadsheets or graphics software can be integrated with DSS.

Increasingly, products originally developed for functions outside the DSS spectrum have had features and interfaces added so that they can be sold as DSS software. For example, easy-to-use spreadsheet packages with self-documentation are available on the market for managerial use in decision making. Many of these packages include data manipulation, graphics and even word processing functions. While there are obvious advantages of combining functions in this way, rarely do such packages have the power of more specialized packages or custom-developed DSS which are designed in-house to fit a particular manager's needs.

Expert systems can also help managers to reach decisions. An expert system is a computer program that draws upon the knowledge of human experts captured in a knowledge base to solve problems that normally require human expertise. Unlike conventional programming, an expert system does not follow an algorithm that details a precise series of steps to yield a precise result. Instead, processing is based on rules called **heuristics**, often called rules of thumb, that state relationships that are likely, but not guaranteed, to yield an outcome in an environment where information is uncertain or incomplete. Consider the thought process of a banker in deciding whether a loan applicant is a good credit risk. After examining hard data, the banker will intuitively evaluate the likelihood of repayment. This is the type of problem that expert systems are designed to address — problems that cannot be reduced to mathematical formulas. Well-designed expert systems imitate the reasoning process of human experts in solving specific problems within specific domains of knowledge.

At present, expert systems exist in only a few limited domains; however, their potential is vast. They may well change the way in which information is collected and evaluated in the future and may even replace some human managers on the job.

As a result of **research in artificial intelligence** (AI), progress is being made in areas such as voice recognition, natural language processing and computer vision that will also have an impact on the managerial role. For example, keyboards on terminals may be replaced with voice input, making it easier for managers to interact with computers. Natural language processing will help to eliminate the need for computer specialists to translate managerial requests for information into programming languages. This will increase the speed with which results are obtained and reduce the 'noise' of communication through an intermediary. Intelligent computer systems are projected for the future with the ability to query a manager to find out what type of information is needed and, based on this determination, self-program for the delivery of the required output.

A word of caution, however. The problems to be solved in artificial intelligence are formidable. As stated by Derek Partridge, a researcher in the field: 'Respect for the complexity and subtleties of human intelligence just keeps on growing.' People working on AI projects continually have to scale down their goals and objectives as they encounter unexpected hurdles. Furthermore, the lead time between AI prototypes and commercial products is proving to be quite lengthy.

Some commentators fear the increased reliance of managers on computers and processed information in decision making. The danger, they say, is that processed data filter out emotion, sentiment, mood and all of the irrational nuances of human situations. Yet effective management and decision making often depend on judgements based on the very elements which have been filtered out. It is argued that the manager who makes intuitive decisions that are just below the level of consciousness often has a clearer vision of reality than managers who base decisions solely on data expressed in words or numbers. After all, not all information that is required for problem solving can be rationally condensed into lists, categories, formulas or compact generalizations.

Quantifying the computer's impact on management decision making

Can the impact of information technology on management be quantified? Jerome Kanter has attempted to do so. He divided management into five functions (planning, organizing, staffing, direction and control) and gave each a number indicating susceptibility to computerization. He also assessed the percentage of time spent in each function by operational, middle and top management. A weighted value for each function was then determined and a computerized

Table 14.2 Calculation of the computerization coefficient for different levels of management

Function	Percentage susceptible to computerization	Top management		Middle management		Operating management	
		Percentage of total job	Weighted value	Percentage of total job	Weighted value	Percentage of total job	Weighted value
Planning	30	70	21.0	20	6.0	5	1.5
Organizing	15	10	1.5	10	1.5	5	1.0
Staffing	25	10	2.5	10	2.5	5	1.5
Direction	5	5	—	20	1.0	20	1.0
Control	80	5	4.0	40	32.0	70	56.0
Computerization quotient			29		43		61

Source: Jerome Kanter, Management-oriented Management Information Systems, Englewood Cliffs, NJ: Prentice Hall, 1982, p. 200

coefficient derived for each level of management (see Table 14.2). According to Kanter's calculations, 29 per cent of top management's functions, 43 per cent of middle management's and 61 per cent of operational management's functions can be computerized (Kanter, 1982, p. 196).

This analysis is simplistic in so far as it does not allow for industry differences or variations over time. Kanter's conclusions are also based on highly subjective weight assignments. Nevertheless, many commentators would argue that Kanter's percentages are reasonable approximations of the actual contribution made by computers to managerial decision making at present. The analysis is also useful because it shows that not all managerial functions can be computerized with ease and that the mix of functions at a given level is what determines the degree of computer assistance.

In coming years, as more operations research models are put into use and as progress is made in artificial intelligence, many functions not currently susceptible to computerization may become so and Kanter's percentages will have to be changed. But we are not yet close to Norbert Weiner's prediction that whatever man can do, computers will do. Managers are still needed to recognize and infer patterns from non-quantifiable variables (especially human variables), interpret information, evaluate divergences between planned and actual performance, and determine corrective actions. Even programmed decision making requires managers initially to think through problems and establish decision rules for problem solutions. As Peter Drucker states:

> We are beginning to realize that the computer makes no decisions; it only carries out orders. It's a total moron, and herein lies its strength. It forces us to think, to set the criteria. The stupider the tool, the brighter the master has to be — and this is the dumbest tool we have. ... It shows us — in fact, it compels us — to think through what we are doing. (Drucker, 1970, pp. 147–8)

Altered span of control and job content

Besides changing the decision-making process, computers have altered managerial **span of control** by changing the number and level of employees a manager supervises. They have also transformed the content of a manager's work. To illustrate, drilling machines were formerly operated by workers following blue-prints: the shopfloor was managed by a supervisor. Today, instruction tape (equivalent of the blueprint) may be fed into numerically controlled machines — machines that do the drilling without worker intervention. The semi-skilled or skilled workers who formerly operated drilling machines have been replaced by professional designers who prepare the instruction tape; the floor supervisor replaced by a worker who monitors production on a machine console. Figure 14.2 compares the role of managers when drilling is automated with traditional drilling operations.

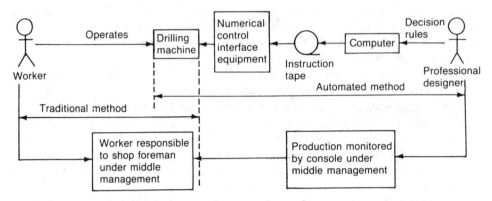

Figure 14.2 *Traditional and computerized approaches to operating a drilling machine*

The emergence of the electronic office is another example of changes in job content and span of control for managers. Word processing has replaced conventional office procedures for the creation of correspondence, documents, reports and memos. Electronic processing speeds computations and retrieval of data while electronic mail speeds inter-office communications. Teleconferencing reduces the need for business travel. These and other office activities listed in Table 14.3 have altered the duties of clerks, secretaries and administrative assistants and, as a consequence, the responsibilities of office managers.

Productivity tools are not limited to the factory floor and clerical operations. They are being introduced in all departments at all organizational levels. Furthermore, information systems to coordinate and control operations now make it possible to manage large enterprises with fewer personnel, particularly at middle management levels. There is evidence that computers are leading to a change in corporate structure, shrinking the traditional management hierarchy.

Another change for managers is that the use of computer systems in all areas of business — accounting, production, marketing, sales — requires managers to manage computer resources within their departments. They must acquire hardware and software; oversee their installation and testing; control quality, privacy, security and systems maintenance; evaluate systems performance; direct employees who work at computer terminals; budget for systems acquisition and operations; design computer facilities; and participate in new systems development. Although trained in business management, managers will undoubtedly have IT personnel in their employ who require supervision. And managers are expected to know how information technology can improve their operations, how to generate the data they need, and how to evaluate the information that computer systems deliver. Chapters in this book cover many of these topics.

All of these changes in the span of control and job content for managers has led to corporate restructuring in many firms. The company's organizational

Table 14.3 *Computer-induced changes in office work*

Area	Without a computer	With a computer
Information handling	Typing	Word processing
Memory	Human	Auxiliary memory of computer
Record-keeping	Manual filing	Computerized
Information retrieval	Manual search and human recall	Computer search and retrieval
Calendar	Manual	Automated, with prompts
Written communication	Postal service	Teleprocessing
Estimation	From experience	Through quantitiative models
Supervision and control	Manual	Exception reporting
Task distribution	Specialization of tasks	Functional and integrated system
Decision making	Judgement, intuition and experience	Testing alternatives, simulation and planning models
Graphics	Manual drawing	Graphic display; interactive displays
Database	Old or current data	Real-time data
Conferences	Attendance (in person)	Teleconferences

hierarchy is altered so that information technology can be absorbed and effectively managed. Planning and implementing an appropriate managerial framework for IT is a new responsibility for top level corporate managers.

Information as a competitive weapon

Most important of all, information technology presents managers with a challenge. They must learn to harness the speed and processing power of computers to achieve business goals and objectives. With computers changing the fundamental nature of industry, altering the structure of markets and transforming daily operations from product design to marketing and sales, opportunities exist to exploit information technology to enhance corporate strength in the marketplace, described next.

Products and services

The life cycle of a product and the speed of its delivery in many industries is being changed by technological advances in computing. With computer-aided design, for example, a computer can produce conventional engineering drawings, make design calculations and simulate operation of the device being designed. Robots, numerical control and process control contribute to manufacturing processes on the factory floor.

Furthermore, with microprocessor chips embedded in goods for sale, we now have a wide range of new products, called **smart products**, that compete on price with traditional goods but provide enhanced service. These products can sense variables in the environment, compute, make choices, and control and time specific activities. One example is a smart postal scale that determines the exact postage for a package being weighed once the destination is keyed by an operator or read by an optical scanner. Other examples of smart products appear in Table 14.4.

The problem for management is how to recoup development costs. The smart product must either have wide market appeal so development costs can be shared by many buyers or have more than one use. To illustrate, a smart clock might be embedded in a thermostat and also sold as part of a security system to lock house doors at night. To use smart products as a competitive weapon, companies must assess customer preferences and needs, design creative products, plan production to keep costs competitive and convince customers that the product is a desirable purchase.

Production economics

There is a major difference between businesses that have computerized ware-housing and inventory control and those that rely on manual operations. The computer helps the former take advantage of economies of scale by monitoring, controlling and coordinating deliveries and by processing warehouse records with speed and accuracy. The administration of the warehouse without a computer too often gets bogged down in paperwork. Warehouse automation is a method used in many businesses today to reduce production costs.

Almost every manufacturing business has areas where **production economics** can be enhanced by information resources. The challenge for the manager is to identify those areas and to implement appropriate information technology. At the same time, the manager must resist pressures to use computers for status or prestige when computer use will not contribute to greater competitiveness in the marketplace.

Market expansion

Communications technology has erased traditional geographic market limitations. By planning to meet the demand for computer goods and services and by looking beyond local markets, managers can gain a competitive advantage for their companies.

To give an example, we now have automatic teller machines, home banking and electronic transfer of funds. Bank managers who have not responded to the changing market for financial services are losing customers to institutions that offer electronic services. Likewise, a large number of hotels and car rental companies today rely on computerized reservation systems. The ability of these companies to service customers throughout the world has contributed to their

Table 14.4 *Examples of smart products*

Product	Description
Taxi meter	Keeps track of charges for as many as five persons sharing a cab, even when passengers are travelling to different destinations. The meter automatically adds luggage-handling charges to each bill
Thermostat	Automates control of heating, ventilation and air-conditioning systems. To prevent energy surcharges during peak demand periods, the thermostat is programmed to switch systems off for short periods of time when energy demand reaches a predetermined level
Crane	Includes a microprocessor-based monitoring system that computes safe machine operation, based on data supplied by the operator. A load chart stored in memory computes variables, such as safe boom acceleration and hook load. The operator can enter constraints such as the location of a power line or wall to be avoided. The range of the crane will be restricted accordingly
Television	Enables viewers to program entertainment for an evening. The correct channel for each program will be automatically selected. Captions for the deaf, transmitted in code and not visible on ordinary television sets, can be decoded and displayed at the bottom of the screen. Programs can be recorded and stored for later replay
Camera	Focus is set by an embedded microprocessor after distance to the subject being photographed is calculated using sonar technology. That is, the camera emits ultrasonic waves, and the length of time it takes for these waves to reach the subject, bounce off, and return to the camera is used by the microprocessor to calculate distance. Camera focus is then automatically adjusted. (More than one microprocessor may be used in a single camera, each performing a different function)
Watch	The wearer can enter dates of importance, such as birthdays and anniversaries. The watch will flash a reminder when each date arrives
Calculator	A sequence of instructions can be programmed for execution when a given key is pressed. Special-purpose calculators are available for estate agents, financial agents, persons planning diets, airline pilots, and so forth. These calculators will perform square roots, logarithms, and other trigonometric functions in a preset sequence according to the use for which the calculator is designed.
Car	Microprocessors in an automobile can be used for control of emissions, engine operation (e.g. air–fuel mixture, ignition timing), door locks, anti-theft alarms, air-conditioning, belt buckling, braking, skidding and speed control. Other uses are vehicle diagnosis, collision avoidance, maintenance analysis and vehicle performance analysis
Materials handler	Uses sensors to inspect certain materials passing on an assembly line. If materials are upside-down or at the wrong angle for the next assembly stage, robot arms will correct the position. Materials can also be scanned and X-rayed in search of structural defects, such as air bubbles, and removed if they fail to meet manufacturing specifications

growth. Competitors who have failed to implement computerized reservation systems of their own have lost market share to those that have.

Reduction of buyer/supplier power

Both buyer and supplier groups, if strong, can demand favourable terms in contract negotiations that reduce the profitability of companies. Information technology can be a weapon used by management to counter the power of these two groups.

Buyers have power when they purchase large volumes relative to a company's total sales. These customers can threaten a company's survival by moving their businesses to competitors, which explains why concessions are given to them at the bargaining table. However, buyer leverage is lost when a company makes switching costs expensive.

To illustrate how information technology can be used by management to diminish **buyer power**, consider a medical supply company that provides online order entry terminals and inventory management software for customers. The order system essentially locks customers into a buyer relationship with the medical company: to switch business to a competitor, customers would have to develop new order procedures. These procedures would then have to be tested and employees would have to be trained in their use. The cost of developing and implementing new procedures rules out an indiscriminate switch.

Information technology can also help a company identify the profit potential of different buyer groups. All industries have some customers that are more expensive to service than others. The problem for management is to identify which buyers bring in profits and which buyers should be pared from customer rosters (or charged more because they are expensive to service) in order to maximize profits. Consider the insurance industry which has traditionally provided full services to all business customers. Today, many insurance companies are building up extensive databases on claims for use in identifying service costs and profitable customer categories. The buyer power of some groups may be diminished because of the information that the computer provides. Here, technology is used as a strategic weapon in buyer selection.

Like buyers, suppliers can reduce a company's potential profits. Suppliers can negotiate concessions in their favour when they control access to sources for raw materials, machinery, capital or labour, or when the cost of turning to an alternative supplier is high. Information technology is providing ways for managers to reduce the power of suppliers by introducing new products, services and distribution channels. For instance, robots are a viable alternative for high-priced labour. In banking, computer systems help managers decide on optimal funds sourcing. (The systems help gather and process data on money markets and provide managers with information regarding the current and future money positions of their institutions.) No longer are bank managers at a strategic disadvantage in dealing with their major supplier — the financial markets.

Creation of entry barriers

When new competitors enter a market, the profits of established firms fall unless demand is growing fast enough to accommodate the new companies. This explains why most industries try to establish conditions that favour existing industry participants and slow or exclude new entrants.

Information technology can be used as a tool by management to create **entry barriers** and deterrents. Suppose a company installs a network to support its multilocational distribution facilities. The network helps to improve operations and, at the same time, makes it hard for a new entrant to be competitive without an equally efficient distribution system. Suppose a company's reputation has been built on its information technology capabilities. A newcomer has a formidable capital barrier to overcome.

Joint ventures

Information technology provides companies with ways to alter their relationships with rivals. It is not always necessary to engage in market warfare to gain a competitive advantage: cooperation may work as well. For example, small rival banks in some towns share ATMs, which helps them stand against large banks in their communities. A strategic advantage may be obtained by sharing software or by establishing computer-to-computer connections with rivals. A modern manager needs to be alert to possible **joint information technology ventures**.

Support of business objectives

Every company has **business objectives**. The challenge for management is to find ways to apply information technology to help realize these objectives. Suppose that high priority is given to the reduction of costs. The implementation of a computer system to transmit and process transactions might contribute to desired savings. Suppose a distinguished product is desired. The use of computerized machine tools might lead to manufacturing precision that no competitor can match.

Since most companies have many demands on their financial and personnel resources, the problem of management is to identify the most cost effective use of information technology to support corporate objectives. There are a large number of options, and Table 14.5 lists sample systems that might be implemented for the objectives just mentioned: lower costs and product differentiation. Similar lists might be compiled for other corporate objectives.

Of course, the burden on management is not limited to selection of appropriate

Table 14.5 *Strategies for cost reduction and product differentiation*

Functional area	Strategies	
	Cost reduction	Product differentiation
Administration	Planning and budgeting models Automation for staff reduction Electronic mail	Office automation for integrative office functions
Product design and development	Product engineering control systems Product budget control system CAD workstations	CAD R&D database access and use
Marketing	Market research report analysis Market distribution control	Econometric models for marketing Telemarketing system Service-oriented distribution system
Operations	Cost control system Process control system Material requirements planning (MRP) Inventory control system	CAM products CAD/CAM Quality control system Customer order-entry system
Sales	Sales control system Sales incentive control Advertising control system	Customer support system Dealer support system Customer/dealer/vendor OLRT system
Computer services	Budget control Cost control	Analysis for competitive advantage

systems. Managers must also oversee their implementation, integrate the use of the systems in the daily operations of the firm and overcome resistance to innovation among employees.

Personnel issues arising from computerization

Thus far, this chapter has focused on ways computers have changed the role of managers and methods of decision making. Before closing the chapter, a few comments are in order on personnel issues arising from computerization that require managerial expertise.

A firm's power base is altered as a result of computerization. According to organizational theorists, four variables are associated with corporate power: links to others, irreplaceability, dependency and uncertainty. In all four areas, information technology scores highly, giving power to computer personnel. Applications such as payroll and accounting have become irreplaceable and link data processing personnel to many functional departments. These departments depend on computing, particularly when integrated systems have been implemented. Computer planning models and programs for control and decision making also reduce uncertainty among users. No wonder computer departments and their personnel have gained so much power.

Shifts in power, however, are accompanied by bruised egos, jealousy and conflict as traditional power bases erode. Management skill in reducing tension and restoring harmonious interpersonal/interdepartmental relationships is taxed to the limit following computerization.

Resentment against IT personnel also stems from the fact that computer departments often win in competition for scarce corporate resources. Computers require major capital investments and large operating budgets. Few departments will admit being less deserving. Should hostility to computer personnel become overt, low priority to job requests may be assigned, a retaliation that reinforces and sustains resentment.

Unrealistic expectations of information users' poorly drawn system specifications or projects that have fallen behind schedule may also be the cause of hostility directed toward computer personnel. Often, computer professionals working in a crisis atmosphere fail to take the time to develop positive relationships with users. Unions may exacerbate existing tensions. *The Times* newspaper first ceased publication, then was sold because of industrial strife over computerization. Modern managers that prove inept in coping with and resolving the social and psychological tensions that accompany computerization may find the very survival of their firms at stake.

Summing up

Computers are changing the nature of a manager's work and altering methods of decision making. Managers are also being displaced by computers, although the threat of unemployment is less acute at top levels of management than at operational levels (see Figure 14.3). There are still too many 'wicked' problems for management to resolve, problems which defy programmed solutions because their variables cannot be easily quantified. However, research in artificial intelligence, data management, linguistics and psychology will undoubtedly expand the role of computers in decision making in the future and lead to further managerial displacement.

The immediate concern of corporate management is to learn how to utilize information technology as a competitive weapon. Opportunities exist to use the technology in the manufacture of products and in the selling of services. The technology can contribute to production economics, market expansion, the reduction of buyer/supplier power, the creation of entry barriers and the formation of alliances. Corporate objectives can also be supported by computer systems.

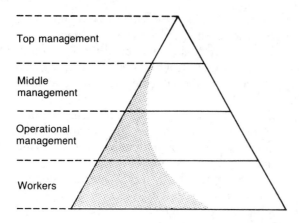

Figure 14.3 *Displacement caused by computerization*

An important role of managers is to develop strategies to take advantage of information technology and to mitigate threats to the company because of use of this technology by rivals.

Traditional organizational structures are not able to respond to growing pressures for more and better information, nor are they able to manage new information technologies effectively.

A reorganization of the firm, the responsibility of top level management, may be necessary for the effective implementation and overseeing of information technology.

Case study: **Missed opportunities**

The findings below are from surveys conducted in the United Kingdom during the 1980s to determine how effectively British managers use information technology (IT). According to sample survey results:

1 One-third of the managers who use information technology daily feel that they do not have adequate knowledge of how IT can help them in their work.

2 Fifty-nine per cent of the respondents believe that top management does not understand how information technology contributes to the business at present.

3 Fifty-three per cent believe they have an inadequate knowledge of how to use available IT systems.

4 Half of the organizations surveyed have no clearly defined strategy for implementing IT.

5 Two-thirds of the respondents believe that IT is not integrated with the corporate plan.

6 Over 40 per cent of the managers surveyed believe their own senior management did not realize what is involved in successfully deploying IT.

7 Only four out of ten managers are confident of their ability to obtain expected benefits from IT.

8 Only 9 per cent of companies surveyed have formulated integrated IT plans to take account

of the single European market. Half of the firms did not believe there is a need to integrate their IT and business plans for 1992. *Source:* These results have been drawn from a variety of surveys. The statistics come from two articles by Ian Meiklejohn in *Management Today*, 'Firms take it to heart', pp. 137–8 and 'Single market, single system' (February 1989), p. 154.

Questions

1 Do you believe that these survey results accurately reflect the use of IT by British managers? Support your position. If you are a student living outside the United Kingdom, would similar results be reported if managers in your own country were surveyed? On what evidence do you rely for your point of view?

2 What conclusions might be drawn from these survey results?

3 David Butler, a management consultant, likens the failure of British managers to conceive and implement appropriate information systems for 1992 to a time bomb ticking away quietly within most companies. He says: 'Instead of [IT] being an instrument to drive the single unified market forward, information systems may become the Achilles heel of the whole process, the single bottleneck that thwarts the process of change.' Comment.

4 Suggest ways to improve management use of information technology.

Case study: Airlines lead in use of information technology

In both Europe and the United States, the airline industry has led other business sectors in the aggressive use of information technology. Deregulation and the industry consolidation which followed are contributing factors to automation of operations. 'As airlines consolidate, merge and get bigger, they get more difficult to manage', says Richard Golaszewski, an industry consultant. 'You have to gain efficiency somewhere, so you have to do more automation.'

Increased competition in the airline industry has also put pressure on major carriers to orchestrate computer activity to improve the quality of operations. For example, automated maintenance scheduling and inventory control of spare parts help the airllines reduce costs and delays, and improve maintenance efficiency and reliability as well. Today's planes even have onboard computers that monitor up to 300 parameters in flight, such as engine temperature and oil consumption — data transmitted to ground computers and processed in search of anomalies.

In addition, crowded skies are forcing the airlines to explore innovative information technologies for routing flights. And in the cockpit, most activities, from the firing of the engines to landing of the aircraft, are under computer control. In effect, the pilot is a systems manager who makes sure that cockpit computers function properly.

Source: Amiel Kornel, 'Airlines lead way in computer uses', *The International Herald Tribune* (15 December 1989), p. 18.

Questions

1 Explain why major airline carriers are aggressive in their implementation of computer technology.

2 How can information technology benefit airline managers in the following areas?
   (a) Products and services.
   (b) Production economics.
   (c) Market expansion.
   (d) Reduction of buyer/supplier power.
   (e) Creation of entry barriers.
   (f) Joint ventures.
   (g) Support of business objectives.

3 Some critics charge that automated flying

raises new dangers in civil aviation. They want pilots to preserve hands-on control of planes, not trusting computer hardware and software to operate reliably in all flight conditions. Discuss the pros and cons of an automated cockpit from management's point of view.

Case study: IT network at Balfour Beatty for a competitive advantage

Balfour Beatty, an international construction group based in the United Kingdom, builds everything from houses to power stations and underseas cabling. With the number of construction contracts reduced in recent years because of recession, the company decided to invest heavily in an IT network to link the computer resources of its twelve operating companies in order to enhance its ability to compete. One of the benefits of the network is to allow the company to collect information on material requirements at scattered construction sites and to order the materials centrally, in bulk, at a cost advantage. The network also facilitates linkage of resources. For example, when Balfour was calculating an estimate for the Channel Tunnel high-speed rail link, the network enabled the project team in Kent to call upon the expertise of a specialist in Edinburgh, and gave the team access to the company's database on component prices for its computerized estimating system on which the tender for a contract based its calculations.

'IT strategy is being driven by commercial necessity', says Richard Meade, IT development manager of Balfour. The key variables in any construction project are cost and speed of completion, areas in which information technology can play a decisive role.

Source: David Dobson, 'Building a brighter future', *Which Computer*, vol. 14, no. 2 (February 1991), pp. 122–4.

Questions

1 As reported by David Dobson, 'A recent report by City accountants KPMG Peat Marwick said that of companies which went into receivership in the last year, close to 25 per cent were in the construction industry. More than ever before construction companies are having to watch the pennies to ensure that they can compete effectively for the limited number of contracts on offer or risk the chance that they may go bust.'

In a period of hard times for the construction industry, why do you think that Balfour Beatty decided to invest heavily in an IT network?

2 Computer resources at Balfour include 75 minicomputers which support over 800 workstations. Plans are being made to add peripherals to the network; for example, the 20 plotters used with computer-aided design (CAD) workstations to provide cable diagrams and design drawings. How would the addition of these plotters to the network contribute to Balfour's competitive advantage?

3 Many large-scale construction projects are joint ventures between a number of firms. How does this fact help explain why paper is still king on most building sites in this age of computers? How might standardized CAD systems help alleviate the paper glut?

4 Give examples of ways, other than those already mentioned, the network may help Balfour compete in the construction industry.

Key words

Artificial intelligence
  research
Business objectives
Buyer power
Competitive weapon
Decision-making
  process

Decision support
  systems (DSS)
Entry barriers
Expert systems
Heuristics
Joint information
  technology ventures

Production economics
Smart products
Span of control
Wicked problems

Discussion questions

1 How do computers benefit management?
2 What negative impact on management have computers had?
3 How can the adverse effects of computers on decision making be minimized? How can benefits be enhanced?
4 How have computers altered decision making at the following management levels?
  (*a*) Top.
  (*b*) Middle.
  (*c*) Operational.
5 Would the impact of computers on management vary with:
  (*a*) Size of firm?
  (*b*) Style of management?
  (*c*) Content of management?
  (*d*) Qualifications of managers?
6 How do decision support systems aid management?
7 How can information technology be used as a competitive weapon by management?
8 What problems do managers have to face when implementing a computerized information system? How can these problems be minimized?
9 Do computers turn managers into conformists? Do managers lose their:
  (*a*) Individuality?
  (*b*) Creativity and innovativeness?
  (*c*) Self-confidence and self-assurance?
  (*d*) Independence in thinking?
  Comment.
10 Computers may solve technical problems for managers, but they create more problems than they solve (including human and social problems). Comment on this statement.

11 How has computer technology affected the quality of decision making? The quality of management?
12 How can a manager's knowledge of computing contribute to:
    (a) Decision making?
    (b) Control of the negative impact of computers?
    (c) Improved efficiency and effectiveness of computer usage?
13 Why do managers feel threatened by computer technology? What can be done to alleviate management fears?
14 Why do many firms need to restructure their companies to accommodate modern information technology?
15 Why are young managers more favourably oriented to computer systems than their seniors?
16 Which levels of management have been most and least affected by computer technology? Why? Do you expect this to change in the near future? Why?

Bibliography

Davenport, T.H. and J.E. Short. 'The new industrial engineering: information technology and business process design', *Sloan Management Review*, vol. 31, no. 4 (Summer 1990), pp. 11–27.

Dertouzos, M.L. 'Building the information marketplace', *Technology Review*, vol. 94, no. 1 (January 1991), pp. 28–40.

Dixon, Paul J. 'Technology issues facing corporate management in the 1990s', *MIS Quarterly*, vol. 13, no. 3 (1989), pp. 247–56.

Drucker, Peter. *Technology, Management and Society*, London: Heinemann, 1970.

Gunton, Tony. *End-user Focus*, Hemel Hempstead: Prentice Hall, 1988.

Gurbaxani, Vijay and Seungjin Whang. 'The impact of information systems on organizations and markets', *Communications of the ACM*, vol. 34, no. 1 (January 1991), pp. 59–73.

Johnson, H. Russell and Shelley R. Carrico. 'Developing capabilities to use information strategically', *MIS Quarterly*, vol. 12, no. 1 (1988), pp. 37–47.

Kanter, Jerome. *Management-oriented Management Information Systems*, Englewood Cliffs, NJ: Prentice Hall, 1982.

Konsynski, Benn R. and Warren McFarlan. 'Information partnership: shared data, shared scale', *Harvard Business Review*, vol. 68, no. 5 (September–October 1990), pp. 114–20.

Napier, H. Albert. 'Enabling technologies for organizations and individuals' in A.M. Jenkins, H.S. Siegle, W. Wojtkowski and W.G. Wojtkowski (eds), *Research Issues in Information Systems — an agenda for the 1990s*, Dubuque, Ia: Wm. C. Brown, 1990, pp. 83–100.

Rockart, John F. and James E. Short. 'IT in the 1990s: managing organizational independence', *Sloan Management Review*, vol. 30, no. 2 (1989), pp. 7–17.

Ryan, A. 'Before you burn out, chill out', *Computerworld*, vol. 24, no. 47 (19 November 1990), pp. 111–12.

Taylor, James R. and Jo Mulamba Katambwe. 'Are new technologies really shaping our organizations?', *Information and Software Technology*, vol. 11, no. 5 (October 1988), pp. 245–51.

15 Global issues related to information management

The world has become a marketplace for information. . . . Computerized data recognizes no border check-points, customs, duty or immigration officers.
Wayne Masden

A basic premise of this textbook is that the assimilation of information technology and astute management of information resources are keys to survival in the modern business world. Information technology (IT) is used to streamline operations and introduce innovative products to the marketplace in order to increase the profitability of the firm. Planning, problem solving, report preparation and business meetings fill the schedules of information managers. Few have time to ponder how to transfer information technology to developing nations or how to control transborder data flow. The issues are remote, not related to daily concerns.

Yet these issues will affect world markets for years to come. Every firm will be affected by the trade policies and regulations placed on the flow of information across national borders that are under consideration today in national legislatures and international organizations. Laws relating to the protection of intellectual property, brain drain, outsourcing and the transfer of technology to the Third World will have an effect on relations with competitors in world markets. The purpose of this chapter is to introduce you to some of the global issues in information management that will shape the business environment of your future.

Transfer of information technology

How can Third World countries, which lack information resources, compete in world markets? This is an issue that festers relationships between the less developed nations of the world and IT-rich countries, many of which were colonial powers in the past. Do developed nations 'owe' the Third World help in building a competitive infrastructure of computer hardware, software and trained IT personnel? Is such an infrastructure necessarily desirable? Is the transfer of IT possible? Feasible? How?

You will find no unanimity of opinion when these questions are debated in international forums, not even among leaders of the Third World. For example, some claim that the transfer of information technology to their countries will spectacularly enhance their process of development. They want to leap-frog into a high-tech future and ask for western assistance in the acquisition of IT. Others, technological pessimists, argue that the transfer of IT will 'reinforce existing social structures, exacerbating politico-economic dependency and the loss of cultural identity'. They fear that computer technology will lead to labour displacement, raising already high levels of unemployment.

While many 'have' nations philosophically accept an obligation to the 'have nots', they point to the failure of many sincere efforts to transfer IT in the past. The lack of specialists and technicians to operate the complex machinery of the introduced technologies is one cause. Legal barriers and resistance to change in the host country are other problems that have stymied 'donor' teams. For example, one group sent to implement an accounting application in a Third World country encountered a law that required the entry of data in special accounting books in order to satisfy the requirements of official auditing. As a result, data from computer printouts had to be entered by hand in these books, negating the benefit of computerization.

Unfortunately, experiences like this are not uncommon. Computer scientist Farhad Mavaddat cautions that technology transfer should be viewed as a transplant operation involving societies as living organisms. Not a simple operation at all. Projects must be selected with care and cautionary measures planned to weaken the rejective forces in the recipient society. Mavaddat concludes that 'it is easier to transfer a technology to a less complex society even if its economic development indicators show a lower value compared to some with complex, traditionalist societies.'

Most of the 'have' nations have democratic systems and market economies. While governments may favour the transfer of technology to the Third World, corporate managers may not. Their interest lies in profits, not the sharing of technology that creates those profits. Corporations willingly participate in the transfer of technology only if it is in their economic interest to do so. In Third World countries, where the need for technical assistance is great, business people typically operate in centralized command economies where government officials mandate corporate policy. The process that business people must set in motion to motivate western corporations to share information technology is simply not understood. Cultural differences as in this example are additional hurdles to IT transfer.

Many experts in information technology believe that domestic research and development are a prerequisite for sound selection, efficient assimilation and successful adaptation of foreign technologies. Third World leaders should plan for a gradual transition to technological independence, they say, not expect to compete with advanced countries in areas like the manufacture of computers, especially those using VLSI (very large-scale integrated circuit) technology, in spite of the social prestige such manufacture will bring. (India and China tried the latter approach, but their mainframes do not meet western standards. South Korea, Taiwan, Singapore and Hong Kong have been successful in the manufacture of microcomputers, but they have the investment capital and technological infrastructure most Third World countries lack.)

Because software development is less capital intensive than hardware manufacture, the software market is cheaper to breach. And developed countries have an interest in training Third World analysts and programmers because of backlogs in software supply. In part, this is attributed to the fact that many of the computer applications in the portfolio of the west are outdated, more than twenty years old, and need replacement. Other applications need to be upgraded to function on and take advantage of advanced hardware architectures. In addition, the market for software is expanding as developing countries play 'catch-up', while old clients demand user-friendly, multi-vendor, integrated and customized solutions to a growing realm of problems. Software demand will be worth an estimated US $340 billion by 1996.

However, software development requires manpower trained in project management, software engineering and advanced techniques of analysis, design and implementation. For example, systems analysts and programmers should be knowledgeable about open systems, telecommunications protocols and network management, graphic libraries, shifting standards relating to file formats and powerful programming languages, like 4GLs (fourth generation language systems). As many as 10 to 100 software engineers may be required to write 50,000 to 500,000 lines of code over a period of 5 to 36 months for major projects, which requires organizational and managerial skills of project managers. Software development is hardly appropriate for a Third World country with limited computer expertise.

Gaining computer expertise

Clearly, the first step in acquiring computer expertise is education. To supplement internal computer science programmes, which are limited in developing countries, many students are sent for study abroad. In 1989, over half of the doctorates granted in the United States in mathematics and computer science went to foreign students. Many of these students looked for jobs in American industry upon graduation in order to gain work experience. Many were hired.

Unfortunately, from the point of view of Third World leaders, many of these students decide to stay abroad, a form of **brain drain** that developing countries can ill afford. Many are aggressively recruiting their nationals to return home. For example, Taiwan pays the airfare home and gives its returning students both money and interest-free loans. The National Taiwan University offers on-the-spot tenured full professorships to lure back qualified nationals. The strategy adopted by Sri Lanka is to create projects with foreign investment and joint collaboration that will present opportunities for career advancement for returnees. Sometimes the courts force the issue. Tata Consulting Service (India) resorted to legal action to force engineers to return after a foreign tour of duty.

With shortages in the IT labour pool in many developed countries, the competition for knowledge workers is increasing worldwide. Brain drain is a problem that will continue to plague the Third World for years to come.

Outsourcing

Another strategy used by developing countries to gain computer expertise is to subcontract work, usually a small segment of a large systems development project. This may include the manufacture of computer parts, data preparation or programming. Often the work is planned, managed and financed by suppliers who favour **outsourcing** to reduce costs. The developing country benefits because such projects provide employment to nationals, help develop a core of knowledge workers through on-the-job training and work experience, and reduce the capital outlay required to enter world information markets.

The outsourcing of data preparation was commonplace in the 1980s. To subcontract a labour-intensive activity like this makes economic sense to western firms because of wage differentials between workers at home and workers in developing countries. (A data entry clerk earns between $2,600 and $3,000 per annum in Barbados or Jamaica while a comparable job commands a salary between $10,000 and $12,000 in the United States.) Data entry clerks in developing countries have also gained a reputation for accuracy not matched by their counterparts in the developed world. Santa Lucia, one country which supports local data preparation, met the requirement of an acceptable turnaround time by constructing a fully digital earth station with telecommunications links to the United States, Canada and Europe. Many countries do data processing for foreign banks, handling electronic transfer of funds and other financial services. The Cayman Islands, Nauru, Vanuatu, the Cook Islands, Maldives, the Marshall Islands and Micronesia are examples.

However, worldwide the outsourcing of data preparation is in decline, in part because of security issues, but primarily because the growing use of online computer systems, like point-of-sales terminals, has reduced the need for offline batch data preparation. New technologies in optical scanning and image and voice processing are also changing the way data are collected, reducing the need for keyed data entry. On the other hand, subcontracts for software development are on the rise. In 1989, an Irish programmer earned approximately $15,000. The salary for a US programmer was twice that amount. No wonder many American firms like to subcontract their programming abroad.

Taiwan, Singapore and Korea are major exporters of software. India has declared software development an economic goal. At present, most of India's software exports are to the United States, largely through **bodyshopping**, a practice of sending engineers abroad to develop software for customers. Bodyshopping has proved to be an easy way to get business, but travel costs are high and the risk is great that nationals posted in America may find more lucrative jobs and resign. One of China's modernization priorities is likewise the development of its software industry. Chinese bids for software projects are low, so that outsourcing to China can be very cost effective for western firms, but the lack of English speakers in China is a disadvantage. Many software contracts are lost to India, where English is widely spoken, as a result.

The downside of software outsourcing from the point of view of corporate managers in developed countries is the danger of piracy. Software piracy may prevent a company from recouping its investment in computer projects and may even undermine its competitiveness. No wonder firms want guarantees that outsourced software will be secure, favouring subcontractors in countries with a legal framework for the protection of intellectual property and computing resources, and legal remedies if project security is breached.

In an international context, the protection of software (and other computer resources) is a very complex issue because of conflicting domestic laws on copyrights, patents, trade secrets and crime. And these laws, if applicable to information (many are not, written to protect tangible property instead), quickly become outdated because of the speed with which the computer revolution is changing the way business is conducted. Even in countries that have participated in the computer revolution from the start, people are only beginning to address the question of what constitutes ethical conduct in computerized business operations. With the world becoming smaller through trade and the flow of information across national borders, there is a growing need for international standards, treaties and laws related to information technology. The lack of these impedes the transfer of technology to the Third World.

Transborder data flow

Transborder data flow is the crossing of information across national boundaries. Coined in the late 1970s to describe the growing international exchange of data, the term is generally associated with the transmission of computer-processed data (or data to be processed by computer following transmission) across frontiers by telecommunications technology; for example, programmed instructions from Paris to Mexico for assembly-line machines, electronic transfer of funds from bankers in London to clients in Hong Kong, technical and scientific information from researchers in Japan to colleagues in Jakarta, reservation data from travel agents in Singapore to Qantas airlines in Australia, or instructions from officials in Houston to astronauts in space. Transborder data flow is vital to world trade.

Restrictions on transborder data flow

However, many nations place **restrictions** on the content of data entering and leaving their countries. They believe that information is power. As stated by Louis Jorvet, a French Magistrate of Justice, 'Information has an economic value and the ability to store and process certain types of data may well give one country political and technological advantage over other countries. This, in turn, may lead to a loss of national sovereignty through supernational data flows.' (Quoted by John Eger in *Datamation*.)

Brazil's National Policy on Informatics is one of the most restrictive regarding transborder data flow. For example, Brazil will allow only Brazilian-made hardware and software within the country (with the exception of Microsoft's disc operating system (DOS)) and prohibits processing by computers outside the country via real-time communications facilities if the same function can be performed internally. France forbids the transmission to data on its natural resources, development plans, government-owned industries and certain economic indicators to data centres outside the country, imposing a fine or five-year prison sentence on data transmission defined by the French government as 'sensitive'. Germany requires that data entering the country be processed by local data processing centres prior to distribution in the country. (This results in redundant processing for preprocessed data.) Taiwan requires that banks and corporations that use international leased circuits hire approved security officers to monitor the content of outgoing data traffic. The Post Office in the United Kingdom has the right to read all transmitted messages, a right that implies that firms must provide their cryptographic codes. Sweden has a Data Inspection Board with powers to approve all transmissions of personal data crossing its borders. Why such restrictive policies? To protect local data processing and government-regulated telecommunications industries (PTTs), to ensure that the privacy rights of citizens are respected, to prevent information leakage that might jeopardize national security, and to control the outflow of domestic economic data that might lead to a loss of economic power.

Third World leaders resent the dominance of the west in forums which decide international communications policies and IT standards. They object to use of information on their nations collected by western satellite systems without their permission, claiming that vast amounts of unscreened private information concerning their countries already reside in western databases. Data monopolization is also a concern: that is, the concentration of scientific and technical information in large databases in the west to which access is limited. The technology of telecommunications raises the spectre of electronic forms of colonialism. It is much less costly to utilize remote computing power than develop domestic information resources. Yet without computing resources of their own, developing countries run the risk of becoming dependent on foreign computer centres and western IT expertise, a dependency that is politically unacceptable. This dependency may also block efforts to advance technologically in fields such as agriculture, transportation, medicine and business, since information technology has spin-off effects. Already, say Third World leaders, computer processing erodes the value of one of the principle assets of their countries: their abundant supply of inexpensive labour. Now, advances in telecommunications, which facilitate transborder data flow, pose an additional threat to their economies. Policies that restrict data outflow are one way to counter this threat.

Regulation of transborder data flow

The problem for world leaders is to establish a framework of laws, treaties and international agreements to protect national interests and keep the potential for conflict inherent in transborder data flow under control. To illustrate conflicts that arise, let us look at the issue of access to financial records. Many countries have financial confidentiality laws and strictly regulate the flow of financial information abroad. For example, the Protection of Business Act of 1978 (South Africa) and Foreign Proceedings Act of 1976 (Australia) prohibit the disclosure of financial and other business-related information to foreign countries. Switzerland and countries like the United Kingdom that host offshore financial centres are known for their bank secrecy laws. In opposition to such confidentiality laws are US law enforcement agencies which claim they need access to protected financial records in order to track down and prosecute international criminals involved in drug money laundering and tax evasion. For the benefit of these agencies, the American government has negotiated a number of treaties to open bank and business records previously kept secret: for example, the USA–Bahamas Legal Assistance Treaty of 1987 and the USA–Cayman Islands Mutual Legal Assistance Treaty of 1986. Belize, Antigua, Grenada, Bermuda and the British Virgin Islands are just a few of the countries which today open financial records, formerly protected by statute, to American scrutiny. Even Switzerland has buckled to American pressure, signing a treaty with the United States that allows Swiss bank officials to lift secrecy in criminal matters.

To supplement bilateral treaties on transborder data flow, international agreements on data flow issues are being worked out in international organizations like the United Nations (UN), Council of Europe, GATT (General Agreement on Trades and Tariffs), ITU (International Telecommunications Union), ISO (International Standards Organization), CCITT (International Telegraph and Telephone Consultative Committee), OECD (Organization of Economic Cooperation and Development) and others. The OECD addressed the protection of personal data in transborder data flows with its 1980 *Guidelines on the Protection of Privacy and Transborder Flows of Personal Data*, a document that covers the collection of data, data quality, security, openness and accountability. Other issues under consideration by international bodies are data standards, copyright protection, legal aspects of competition, computer criminality, communication-based services, value-added services, satellite surveillance, security and trade sanctions, to name but a few.

The ownership of data is a key point of contention. Are data transmitted from one country to another the property of the sender or the receiver? If retransmitted to a third party, does the destination country own that data? Data taxation is another thorny issue. If incoming or outgoing data are taxed, will the cost of data transmission jeopardize world trade? (Italy is one country with a surcharge on transborder data flow.) Debt-ridden countries may decide data taxation is a good source of revenue.

Data flows are supported by satellite, microwave, radio, coaxial cables and laser communications. Standards for these telecommunications lines and licensing rules are technical matters that require international cooperation. In many nations, a government monopoly regulates and controls internal telecommunications services as well as services to other countries; other nations allow competition between privately owned licensed carriers. In formulating regulations for telecommunications, the interests of governments, multinational corporations, telecommunications equipment suppliers and carriers must all be reconciled. There is also the problem of protocols for telecommunications gateways to allow rapid and decipherable communications between different computer systems and dissimilar data networks. One organization working on this problem is the ITU which is currently setting protocols for a global network of high-speed pipelines that will combine text with video, voice and facsimile transmissions in digital media, called the Integrated Services Digital Network (ISDN). In opposition are countries and vendors that have billions of pounds invested in analogue technology.

Security and data integrity

All business people have concerns about data availability, quality, timeliness, accuracy, reliability, privacy and security, as we discussed in Part Two of this book. Transborder data flow just adds to these worries. How reliable is the collection and processing of data in volatile regions of the world? Ethnic, religious or political strife could spell disaster for corporations dependent on foreign data if telecommunications are disrupted, computer facilities sabotaged or data integrity compromised. Terrorist groups, such as the Committee to Liquidate and Hijack Computers and Action Directe in France have already targeted computer facilities in Europe. Third World computer installations are particularly vulnerable to attack in unstable regions where anger exists against technological competition from the west. Nationalization accompanied by the seizure of proprietary data banks is a threat in socialist-inclined countries. Many countries involved in offshore data processing and international financial services are subject to hurricanes (Jamaica, the Cayman Islands), volcanos (Philippines), earthquakes (the Pacific rim) and epidemics that can cause disruption, work delays, destruction and loss of personnel. With global networks, any terminal in the world can be the source of infection from viruses, worms, Trojan horses, trap doors and logic bombs (all names of malicious software code inserted in programs to interfere with, or destroy, programs or data). In 1987, a virus introduced in Darmstadt, West Germany, penetrated IBM's message system, infecting hundreds of IBM mainframes throughout the world, causing gridlock. As you can see, problems related to computer system security are magnified when processing nodes are integrated into worldwide networks.

Summing up

Information and telecommunications technologies play an important role in world trade, helping to define markets, design and manufacture products, sell goods, transport commodities and exchange payments. At each stage of the trade cycle, data are recorded, stored and processed by IT with output delivered to managers, workers and clients largely by telecommunications. To be competitive in world markets, business people in all countries need access to information technologies. Do developed nations have an obligation to help the Third World gain the technical know-how and the resources they lack? How can the transfer of technology be achieved? The **North–South dialogue** (so named to describe discussions between developed 'rich' nations, most of which lie in the northern hemisphere, and developing countries found primarily in the southern hemisphere) addresses these questions. While the obligation of the 'haves' to the 'have nots' is generally acknowledged, there is no consensus on the extent of this obligation or how technological parity can be achieved. Many governments are currently addressing these issues in bilateral trade negotiations and in world forums like the UN, Council of Europe, ISO, GATT and OECD. Corporate managers should initiate and participate in a discussion of these issues in their communities, register their views with government representatives, formulate proposals for rules and regulations governing world trade with business colleagues and lobby for passage of legislation and treaties that reflect these views; that is, play a leadership role in shaping the business and IT environment of the future.

The same holds true on matters regarding transborder data flow. The issues here are often highly technical. So corporate technical expertise and business acumen relating to the cost of proposals, their practicality, legal ramifications and the impact on trade, can be particularly helpful to representatives responsible for hammering out standards and regulations governing data flows.

A definitive settlement of the issues of technology transfer and transborder data flow will never be achieved because information and telecommunications technologies are continually changing through research and development. In addition, the number of applications for these technologies is expanding. Finally, issues of IT transfer and transborder data flow are resolved in bilateral, regional and international forums where world views and national interests continually shift, and where power politics complicate negotiations. IT managers must remain alert to these interest and power shifts and adapt to them.

Case study: A computerized agricultural credit system for Malawi

Voluntary Services Overseas (VSO), an aid agency which sends programmers and analysts to the Third World to work on development projects, is gaining a wealth of experience on the problems involved in the transfer of IT. For example, they sent Ian Wood to Malawi to work in the Ministry of Agriculture on a program to handle farm credit given to small farmers to buy seeds, equipment and fertilizers — loans to be paid back after harvest. Lost money because of records going astray and corruption were the principal reasons the government favoured the replacement of manual record-keeping with computerization. Wood spent two and a half years working on the development of an accounting system that ran on a Burroughs B20 micro to automate credit record-keeping. Although Wood trained local people to use the new system, no one in the department had sufficient skills to learn how to program it. Says Wood, 'In Malawi, government staff do not get paid well, so anyone with computer skills moves into the private sector.' He believes that the system was abandoned after he left the country.

Source: 'Developing IT skills in the Third World', *Computing* (15 June 1989), pp. 20–1.

Questions

1 Why did this attempt to develop a computerized credit system ultimately fail?
2 What factors were needed for the project's success?
3 What responsibility does VSO have for the project's failure? What responsibility for failure lies with the Ministry of Agriculture? With Wood? What should have been done differently by the parties involved?
4 How does this project exemplify problems inherent in the transfer of information technology?
5 Do developed countries have an obligation to transfer information technology to developing countries in projects like this one? Discuss.

Case study: Transborder data flow

At first, transborder data flow was mainly by air freight. Companies sent back office paperwork, such as credit card applications, to facilities abroad where keypunch operators entered the data on magnetic tape. This tape was then returned by air for processing.

Soon, however, the return leg became electronic. American Airlines was one of the first to exploit telecommunications in this manner, sending ticket stubs by plane to the Caribbean island of Barbados for keyboard entry, with the computerized data returned via a satellite link. New York Life Insurance Co. likewise relies on overseas data entry, sending medical and dental claims by Aer Lingus to a processing centre in Ireland. There, claims adjusters work at terminals linked in real-time by fibre-optic line to the company's mainframe in New Jersey, making decisions on which claims to pay and how much. Texas Instruments employs 160 Indian technicians in an eight-storey facility in Bangalore, India, for the development of computer software and the design of integrated circuits. A satellite dish on the roof is used to export their work electronically to the United States.

Source: John Burgess, 'White-collar jobs go offshore', *International Herald Tribune* (7 October 1991), p. 17.

Questions

1 Why is the physical proximity of white-collar workers to their bosses less and less relevant?

2 According to Sal Anfora, a senior claims consultant at New York Life, 'It's about 25 to 30 per cent less expensive to pay claims over in Ireland than it is in the United States, mostly due to lower salaries.' What will happen to Irish workers when their salary structure improves? When Third World countries with even lower wage scales get the expertise and telecommunications infrastructure to be competitive with Irish claims adjusters? Will the Irish economy benefit from telecommunications only temporarily? Discuss.

3 What are some of the costs involved in sending work abroad? What problems might arise that would not occur if workers were closer to headquarters? Use the examples in this case to illustrate the problems.

4 Do you believe that setting up foreign shops, or subcontracting work abroad, is a growing trend in information industries? If so, what are the reasons for this trend? If not, what factors mitigate against outsourcing in world markets?

5 Do you believe that outsourcing benefits developing countries? How? What are the benefits to the contractor?

Case study: Computerized ID system

As part of Thailand's programme to computerize social services, the government is developing a population database containing information on its 65 million citizens. Every Thai national over 15 years old will be issued a personal identification card with his or her photo, pertinent data (name, address, and so on) and ID number to carry at all times. This card will simplify state services, such as school enrolment and receipt of medical care. Behind the card is a $50 million computer system that will allow bureaucrats to create a personal dossier on the card holder from files in disparate government offices. By entering the ID from the card on a keyboard, the holder's address, marital status, education, occupation, income, nationality, religion, family history, tax return, fingerprints and criminal record can be brought to the computer screen.

Source: Philip Elmer-Dewitt, 'Peddling Big Brother', *Time* (24 June 1991), p. 62.

Questions

1 Thailand's population database system is opposed by civil libertarians. Why do you think they might object to the system? Describe ways in which population databases like this one might be abused?

2 Taiwan is awarding contracts worth $270 million for its own 'residential-information system'. Unisys, Digital Equipment Corp., NEC and ICL have submitted bids. Do you think the company that wins the bid has any responsibility for the way in which the technology they provide will be used? Explain your point of view.

3 If you were manager of a multinational company asked to supply information technology to the Third World, would you be concerned about the application of that technology? Would you base your business decision on whether the transfer of technology would be moral? Ethical? Discuss.

4 Israel uses a work-permit card system running on US equipment to monitor the movements of Palestinians living in the occupied territories. Until recently, South Africa employed pass-card and fingerprint systems, run on IBM and ICL computers, to enforce travel restrictions on blacks. Could these western manufacturers prevent this surveillance use of their equipment? How?

5 Should surveillance systems be produced by the west? Would you participate in their design? Should western governments outlaw the sale of relational database systems that might be used for population surveillance to countries without basic constitutional safe- guards on personal privacy? Discuss the issues in this dilemma.

Key words

Bodyshopping	Outsourcing	Transborder data flow
Brain drain	Restrictions on	Transfer of information
North–South dialogue	transborder data flow	technology

Discussion questions

1 What preconditions are necessary for the transfer of technology to the Third World?
2 Do you believe that advanced countries have an obligation to assist the Third World in gaining computer expertise? Do developing nations have a right to be given advanced technology? Discuss.
3 Will computerization change the life style in developing countries? How? Change the style of business management in developing countries? How?
4 What factors make it difficult for developing countries to compete in:
   (*a*) The manufacture of hardware?
   (*b*) The development of software?
   (*c*) The development of applications?
5 What is brain drain? Who benefits, who loses, from brain drain? What responsibility do developed countries have towards the Third World to stop brain drain?
6 What is the meaning of the term outsourcing in a computer environment?
7 What are the benefits and disadvantages of outsourcing to developed countries? To developing countries? To vendors?
8 How can differences in domestic laws regarding copyrights, patents and trade secrets affect world trade? Cite specific trade disputes in your answer.
9 How did transborder data flow occur prior to the telecommunications revolution? Why are transborder data flow issues today more pressing than in the past?
10 Give examples of controversy arising from transborder data flows.
11 Why are restrictions placed on transborder data flow? What purposes do they serve?
12 In many parts of the world, you cannot set up a satellite dish and bypass the local phone company. Why?
13 What are the benefits of a government monopoly of telecommunications,

such as the European PTTs? How do such monopolies affect world trade? The management of a multinational corporation?

14 What is your definition of electronic colonialism? Do you believe that electronic colonialism exists? Is a major issue of the 1990s? Cite examples.

15 How are the representatives of your country chosen in organizations like GATT and the ISO? Does the business community in your country have a voice in trade negotiations? Should the business community have a greater role in these negotiations? Explain your point of view.

16 Explain why transborder data flow adds to concerns about data availability, quality, timeliness, accuracy, reliability, privacy and security.

17 How can a multinational company protect itself from computer viruses introduced from abroad?

18 What are the primary concerns of your national leaders regarding IT transfer and transborder data flow? Are there party differences among your politicians on these issues? Discuss.

19 Describe how the issues of IT transfer and transborder data flow affect business people in your community.

Bibliography

Akinlade, T.O. 'Software engineering in a developing country', *Information Technology for Development*, vol. 5, no. 1 (1990), pp. 69–72.

Byram, Tamara J. 'Computer protection against foreign competition in the United States', *Computer/Law Journal*, vol. 10, no. 3 (October 1990), pp. 370–92.

Eger, John. 'Transborder flow', *Datamation*, vol. 24, no. 12 (November 1978), p. 50.

Erstling, Jay A. 'The Semiconductor Chip Protection Act and its impact on the international protection of chip design', *Rutgers Computer and Technology Law Journal*, vol. 15, no. 2 (1989), pp. 303–49.

Grewlich, Klaus W. 'Transborder data flows: a field of action for foreign trade diplomacy', *Information Age*, vol. 11, no. 2 (April 1989), pp. 67–71.

Farr, Evan H. 'Copyrightability of computer-created works', *Rutgers Computer and Technology Law Journal*, vol. 15, no. 1 (January 1989), pp. 63–80.

Guynes, Jan L. 'The impact of transborder data flow regulation', *Data Communications*, vol. 7, no. 3 (Summer 1990), pp. 70–3.

Lee, Susan. 'Train 'em and keep 'em here', *Forbes*, vol. 147, no. 11 (27 May 1991), pp. 110–16.

Madsen, Wayne. 'Effect of transborder data flow upon information security and integrity', *Information Age*, vol. 11, no. 9 (July 1989), pp. 131–8.

Mavaddat, Farhad. 'Transferring and transplanting technologies? The case for informatics technology', *Information Technology for Development*, vol. 1, no. 2 (1989), pp. 91–7.

Rappaport, Andrew S. and Shmuel Halevi. 'The computerless computer company', *Harvard Business Review*, vol. 69, no. 4 (July–August 1991), pp. 69–80.

Schware, Robert. 'Software for developing countries: major issues in the 1990s',

Information Technology for Development, vol. 5, no. 2 (1990), pp. 101–7.

Sharif, M. Nawaz. 'Technological leapfrogging implications for developing countries', *Technological Forecasting and Social Change*, vol. 36, no. 2 (1989), pp. 201–8.

Shields, Peter and Jan Servaes. 'The impact of the transfer of information technology on development', *Information Society*, vol. 6, nos 1–2 (1989), pp. 47–57.

Varma, Kirtimaya. 'Challenges and new pastures', *Information Technology* (India) (June 1991), pp. 66–8.

Woodrow, R. Brian. 'Telecommunication and information networks: growing international tensions and their underlying causes', *The Information Society*, vol. 6, no. 3 (1989), pp. 117–25.

16 The future of computing

Did we come here to laugh or cry?
Are we dying or being born?
Carlos Fuentes

Many new technologies will shape tomorrow. Genetic engineering, holography, robotics and space science are examples. But perhaps the greatest impact on the entire fabric of society will come from the integration to telecommunications and computing. The French have coined the term 'telematique' to describe this integration, the English version being 'telematic'. Our future will be a **telematic society** in which not only the workplace but also the daily lives of citizens will be transformed.

In this chapter we look at advances in hardware and software for a new generation of computer systems that will usher in the telematic society. We then examine how these advances will impact on business and IT management. For instance, organizations may evolve into structured networks leading to shifts in the base of corporate power. Though managers will be aided in decision making by intelligent computer systems, new legal, ethical, and social issues will arise, like deskilling and worker displacement, as the workforce is transformed by a rise in the number of knowledge workers.

Alternate scenarios of a telematic society will bring the chapter to a close.

Looking ahead

The ability to look ahead is a rare gift, certainly not a science. Too often predictions fail to match the reality of the future. The British Parliament failed to recognize the merit of Thomas Edison's incandescent lamp, suggesting in 1878 that the idea might be 'good enough for our transatlantic friends but unworthy of the attention of practical or scientific men.' Franklin Roosevelt, the US president during the Second World War, was also far off the mark with his 1922 prediction, 'It is highly unlikely that an airplane, or a fleet of them, would ever successfully sink a fleet of Navy vessels under battle conditions.'

In the field of computer science, many early predictions have likewise proved erroneous. For example, Howard Aiken, who developed Mark 1, the first large-scale digital computer, predicted in the 1940s that there would be no commercial future in building computers. IBM assumed the market for electronic computers would be limited when it launched its 701 series in the early 1950s. Only eighteen computers were planned on the expectation that that number would saturate the market.

Although we smile with hindsight, many of us are sceptical about talk of a telematic society in the future. Why should we listen to technological forecasts? They have been wrong in the past.

The reason is that we must try to anticipate the future so that our society has time to plan for change. Perhaps technological advances will require revision of our educational systems in order to provide young people with skills for the workplace of tomorrow. Perhaps computer networks will create international banking systems and markets that necessitate new types of controls, forcing a redefinition of the roles of local and national governments in relation to international institutions. Perhaps laws will have to be revised and attitudes changed. Because social change proceeds slowly, we must begin to lay the groundwork for the future today. That is why we need to forecast technological innovation in computing and analyze how such innovation will affect business organizations, the management of computing and the labour force. If this chapter stimulates a discussion of the future of computer technology and the social implications of that technology, it will serve a useful purpose.

Future directions in computing

The first four generations of computers have all shared a single basic design: the von Neumann processor that executes simple instructions in sequence. Improvements have come by making individual parts run faster and by increasing storage capacity, and these improvements have been impressive indeed. Conventional systems able to execute 100 million sequential instructions per second and access gigabytes (billions of bytes) of memory are now being marketed.

However, increased processing speed cannot overcome a basic limitation of the **von Neumann approach**: the inefficiency of serial processing. In an image processing application in which a hundred operations must be applied to millions of individual picture elements (pixels), most of the processing time is spent retrieving and storing data with relatively little time devoted to computation. For applications like this with vast amounts of data for processing, multiprocessors that work in parallel should speed output. New computer architectures to replace the von Neumann processor are a major focus of research.

However, researchers recognize that faster processing speed does not guarantee that problems can be quickly solved. Problem solutions may be obscured by the tons of output that a fast computer can generate. Systems designers are now addressing the issue of information indexing and data management so that users in the future will not be overwhelmed by information glut. New software concepts are also being developed that enable computers to do more than fulfil the predetermined information needs of users. They help users recognize problems, draw problem boundaries, access data relevant to problem solutions, and then manipulate the data or perform appropriate computations.

In 1981 the Japanese announced an ambitious plan for a **fifth generation computer**, components of which are illustrated in Figure 16.1, scheduled to reach the market in the 1990s. Artificial intelligence was to be a major feature of the computer. In addition, large-scale integrated circuits, advanced computer

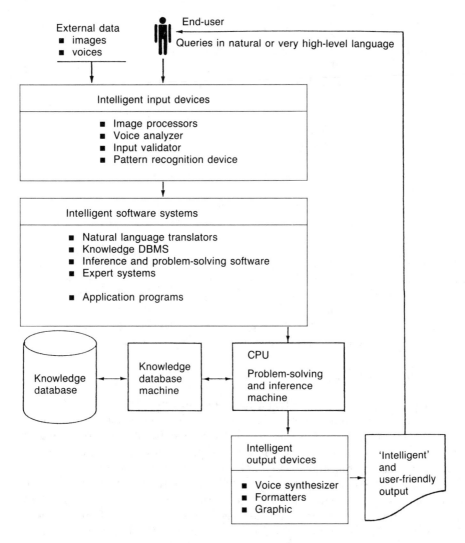

Figure 16.1 *Overview of the proposed Japanese fifth generation computer system*

Table 16.1 *Areas of research for fifth generation computers*

Hardware architecture	Gallium arsenide chips
	ULSI (ultra-large-scale integration)
	High speed numerical computation
	Database machines
	Distributed function architecture
	Wafer-scale chip
Software systems	Intelligent programs
	Intelligent problem-solving and inference system
	Intelligent interface software
	Natural language communication systems
	Question—answer systems
Systems technology	Knowledge database management system
	Intelligent input/output system
	Image recognition
	Speech understanding
	Expert systems
	Online testing
	Fault logging
	Self-diagnosis
Systems organization	Priority of human factors
	Mechanism for influencing perceptions
	Improved user interface and communication facilities
	Maximize effectiveness, but not necessarily efficiency

architectures and improved human—machine interface were planned. The United States and Europe, in turn, announced research plans to develop fifth generation computing systems of their own. (See Table 16.1 for a partial list of research topics for these new systems.) Because of the complexity of technical problems for these new systems, fifth generation systems have still not met their goals. We look next at advances that have been made and research in progress.

Ultra-large-scale integrated circuits

Integrated circuits with circuit lines a mere **micron** thick (a human hair is 100 microns thick) now make it possible to produce quarter-inch-square chips containing more than a million transistors, four times the number of transistors contained on 256K memory chips. Already sample quantities of next-generation computer chips using half-micron geometries are being built in development labs and should be produced in volume in the 1990s. Quarter-micron chips containing tens of millions of transistors are a real possibility by the turn of the century.

What does this mean to the computer user? That the power of all computers will dramatically increase. Within a few years, one superchip will be able to do the work of today's mainframes, while the power of a supercomputer may be packaged on a slice of silicon about the size of a credit card. In the United States, the Department of Defense has funded a large share of superchip research to enhance the intelligence of military communications and weapons systems. As a result, applications for the chips will be primarily for military use in the immediate future. But 'successor technologies' should 'spill over' into the commercial realm within a decade. In particular, companies that process enormous amounts of data should benefit, like chemical plants and oil refineries which rely on computers for industrial process control. The artificial intelligence capability of computers, which requires considerable computational power, will also be enhanced. With more circuitry per chip, computers will become smaller in size and computing costs should drop significantly.

Reduced circuit size also allows chips to carry spare parts to overcome flaws introduced in manufacturing. Built-in software is under development to detect non-functioning elements, then reconfigure the circuitry to bypass the fault. This **self-repair capability** should improve computer reliability, extend the life of chips, and add to the usefulness of systems in remote or inaccessible locations, like satellites in orbit.

However, increased circuit density creates problems of heat dissipation, so researchers are looking for new materials and revolutionary designs to replace silicon chips in widespread use today. **Gallium arsenide** is one alternative, a material which allows electrons to be moved at lower voltage and four times faster than silicon. Work is also progressing on **biochips**, microchips made of proteins; **optical chips**, integrated circuits using a combination of silicon, gallium arsenide, and fibre optics; **high-electron mobility transistors**, a high-speed device that produces extremely high switching times when cooled to 77° Kelvin; and **ballistic transistors**, chips with the potential to switch at 10 femtoseconds (1 femtosecond equals 1 quadrillionth of a second).

Present design and fabrication techniques are inadequate for the large-scale manufacture of superchips like these. The development of ultra-large-scale integration tools to support the production of experimental chips and wafers is therefore essential for fifth generation products.

Advanced computer architectures

As mentioned earlier, fifth generation computers will be high-performance **multiprocessor systems** made of small specialized processors that operate in parallel, allowing the system to perform many operations at once. A control unit will integrate the work of these processors, each dedicated to solving a portion of the problem at hand. The component configuration of these systems will vary according to the needs of the user. Should a vision system be required, this system will be added just as we add components to a stereo system today.

Much research still needs to be done on multiprocessor architectures. The goal of usable, highly functional systems that increase speed of processing as more components are added remains illusive. This goal is dependent on **concurrent** or **parallel programming** — that is, programming system components so that they execute two or more processes simultaneously — which no one yet knows how to do well. In addition, there is still only a limited understanding of **task decomposition**, which is the process of deciding how to subdivide a complex problem into small segments for parallel processing. Multiprocessor experiments to date have shown that additional processors may decrease performance because of the 'too many cooks' syndrome. In effect, the processors start tripping over each other's toes.

Disk storage is another area of system architecture under research. Two promising technologies should contribute to increased memory: optical storage and vertical magnetic recording.

AI and intelligent problem-solving systems

Researchers in **artificial intelligence (AI)** focus on machine equivalents of human processes such as pattern recognition (vision, voice, image, language), relevance extraction, deduction, discovery techniques and optimization of goals. They hope to improve the capability of computer systems to perform operations associated with human intelligence: for example, the selection of appropriate lines of reasoning to solve complex problems or the search for and retrieval of relevant data for problems at hand.

Work is in progress on the building blocks of such intelligent computer systems: inference engines, knowledge bases and knowledge-based management systems. (An inference engine is software that provides strategies to draw inferences and produce solutions to problems under analysis. A knowledge base is a database consisting of a body of expert knowledge on a particular subject plus context data built up by the system about the situation in which the problem arises. A knowledge-based management system automatically organizes, controls, updates and retrieves relevant knowledge stored in computer memory.)

The intelligence of fifth generation systems will also depend on advanced input equipment with enhanced sensory capability: for example, the ability to recognize and interpret patterns in the environment and the ability to conduct a meaningful dialogue with the user in a natural language. Likewise, output will be delivered by intelligent devices such as voice synthesizers or formatters that automatically determine how best to present numbers, text and graphic information for display.

Intelligent programming is projected for the future that will enable users to tell the computer what to do, not how to do it. The computer itself will write the 'how to' instructions according to software that gives the machine instructions about writing programs. That is to say, the computer will take over the burden of programming. The ultimate goal of intelligent programming will be to automate conversion of problems into efficient computer solutions. End-users will merely present problems to the computer in English or another natural language, and let the machine determine the nature of each problem and how best to solve it.

(Software will, of course, direct the machine in making this determination.) Then the computer will program itself for the solution.

Artificial intelligence is a controversial field. Some critics believe that intelligent machines will undermine the importance of human accomplishments. They fear that people may begin to feel subservient to machines and no longer value human life, or that intelligent machines may so threaten mankind's self-image that pathological behaviour results. We should call a halt to further research in AI, they argue, until we have studied the social, psychological, ethical and human implications of developing machines with problem-solving capabilities that surpass human capabilities in many domains. Let us identify and specify worthy national goals for AI instead of pursuing AI research blindly without knowledge or concern for the consequences. As stated by Joseph Weizenbaum, an eminent computer scientist, there are certain tasks which computers *ought* not do even if computers *can* be made to do them.

Those who oppose restrictions on AI research argue that the benefits of AI to society may outweigh the harm of ill-conceived AI applications. And they question how are we to know the potential of the field without continued research efforts. Yet they acknowledge that given the known limitations of the current technology, AI problems for computer solution should be selected with care and AI technology applied in a well-thought-out way. And they recognize that there are many technical aspects of AI that we don't yet know how to solve, societal problems that a radical change in technology always engenders, and ethical problems caused by the introduction of a new species of intelligence into our midst.

Networks

Fundamental to fifth generation computing will be **networks** that enable computers at dispersed locations to share hardware, software and data resources. Computers will be connected to local area networks (LANs), and these networks will be interconnected in regional, national and international networks in turn.

With advances in semiconductor and telecommunications technologies, solutions to many of the hardware problems related to networks are expected in the near future. For example, ISDN (integrated services digital network) promises the ability to transmit voice, data, and image messages in a single digital data stream. Progress toward the implementation of international telecommunications standards is also being made.

In the past, software to interface between computers built by different manufacturers was lacking which restricted the usefulness of networks. But this problem is also being resolved. Both computer users and computer companies are working towards agreement on networking **protocols** ('rules of the road' that regulate the flow of data among different computers on a network), user interfaces and operating systems so that the concept of open systems can become a reality. (An **open system** means that a common set of software can be easily transferred from one brand of computer to another.) The advantage to computer customers is that they will no longer be wed to a single computer manufacturer because of the investment they have made in software and training for proprietary systems. When upgrading or purchasing new equipment, they can switch brands yet still access all network resources. In addition, the cost of writing customized applications software will drop since multiple operating systems will be in use. According to some industry observers, the open systems concept is the most fundamental change in the computer industry in thirty years.

Applications of advanced technology

Advances in information technology will have an impact in all fields of endeavour. Table 16.2 lists some of the applications we can expect in retailing, manufacturing and office automation, education, health care, aerospace and transportation. Even our homes will be transformed as computers become master controllers of the environment, monitoring heating/cooling, security and even our appliances. Should leaks, plugged drains, or short circuits occur, the computer will identify the potential problem and provide fix-it advice. (If needed repair information is not in computer memory, the master controller will consult the computer of a neighbour or search a remote database for the information.)

Imagine a house where the master computer shuts off stove heat when food begins to burn. Where food supplies are monitored and shopping lists automatically prepared when food stocks are low. Where menus are recommended for well-balanced meals to include favourite recipes. Where white noise is automatically generated to block out street sounds if the room occupant

Table 16.2 *Applications for the 1990s*

Retailing	Greater use of intelligent optical scanning and home-shopping
Manufacturing	Integration of CIM, fuzzy logic, intelligent robots and intelligent control
Office	Greater integration of work, image and voice processing with pen-based input and optical scanning
	More teleconferencing
Education	Worldwide intregration of multimedia, with 3-dimensional graphics and animation
Health care	Surgery and treatment by intelligent robots
	Greater spatial resolution and 3-dimension reconstruction of MRI (magnetic resonance imaging)
Aerospace	Smaller and cheaper satellites
	Unmanned computer-controlled vehicles
	Smarter equipment, weapons and reconnaissance
Transportation	Computer controlled take-off, flying and landing and air-traffic control
	Integrated computerized scheduling, ticketing and baggage control
	Computer control of future space shuttle and space stations
	Computerized trains and automobiles

is studying or where temperature is lowered if someone is sleeping. Where robots perform household chores such as vacuuming, mowing the lawn, ironing clothes and preparing meals. For a trip, the master controller will check the weather, make reservations, write tickets, arrange payment through EFT, provide information on local customs, present a screen preview of sights you will see, and organize a quick language course with videotapes so you can learn phrases you will need in your travels. The computer will even be able to carry on a conversation when you want to talk, adjusting to your mood, telling jokes to cheer you or gossip if you so choose.

This scenario is not as fanciful as you may think. The technology is already on the drawing boards. However, technological feasibility is not all that is needed to make such houses a reality. Entrepreneurs must produce the hardware and software at a reasonable price, the systems must operate efficiently and effectively, and the idea of a master controller for homes must have public appeal.

Impact on managers

Since this is a textbook for students of management, let us examine how technological advances in information science will affect business and IT managers in the future.

As you have learned in earlier chapters, the advent of computers has made changes in the way work is done. The future may accelerate change, but most of the managerial challenges in the years ahead will simply be the extenuation of challenges encountered in the recent past. Notice that the topics in Table 16.3 — issues and problems for managers of the future — have already been introduced in this textbook as ongoing problems of management in a computerized society. Nevertheless, a few comments are in order on what lies ahead.

Intelligent systems

'Intelligence' will be added to conventional management information, executive information systems and decision support systems in a fifth generation computing environment. That is to say, subsystems that incorporate artificial intelligence will be added to computer systems used to help business and corporate managers:

- Communicate and interact with the hardware and software.
- Recognize and state problems to be solved.
- Specify goals and constraints.
- Format input.
- Select appropriate models to reach problem solutions.
- Access information stored in knowledge bases.
- Interpret output by presenting it in a format that is easy to understand and assimilate.

Table 16.3 *Issues and responsibilities facing managers in the future*

Network administration including the evolving of ISDN
Management of end-user computing
Implementing of user-friendly systems
Continued monitoring of security and protecting privacy
Planning and implementing best use of graphics
Planning and implementing best use of AI
Integration of data, voice and word processing
Functional horizontal and vertical integration including DSS and data processing
Using information technology to improve firms' competitive position
Aligning IS planning with organizational goals and objectives
Effective planning and use of computer resources
Effective planning and implementation of automation in office and executive suite
Improving quality and productivity of software development
Replacement and phasing out of old systems and applications
Absorbing and diffusing changing computer technology
Planning adequately for disasters and recovery from failures
Finding appropriate combination and organization structure from among
    centralized, distributed and information centre strategies
Attracting and retaining professionals in computing
Identifying applications and opportunities for information to improve firm's
    competitive use
Manage information as a corporate resource

To illustrate these advantages, suppose an organization has a slump in sales. The manager's job is to determine the cause and develop strategies to reverse the trend. With conventional information systems, so much information is generated that managers often lose their focus and waste time sifting through masses of irrelevant, non-essential data in their search for problem solutions.

A fifth generation system, on the other hand, will narrow the parameters of the problem and direct the manager to specific information of interest. Suppose the manager inputs the command, 'Give me Liverpool sales data'. Through prompts and a dialogue the system might help the manager reformat the request to, 'Give me a product listing where slippage has been greater than 5 per cent during the period 15 April–15 June 1995 in Liverpool'.

In addition, the system will be capable of drawing inferences to assist the manager in evaluating information and may call upon an expert subsystem to reach cause–effect conclusions. Future information systems may also store profiles of managers that describe their backgrounds and experience so that the level of technicality and sophistication of the computer response can be customized to the individual interacting with the system.

Integration

Integrated systems will be the norm as technical issues of connectivity and standards are resolved. In the office, electronic mail will be integrated with data,

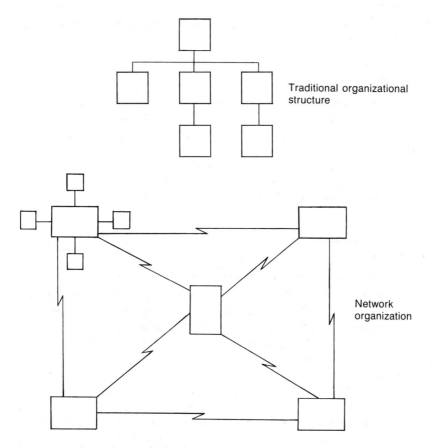

Figure 16.2 *Change in organizational structure*

word, voice and image processing. Retrieval of information from institutional databases will be possible from computers of different sizes and makes regardless of network location. Horizontal integration will link factory, office and professional subsystems: vertical integration will provide top level managers with operational data for planning and control. From a single terminal, a manager will have access to all corporate information resources, and to external databases and utilities for hardware/software enhancements if desired.

Networking will inevitably change organizational structure since processing nodes will be interconnected, as illustrated in Figure 16.2, upsetting traditional management hierarchies. The pyramid structure of management (operations, control and planning) may actually negate advantages of fifth generation systems by requiring that information filter through layers of management before policy decisions are made. Instead, an information network-style management may evolve that allows individuals to exchange ideas and knowledge without channelling communications through a restrictive bureaucracy. One might characterize these changes as evolution from a managerial society to an entrepreneurial society.

Faster processing, lower costs

The speed of fifth generation processing will help reduce the length of time managers require to collect information, analyze it and reach decisions. One hopes that the result will be more timely decisions and greater responsiveness to environmental changes.

When the power of a present-day supercomputer can be acquired for the cost of a microcomputer, small organizations, even individuals, will have the ability to process vast amounts of data. No one will be excluded from the information revolution.

Shifting responsibilities

With advanced technology, tools for the development of computer systems will become easier to use and computer systems themselves will require less technical skill to manage. The result will be a shift in responsibility for the management of computing from computer professionals to functional department managers. They will have to plan for the acquisition of computer resources and their organization, operation, maintenance, and security.

The key to successful use of the new technology will be the **education** and **training** of both managers and end-users. Unfortunately, most schools and universities are not adequately preparing students for a computerized future. If people enter the workforce without a computer background, employers will have to educate them about computer systems. In Chapter 2 we discussed one organizational structure for this purpose: the information centre.

Workforce adjustments

Computer advances have added a new class of workers to the workforce: **knowledge workers** (see Figure 16.3). These are people who develop information systems; collect, organize, store, analyze, present and distribute knowledge; and make decisions based on that knowledge. With each advance in the electronic handling of information, the number of information occupations has grown.

Workforce characteristics have altered as jobs have been transformed in this information age. With networks to connect the knowledge worker's terminal to others, the physical presence of employees at a central office is less important than in the past, leading to decentralization in many companies and new work modes like flexible work hours and telecommuting. One forecast is that knowledge workers will change the economics of mass markets, large organizations and

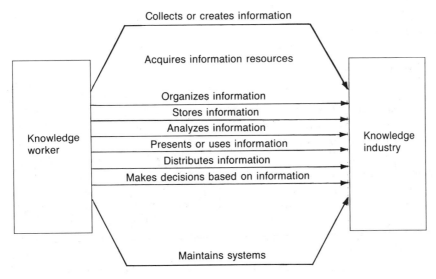

Figure 16.3 *Jobs performed by knowledge worker*

corporate enterprises, making small companies with specialized markets profitable and better able to meet customer demands for individualized service.

Since the planning and implementation of computer systems often have a long lead time, there may be time for management to retrain workers, restructure jobs and transfer employees to other duties when a computer system under development threatens jobs. (With prototyping and new development tools to speed the process of systems analysis and design, this lead time is shrinking.) Many companies have formalized in-house training programmes to upgrade the skills of workers so that they can switch to new jobs when displaced by automation. Others allow employees to attend outside classes on company time. Some provide individual counselling, job referals, monetary compensation for relocation, early retirement, or others schemes to soften the impact of innovation that involves deskilling or large-scale labour shedding.

Nevertheless, **displacement** and **unemployment** because of fifth generation computing will undoubtedly occur in the future. Most corporate managers and labour leaders agree that they cannot handle the problems of technological unemployment alone and turn to national governments for help, recommending that policy be formulated at the national level to deal with human resources. For example, the government might shift priorities from welfare to job creation or establish protectionist policies for new industries. Government also has the power to increase public spending, to add to the money supply, to revise tax laws, to extend benefits to people out of work, and to create civil service jobs, all of which have a bearing on employment.

New legal and ethical dilemmas

Although legislators recognize that it is their responsibility to write appropriate laws to help fight computer crime and to provide a **legal framework** for business operations, they cannot keep pace with the speed of technological development in the computer industry. As a result, business and IT managers are not always aware of the legal ramifications of computer policies in their companies and knowledge workers are often uncertain regarding their rights and responsibilities.

For example, the legal liability is unclear when a computer program fails and thereby inconveniences or harms a customer. Who is responsible? The analyst who designed the program? The programmer who used faulty logic? The corporate manager who approved the project? The IT manager who implemented the project? To resolve liability disputes in many countries, laws that are not explicitly written for liability in a computerized environment must be interpreted by the courts. Similar problems arise with regard to computer crime and the protection of hardware/software under patent, copyright, and trade secret laws. No wonder there is so much litigation in the computer field. Managers often have difficulty assessing whether the actions they take are legal or not, a problem that will be exacerbated by fifth generation computing.

Computer ethics, a subject with legal overtones, has received little public attention and is taught in few schools and universities at the present time. Ethical standards for working in a computer environment are lacking. Software piracy is widespread, privacy rights of individuals are often infringed with impunity, unauthorized use of computer resources is commonplace and computer crime is on the rise. A major responsibility of business and IT managers is to raise employee sensitivity to information malpractice, intellectual property rights, equal access to information, and other issues of ethical conduct and to promote the development of ethical standards, the foundation on which professionalism is built.

Many computing organizations like the Data Processing Management Association (DPMA) and Association of Computer Machinery (ACM) have adopted codes of ethics for their memberships. See Figure 16.4 for the code of ethics of the Data Processing Management Association in the United States. However, these codes have little force since computer professionals do not need a licence to work. (Code violations can only lead to threatened expulsion from the organization.) Nevertheless, the codes serve a useful purpose: they help make professionals aware of their responsibilities in computer environments and provide some guidance in ways to deal with difficult ethical situations. Business and IT managers should study these codes and educate themselves regarding business computer ethics by attending seminars and reading articles on the

DPMA Code of Ethics*

I acknowledge:

That I have an obligation to management, therefore, I shall promote the understanding of information processing methods and procedures to management using every resource at my command.

That I have an obligation to my fellow members, therefore I shall uphold the high ideals of DPMA as outlined in its International Bylaws. Further, I shall cooperate with my fellow members and shall treat them with honesty and respect at all times.

That I have an obligation to society and will participate to the best of my ability in the dissemination of knowledge pertaining to the general development and understanding of information processing. Further, I shall not use knowledge of a confidential nature to further my personal interest, nor shall I violate the privacy and confidentiality of information entrusted to me or to which I may gain access.

That I have an obligation to my employer whose trust I hold, therefore, I shall endeavor to discharge this obligation to the best of my ability, to guard my employer's interests, and to advise him or her wisely and honestly.

That I have an obligation to my country, therefore, in my personal, business and social contacts, I shall uphold my nation and shall honor the chosen way of life of my fellow citizens.

I accept these obligations as a personal responsibility and as a member of this asociation. I shall actively discharge these obligations and I dedicate myself to that end.

* Adopted by DPMA Executive Council, November 1981.

DPMA Standards of Conduct*

These standards expand on the Code of Ethics by providing specific statements of behavior in support of each element of the Code. They are not objectives to be strived for, they are rules that no true professional will violate. It is first of all expected that information processing professionals will abide by the appropriate laws of their country and community. The following standards address tenets that apply to the profession.

In recognition of my obligation to management I shall:

- Keep my personal knowledge up-to-date and insure that proper expertise is available when needed.
- Share my knowledge with others and present factual and objective information to management to the best of my ability.
- Accept full responsibility for work that I perform.
- Not misuse the authority entrusted to me.

* Adopted by DPMA Executive Council, November 1981.

- Not misrepresent or withhold information concerning the capabilities of equipment, software or systems.
- Not take advantage of the lack of knowledge or inexperience on the part of others.

In recognition of my obligation to my fellow members and the profession I shall:

- Be honest in all my professional relationships.
- Take appropriate action in regard to any illegal or unethical practices that come to my attention. However, I will bring charges against any person only when I have reasonable basis for believing in the truth of the allegations and without regard to personal interest.
- Endeavor to share my special knowledge.
- Cooperate with others in achieving understanding and in identifying problems.
- Not use or take credit for the work of others without specific acknowledgement and authorization.

►

- Not take advantage of the lack of knowledge or inexperience on the part of others for personal gain.

In recognition of my obligation to society I shall:

- Protect the privacy and confidentiality of all information entrusted to me.
- Use my skill and knowledge to inform the public in all areas of my expertise.
- To the best of my ability, insure that the products of my work are used in a socially responsible way.
- Support, respect and abide by the appropriate local, state, provincial and Federal laws.
- Never misrepresent or withhold information that is germane to a problem or situation of public concern nor will I allow any such known information to remain unchallenged.
- Not use knowledge of a confidential or personal nature in any unauthorized manner or to achieve personal gain.

In recognition of my obligation to my employer I shall:

- Make every effort to ensure that I have the most current knowledge and that the proper expertise is available when needed.
- Avoid conflict of interest and insure that my employer is aware of any potential conflicts.
- Present a fair, honest and objective viewpoint.
- Protect the proper interests of my employer at all times.
- Protect the privacy and confidentiality of all information entrusted to me.
- Not misrepresent or withhold information that is germane to the situation.
- Not attempt to use the resources of my employer for personal gain or for any purpose without proper approval.
- Not exploit the weakness of a computer system for personal gain or personal satisfaction.

Figure 16.4 *DPMA Code of Ethics* and DPMA Standards of Conduct**

subject. They will then be able to play a leadership role at work in establishing an ethical foundation for fifth generation computing to come.

A telematic society

We are already in the first stages of a telematic society (see Figure 16.5). Automated offices and factories are reshaping the workplace: electronic homes, telebanking, teleshopping and electronic mail are changing the way we live. We are beginning to wire our cities in local area networks for information resource sharing and making progress in communications protocols and standards for national networks. In Japan, the government has adopted a national strategy to strengthen the country's regional economies through development of new high-tech centres linked together, called the **technopolis strategy**. The question we must ask while we still have a chance to change the direction of the future is: Will quality of life in a telematic society be improved?

Optimists see freedom from drudgery, intelligent management of natural resources, and the elimination of war and poverty in a telematic future. They predict a new Renaissance since more time will be available for cultural pursuits.

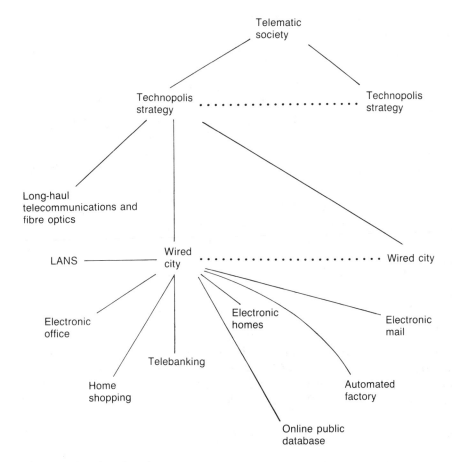

Figure 16.5 *A telematic society*

Access to the world's knowledge will contribute to mankind's understanding of the universe, they say. Interactive communication tools will stimulate empathy with others and help bind human ties. The home will again become the focus of daily life, promoting family togetherness. National boundaries will lose their importance as a world community is born.

Pessimists see illiterates glued to game shows on video screens in the world of tomorrow, waited on hand and foot by domestic robots. They see responsibility for managing cities, running factories, growing crops, and distributing goods and services delegated to intelligent computers. Surveillance systems with little regard for personal privacy will be the norm. Individuals, they say, will sever all ties with the human race in favour of computer companionship since computers will indulge every selfish wish. With self-selective media, people will filter out unwelcome news, preferring to live with virtual realities — that is, with imaginary constructions of the world — rather than with physical realities.

In *The Third Wave* Alvin Toffler sees a middle course for society, a **practopia** that is neither the best nor worst of all possible worlds. He sees,

> A civilization no longer required to put its best energies into marketization. A civilization capable of directing great passion into art. A civilization facing unprecedented historical choices — about genetics and evolution, to choose a single example — and inventing new ethical or moral standards to deal with such complex issues. A civilization, finally, that is at least potentially democratic and humane, in better balance with the biosphere and no longer dangerously dependent on exploitive subsidies from the rest of the world. (Toffler, 1989, p. 375)

Clearly, information technology itself will not decide our future. It is the way technology is used that will decide the quality of life in the years ahead. We must begin now to construct a society that can meet the revolutionary challenges of advanced technology. We have a destiny to create.

Summing up

Research on fifth generation systems is underway. By the end of this century we should have computers with ultra-large-scale integrated circuits, advanced computer architectures, machine intelligence and improved human–machine interfaces linked in local, national and worldwide networks. (See Table 16.4 for

Table 16.4 *A forecast of computer technology for the year 2000*

Superconductivity parallel architectures
40–50 million component chips
25–45 MIPS (million instructions per second) on microcomputers
High resolution flat screens
Speech synthesis
Continuous speech recognition
ISDN (integrated services digital network) for integreated voice, data and image
    transmission
Extensive use of expert systems
Machine translation of selected natural languages
Natural language, intelligent, user-friendly interfaces
Programming without programmers
Very high level dialogue programming languages
Effective end-user computing
Advanced optical character recognition
Secure user identification
Price of hardware still dropping 5–10 per cent per year
Flat screens using FED (field emission display) technology

a list of advances we can expect by the year 2000.) Our telematic future will require a redefinition of work, leisure, home and community.

However, not all of the predictions made in this chapter will come to pass. Some of the goals of fifth generation computers may prove technologically unfeasible or too expensive to implement. Limited resources, government regulatory schemes or interference (for example, unfavourable tax policies), high risk of realizing capital investments, product development priorities in other fields, lack of markets, legal restrictions and user resistance are factors that may affect the speed and direction of change.

Since business and IT managers often serve in a leadership role in their communities as well as at work, they will have a prominent position in shaping our telematic future. Planning must begin now for the computerized society to come. As stated by Ashley Montagu and Samuel Synder:

> Many deplore the computer and some even fear it as more monster than machine. Whatever we think of it, however, we must adjust to it. This does not imply resignation, but rather that we must understand the true nature of this latest of man's inventions and learn how its powers can be combined with our own abilities to be used to the best advantage of humanity (Montagu and Synder, 1972, pp. 1–2)

We hope this book has helped to prepare you for the challenges ahead.

Case study: Modular manufacturing

For the last 75 years, manufacturers have copied Henry Ford's mass-production methods, relying on assembly lines to make things. The problem is, assembly lines are expensive to build, so a large number of identical items must be produced to keep the sale price low.

With information technology, new generation flexible manufacturing systems are beginning to replace the assembly line. Today, subcontractors with computerized machining centres can economically produce batches of 50 instead of 50,000, so instead of manufacturing various bits and pieces for the assembly line of a major manufacturer, they supply whole modules of the end product. In effect, the actual manufacturing process 'is being pushed back up the line to faceless subcontracting firms'. The end product is fashioned by mixing and matching these modular components.

Although no one knows where this is leading, a revolution in manufacturing is in the making.

Source: 'Design it yourself', *The Economist*, vol. 312, no. 7613 (29 July 1989), pp. 14–15.

Questions

1 In principle, modular manufacturing should lower the cost of entry into mass-market businesses. Why?

2 Do you believe that modular manufacturing will favour companies that are sensitive to what customers might and do want? How?

3 How does information technology contribute to modular manufacturing?

4 How do the roles of corporate and IT managers change when a factory switches from a conventional assembly line to modular manufacturing?

5 As stated in *The Economist* article, today 'Bosch has a grip on the market for fuel-injection systems for European cars. GKN reigns supreme in supplying the constant-velocity joints needed to drive a vehicle's front wheels.' Do you agree that modular manufacturing might foster the rise of monopoly suppliers? Hamper innovation and imaginative new designs? Benefit the consumer? The manufacturer? Help suppliers in developing countries? Explain.

6 What positive effects might modular manufacturing have on society? What negative effects? Should we begin to prepare now for a future when production lines as we know them today are obsolete? How?

Case study: Automated autoways

Imagine a motorway packed with cars safely travelling at 65 mph yet spaced only one and a half feet apart. The cars are kept in position by on-board computers which adjust steering in response to signals from the roadside and brake automatically if cars in front slow down. Since computers can react faster than humans do, travel would be safer. Fuel would be saved by travelling at a fairly constant speed and in a line, which reduces wind resistance. And more cars could fit into a given stretch of roadway during rush hour without the danger of gridlock.

In Western Europe, a project is underway to bring this fanciful scenario closer to reality. Government agencies, researchers in universities, and some thirteen car manufacturers are cooperating in PROMETHEUS (Program for European Traffic with Highest Efficiency and Unprecedented Safety). This project, begun in 1986, is to develop 'electronic devices for cars, wired-up roads, and systems to improve communication between a car and the road, other cars, and its driver.'

Some prototype systems are already being tested. For example, in Wolfsburg, Germany, beacons near traffic lights send signals to passing cars, telling drivers what speed will catch the next light while it is green. A fleet of 265 demonstration cars in London are guided around the city by a system that allows a driver to punch in his order starting point and destination. Information on the best route to avoid traffic jams and obstacles is then displayed on a monitor.

Source: 'The boulevard of dreams', *The Economist*, vol. 308. no. 2569 (24 September 1988), p. 131–2.

Questions

1 Are automated motorways a long way off? How far in the future? What progress towards automated motorways do you expect in the near future? Will electronics ever free up motorways and unlock city arteries?

2 What is holding up the implementation of automated motorways? Lack of the necessary technology? Lack of financial resources? Lack of will? Some other reason?

3 Who should invest in the technology of automated motorways? How can this group recoup its investment?

4 Are automated motorways a good idea? Will they benefit society? How? What problems will they pose? Explain.

5 What are the roles of corporate managers and IT managers in this revolution?

Key words

Artificial intelligence
  (AI)
Ballistic transistors
Biochips
Computer ethics
Concurrent
  programming
Displacement
Education
Fifth generation
  computer systems
Gallium arsenide
High-electron mobility
  transistors

Integrated systems
Intelligent
  programming
Intelligent systems
Knowledge workers
Legal framework for
  computing
Micron
Multiprocessor systems
Networks
Open system
Optical chips
Parallel programming

Practopia
Protocols
Self-repair capability
Task decomposition
Technopolis strategy
Telematic society
Training
Unemployment
Von Neumann
  approach
Workforce
  characteristics

Discussion questions

1 What is a telematic society? Is all this talk about a wired society pure
   conjecture or are we near implementation?
2 Why is it difficult to make predictions regarding the future of computing?
3 How will fifth generation computer systems differ from the preceding
   generations? Describe developments that can be expected in the coming
   decade in:
   (a) Integrated circuits.
   (b) Computer architecture.
   (c) Software.
4 What are the advantages and disadvantages of intelligent programming?
5 What advances in user interfaces are proposed for fifth generation
   systems?
6 Discuss applications that will be feasible in the near future as a result of
   advances in computer technology.
7 In your country what role should the following groups play in preparing
   for a wired society:
   (a) Federal/national government?
   (b) Business?
   (c) Churches?
   (d) Universities?
   (e) Clubs or special-interest groups?
   (f) Computer industry?

8 Do you look to the future of computing with anticipation or dread? Explain. How will a wired society affect:
   (a) Quality of life?
   (b) Environment?
   (c) Economics?
   (d) Education?
   (e) Leisure?
9 Discuss six negative effects of computers on society that you foresee in the future.
10 How do you think computers in the year 2000 will affect:
   (a) Privacy?
   (b) The work week?
   (c) Housekeeping?
   (d) Education?
   (e) Recreation?
   (f) Transportation?
11 Comment on the following statement: The passage of statutes is too slow a process to be responsive to the fast moving and dynamic computer industry.
12 What priorities would you give to fifth generation research? Why? Are there some research objectives that you think should be abandoned because they are not in the interest of society? Which ones?
13 What will be the impact of fifth generation computer systems on IT management? How will the roles and responsibilities of business managers and IT managers change by the year 2000?
14 How can business organizations and IT managers prepare for the social change that information technology will bring?
15 Is computer knowledge important for business managers? Why? To what extent? How can computer literacy of management be achieved?
16 It has been charged that the developed western nations want to use information technology to exploit the rest of the world. The term 'information imperialism' is used in this context. Do you think the charge is valid?
17 How will fifth generation computer systems affect:
   (a) Accounting?
   (b) Advertising?
   (c) Marketing?
   (d) Production?
   (e) Personnel management?
   (f) The location of a business?
18 What effect do you think fifth generation computing will have on employment in your country? Do you foresee massive unemployment resulting from computerization? What measures should be taken now to prevent high levels of unemployment?

19 Is unemployment a price that must be paid for the benefits of high technology?

20 Do you perceive computers as a threat to your future with regard to employment possibilities? Explain.

21 Do you think that lack of ethical computer behaviour is a problem in the workplace? Why? What measures would you recommend to improve standards of conduct? What should be the role of IT managers in this respect?

Exercises

1 Research bills that are currently before your national legislature that specifically relate to computing. Present arguments for and against the proposed legislation. Discuss the likely impact on society if this legislation is passed.

2 Read about a recent union strike in which computer use was at issue. Discuss the position of both sides in the dispute. If you were the arbitrator in the case, what would your decision be? State your reasons.

3 You are an employer about to implement a computer system that will displace 200 workers. Write the criteria you will use to decide which employees to let go. State your assumptions.

4 Make a list of the most important social issues in your country that are directly related to our growing dependency on computers. Rank these issues in order of importance to IT managers from your point of view.

5 Research computer applications that have recently been put on the market that incorporate fifth generation technologies. Describe five such applications.

6 Imagine that you are a school superintendent. What revisions would you make to the school curriculum for children 6–18 years old to help students prepare for a computerized future? Explain your assumptions.

7 Discuss the ethical issues in the following scenarios.

(a) A company buys one copy of a microcomputer software package, duplicates the disk and distributes copies to employees who want to use the software.

(b) A student taking a computer science class gives his password to a friend who wants to use the word processing capability of the university's computer to write a term paper.

(c) A programmer gives a copy of a program she wrote for her employer to a friend working at another organization.

(d) A psychology professor has conducted a study on drug use by students, promising his subjects that the data will be kept confidential. Test data from the study are processed by a student assistant on the university's mainframe.

(e) An employee discovers a computer bug that is causing inaccurate output. When brought to the attention of her supervisor, the employee is told that the problem is inconsequential and to ignore it.

(f) A student uses computer time at the university to do (1) personal work or (2) work as a part-time employee of a business in town.

Bibliography

Carlyle, R.M. 'Toward 2017', *Datamation*, vol. 33, no. 18 (15 September 1987), pp. 142–54.

Dertouzos, Michael L. 'Building the information market place', *Technology Review*, vol. 94, no. 1 (January 1991), pp. 29–40.

Foley, James D. 'Interfaces for advanced computing', *Scientific American*, vol. 257, no. 4 (October 1987), pp. 127–35.

Fondersmith, John. 'The downtown 2040: making cities fun', *The Futurist*, vol. 22, no. 2 (April 1988), pp. 9–17.

Frenkel, Karen A. 'The next generation of interactive technologies', *Communications of the ACM*, vol. 32, no. 7 (July 1989), pp. 872–82.

Gunton, Tony. 'The demands of the organization', Chapter 2, *Infrastructure: Building a Framework for Corporate Information Handling*, London: Prentice Hall, 1989, pp. 35–61.

Harris, Richard. 'The database industry: looking into the future', *Database*, vol. 11, no. 5 (October 1988), pp. 42–8.

Huws, Ursula. 'Telework: projections', *Futures*, vol. 23, no. 1 (January/February 1991), pp. 135–57.

Knorr, Eric. 'Software's next ware: putting the user first', *PC World*, vol. 8, no. 1 (January 1990), pp. 134–43.

Malone, T.W., JoAnne Yates and Robert I. Benjamin. 'Electronic markets and electronic hierarchies', *Communications of the ACM*, vol. 36, no. 6 (June 1987), pp. 484–97.

Maybury, Mark T. 'The mind matters: artificial intelligence and its societal implications', *IEEE Technology and Societal Magazine*, (June/July 1990), pp. 7–14.

Mehte, Angeli. 'The fifth generation goes soft', *Datamation*, International Edition, vol. 35, no. 9 (1 May 1989), pp. 80.2–.9.

Montagu, Ashley and Samuel Synder. *Man and the Computer*, Philadelphia: Auerbach, 1972.

Mujjumder, D. Dutta. 'Fifth generation computer systems', *Telematics India*, (November 1989), pp. 25–31.

Reed, Sandra R. 'Technologies for the 1990s'. *Personal Computing*, vol. 14, no. 1 (January 1990), pp. 66–9.

Rockart John F. and James E. Short. 'IT in the 1990s: managing organizational independence', *Management Review*, vol. 30, no. 2 (Winter 1989), pp. 7–12.

Seitz, Konrad. 'Creating a winning culture', *Siemens Review* vol. 58, no. 2 (March/April 1991), pp. 37–9.

Spence, Malcolm D. 'A look into the 21st century: people, business, and computer', *Information Age*, vol. 12, no. 2 (April 1990), pp. 91–9.

Toffler, Alvin. *The Third Wave*. New York: William Morrow, 1980.

Zuboff, Shoshana. *In the Age of the Smart Machine*. New York: Basic Books, 1988.

Selected list of technical abbreviations and acronyms

ADP Automatic Data Processing
AFIPS American Federation of Information Processing System
AI Artificial Intelligence
ALGOL ALGOrithmic Language
ALU Arithmetic and Logic Unit
ANSI American National Standards Institute
APL A Programming Language

BASIC Beginner's All-purpose Symbolic Instruction Code

COBOL COmmon Business-Oriented Language
CODASYL Conference On DAta SYstems Languages
COM Computer Output on Microfilm, or Microfiche
CPE Computer Performance Evaluation
CPM Critical Path Method
CPU Central Processing Unit
CRT Cathode Ray Tube
CSF Critical Success Factor

DBA DataBase Administrator
DBMS DataBase Management System
DDL Data Definition Language
DDP Distributed Data Processing
DED Data Element Dictionary
DED/D Data Element Dictionary/Directory
DED/DD Data Element Dictionary/Data Directory
DES Data Encryption Standard
DPMA Data Processing Management Association
DRAM Dynamic Random Access Memory
DSS Decision Support System

EAM Electrical Accounting Machines
EDM Event-Driven Monitor

EDP Electronic Data Processing
EFT Electronic Fund Transfer
EPROM Erasable Programmable Read-Only Memory

FIPS Federation of Information Processing Standards
FM Facilities Management
FORTRAN FORmulae TRANslator
4GL Fourth(4)-Generation Language

IBM International Business Machines Corporation
ICL International Computers Limited Great Britain
IEEE Institute of Electrical and Electronics Engineers
I/O Input/Output
IRM Information Resource Management
IS Information Systems
ISBN International Standard Book Number
ISO International Standards Organization
ITF Integrated Test Facility
ITT International Telephone and Telegraph Corporation

JDS Job Diagnostic Survey

KOPS Thousands (K) of Operations Per Second
KWIC Key Word In Context
KWOC Key Word Out of Context

LISP LISt Processing
LOC Lines Of Code
LSI Large-Scale Integration

MBO Management By Objective
MIC Magnetic Ink Character
MICR Magnetic Ink Character Recognition
MIPS Millions of Instructions Per Second
MIS Management Information System
MQA Management Quality Assurance
MRP Material Resource Planning

NBS National Bureau of Standards

OECD Organization of Economic Cooperation and Development
OEM Original Equipment Manufacturers
OLRT OnLine Real-Time

PCM Plug-Compatible Manufacturer
PERT Program Evaluation Review Technique
PL/1 Programming Language 1
PTF Parallel Test Facility
PV Present Value

RAM Random Access Memory
R&D Research and Development
RJE Remote Job Entry
RPG Remote Program Generator

SCERT System and Computer Evaluation and Review Technique
SDLC Synchronous Data Link Control
SLA Service-Level Agreement
SNA Systems Network Architecture

TDM Time-Driven Monitor

UPC Universal **Product** Code
UPS Uninterruptible Power Supply

WP Word Processing

Glossary

This glossary has operational definitions of terms that are needed for understanding the management of computing and information resources. Since precise and formal technical definitions all too often obscure meanings, the definitions in this list have been written in simple terms in order to facilitate understanding. As stated in Chapter 1, this text requires a general knowledge of computing. In this glossary you will find definitions of many basic computing terms that you should know, but perhaps need to review.

Readers in the United States wishing a complete technical glossary of computer terms should consult dictionaries such as the *American Standard Vocabulary of Information Processing* published by the American National Institute of Standards. In the United Kingdom, a popular reference is *Complete Encyclopedia of Information Technology* 3rd edition by Adrian V. Stakes with approximately 3,000 terms.

Access the manner in which files or data sets are referred to by the computer. See *direct access, random access* and *remote access*.

Access time the period of time between a request for information and the availability of that data.

Algorithm a step-by-step process for the solution of a problem in a finite number of steps. Usually developed in an outline or by a tool of analysis before coding begins.

American National Standards Institute (ANSI) an organization sponsored by the Business Equipment Manufacturers Association (BEMA) for the purpose of establishing voluntary industry standards.

Analog computer (1) a computer in which analog representation of data is mainly used; (2) a computer that operates on analog data by performing physical processes on these data. Contrast with *digital computer*.

Analyst see *systems analyst*.

Application program a program written for or by a user that applies to the user's own work.

Application software software programs that perform a specific user-oriented task, such as line balancing or payroll. Application software can be either purchased as a package or custom designed by a programmer.

Artificial Intelligence (AI) the ability of a computer to imitate certain human actions or skills, such as problem solving, decision making, perception, and learning.

Audit trail the procedure of tracing the steps in processing data to ensure that results are within either expected or standardized limits.

Auditing around the computer checking output for a given input.

Auditing through the computer checking both input and computer processing. May use test data, auditor-prepared programs, auditor software packages, or audit programming languages.

Auditor person authorized to make a formal periodic examination and check of accounts or financial records to verify their correctness. A computer auditor may also be assigned to verify the correctness of computer information processing to ensure that processing conforms to the firm's goals, policies, and procedures (such as policies with regard to security and privacy).

Authentication verifying the user's right to access a requested file or portion of the database.

Authorization verifying the type of access permitted, such as read, write, update, or no access.

Auxiliary storage (1) data storage other than main storage. For example, storage on magnetic tape or direct-access devices. Synonymous with external storage and secondary storage; (2) a storage that supplements another storage. Contrast with *main storage*.

Backup (1) one or more files copied onto a storage medium for safekeeping should the original get damaged or lost; (2) redundant equipment or procedures used in the event of failure of a component or storage medium.

BASIC (Beginner's All-purpose Symbolic Instruction Code) a relatively easy-to-use programming language that is available in many small computer systems.

Batch processing a traditional method of data processing in which transactions are collected and prepared for processing as a single unit.

Benchmark a point of reference from which measurements can be made.

Capacity planning planning an adequate and efficient mix of resources in order to sustain the level of information services expected by corporate management for workloads of the future.

Card reader a device that senses and translates into machine code the holes in punched cards.

Cathode ray tube (CRT) an electronic vacuum tube, such as a television picture tube, that can be used to display graphic images, text, or numercial data on visual display terminals.

Central processing unit (CPU) the part of the computer that controls the execution and interpretation of the machine language processing instructions.

Character any letter, number, symbol, or punctuation mark.

Check a process for determining accuracy.

Check digit a digit added to a set of digits and used for the purpose of checking the accuracy of input data.

Checkpoint (1) a place in a routine where a check, or a recording of data for restart purposes, is performed; (2) a point at which information about the status of a job and the system can be recorded so that the job step can be later restarted.

Chip a thin semiconductor wafer on which electronic components are deposited in the form of integrated circuits.

COBOL (Common Business-Oriented Language) a high-level programming language designed for business data processing.

Code (1) in data processing, the representation of data or a computer program in symbolic form according to a set of rules; (2) in telecommunications, a system of rules and conventions according to which the signals representing data can be formed, transmitted, received and processed; (3) to write a routine.

Common database pooled data integrated for common use as a shared resource.

Compatibility (1) the ability of an instruction, program, or component to be used on more than one computer; (2) the ability of computers to work with other computers that are not necessarily similar in design or capabilities.

Computer a system designed for the manipulation of information, incorporating a central processing unit (CPU), memory, input/output (I/O) facilities, power supply and cabinet.

Computer code a machine code for a specific computer.

Computing system a central processing unit, with main storage, input/out channels, control units, direct-access storage devices and input/output devices connected to it.

Configuration the group of devices that make up a computer or data processing system.

Console that part of a computer used for communication between the operator or maintenance engineer and the computer.

Constraint a restriction.

Contingency planning planning for disaster or some abnormal shutdown of operations for an extended period of time.

Control unit (1) the part of the central processing unit that directs the sequence of operations, interprets coded instructions and sends the proper signals instructing other computer circuits to carry out the instructions; (2) a device that controls the reading, writing, or display of data at one or more input/output devices.

Computer utility a service facility that provides computatonal capability that is generally accessed by means of data communication.

Conversion (1) the process of changing from one method of data processing to another or from one data processing system to another; (2) the process of changing from one form of representation to another (e.g. to change from decimal representation to binary representation).

Core storage a form of high-speed storage using magnetic cores.

Corporate strategic plan states goals and objectives and charts the direction of the organization for the coming four to five years.

CRT display device a display device on which images are produced on a cathode ray tube.

Cryptography the art of writing or deciphering messages in code.

Custom software tailor-made computer programs prepared for a specific purpose. Contrast with *packaged software*, in which the programs are written for general purposes.

Data facts, numbers, letters and symbols that become usable information when processed.

Data acquisition the process of identifying, isolating and gathering source data to be centrally processed in a usable form.

Data bank a comprehensive collection of libraries of data. For example, one part of an invoice may form an item, a complete invoice may form a *record*, a complete set of such records may form a *file*, the collection of inventory control files may form a *library*, and the libraries used by an organization are known as its *data bank*.

Database a collection of interrelated data files or libraries organized for ease of access, update, and retrieval.

Database administrator (DBA) a person with delegated authority to coordinate, monitor and control the database and related resources, including the *data element dictionary (DED)* and *data directory (DD)*.

Database management system (DBMS) a generalized set of computer programs that control the creation, maintenance and utilization of the databases and data files of an organization.

Data collection (1) a telecommunications application in which data from several locations are accumulated at one location (in a queue or on a file) before processing; (2) accumulation of data in a form usable by computer.

Data directory (DD) lists or tables that facilitate quick reference to pertinent information regarding an information system using a *data element dictionary (DED)*.

Data element a fact or observation collected and recorded as data.

Data element dictionary (DED) defines data elements by use of descriptors that identify characteristics, attributes and other related information concerning the data element.

Data layout sheet used in planning the physical space of data (field width) in data records.

Data management a major function of operating systems that involves organizing, cataloguing, locating, storing, retrieving and maintaining data.

Data manager software that describes the logical and physical organization of the database and enables manipulation of the base by programmers.

Data network telecommunications network designed specifically for data transmission.

Data organization the arrangement of information in a data set. For example, sequential organization or partitioned organization.

Data processing (DP) the manipulation of data by following a sequence of instructions to achieve a desired result.

Data processing system a network of machine components capable of accepting information, processing it according to a plan and producing the desired results.

Data security protection of computerized information by various means, including cryptography, locks, identification cards and badges, restricted access to the computer, passwords, physical and electronic backup copies of the data, and so on.

Data structure the manner in which data are represented and stored in a computer system or program.

Data transmission the sending of data from one part of a system to another part.

Decision support systems (DSS) computerized applications used by management for decision making. These applications often use mathematical and statistical models, such as linear programming, critical path method (CPM), or program evaluation review technique (PERT) models included in operations research and management science.

DED/DD committee committee that takes responsibility for the content and control of data in an information system.

Dedicated describes a computer or piece of hardware assigned exclusively to one task.

Device in computers, a piece of hardware that performs a specific function. Input devices (e.g. keyboard) are used to get data into the central processing unit. Output devices (e.g. printer or display monitor) are used to take data out of a computer in some usable form. Input/output devices (e.g. terminal or disk drive) are able to perform both input and output of data.

Digital the representation of data using a discrete medium, such as sticks, markers, bits, or anything that is counted to determine its value.

Digital computer a computer that operates on digital data by performing arithmetic and logical operations on the data. Contrast with *analog computer*.

Direct access (1) retrieval or storage of data by a reference to its location on a volume, rather than relative to the previously retrieved or stored data; (2) pertaining to the process of obtaining data from or placing data into storage where the time required for such access is independent of the location of the data most recently obtained or placed in storage; (3) pertaining to a storage device, such as magnetic disk or drum, in which the access time is effectively independent of the location of the data. Synonymous with *random access*.

Disk a circular plate with magnetic material on both sides. This plate rotates for the storage and retrieval of data by one or more 'heads', which transfer the information to and from the computer. The computer-readable information may be placed on a floppy or a rigid (hard) disk and may have information on one or both sides. Also known as diskette or disc.

Display unit a terminal device that presents data visually, usually by means of a cathode ray tube (CRT).

Distributed database a database needed for local processing and kept by the processing centre at a distributed *node*.

Distributed data processing (DDP) the arrangement of computers within an organization in which the organization's computer complex has many separate computing facilities all working in a cooperative manner, rather than the conventional single computer at a single location. Frequently, an organization's central files are stored at the central computing facility, with the geographically dispersed smaller computers calling on the central files when they need them.

Distributed network a network in which all node pairs are connected, either directly or through redundant paths through intermediate *nodes*.

Documentation (1) the creating, collecting, organizing, storing, citing and disseminating of documents or the information recorded in documents; (2) a collection of documents or information on a given phase of development, or all development documentation of an information system.

Downtime the period during whch a computer is not operating.

Edit to modify the form or format of data. For example, to insert or delete characters such as page numbers or decimal points.

Effectiveness system readiness and design adequacy. Effectiveness is expressed as the probability that the system can successfully meet an operational demand within a given time when operated under specified conditions.

Efficiency the ratio of useful work performed to the total energy expended. A system is efficient if it fulfils its purpose without waste of resources.

Electronic data processing (EDP) processing of data largely performed by electronic devices.

Encrypt to encipher or encode.

End-user person who uses final computer output.

Ergonomics the science of human engineering which combines the study of human body mechanics and physical limitations with industrial psychology. See *human factors*.

Facilities management (FM) the use of an independent service organization to operate and manage a data processing installation.

Fail-safe ability to continue operations in spite of breakdown, because backup processing exists.

Fail-soft ability to continue operations in spite of breakdown but with a degraded level of operations.

Feasibility study an analysis to determine whether or not desired objectives of a proposed (information) system can be achieved within specific constraints.

Feedback the return of part of the output of a machine, process, or system to the computer as input for another phase, especially for self-correcting or control purposes.

Field in a record, a specified area used for a particular category of data.

File a logical collection of data, designated by name and considered as a unit by a user. A file consists of related *records*. For example, a payrole file (one record for each employee showing rate of pay, deductions, etc.) or an inventory file (one record for each inventory item showing the cost, selling price, number in stock, etc.).

File layout the arrangement and structure of data in a file, including the sequence and size of its components.

File maintenance updating the file to reflect changes in information. Data might be added, altered, or deleted. File maintenance also refers to reorganizing files, deleting records that are no longer in use, etc.

Financial feasibility whether or not funds are available to meet expected costs.

Format a specific arrangement of data.

Fount a family or assortment of characters of a given size and style. For example, large print for preparing transparencies and italicized print for emphasis.

General-purpose computer a computer designed to handle a wide variety of problems.

Hardware the electronic circuits, memory and input/output components of a computer system. Components made of steel or metal that one can see and touch. Contrast with *software*.

Hash total a summation, for checking purposes, of one or more corresponding fields of a file that may be in different units.

Heuristic pertaining to exploratory methods of problem solving in which solutions are discovered by evaluation of the progress made toward the final result. Contrast with *algorithm*.

Hierarchy of data a data structure consisting of sets and subsets such that every subset of a set is of lower rank than the data of the set.

High-level language a programming language in which the statements represent procedures rather than single machine instructions. FORTRAN, COBOL and BASIC are three common high-level languages. A high-level language requires a compiler or interpreter.

Horizontal integration the integration of functional information subsystems (e.g. production, marketing and finance) at one level of an organization (e.g. operations, control or planning).

Host computer a computer and associated software that, although run as a separate entity, can be accessed via a network.

Human factors physiological, psychological and training factors to be considered in the design of hardware and software and the development of procedures to ensure that humans can interface with machines efficiently and effectively.

Information data that are processed and transformed into a meaningful and useful form.

Information centre an organizational structure maintained by computer personnel to provide the end-user with technical advice and training.

In-house a system for use only within a particular company or organization, where the computing is independent of any external service.

Input (1) the data that are entered into programs; (2) the act of entering data into a computer; (3) data used by programs and subroutines to produce output.

Input device any machine that allows entry of commands or information into the computer. An input device could be a keyboard, tape drive, disk drive, microphone, light pen, digitizer, or electronic sensor.

Input/output (I/O) that part or procedure of a computer system that handles communications with external devices.

Inquiry a request for information from storage. For example, a request for the number of available items or a machine statement to initiate a search of library documents.

Installation process of installing and testing either hardware or software or both until they are accepted.

Intelligent terminal a terminal that is programmable and can process its messages. For example, checking validity of input data.

Interactive term commonly used to describe a software program that provides give-and-take between the operator and the machine. The program may ask a question to elicit a response from the operator or present a series of choices from which the operator can select. Also referred to as *conversational*.

Interface the juncture at which two computer components (hardware and/or software) meet and interact with each other. Also applies to human—machine interaction.

Iterate to execute repeatedly a loop or series of steps. For example, a loop in a routine.

Job a specified group of tasks prescribed as a unit of work for a computer. By extention, a job usually includes all necessary computer programs, linkages, files and instructions to the operating system.

K computer shorthand for the quantity 1,024, which is 2^{10}. The term, usually used to measure computer storage capacity, is approximated as 1,000.

Key in a record, a field of data that is used for accessing the record.

Key data element data element used to link files.

Keyboard the panel of keys that is connected to a computer and used to enter data. It looks similar to the keyboard of a typewriter.

Language see *programming language*.

Large-scale integration (LSI) the combining of about 1,000 to 10,000 circuits on a single chip. Typical examples of LSI circuits are memory chips, microprocessors, calculator chips and watch chips.

Lease a contract by which one party gives another the use of hardware for a specified time for a payment.

Librarian person in charge of data, programs and documentation in the computer library.

Logging recording of data about events that occur in time sequence.

Main memory the computer's internal memory contained in its circuitry, as opposed to peripheral memory (tapes, disks).

Main storage (1) the general-purpose storage of a computer. Contrast with *auxiliary storage*; (2) all program-addressable storage from which instructions may be executed and from which data can be loaded directly into registers.

Mainframe a large general-purpose computer with fast processing time.

Maintenance any activity intended to eliminate faults or to keep hardware or programs in satisfactory working condition. Includes tests, measurements, replacements, adjustments and repairs.

Malfunction the effect of a fault or unexpected functioning.

Management information system (MIS) a computerized information system that processes data to produce information to aid in the performance of management functions.

Mark-sense to mark a position with an electrically conductive pencil for later conversion to machine-readable form.

Master file a file that is either relatively permanent or is treated as an authority in a particular job.

Master schedule used to schedule batch processing.

Match to check for identity between two or more items of data.

Matrix a commonly used method of storing and manipulating data. A matrix format consists of rows and columns of information.

Matrix organization borrows staff from functional divisions — staff that is responsible to the project manager for the life of a project.

Maximum separation principle that the generation of information must be separate from its flow.

Metrics measures that are quantified numerically and claim useful accuracy and reliability that are used in performance evaluation.

Microcomputer a small but complete microprocessor-based computer system, including central processing unit (CPU), memory, input/output (I/O) interfaces and power supply.

Microfiche a sheet of microfilm on which it is possible to record a number of pages of microcopy.

Microprocessor an integrated-circuity implementation of a complete processor (arithmetic logic unit, internal storage and control unit) on a single chip.

Millisecond one thousandth of a second.

Minicompany approach when auditing, use of a representative set of data to represent a company. Allows audit independent of live data stream.

Minicomputer a small (for example, desktop size) electronic, digital, stored-program, general-purpose computer.

Monitor (1) a microcomputer program that directs operations of the hardware; (2) may also refer to a video display.

Nanosecond a billionth of a second. Most computers have a cycle time of hundreds of nanoseconds. High-speed computers have a cycle time of around 50 nanoseconds.

Network an interconnection of computer systems, terminals, and communications facilities.

Node (1) an end point of any branch of a network, or a junction common to two or more branches of a network; (2) any station, terminal, terminal installation, communications computer, or communications computer installation in a computer network.

Offline used to describe equipment that is neither connected to nor under the control of the central processing unit.

Offloading the transference of processing from one system to another.

Online directly connected to the computer and in operational condition.

Online processing processing of input data in random order without preliminary sorting or batching. Contrast with *batch processing*.

Online system in teleprocessing, a system in which the input data enters the computer directly from the point of origin or in which output data is transmitted directly to where it is used.

Operating system a collection of programs for operating the computer. Operating systems perform housekeeping tasks, such as input/output between the computer and peripherals and accepting and interpreting information from the keyboard.

Original equipment manufacturer (OEM) a term commonly used to refer to a computer sales organization that has an arrangement to package and sell a manufacturer's product.

Output (1) any processed information coming out of a computer via any medium (print, cathode ray tube, etc.); (2) the act of transferring information to these media.

Output device a machine that transfer programs or information from the computer to some other medium. Examples of output devices include tape, disk and bubble memory drives; computer printers, typewriters and plotters; the computer picture screen (video display); robots; and sound-synthesis devices that enable the computer to talk and/or play music.

Packaged software a program designed to be marketed for general use that may need to be adapted to a particular installation.

Parallel conversion operating a new system in a test mode before the old system is fully phased out.

Parity a 1-bit code that makes the total number of bits in the word, including the parity bit, odd (odd parity) or even (even parity). Used for error detection during data transmission.

Password a secret identification code keyed by the user and checked by the system before permitting access. Each user or group of users has a unique password.

Peripheral any unit of equipment, distinct from the central processing unit, that may provide the system with outside communication.

Peripheral-bound describes a system that is backlogged because of the slowness of peripheral equipment.

Portability property of software that permits its use in another computer environment.

Price differentiation pricing a product to help favoured customers or damage specific competitors: a strategy to enter and/or capture a desired market share.

Price tying combining two or more products or services (hardware, software, education, documentation, and consulting) in a single price package.

Primitive data synonymous with raw data.

Printer a computer output device that produces computer output on paper.

Priority a rank that is assigned to a task and that determines its precedence in receiving system resources.

Proactive information centre an information centre that aggressively seeks to introduce new technology to enhance employee performance in computing.

Process chart a document used to collect information on each step of a process. Used in systems development to analyze procedures to be computerized.

Processor in hardware, a data processor.

Program a sequence of instructions directing a computer to perform a particular function; a statement of an algorithm in a programming language.

Program error any mistakes or problems in a computer program that keep the computer from performing the proper computations.

Program library a collection of debugged and documented programs.

Programmer person who writes programs.

Programmer's manual descriptions of programs.

Programming language a set of symbols and rules that can be used to specify an algorithm in a computer-executable form.

Project management in information systems development, the planning, coordination and control of activities during the development, from the feasibility study through conversion.

Project organization the creation of a separate organizational unit for the sole purpose of completing a project.

Protocol the rules governing how two pieces of equipment communicate with one another.

Prototype an original, unrefined version of an information system, developed interactively by user and analyst.

Random access an access method whereby each record of a file or location in memory can be accessed directly by its address.

Reactive information centre information centre that models its services around identifiable user demand.

Read to accept data from a disk, card, etc., for storage and/or processing.

Real-time describes a system that processes in synchronization with the actual occurrence of events.

Record a collection of data items, stored on a disk or other medium, that may be recalled as a unit. Records may be fixed or variable in length. One or more records usually make up a *data file*.

Recovery re-establishment of operations following breakdown of the central processing unit or input/output devices.

Redevelopment recycling the development cycle for major modification of an information system.

Remote access pertaining to communication with a data processing facility by one or more stations that are distant from that facility.

Remote job entry (RJE) submission of job control statements and data from a remote terminal, causing the jobs described to be scheduled and executed as though encountered in the input stream.

Replicated distributed database a duplicate segment of a database, needed for local processing and stored at the local site.

Report program generator (RPG) a computer programming language that can be used to generate object programs that produce reports from existing sets of data.

Resistance in the context of information systems, the act of opposing change brought about by the use of computers.

Response time the time required for the system to respond to a user's request or to accept a user's inputs.

Run the execution of a program by a computer on a given set of data.

Security prevention of access to or use of data, documentation, or programs without authorization.

Semiconductor a substance whose conductivity is poor at low temperatures but is improved by the application of heat, light, or voltage.

Sensor any device that monitors the external environment for a computer. Types of sensors include photoelectric sensors that are sensitive to light: image sensor cameras that can record visual images and transform them into digital signals; pressure sensors that are sensitive to any kind of pressure; sensors that record infrared information; and ultrasonic transducers that produce a high-frequency sound wave that bounces off objects and lets the computer calculate the distance between itself and those objects.

Separation of responsibility a management control technique that can be applied to management of information systems. The information system is divided into functions, and employees are assigned duties and responsibilities that do not cross functional lines.

Sequence (1) an arrangement of items according to a specified set of rules; (2) in sorting, a group of records whose control fields are in ascending or descending order according to the collating sequence.

Service bureau provides computing services to customers.

Service-level agreement (SLA) a document that guarantees a given level of service to users in terms of transaction volumes, response times and other service criteria.

Simulation a computerized reproduction, image, or replica of a situation or set of conditions.

Software a general term for computer programs involved in the operation of the computer.

Software maintenance the adjustment of an existing program to allow acceptance of new tasks or conditions (e.g. a new category of payroll deduction) or to correct previously undiscovered errors detected by users.

Sort (1) a procedure to reorder data sequentially, usually in alphabetic or numeric order; (2) the action of sorting.

Stand-alone system a computer system that does not require a connection to another computer.

Storage the general term for any device that is capable of holding data that will be retrieved later.

Strategic plan for information processing states information processing goals and objectives.

Subsystem a secondary or subordinate system, usually capable of operating independently.

System usually refers to a group of related hardware and/or software designed to meet a specific need.

System life cycle development methodology a set of prescribed activities for the development of an information system. Includes a feasibility study, user specifications, design, implementation, testing, and conversion.

Systems analysis the analysis of an activity to determine precisely what must be accomplished and how to accomplish it.

Systems analyst an individual who performs system analysis, design and many related functions in the development and maintenance of an information system.

Systems manual general information (an overview, not details) on a system and its objectives.

Tape inexpensive mass-storage medium. Must be accessed sequentially.

Task a program in execution.

Telecommunications (1) pertaining to the transmission of signals over long distances, such as by telegraph, radio, or television; (2) data transmission between a computing system and remotely located devices via a unit that performs the necessary format conversion and controls the rate of transmission.

Teleprocessing the processing of data that is received from or sent to remote locations by way of telecommunications lines.

Throughput a measure of the amount of work that can be accomplished by the computer during a given period of time.

Time-sharing a method of sharing the resources of the computer among several users so that several people can appear to be running different computer tasks simultaneously.

Transposition the interchange of position. May be an exchange of data positions (e.g. 15 instead of 51).

Turnaround document document produced as output that becomes input when user supplies additional data on the document.

Turnaround time the measure of time between the initiation of a job and its completion by the computer.

Turnkey vendor one who provides a complete system including the computer, software, training, installation and support.

Update to modify a master file with current information according to a specified procedure.

User friendly descriptive of both hardware and software that are designed to assist the user by being scaled to human dimensions, self-instructing, error-proof, etc.

User's manual procedures for use of an information system written in terms that users understand.

Utility program a program used to assist in the operation of the computer (e.g. a sort routine, a printout program, a file conversion program). Generally, these programs perform housekeeping functions and have little relationship to the specific processing of the data.

Validation process of checking compliance of data with preset standards and verifying data correctness.

Value pricing charging a high markup for an indispensable product to cover low profit margins for other products in the company's line.

Variable a quantity that can assume any of a given set of values.

Vendor a supplier or company that sells computers, peripherals, or computer services.

Very large-scale integration (VLSI) in practice, the compression of more than 10,000 transistors on a single chip.

Width of field the amount of space allowed for data in a data record.

Wiretapping electromagnetic pickup of messages off communication lines.

Word processor a text editor system for electronically writing, formatting and storing letters, reports, and books prior to printing.

Index